THE BIBLE AS CHRISTIAN SCRIPTURE

Society of Biblical Literature

Biblical Scholarship in North America

Number 25

THE BIBLE AS CHRISTIAN SCRIPTURE
The Work of Brevard S. Childs

THE BIBLE AS CHRISTIAN SCRIPTURE

THE WORK OF BREVARD S. CHILDS

Edited by

Christopher R. Seitz

and

Kent Harold Richards

with editorial assistance
from Robert C. Kashow

Society of Biblical Literature
Atlanta

THE BIBLE AS CHRISTIAN SCRIPTURE
The Work of Brevard S. Childs

Copyright © 2013 by the Society of Biblical Literature

All rights reserved. No part of this work may be reproduced or transmitted in any form or by any means, electronic or mechanical, including photocopying and recording, or by means of any information storage or retrieval system, except as may be expressly permitted by the 1976 Copyright Act or in writing from the publisher. Requests for permission should be addressed in writing to the Rights and Permissions Office, Society of Biblical Literature, 825 Houston Mill Road, Atlanta, GA 30329 USA.

Library of Congress Cataloging-in-Publication Data

The Bible as Christian scripture : the work of Brevard S. Childs / edited by Christopher R. Seitz and Kent Harold Richards.
   p. cm. — (Society of Biblical Literature biblical scholarship in North America ; no. 25)
   ISBN 978-1-58983-713-3 (paper binding : alk. paper) — ISBN 978-1-58983-714-0 (electronic format) — ISBN 978-1-58983-884-0 (hardcover binding : alk. paper)
   1. Bible. Old Testament—Criticism, interpretation, etc. 2. Bible. Old Testament—Theology. 3. Bible. Old Testament—Canon. 4. Childs, Brevard S. I. Seitz, Christopher R. II. Richards, Kent Harold.
   BS1192.B534 2013
   220.6092—dc23   2013028634

Printed on acid-free, recycled paper conforming to
ANSI/NISO Z39.48-1992 (R1997) and ISO 9706:1994
standards for paper permanence.

Contents

Preface
Christopher R. Seitz vii

Abbreviations ix

Works of Brevard Springs Childs xiii

Tribute to Brevard S. Childs, at the International SBL Meeting
in Vienna, Austria
Christopher R. Seitz 1

Brevard Childs and Form Criticism
David L. Petersen 9

The Wrath of God at Mount Sinai (Exod 32; Deut 9–10)
Jörg Jeremias 21

The Contrastive Unity of Scripture: On the Hermeneutics of
the Biblical Canon
Bernd Janowski 37

Brevard Childs as a Historical Critic: Divine Concession
and the Unity of the Canon
Stephen B. Chapman 63

Theological Interpretation, the Historical Formation of
Scripture, and God's Action in Time
Neil B. MacDonald 85

Faith Seeking Canonical Understanding: Childs's Guide to
the Pauline Letters
Leander E. Keck 103

Childs and the History of Interpretation
   Mark W. Elliott 119

Biblical Theology and the Communicative Presence of God
   Murray A. Rae..137

The Doctrine of God is a Hermeneutic: The *Biblical Theology*
of Brevard S. Childs
   C. Kavin Rowe 155

A Shared Reality: Ontology in Brevard Childs's Isaiah Commentary
   Mark Gignilliat 171

A Tale of Two Testaments: Childs, Old Testament Torah,
and *Heilsgeschichte*
   Don Collett..185

Reflections on the Rule of Faith
   Leonard G. Finn 221

Childs and the Canon or Rule of Faith
   Daniel R. Driver 243

Psalm 34: Redaction, Inner-Biblical Exegesis and the Longer Psalm
   Superscriptions—"Mistake" Making and Theological Significance
   Christopher R. Seitz..279

Allegory and Typology within Biblical Interpretation
   Brevard S. Childs...299

Contributors...313

Index of Ancient Sources..317

Index of Modern Authors...323

Preface

This volume has been prepared at the suggestion of Kent Richards. Professor Childs was honored with two Festschriften on the occasion of his sixty-fifth and seventy-fifth birthdays, and indeed I was the editor of the second of these. I want to acknowledge the help of my St. Andrews colleague Mark Elliott. At the Vienna SBL Meeting following the death of Brevard Childs, Mark helped me think about constructing this particular tribute.

I decided, rather than seeking contributions from former students and focusing on the Old Testament alone, to include a sample of historical, theological, New Testament, and other essays. I also wanted a more international sample, so we have essays on theological aspects of Childs's work from Murray Rae of New Zealand and Neil MacDonald of London; New Testament essays from Kavin Rowe and Leander Keck; chapters on the history of interpretation from Mark Elliott of St. Andrews and myself; Old Testament contributions from Bernd Janowski (Tübingen), Jörg Jeremias (Marburg), David Petersen (Emory), and Stephen Chapman (Duke). Younger scholars, who had listened to Childs lecturing for several seasons at St. Andrews, were also chosen to contribute (Don Collett, Daniel Driver and Mark Gignilliat). The essay on the rule of faith, a significant theme in Childs's work, is supplied by Leonard Finn. I am indebted to Mr. Robert Kashow for his editorial and clerical help with this project. Further thanks go to Jonathan Reck, who kindly prepared the indices for this volume. Daniel Driver of Toronto translated the essay of Professor Janowski and also provided the bibliographical data for Professor Childs. I am grateful to Bob Buller for his willingness to stick with this project through a transitional season at SBL.

I have decided to include the tribute I gave to Professor Childs at Vienna and leave it in its original oral form. I have also included an essay of my own in relation to Childs's observations on the psalm titles (1971).

Offering his own tribute to Childs in Vienna, James Kugel remarked that a rabbi once said, "I learned much from my teachers, much from my colleagues, but most from my students." Kugel then paused and said he didn't think that was true at all. "No, I learned the most from colleagues." Childs had been that kind of colleague for him at Yale. He was for many years that kind of colleague for me as well.

Christopher R. Seitz

Abbreviations

AB	Anchor Bible
ABD	*Anchor Bible Dictionary*. Edited by David Noel Freedman. 6 vols. New York: Doubleday, 1992.
ANF	*The Ante-Nicene Fathers*. Edited by Alexander Roberts and James Donaldson. 1885–1887. 10 vols. Repr., Peabody, Mass.: Hendrickson, 1994.
ANQ	*Andover Newton Quarterly*
BBB	Bonner biblische Beiträge
BETL	Bibliotheca Ephemeridum theologicarum Lovaniensium
BEvTh	Beiträge zur evangelischen Theologie
Bib	*Biblica*
BibSem	Biblical Seminar
BibThom	Bibliothèque Thomiste
BiOr	*Bibliotheca Orientalis*
BLE	*Bulletin de littérature ecclésiastique*
BN	*Biblische Notizen*
BThSt	Biblische Studien
BTONT	Brevard S. Childs, *Biblical Theology of the Old and New Testaments: Theological Reflections on the Christian Bible*. Minneapolis: Augsburg Fortress, 1992.
BZ	*Biblische Zeitschrift*
BZAW	Beihefte zur Zeitschrift für die alttestamentliche Wissenschaft
BZNW	Beihefte zur Zeitschrift für die neutestamentliche Wissenschaft und die Kunde der älteren Kirche
CBET	Contributions to Biblical Exegesis and Theology
CBOT	Coniectanea biblica. Old Testament series
CBQ	*Catholic Biblical Quarterly*
CTM	*Concordia Theological Monthly*
CurBS	*Currents in Research: Biblical Studies*

ECCA	Early Christianity in the Context of Antiquity
EdF	Erträge der Forschung
EHS	Europäische Hochschulschriften
EKKNT	Evangelisch-katholischer Kommentar zum Neuen Testament
EvK	*Evangelische Kommentare*
EvT	*Evangelische Theologie*
ExAud	*Ex auditu*
FAT	Forschungen zum Alten Testament
FRLANT	Forschungen zur Religion und Literatur des Alten und Neuen Testaments
GAT	Grundrisse zum Alten Testament
GNT	Grundrisse zum Neuen Testament
HBS	Herders Biblische Studien
HBT	*Horizons in Biblical Theology*
Int	*Interpretation*
ITS	Innsbrucker theologische Studien
JBL	*Journal of Biblical Literature*
JBTh	*Jahrbuch für biblische Theologie*
JSOT	*Journal for the Study of the Old Testament*
JSOTSup	Journal for the Study of the Old Testament Supplement Series
JSS	*Journal of Semitic Studies*
JTI	*Journal of Theological Interpretation*
JTS	*Journal of Theological Studies*
KStTh	Kohlhammer Studienbücher Theologie
KuI	*Kirche und Israel*
LSTS	Library of Second Temple Studies
LThK	*Lexikon für Theologie und Kirche*. 3rd ed. Edited by Walter Kasper. Freiburg: Herder, 1993–2001.
ModTheo	*Modern Theology*
MTV	Münstersche theologische Vorträge
NTD	Das Neue Testament deutsch
NZSTh	*Neue Zeitschrift für Systematische Theologie und Religionsphilosophie*
OBT	Overtures to Biblical Theology
OrChrAn	Orientalia christiana analecta
OTL	Old Testament Library
OTS	Old Testament Studies

PL	Patrologia Latina. Edited by Jacques-Paul Migne. 217 vols. Paris: Migne: 1844–1855.
ProEccl	Pro Ecclesia
PTR	Princeton Theological Review
QD	Quaestiones disputatae
RB	Revue biblique
RelS	Religious Studies
RGG	Religion in Geschichte und Gegenwart. Edited by Hans Dieter Betz, Don S. Browning, Bernd Janowski, and Eberhard Jüngel. 8 vols. Tübingen: Mohr Siebeck, 1998–2005.
RHPR	Revue d'histoire et de philosophie religieuses
SBAB	Stuttgarter biblische Aufsatzbände
SBET	Scottish Bulletin of Evangelical Theology
SBLDS	Society of Biblical Literature Dissertation Series
SBLSymS	Society of Biblical Literature Symposium Series
SBS	Stuttgarter Bibelstudien
SBT	Studies in Biblical Theology
SDSSRL	Studies in the Dead Sea Scrolls and Related Literature
SHS	Scripture and Hermeneutics Series
SJT	Scottish Journal of Theology
SMRT	Studies in Medieval and Reformation Thought
SNTU	Studien zum Neuen Testament und seiner Umwelt
SSEJC	Studies in Scripture in Early Judaism and Christianity
ST	Studia theologica
STDJ	Studies on the Texts of the Desert of Judah
STI	Studies in Theological Interpretation
StZ	Stimmen der Zeit
ThBeitr	Theologische Beiträge
ThPQ	Theologisch-Praktische Quartalschrift
ThRev	Theologische Revue
ThTo	Theology Today
TQ	Theologische Quartalschrift
TRE	Theologische Realenzyklopädie. Edited by Gerhard Krause and Gerhard Müller. 36 vols. Berlin: de Gruyter, 1976–2004.
TZ	Theologische Zeitschrift
UTB	Uni-Taschenbücher
VG	Verkündigung und Forschung

VGWTh	Veröffentlichungen der Wissenschaftlichen Gesellschaft für Theologie
VT	*Vetus Testamentum*
WMANT	Wissenschaftliche Monographien zum Alten und Neuen Testament
WUNT	Wissenschaftliche Untersuchungen zum Neuen Testament
ZAW	*Zeitschrift für die alttestamentliche Wissenschaft*
ZNT	*Zeitschrift für Neues Testament*
ZThK	*Zeitschrift fuer Theologie und Kirche*

Works of Brevard Springs Childs

With the exception of reviews, which represent only a sampling, the following is a complete bibliography of Brevard Childs's published works. Those with an interest in unpublished letters and papers should not miss the Brevard S. Childs Manuscript Collection, housed in the Princeton Theological Seminary archives. A finding guide may be found in the Seminary's online catalog.

Dissertation and Books

"Der Mythos als theologische Problem im Alten Testaments." Basel, 1953. Resubmitted as "A Study of Myth in Genesis I–XI." ThD diss., Basel, 1955. Revised and published as:
Myth and Reality in the Old Testament. SBT 27. London: SCM, 1960. 2nd ed. London: SCM, 1962.
Memory and Tradition in Israel. SBT 37. London: SCM, 1962.
Isaiah and the Assyrian Crisis. SBT 2/3. London: SCM, 1967.
Biblical Theology in Crisis. Philadelphia: Westminster, 1970.
The Book of Exodus: A Critical, Theological Commentary. OTL. Philadelphia: Westminster, 1974.
Old Testament Books for Pastor and Teacher. Philadelphia: Westminster, 1977.
Introduction to the Old Testament as Scripture. Philadelphia: Fortress, 1979.
The New Testament as Canon: An Introduction. Philadelphia: Fortress, 1984.
Old Testament Theology in a Canonical Context. Philadelphia: Fortress, 1985.
Biblical Theology of the Old and New Testaments: Theological Reflection on the Christian Bible. Minneapolis: Fortress, 1992. Translated into German by Manfred and Christiane Oeming, with a preface by

Christoph Dohmen, as *Die Theologie der einen Bibel.* 2 vols. Freiburg: Herder, 1994–1996.

Biblical Theology: A Proposal. Minneapolis: Fortress, 2002.

Isaiah: A Commentary. OTL. Louisville: Westminster John Knox, 2001.

The Struggle to Understand Isaiah as Christian Scripture. Grand Rapids: Eerdmans, 2004.

The Church's Guide for Reading Paul: The Canonical Shaping of the Pauline Corpus. Grand Rapids: Eerdmans, 2008.

ARTICLES AND SELECT PAPERS

1955–1959

"A Study of Glory." *Mission House Seminary Bulletin* 2 (1955): 34–43.

"Jonah: A Study in Old Testament Hermeneutics." *SJT* 11 (1958): 53–61.

"Prophecy and Fulfillment: A Study of Contemporary Hermeneutics." *Int* 12 (1958): 257–71.

"The Enemy from the North and the Chaos Tradition." *JBL* 78 (1959): 187–98.

1960–1969

"Adam," "Eden, Garden of," "Eve," "Orientation," "Tree of Knowledge, Tree of Life." In *The Interpreter's Dictionary of the Bible.* Edited by George Arthur Buttrick et al. 4 vols. Nashville: Abingdon, 1962.

"A Study of the Formula, 'Until This Day.'" *JBL* 82 (1963): 279–92.

"Interpretation in Faith: The Theological Responsibility of an Old Testament Commentary." *Int* 18 (1964): 432–49.

"The Birth of Moses." *JBL* 84 (1965): 109–22.

"A Survey of Recent Books in Old Testament." *Yale Divinity News* 62/3 (1965): 13–14.

"Deuteronomic Formulae of the Exodus Traditions." Pages 30–39 in *Hebräische Wortforschung: Festschrift zum 80. Geburtstag von Walter Baumgartner.* Edited by George W. Anderson, P. A. H. de Boer, G. R. Castellino, Henri Cazelles, E. Hammershaimb, H. G. May, and W. Zimmerli. VTSup 16. Leiden: Brill, 1967.

"Karl Barth as Interpreter of Scripture." Pages 30–39 in *Karl Barth and the Future of Theology: A Memorial Colloquium Held at Yale Divinity*

School January 28, 1969. Edited by D. L. Dickerman. New Haven: Yale Divinity School Association, 1969.

"Psalm 8 in the Context of the Christian Canon." *Int* 23 (1969): 20–31.

1970–1979

"A Traditio-historical Study of the Reed Sea Tradition." *VT* 20 (1970): 406–18.
"Psalm Titles and Midrashic Exegesis." *JSS* 16 (1971): 137–50.
"Midrash and the Old Testament." Pages 45–59 in *Understanding the Sacred Text*. Edited by John Reumann. Valley Forge, Pa.: Judson, 1972.
"The Old Testament as Scripture of the Church." *CTM* 43 (1972): 709–22.
"A Tale of Two Testaments." *Int* 26 (1972): 20–29.
"The Etiological Tale Re-examined." *VT* 24 (1974): 387–97.
"The Old Testament as Narrative." *Yale Alumni Magazine* 38.4 (Jan 1975): 30–32.
"God Leads a People to Freedom: Studies in Exodus." *Enquiry* 9 (1976): 1–33.
"Reflections on the Modern Study of the Psalms." Pages 377–88 in *Magnalia Dei: The Mighty Acts of God: Essays on Bible and Archaeology in Memory of G. E. Wright*. Edited by Frank Moore Cross, Werner Lemke, and Patrick D. Miller. New York: Doubleday, 1976.
"The Search for Biblical Authority Today." *ANQ* 16 (1976): 199–206.
"The Sensus Literalis of Scripture: An Ancient and Modern Problem." Pages 80–93 in *Beiträge zur alttestamentlichen Theologie: Festschrift für Walther Zimmerli zum 70. Geburtstag*. Edited by Walther Zimmerli, Herbert Donner, Robert Hanhart, and Rudolf Smend. Göttingen: Vandenhoeck & Ruprecht, 1977.
"Symposium on Biblical Criticism" [response to Paul Minear]. *ThTo* 33 (1977): 358–59.
"The Canonical Shape of the Book of Jonah." Pages 122–28 in *Biblical and Near Eastern Studies: Essays in Honor of William Sanford LaSor*. Edited by Gary A. Tuttle. Grand Rapids: Eerdmans, 1978.
"The Canonical Shape of the Prophetic Literature." *Int* 32 (1978): 46–55. Reprinted as pages 41–49 in *Interpreting the Prophets*. Edited by James Mays and Paul Achtemeier. Philadelphia: Fortress, 1987. Reprinted as pages 513–22 in *"The Place is Too Small for Us": The Israelite Prophets*

in Recent Scholarship. Edited by Robert P. Gordon. Winona Lake, Ind.: Eisenbrauns, 1995.
"The Exegetical Significance of the Canon for the Study of the Old Testament." Pages 66–80 in *International Organization for the Study of the Old Testament Congress Volume.* VTSup 29. Leiden: Brill, 1978.
"Background Material on Exodus." In "Studies in Exodus and Psalms," by John A. Bowe. New Ventures in Bible Study 1/2 (Winter 1978–1979): 3–64.

1980–1989

"On Reading the Elijah Narratives." *Int* 34 (1980): 128–37.
"A Response [to James Mays et al.]." *HBT* 2 (1980): 199–211.
"Response to Reviewers of Introduction to the OT as Scripture." *JSOT* 16 (1980): 52–60.
"Differenzen in der Exegese: Biblische Theologie in Amerika." *Evangelische Kommentare* 14 (1981): 405–6.
"Some Reflections on the Search for a Biblical Theology." *HBT* 4 (1982): 1–12.
"Wellhausen in English." *Semeia* 25 (1982): 83–88.
"Anticipatory Titles in Hebrew Narrative." Pages 57–65 in vol. 3 of *Isac Leo Seeligmann Volume: Essays on the Bible and the Ancient World.* Edited by A. Rofé and Y. Zalovitch. 3 vols. Jerusalem: E. Rubinstein, 1983.
"Gerhard von Rad in American Dress." Pages 77–86 in *The Hermeneutical Quest: Essays in Honor of James Luther Mays on his 65th Birthday.* Edited by Donald G. Miller. Allison Park, Pa.: Pickwick, 1986.
"Die Bedeutung des Jüdischen Kanons in der Alttestamentlichen Theologie." Pages 269–81 in *Mitte der Schrift?: Ein jüdisch-christliches Gespräch—Texte des Berner Symposions vom 6–12 Januar 1985.* Edited by Ulrich Luz, Martin Klopfenstein, Emmanuel Tov, and Shemaryahu Talmon. Translated by Ulrich Luz and Eva Ringler. Judaica et Christiana 11. Frankfurt: Peter Lang, 1987.
"Death and Dying in Old Testament Theology." Pages 89–91 in *Love and Death in the Ancient Near East.* Edited by John H. Marks and Robert M. Good. Guilford, Conn.: Four Quarters, 1987.
"Die theologische Bedeutung der Endform eines Textes." *TQ* 167 (1987): 242–51.
"Biblische Theologie und christlicher Kanon." Pages 13–27 in *Zum Problem des biblischen Kanons.* Edited by Ingo Baldermann, Ernst Dass-

man, Ottmar Fuchs, Berndt Hamm, Otfried Hofius, Bernd Janowski, Norbert Lohfink, Helmut Merklein, Werner H. Schmidt, Günter Stemberger, Peter Stuhlmacher, Michael Welker, and Rudolf Weth. JBTh 3. Neukirchen-Vluyn: Neukirchener, 1988.

"Karl Barth: The Preacher's Exegete." Paper presented at The Lyman Beecher Lectureship on Preaching, Yale University. New Haven, 1989.

"Reflections on the Reissue of William Perkins's Commentary on Galatians." Pages xiv–xvi in William Perkins, *A Commentary on Galatians*. Edited by Gerald T. Sheppard. Pilgrim Classic Commentaries. New York: Pilgrim, 1989.

"The Struggle for God's Righteousness in the Psalter." Pages 255–64 in *Christ in Our Place*. Edited by Trevor Hart and Dan Thimell. Allison Park, Pa.: Pickwick, 1989.

1990–1999

"Analysis of a Canonical Formula: 'It Shall be Recorded for a Future Generation.'" Pages 357–64 in *Die hebräische Bibel und ihre zweifache Nachgeschichte*. Edited by Erhard Blum, Christian Macholz, and Ekkehard W. Stegemann. Neukirchen-Vluyn: Neukirchener, 1990.

"Critical Reflections on James Barr's Understanding of the Literal and the Allegorical." *JSOT* 46 (1990): 3–9.

"Die Bedeutung der hebräischen Bibel für die biblische Theologie." *TZ* 48 (1992): 382–90.

"Leander E. Keck: A Tribute." Pages xix–xxi in *The Future of Christology: Essays in Honor of Leander E. Keck*. Edited by A. Malherbe and W. Meeks. Minneapolis: Fortress, 1993.

"Biblical Scholarship in the Seventeenth Century: A Study in Ecumenics." Pages 325–33 in *Language, Theology, and the Bible: Essays in Honour of James Barr*. Edited by Samuel E. Balentine and John Barton. Oxford: Clarendon, 1994.

"Old Testament in Germany 1920–1940: The Search for a New Paradigm." Pages 233–46 in *Altes Testament, Forschung und Wirkung: Festschrift für Henning Graf Reventlow*. Edited by Peter Mommer and Winfried Thiel. Frankfurt: Peter Lang, 1994.

"Die Beziehung von Altem und Neuem Testament aus kanonischer Sicht." Pages 29–34 in *Eine Bibel—Zwei Testamente: Positionen biblischer Theologie*. Edited by Christoph Dohmen and Thomas Söding. Translated by U. Dohmen. Paderborn: Ferdinand Schöningh, 1995.

"Old Testament Theology." Pages 293–301 in *Old Testament Interpretation: Past, Present, and Future*. Edited by James L. Mays, David L. Petersen, and Kent Harold Richards. Edinburgh: T&T Clark, 1995.
"On Reclaiming the Bible for Christian Theology." Pages 1–17 in *Reclaiming the Bible for the Church*. Edited by Carl E. Braaten and Robert W. Jenson. Grand Rapids: Eerdmans, 1995.
"Retrospective Reading of the Old Testament Prophets." *ZAW* 108 (1996): 362–77.
"Does the Old Testament Witness to Jesus Christ?" Pages 57–64 in *Evangelium, Schriftauslegung, Kirche: Festschrift für Peter Stuhlmacher zum 65. Geburtstag*. Edited by Peter Stuhlmacher, Scott J. Hafemann, Jostein Ådna, and Otfried Hofius. Göttingen: Vandenhoeck & Ruprecht, 1997.
"The Genre of the Biblical Commentary as Problem and Challenge." Pages 185–92 in *Tehillah le-Moshe*. Edited by Mordechai Cogan, Barry L. Eichler, and Jeffrey H. Tigay. Winona Lake, Ind.: Eisenbrauns, 1997.
"Interpreting the Bible Amid Cultural Change." *ThTo* 54 (1997): 200–11.
"Toward Recovering Theological Exegesis." *ProEccl* 6 (1997): 16–26.
"Jesus Christ the Lord and the Scriptures of the Church." Pages 1–12 in *The Rule of Faith: Scripture, Canon, and Creed in a Critical Age*. Edited by Ephraim Radner and George Sumner. Harrisburg, Pa.: Morehouse, 1998.
"The Nature of the Christian Bible: One Book, Two Testaments." Pages 115–25 in *The Rule of Faith*. Edited by Ephraim Radner and George Sumner. Harrisburg, Pa.: Morehouse, 1998.
"The One Gospel in Four Witnesses." Pages 51–62 in *The Rule of Faith*. Edited by Ephraim Radner and George Sumner. Harrisburg, Pa.: Morehouse, 1998.
"The Almost Forgotten Genesis Commentary of Benno Jacob." Pages 273–80 in *Recht und Ethos im Alten Testament—Gestalt und Wirkung: Festschrift für Horst Seebass zum 65. Geburtstag*. Edited by Stefan Beyerle, Günter Mayer, and Hans Strauß. Neukirchen-Vluyn: Neukirchener, 1999.
"Hermeneutical Reflections on C. Vitringa, Eighteenth-Century Interpreter of Isaiah." Pages 89–98 in *In Search of True Wisdom: Essays in Old Testament Interpretation in Honour of Ronald E. Clements*. Edited by Edward Ball. Sheffield: Sheffield Academic, 1999.

2000–2006

"Allegory and Typology within Biblical Interpretation." Paper presented at St Mary's College, University of St Andrews. St Andrews, 2000.
"Toward Recovering Theological Exegesis." *ExAud* 16 (2000): 121–29.
"A Tribute to the Book List of SOTS." Pages 90–94 in *Reading from Right to Left: Essays on the Hebrew Bible in Honour of David J. A. Clines*. JSOTSup 373. Edited by J. Cheryl Exum and H. G. M. Williamson. London: Sheffield Academic Press, 2003.
"Critique of Recent Intertextual Canonical Interpretation." *ZAW* 115 (2003): 173–84.
"The Canon in Recent Biblical Studies: Reflections on an Era." *ProEccl* 14 (2005): 26–45. Reprinted as pages 33–57 in *Canon and Biblical Interpretation*. Edited by Craig Bartholomew, Robin Parry, and Scott Hahn. Grand Rapids: Zondervan, 2006.
"Speech-Act Theory and Biblical Interpretation." *SJT* 58 (2005): 375–92.

Select Reviews

Review of James Barr, *Semantics of Biblical Language*. *JBL* 80 (1961): 374–77.
Review of Martin Noth, *Exodus: A Commentary*. *JBL* 81 (1962): 428.
Review of Gerhard von Rad, *Genesis: A Commentary*. *JBL* 81 (1962): 103.
Review of Lothar Perlitt, *Vatke und Wellhausen*. *JBL* 84 (1965): 470.
Review of Gerhard von Rad, *The Problem of the Hexateuch and Other Essays*. *JBL* 85 (1966): 390.
Review of Otto Eissfeld, *The Old Testament: An Introduction*. *JBL* 85 (1966): 130.
Review of Werner Klatt, *Hermann Gunkel: Zu seiner Theologie der Religionsgeschichte und zur Entstehung der formgeschichtlichen Methode*. *JBL* 88 (1969): 508–9.
Review of Hans-Joachim Kraus, *Geschichte der historisch-kritischen Erforschung des Alten Testaments*. *JBL* 89 (1970): 96–98.
"A Call to Canonical Interpretation." A review of James Sanders, *Torah and Canon*. *Int* 27 (1973): 88–91.
Review of Gerhard von Rad, *Genesis: A Commentary*. *Religious Studies* 10 (1974): 360–62.
Review of Otto Kaiser, *Introduction to the Old Testament*. *JSS* 22 (1977): 220–21.

Review of Walther Zimmerli, *Old Testament and the World. ThTo* 34 (1977): 130–32.
Review of Rolf Rendtorff, *Das überlieferungsgeschichtliche Problem des Pentateuch. JBL* 97 (1978): 272–73.
Review of James Crenshaw, *Gerhard von Rad. JBL* 100 (1981): 460.
Review of James Smart, *The Past, Present, and Future of Biblical Theology. JBL* 100 (1981): 252–53.
Review of James Barr, *Holy Scripture: Canon, Authority, Criticism. Int* 381 (1984): 66–70.
Review of Michael Fishbane, *Biblical Interpretation in Ancient Israel. JBL* 106 (1987): 511–13.
Review of Walter Brueggemann, *Theology of the Old Testament: Testimony, Dispute, Advocacy. SJT* 53 (2000): 228–33.

Tribute to Brevard S. Childs at the International SBL Meeting in Vienna, Austria

Christopher R. Seitz

Upon return from his customary spring residence in the United Kingdom, Brevard Springs Childs took a serious fall at their Connecticut home, from which, after a week in the hospital, he never recovered. He was eighty-three years old and had suffered from the after-effects of Lyme disease for many years, but was in reasonably good health and had just finished a manuscript project in Cambridge, England. So it was a shock to those of us who knew him and stayed in touch with him to learn of his death. SBL Executive Director Kent Richards very kindly asked me to pay him tribute. I am not sure I am competent to do that, and I am very sure an event like this would have made Childs wince. Childs was an intensely private man who preferred that his work speak for itself.

Much could be said at a section like this. This is all the more true with a figure like Brevard Childs who wrote in such a wide variety of forms: on both testaments; on the history of the discipline; on theological, historical, and methodological questions; on *Receptionsgeschichte*; on Isaiah and Exodus in extensive commentary treatments; on Biblical Theology; and before his untimely death, on the Pauline letter collection. I have written myself on Childs's contributions, and have recently published a long evaluation of the canonical approach, and I do not care to go over old ground here. If nothing else were said about Childs the scholar, it would be that he always sought the outer limits of a project, and did not rest until he could convey something both of the details and the comprehensive whole of a thing. I have never encountered a more curious mind. That also meant he was frequently misunderstood, sometimes very sympathetically, other times less so—quite apart from those who did understand and just disagreed!

What I would like to do is focus on one general theme, appropriate to this setting. *Childs and the formal discipline of biblical studies.* Childs believed in the necessary role of the academic discipline of biblical studies, as essential to the church's critical engagement with culture and for its own internal welfare. Childs loved the idea of a formal discipline of academic biblical studies, and always tried to honor it by attending to its phases with care and with critical insight. Part of this was simply the historian in him: Childs knew that at every period of the church's life there was manifested the formal concern for thinking seriously about the Bible: in commentary, introduction, hermeneutics, homiletics, apologetic. The great figures of the church's life—and of Judaism—were biblical scholars, and that was what I believe he saw as his own vocation and calling.

So there was in Childs a deep appreciation for learning and study, as a Christian discipline and virtue, coupled with the sense that this would be hard work, spiritually and practically. I can recall on numerous occasions receiving unwanted support from Childs, in the form of accounts of the struggles of this or that scholar or churchman in this or that period. Like most people, I wanted the politics of academic life to go my way; Childs wanted politics to be endured for the sake of the discipline of biblical studies, knowing that the joy of the Christian life could only be known through suffering and perseverance. He had history on his side in mounting this case.

I first encountered Childs in the pages of his 1974 Exodus commentary. I was studying in seminary, and then at the University of Munich, and I wanted a teacher who could demonstrate mastery of the most difficult questions of methodology and interpretation. That commentary struck me as an example of enormous hard work, if not always straightforward insight. It was not an easy commentary to use, and this had to do with its ambition. To my mind, this was its appeal. But it was also able to be used with profit by the preacher or Sunday school teacher.

A second and related memory was of attending my first SBL meeting. It was in 1982, and a group of us poor graduate students trundled down from New Haven to the New York Hilton. The session I remember was on Childs's *Introduction to the Old Testament as Scripture.* Assembled were the great and the good, the gladiator class of *Alttestamentler*: Bernard Anderson, Norman Gottwald, Jim Mays, Paul Hanson, Pat Miller, maybe Rolf Knierim (my memory is cloudy). As was typical of Childs, he did not attend. In addition to whatever allergies he had to such events, he was, I later learned, already hard at work on the *Introduction to the New Testa-*

ment and his mind had, as always, moved on. Strange it may seem to those who did not know him, Childs never discussed his own work in seminars and never promoted his theories or held forth on his own ideas. Instead, he listened carefully and taught his students to think critically. I am sure he viewed panel discussions of his work as too personal. (Those of us who have the idea that assigning our own publications to students is a good idea must learn the hard way.)

At the time I was surprised at the vehemence of the reaction to his 1979 publication, which ranged from mildly bemused to aggressively negative. My sense was that Childs was viewed as having somehow abandoned the disciplines of OT study (source, form, tradition, and redactional study) in the name of something called—wait for it—"scripture," and that, in the minds of some, this could only amount to piety, harmonization, false trails leading to the final form, and so forth. In other words, it amounted to a repudiation of critical foundations. I had not read the book, and did not recognize Childs in these reactions. The Childs I knew from the classroom had not tossed aside the critical skills shown in the Exodus commentary. When I did read *IOTS* I confess I did not understand it, and also did not recognize it as an introduction. But I could never accept that Childs had gone into a strange country. I assumed it was a book I would have to return to later when my Ph.D. seminars and dissertation were behind me.

I mention this because, twenty-five years later, the scene has changed dramatically. There was nothing, not even in Gottwald's *Tribes of Yahweh*, of the present character of social scientific methods or reader response—concern with matters in front of the text, in the community or the reader, or in the text's latest phases of alleged social construction and constructing. Ironically, it would be Childs who, at the end of the day, probably looked far more like a conservator of academic methodology and the disciplines of critical analysis, in their source to form to tradition to redaction phases, than like their opponent or their dismantler, in the name of the Old Testament "as scripture."

It is important to reflect briefly on the development of critical theory as it moved through alleged phases, what Koch could in the late 1960s optimistically describe as clear "extensions" of previous methods. Here, I believe, we find the unique contribution of Brevard Childs as an Old Testament scholar, that is, in his particular understanding of the nature of critical theory and its role in biblical interpretation and hermeneutics. In a word, Childs accepted critical observations in a local and non-comprehensive sense, using that which he believed appropriate to the biblical texts in question, and so tuned rightly to some dimension of proper interpretation. In that sense, he could accept something like sources in Genesis, because he acknowledged the way that Gen 1 and Gen 2–3 diverged at key points. The real question was what to make of the seam joining them and its larger effect on both texts.

Or, in his treatment of the crux regarding "this will be the sign for you" in Exod 3, he could accept the form-critical analysis of Gunkel and his students, and believe that the original sign, found in the oral tradition, was the bush; but that in the development of the traditions, in their literary form, a vestige of the older oral tradition had not been cleaned up or smoothed over. Examples like this—in the Psalms, the prophets, the Gospels, or the letters of Paul—could be multiplied.

In his work on the canonical shape, Childs was endeavoring to understand how the final form makes its particular sense. Recourse to aspects of critical theory would here manifest their usefulness. What one could not find in Childs was a sense that the phases of critical theory revealed a kind of *comprehensive usefulness of the methods in their entirety*. Their results were far more partial and provisional. Moreover, one had to exercise enormous caution in moving from one part of the canon to another. I recall finishing a dissertation on Jeremiah, in which I made heavy use of redaction criticism in order to understand the maturing form of the developed text. When I went to Isaiah to understand its final form, these methods did not work in the same way. Yet simply appealing to the synchronic shape of the final sixty-six chapters brought reactions of disdain from Childs. What was at issue was accepting the limitations of an honest account of the state of research in question for a given work, and seeking to move beyond impasses revealed precisely because of the limitations of the methods, and especially of asking them to go beyond their proper, more limited, remit.

The irony here is that by being used selectively and critically, these critical methods retained a more enduring character in Childs's work than in many others. I think there are several explanations for this, and one has been mentioned already. Childs wanted method to serve the purpose of helping him understand the theological implications of the final form of the text, not for the reproduction of a full scale history of religion behind the text or a seamless tradition-history straddling it. Neither religion nor an account of what von Rad called trying to understand "what Israel thought about Yahweh" interested Childs as ultimate affairs. This meant that method was at the service of understanding a *given*, not something to be retrieved or reconstructed: the given of the biblical text in its complex final form.

So method was not a project intended to make independent and comprehensive sense, but to serve a specific purpose: understanding the complexity of the biblical text in the form in which it lies before us. That there was a depth dimension was a given for Childs. This understanding meant that he accepted his own particular historical location in the twentieth and twenty-first centuries where this dimension had been rightly brought into focus. He did not seek to imitate previous interpreters, but only to learn from them. The specific cultural challenge of historical reference was one given in a particular form for the generation Childs knew himself to be a part of, and that challenge had to be faced on its own terms, and then transformed in the light of the biblical text's own special brokering of history.

Consider as well another problem in the development of critical methods: the desire to have them cooperate at maximal levels from one phase to the next. Childs did not ask the form-critical concern with origins and small oral units to magically join up with an inquiry starting at the other end, that is, literary sources revealed by attention to problems in the final form of the literature. The grand consensus of von Rad and Noth on this matter never really attracted Childs, and in the end he treated these phases as tools to be used where useful, and not organic products whose success demanded a seamless edifice. Of Bernard Anderson's bestselling *Understanding the Old Testament*, Childs could remark: it's better than the Bible. One could say that as well about efforts to smooth over the serious differences that quite properly divided phases of critical inquiry.

And of course these "better than the Bible" edifices don't last, probably because of their tendency to overreach. Jeremias has shown in a recent article how profoundly un-durable were the major planks in the von Radian and Nothian edifice: *Klein Credo*, sacral league, Solomonic enlightment, Yahwist as theologian, Wisdom as Israel's answer, the Hexateuch, and so on. It all made a kind of sense as an independent project once upon a time. But one could well ask whether even von Rad's own Genesis commentary really required this enormous critical prolegomena. Childs was more interested in which aspects of critical method genuinely assisted us in hearing the biblical text. Far more intriguing to my mind, therefore, were von Rad's final ruminations about the effects of the joining of sources, although this joining blunted the profile he had wished to give to the Yahwist. Von Rad had the courage to entertain the question, but not to pursue it with any vigor, due to his enormous investment in the grand consensus of thirty years of work. Childs, it seems to me, took the best of von Rad and moved on to areas von Rad would have seen as proper extensions of his ideas.

An opposite problem can also arise in the formal discipline of biblical studies. When a grand consensus fails, the danger is in thinking that one can free oneself from problems by developing a kind of selective amnesia about what previous phases had properly identified. At present there is a tremendous interest in a kind of neo-*Literarkritik*, focused on the final redactional stitching and the forces responsible for these, often at a high level of abstraction. I have in mind the work of Kratz, Steck, Kaiser, and others. Almost absent is any confidence about historical depth and the way form-criticism could posit an original tradition, figure, or saga. Childs never tried to recast these with great precision, but saw the reality to which the text referred in more general ways, never denying that something quite specific had triggered the development of the tradition. To choose a metaphor from Scotland: His concern was with single malt, not peat, barley, or water. But no whiskey can be made without these.

To conclude: It is something of an irony that the man who in 1982 was seen as a threat to historical-critical theory now retains far more of the historical depth of the biblical text precisely because of his concern to understand the final form. In *IOTS* there is a real Hosea, who married a real Gomer, in order to give a real message to the northern kingdom about real problems in their understanding of fertility, worship, and the nature of God's care. That this realist critique becomes a metaphor capable of extension to Judah, through a Judah redaction, and to future generations, through a closing appeal to wisely learn from the past, erases neither the original Hosea and Gomer nor the specific word given by God to that time and place. Childs was interested in the way the word of God *given in time* was a word *for the times*. This is what he saw the Bible demonstrating in its final form, through a careful analysis of it armed with all the tools of critical theory available to him. And this attention to history through time also animated his interest in the Bible's use in the church catholic through the ages, up to and including our own specific age. It would be wrong to call Childs unhistorical, and right to call him historical, but only in the most far-ranging sense.

Above all I will miss the confidence Childs had in sketching the character of the discipline, all the while interrogating and pressing it. There was in him a confidence that formal study of the Bible needed to happen in serious, public, disciplined ways, and that the church would then need to think through and commend what it was able to commend, with confidence, just as would the academy. Childs wanted the church to remain committed to serious biblical study, taking up with confidence challenges brought by cultural location, but always believing the Bible had a way of reframing such challenges according to the purposes of God. What worried him was a cleavage opening up, leaving the church and the academy each to do their thing, both becoming the lesser for it.

For Childs it was a mistake to look behind the Bible or too far in front of it, precisely because the final form of the text had sufficient riches for the church's life, to sustain and renew it. In its final form, the Bible offered a complete and ready-made set of problems to work through, and challenges sufficient for a lifetime and more—especially for someone seeking a comprehensive account. Never one to work as a quartermaster, Childs always had a comprehensive account in view.

It's a privilege to pay tribute to a teacher, a colleague, and a friend. I am sure this talk would have made Childs very restless unless it failed to commend the vocation that was his own, with attention to both its challenges and its hopefulness. I know he will be greatly missed, by family, friends, students, colleagues, and those who were challenged by his writings.

A verse from the Psalms comes to mind when I think of the contribution of Brevard Springs Childs, the man and the scholar. לֹא לָנוּ יְהוָה לֹא לָנוּ כִּי־לְשִׁמְךָ תֵּן כָּבוֹד, "Not to us, Lord, not to us, but to your name be the glory."

Brevard Childs and Form Criticism

David L. Petersen

To those casually familiar with biblical studies, the name of Brevard Childs is often associated both with an assessment of the biblical theology movement and with "canonical criticism." Such a response is understandable. However, I leave it to others to reflect on those features of Childs's work. The purpose of this essay is to assay Childs as one who worked from the perspective of form criticism, which, I shall suggest, is linked to his readings of biblical literature from a canonical perspective.

When Childs graduated from Princeton Seminary in 1950, the discourse of form criticism was not regularly prominent in the work of North American biblical scholars. However, his decision to pursue his graduate education at the University of Basel put him in proximity, both at Basel itself and at the German universities in which *Gattungs-* or *Formgeschichte* was a prominent mode of analysis. His teacher at Basel, Walter Baumgartner, had been a student of Hermann Gunkel, one of the definitive pioneers of form criticism. Further, the 1950s were a time when scholars such as von Rad, Westermann, and Zimmerli were writing from a form-critical perspective.[1] One might, therefore, have expected Childs to have been influenced immediately by such work. That appears not to have been the case.[2]

---

1. Childs identified Eichrodt, von Rad, and Zimmerli, among others, as his teachers (*Old Testament Theology in a Canonical Context* [Philadelphia: Fortress, 1986], xiii). It should also be noted that two German scholars, Erhard Gerstenberger and Walther Zimmerli, who often worked from a form-critical perspective, were at Yale during Childs's early tenure there. One may infer that he continued to be influenced by German form-critical scholarship from such personal contacts.

2. One must, however, reckon with his self-referential statement: "Having been trained in the form-critical method" (Brevard S. Childs, *Introduction to the Old Testament as Scripture* [Philadelphia: Fortress, 1979], 75).

Childs appears to have appropriated form-critical work over a period of time. In order to observe this development, it is appropriate to examine some of his early publications. His dissertation was revised and published in English as *Myth and Reality in the Old Testament*.[3] This volume was, in many ways, a theological study, as the final chapter, "The Theological Problem of Myth," suggests. However, it was also a volume in which Childs's form-critical sensibilities were in evidence. One sentence is telling: "In saga, in legend, the broken myth, through these unhistorical vehicles as well as through the historical, Israel articulated her understanding of her existence."[4] These "unhistorical vehicles" could be viewed as construals of reality. However, they could also be understood as literary forms: saga, legend, and (broken) myth. Further, it is not surprising that those terms would appear in lists compiled by other scholars of *Gattungen* found in Hebrew prose literature.

The foregoing statement reflects work present in the book's first chapter. When setting up the project, Childs distinguished between "broad" and "narrow" definitions of myth. He deemed the latter to be "form-critical."[5] And he disagreed with this characterization, which he attributed to the brothers Grimm and Gunkel. His primary argument against the form-critical definition of myth was that it defined myth "too exclusively as a literary product." As a result, Childs wanted to think about myth in *"phenomenological"* terms, as "an understanding of reality," a reality that he contended stood in conflict with "Old Testament reality." Though there is literature of mythic origin in the OT, it has been "altered" or "broken." In sum, though he occasionally used form-critical categories, Childs's approach in *Myth and Reality in the Old Testament* was not essentially form-critical. Myth was for him not a *Gattung* but a way of being in the world.

His second book, *Memory and Tradition in Israel*, marks a significant change.[6] When examining the categories "God Remembers" and "Israel Remembers," he begins by analyzing the semantic range of the Hebrew word *zkr*. Immediately, therefore, he broaches the question of how to pro-

---

3. Brevard S. Childs, *Myth and Reality in the Old Testament* (SBT 27; London: SCM, 1960).
4. Ibid., 103.
5. Ibid., 15.
6. Brevard S. Childs, *Memory and Tradition in Israel* (SBT 37; London: SCM, 1962).

ceed with the analysis. What he writes may serve as a programmatic statement about the significance of form criticism for his work:

> The task of tracing the development of a term presents the exegete with a basic methodological decision. What is the proper method of approach? The method most frequently employed for a critical word study is to arrange the occurrences of the word in a chronological sequence according to literary sources, and then attempt to discover a development in usage. Many of the articles in Kittel's *Wörterbuch* are classic examples of this method. How can one accurately trace the development of a term in a living oral tradition solely based on chance occurrences in the literary level? Is there not danger that the artificial order of the literary sources be imposed upon material that may have another structure entirely?
>
> The form-critical approach, which has been developed with such precision in recent German Old Testament scholarship, attempts to avert these dangers by penetrating to the oral tradition. By examination of the form a word is set within the living context of an ancient tradition ... this study will attempt to employ this critical method in tracing the development of the phrase "God remembers."[7]

Four things are noteworthy in these paragraphs. First, Childs was overtly concerned to identify a method appropriate for a particular kind of investigation. Second, form criticism is deemed a "critical method." That does not mean, however, that it cannot be used to address theological issues. Third, Childs deems it immune from the problems associated with theological word study approaches. Finally, at this period in Childs's work, form criticism provides access to "living oral tradition."

Childs then proceeded to examine the language of the deity remembering. He discovered that imperative verbs for *remember* occurred in complaint psalms, whereas finite verbs were present in hymns. The standard examples are termed "unbroken." Things change when the discourse of *remembering* appears in the confessions of Jeremiah and in Job. Here, that discourse appears in dialogues. Even more distinctive is the language of remembering in prophetic literature (e.g., Hos 6:11b–7:2). Whereas the call for God to remember in psalms of complaint could lead to God's positive response to an Israelite, the notion of God's remembering in the books of Hosea and Jeremiah could lead to devastating judgment. For Childs, to

---

7. Ibid., 34.

assay God as one who remembers, one must think form-critically about the texts in which such verbiage appears.

In 1963, Childs published an article that exemplified his use of form criticism.[8] However, in contrast to *Memory and Tradition in Israel*, here he focused more on a formula than on larger entities such as psalms or prophetic oracles. The well-known conclusion was that the formula "until this day" was regularly a redactional addition to an earlier tradition. To this extent, the article appears to be primarily redaction-critical in its orientation. However, that conclusion was only made possible by a form-critical argument early on in the article. At the outset, he was concerned to analyze "the etiological story," which he characterized as a "genre." In attempting to move beyond the scholarly impasse in reflection about the historical character of this literature, he first examined the formula "until this day," focusing on the etymological etiology. He discerned a "pure, unbroken form" of the formula in Josh 7:26; Judg 18:12; and 2 Chr 20:26, consisting of the adverb *therefore* (*'l-kn*) followed by the verb *qr'* in the frequentative perfect and then the phrase "until this day." Other examples of the form, e.g., Deut 3:14; 2 Sam 6:8, deviate in one way or another from that form, and are therefore deemed to represent divergences from it. For example, the verb *qr'* appears as a *waw* consecutive imperfect reporting a completed rather than a "frequentative" action. Elsewhere (e.g., Gen 19:37; 26:33), the formula has been used to modify a noun or pronoun instead of a verb. The move is significant. Instead of explaining the reason for a word, the formula "becomes an archaeological note which expresses the extension in time of a past phenomenon into the present." He then surveyed other types of etiologies and observed the same "breakdown in form" that he had discerned in the etymological etiology.

In order to explain these diverse uses of the formula in the final section of the article, Childs hoped to identify the *Sitz im Leben* of the biblical formula. By appealing especially to the work of Herodotus, he maintained that the divergent formulae reflect the hands of redactors who are adding "personal testimony" to the traditions that they had received.

There was far less emphasis in this essay on discovering "oral tradition" than on understanding the nature of a literary form/formula and the ways in which it was used in redactional activity. Common to both *Memory*

---

8. Brevard S. Childs, "A Study of the Formula, 'Until This Day,'" *JBL* 82 (1963): 279–92.

and Tradition in Israel and "A Study of the Formula, 'Until this Day'" was a distinction between unbroken and broken form. Only by attending to the "pure form" was it possible to discern the unusual, and often theologically provocative, occasions when the form deviated from the norm.

Gerald Sheppard, a former student of Childs, once wrote, "In the 1960s C. became known for his skills in form criticism and traditio-historical studies as well as his critique of failings in the older biblical theology movement."[9] This statement is particularly apt, since it was during the early 1960s that Childs published studies, both in articles and in one monograph, that were overtly form-critical in character. That same focus had not been apparent in work prior to that time.

Childs's use of form-critical analysis continued. It is thoroughly integrated into his commentary devoted to the book of Exodus. When writing the commentary's introduction, Childs described one section of the commentary as follows: "In this section a form-critical, traditio-historical analysis is offered which seeks to explore the early forces at work in the shaping of the oral tradition."[10]

An example will help readers understand the character of his form-critical approach to exegesis. When examining Exod 3:1–4:17, Childs created several subsections for his work. The phrase "form criticism" appears in several of the rubrics that introduce these subsections. Childs's treatment of these verses falls into the following parts: (1) textual and philological notes; (2) literary, form-critical, and traditio-historical problems; (3) Old Testament context; (4) New Testament context; (5) history of exegesis; and (6) theological reflection. Virtually all of his "critical" work on the text took place under the second of these categories.[11] It soon becomes clear that this second section includes a broad range of critical perspectives. For example, subsection B is titled "The Problem of Sources"; subsection C, "Form-Critical and Tradition-Critical Analysis of 3.1ff."; and subsection D, "A Form-Critical Study of Ex. 3.12." Two of the sections mention form criticism overtly. In one it is linked with tradition history; in the

---

9. Gerald T. Sheppard, "Childs, Brevard," in *Dictionary of Biblical Interpretation* (ed. John H. Hayes; Nashville: Abingdon, 1999), 1:178.

10. Brevard S. Childs, *The Book of Exodus: A Critical, Theological Commentary* (OTL; Philadelphia: Westminster, 1973), xiv. That "section" also included source- and redaction-critical perspectives.

11. Ibid., 51–71.

other it stands alone.[12] When working with these two analytical categories, Childs first proceeded to characterize Exod 3:1–4:17 as a call narrative. He then attempted to discern the *Sitz im Leben* of that "fixed form." After reviewing various proposals, he contended, "The setting of Ex. 3 is the prophetic office."[13] Put another way, the form had been preserved by the way in which prophets were installed into a particular office. At that point he moved to consider "tradition," attempting to place what he deemed to be a prophetic form within the larger context of the development of Israelite literature. His approach was dialectical. On the one hand, he suggested that Israelite writers knew that Moses initiated a new role, one in which he was commissioned to communicate a message to another party. This distinguished him from the patriarchs who, though they communicated with the deity, were not asked to function as messengers. On the other hand, Exod 3 "echoed" the experiences of Israel's prophets, which meant that traditions about prophets who lived later than Moses had influenced this portrayal of Moses' call. One may draw back from this analysis and learn that the use of these two critical perspectives was sequential. Childs first made a judgment about the form of this literature and only then posed a question about the way in which it was related to Israelite tradition(s).

The other section in which form-critical perspectives are overtly at work focuses on a single verse, Exod 3:12. In the phrase "this shall be the sign for you," to what does "this" refer? Childs proposed to answer what appears to be a grammatical question with "a fresh form-critical study." This study involved assessing narratives in which a sign is given. Childs noted two basic "patterns." In one, labeled "A," the sign preceded that which was promised. In the other, labeled "B," the sign confirmed a present act and did not relate directly to what was promised. Then Childs returned to Exod 3:12, observing that it reflects neither of these patterns. He argued that the meaning of this verse had been affected by "the development of the tradition." An early etiological tradition about a burning bush had been integrated into a call narrative. Hence, "this" refers to the burning bush and not to a sign provided in response to the prophet's objection. Here, though Childs claimed to be offering a form-critical study, it is clear

---

12. This approach differs from that in some of the Biblischer Kommentar volumes, in which form criticism routinely stood alone, e.g., in English translation, Hans Walter Wolff, *Hosea: A Commentary on the Book of the Prophet Hosea* (Hermeneia; Philadelphia: Fortress, 1974).

13. Childs, *Exodus*, 55.

that the "thesis" he offered relied as well on study of the tradition-historical character of the text. He as much as recognized this when he wrote, "In sum, the problem of the sign in Exod 3:12 has arisen because of its history of tradition."[14]

In sum, whether Childs claimed to be linking form-critical work with other modes of critical inquiry or not, he regularly integrated form criticism with other approaches to the text. His work was methodologically eclectic, drawing on the full variety of critical biblical scholarship of the time.

It is instructive to compare the sort of work that appeared in the commentary on Exodus with that which appeared in his commentary on Isaiah. Though published in the same commentary series as his volume on Exodus, the analytical categories had changed. This was no doubt due to his own views about attention to method, which had been so prominent in his earlier work. One sentence from the commentary's preface underscores this change: "I have tried to keep abreast of the changing approaches to the book, which have moved through numerous stages of literary-critical, form-critical, redactional, and rhetorical analysis. I have learned much from each, yet I am also conscious that an eclectic mixing of methods does not offer a real solution."[15] Perhaps most striking is Childs's distancing from the sort of the work of which he had been a practitioner. During the 1960s he had not simply kept up, but had written incisively using the perspectives of form criticism, among others. Now he had, in effect, characterized those approaches as the work of others, whereas he intended to work from the new perspectives he identified in the commentary's introduction. Needless to say, these new perspectives do not include the categories present in the sentence just quoted.

It is useful to compare Childs's analysis of Isaiah's call narrative with that of his assessment of Moses' call. The first major rubric, "The Critical Debate," stood in the place of the first rubric in the Exodus commentary, "Literary and Form-critical Analysis." Childs identified several issues that he thought made up the agenda of the critical debate, the second of which is "The Form-Critical Debate."[16] In this section, Childs distinguished between those who think Isa 6 is a commissioning narrative, such as one

---

14. Ibid., 60.
15. Brevard S. Childs, *Isaiah: A Commentary* (OTL; Louisville: Westminster John Knox, 2001), xii.
16. Ibid., 52–53.

finds in 1 Kgs 22, and those who construe it as a call, similar to Exod 3 and Judg 6. In the latter cases, an individual is "called" whereas in the former, the individual volunteers. Having delineated these positions, he maintained, "the issue at stake is more complex than usually considered." He deemed Isa 6 to include material not present in a commissioning scene, that is, the lengthy introduction. He wrote:

> When Isaiah beholds God, he confesses in complete awe his own sin and guilt, and only after he has been cleansed is the commission delivered to him. In a word, Isaiah's role is, in some important sense, paradigmatic. His experience of "death and rebirth" is constitutive of his role in this chapter. … As a consequence, the currently formulated polarity between call and commission does not address adequately the theological dimension of the text and needs to be approached from a different theological perspective.[17]

At this point, Childs seems to have moved beyond concerns typical of form criticism to concerns that he, at least, construed as "theological." Later, in the Exposition, Childs worked out the theological implications of these verses.[18] Though he identified them there as a "commission," the form-critical debate did not play a prominent role in his theological analysis of Isa 6.

I have argued that Childs, though in no overt sense a forerunner of what one might characterize as the literary critical study of the Bible, was nonetheless sensitive in the 1960s and 1970s to the significance of literary forms and their distinctive features. His attention to "form," or at least to the vocabulary of form, continued beyond those decades. However, the term was embedded in a new discourse, that of "canonical form."[19] One might suggest that the logic of form criticism was at work even in this next phase of Childs's work. Canon was, after all, a "form." It was a distinctive kind of literature with identifiable features. For Childs, those included the sense of the biblical canon as a "theological whole."

Childs charted his ideas about the "formfulness" of biblical literature most thoroughly in *Introduction to the Old Testament as Scripture*. In that volume, he discussed "the canonical form of the Old Testament" and "the

---

17. Ibid., 53.
18. Ibid., 54–60.
19. That phrase appears, for example, in his *Isaiah*, 5.

canonical shape of the literature." Those phrases appear to be interchangeable.[20] In developing this approach to the Bible, Childs identified different entities whose "shape" he could discuss. The smallest such entity was the biblical book, the largest was "the form of the Christian Bible."[21] Between those two poles stood the three canonical components of the Jewish Bible: Torah, Prophets, and Writings. One can therefore contend that Childs had undertaken a sort of canonical form-critical analysis and, in so doing, had identified different genres of scriptural forms: books, canonical construals (e.g., Writings), Jewish scriptures, and Christian Bible.[22]

Childs deemed each of the canonical entities worthy of analysis. For example, he assayed the Pentateuch to determine its "form and function." On the one hand, he argued that "the final biblical editor" saw each of the first five books of the Bible as "separate entities."[23] On the other hand, he maintained that the Pentateuch had a final form that was more than the simple combination of those originally distinct books. Childs maintained, for example, that the book of Genesis had been redacted in a way that contributed to this pentateuchal coherence. He wrote:

> Yet it is also evident that the patriarchal material has not just been accidentally attached to the story which follows, but is integrally connected. Indeed, the patriarchal stories have been consistently edited in such a way as to point to the future.... Clearly Genesis was conceived of by the final redactor as the introduction to the story of Israel which begins in Exodus.[24]

His treatments of individual biblical books were of a similar kind. Redaction played an important role. His assessment of the book of Joel offers a characteristic example. He agreed with Wolff, who argued that the book,

---

20. Childs, *Introduction to the Old Testament as Scripture*, 71.
21. Ibid., 671.
22. One good place to read Childs's views on the shape of the Christian Bible is *Biblical Theology of the Old and New Testaments: Theological Reflection on the Christian Bible* (Minneapolis: Fortress, 1993). Childs does not appear to have written extensively on the notion of a biblical book. Cf. Ehud Ben Zvi, "The Prophetic Book: A Key Form of Prophetic Literature," in *The Changing Face of Form Criticism for the Twenty-First Century* (ed. Marvin Sweeney and Ehud Ben Zvi; Grand Rapids: Eerdmans, 2003), 276–97.
23. Childs, *Introduction to the Old Testament as Scripture*, 129.
24. Ibid., 130.

though a literary "unity," reflects diverse authorial hands. Childs construed the redactional work as part of the canonical process: "The crucial canonical shaping occurred when an editor took up this prophecy and fashioned it into a message for future generations."[25] Childs also thought it noteworthy that this editor referred to earlier prophetic literature when updating Joel's original message. This kind of allusion also contributed to the canonical form of the book.

If, as Childs held, it is appropriate to think about canon as a form, then one could ask questions about the *Sitz im Leben* that created and preserved this form. For Childs, that setting in life was not difficult to identify; it was the community of faith. That community of faith, existing over centuries, was responsible for "the canonical process." The community "shaped" or gave form to the literature that had been or was being written. It was the community, and not simply a redactor, that "created" the Pentateuch. The setting in life for the creation of scripture, whether in smaller or larger entities, was the religious community, whether Israelite, Jewish, or Christian.

Several concluding remarks are in order. First, just as Child rejected the notion that he should be known as a canonical critic, one should assume that he would have also rejected calling himself a form critic. He would have agreed that he used form-critical perspectives in his work as a biblical scholar, but he would have also maintained that he deployed other critical perspectives as well, notably tradition history and redaction criticism. Form criticism belonged to the full range of methods that a responsible scholar would use when analyzing biblical literature.

Second, Childs's work as a form critic was formative for individuals who were enrolled in Yale's Ph.D. program relatively early in his tenure there. Though Childs did not serve as the dissertation adviser for all those who graduated from that program, he influenced those students in consequential ways. The following representative scholars, notably form-critical in their orientation in the works cited here, are emblematic of his impact: George Coats, *Saga, Legend, Tale, Novella, Fable: Narrative Forms in the Old Testament*;[26] Burke Long, *The Problem of Etiological Narrative in the*

---

25. Ibid., 39.
26. George Coats, ed., *Saga, Legend, Tale, Novella, Fable: Narrative Forms in the Old Testament* (JSOTSup 85; Sheffield: JSOT, 1985).

Old Testament;[27] Roy Melugin, *The Formation of Isaiah 40–55*;[28] and Gene Tucker, *Form Criticism of the Old Testament*.[29]

In sum, as a biblical scholar, Brevard Childs was deeply concerned with using methods and perspectives appropriate to the biblical literature that he was examining. His sense of what was appropriate evolved during the course of his career, moving from what he himself identified as "critical" problems to those that might be characterized as "theological." As a part of this development, his focus on "form" changed. In his earlier years, he was concerned about the forms that one might find within biblical books, both in their "unbroken" and "broken" states. In later years, he was far more concerned about the canonical form (and forms) of biblical literature. To that extent, one might claim that he never strayed from his longstanding concern to identify the form of the literature he was reading and to interpret it as that form or shape demanded.

---

27. Burke Long, *The Problem of Etiological Narrative in the Old Testament* (BZAW 108; Berlin: Töpelmann, 1968).

28. Roy Melugin, *The Formation of Isaiah 40–55* (BZAW 141; Berlin: de Gruyter, 1976).

29. Gene Tucker, *Form Criticism of the Old Testament* (Philadelphia: Fortress, 1971).

The Wrath of God at Mount Sinai (Exod 32; Deut 9–10)[*]

Jörg Jeremias

Characteristically, Brevard S. Childs's preface to his Exodus commentary begins: "The purpose of this commentary is unabashedly theological. Its concern is to understand Exodus as scripture of the church."[1] Yet, he adds at once, "a rigorous and careful study of the whole range of problems" that historical-critical reading of the Bible had developed since the eighteenth century should be prerequisite. His training in Basel under Walter Baumgartner had prepared him excellently for such exegesis, but the theological impetus was his own. It implied "a continuous wrestling with the history of interpretation and theology," including "rabbinics, New Testament, patristics, medieval and Reformation studies, philosophy and dogmatics," even if, of course, "there are gaps and deficiencies in one man's attempt."[2]

Childs's primary intention was not to introduce revolutionary new ideas into the interpretation of the book of Exodus, but "to shift the scale of priorities" in exegesis (x). "In my judgment, the study of the prehistory [of a given text] has its proper function within exegesis only in illuminating the final text" (xv). More important for Childs was "the heart of the commentary" which he called "Old Testament context," dealing with "the

---

[*] When I came to Yale as a student in 1960 working for my Master's degree, my first course with the young Professor Brevard S. Childs was on Exodus. At the same time both of us read the Mekhilta on Exodus under the guidance of Judah Goldin. Thus, for me it was evident that I should choose the book of Exodus as my subject in his memorial volume.

1. Brevard S. Childs, *Exodus: A Critical, Theological Commentary* (OTL; Philadelphia: Westminster, 1974).

2. Ibid., ix–x.

text in its final form," not the least aiming at the usefulness of the commentary for a preacher (xiv). Yet this interpretation of the final form of the text is by no means an easy enterprise. It presupposes every step of historical-critical exegesis, and it "knows" already the partners with whom it has to talk: "New Testament context" and "theological reflection."

In an ambitious enterprise like Childs's commentary on Exodus, it is evident that "gaps and deficiencies in one man's attempt" are inevitable not only concerning the history of exegesis, but also concerning the interpretation of the final form of the text. By pointing to an aspect of Exod 32 that is missing in Childs's exegesis, the present writer does not aim at criticizing Childs, but at continuing his intention in his own spirit. The texts we try to understand are far beyond our understanding; nobody is able to exhaust them. Yet my interpretation will bear a stronger accent on historical-critical research. According to my conviction, it is the complex growth of biblical texts and biblical tradition during centuries that led to a complex set of meanings in a given text. Already in biblical times texts were heard and read with different nuances. As far as we are able to grasp, these differences can't be unimportant for our own interpretation of the text, because "it is incumbent upon each new generation to study its meaning afresh, to have the contemporary situation of the church addressed by its word" (xiii).

1.

A synchronic reader of the Old Testament starting with the creation of the world in Gen 1 meets the "wrath of God" against his own people for the first time in the story of the golden calf in Exod 32. He or she will notice quickly that this new kind of divine reaction draws one's attention to a new dimension of human guilt: still at Sinai, having just experienced God's basic revelation, in the moment of Moses' absence, Israel urges Aaron "to make" a god. For Israel, the living God is obscure and must be interpreted by Moses. The golden calf is visible and evident; it needs no interpretation. In the very hour of his fundamental revelation, the true God is refused by his people, who long for a god fitting their own taste and who is easy to handle. In his reaction, God's anger burns and he wants to devour his people.

God's wrath is mentioned three times in Exod 32, though only in one limited passage (32:10–14). And this passage is a later (Deuteronomistic) addition to Exod 32 (see below). There was an early version of the story of the golden calf which did not know of the wrath of God. On the other hand, the importance of the notion of God's wrath at Sinai for the whole Old Testament becomes evident when the parallel text in Deut 9–10 (9:7–10:11) is taken into account. While Moses here reflects upon his experience with Israel during his lifetime, *the wrath of God upon his people has become the one and only subject* (Deut 9:7, 8, 18, 19, 20, 22; cf. 10:10) dominating Moses' thought "since I have known you" (9:24). Once detected, the wrath of God becomes a power that threatens Israel not only at the incident of the golden calf, but during their whole existence. It is Deut 9–10, with its stress on the wrath of God, that urges the reader of Exod 32 to focus interest on this subject too, especially since Exod 32 and Deut 9–10 run parallel not only in their general thought but also in many details and even in many common phrases (see below). Thus, Exod 32 cannot be interpreted without an eye on Deut 9–10, and vice versa.

What exactly is divine wrath? Instead of giving a comprehensive definition, I want to limit myself to a double differentiation that is decisive for my understanding of Exod 32 and Deut 9–10[3]:

(1) Divine wrath is basically different from human wrath in that it is never arbitrary. A human being in great anger does not know what he or she is doing; he or she is out of control. In the narratives of the OT God is never out of control in this sense. On the contrary, his wrath is a sign of exceeding human guilt. Only much later—in the book of Job—does the question arise whether God may be angry without corresponding guilt. It is answered in a negative way; if God would be enraged without adequate reason, that is, quite arbitrarily, he would be no longer the God of the Bible.

(2) Divine wrath is basically different from divine punishment. Divine punishment stands in a clear and indisputable relation to the guilty act to which it reacts. It is moderate and limited. In contrast, God's wrath is immoderate and unlimited. In most cases its effect is total destruction. It is limited only in terms of time; it comes and ends. But because of its destructive nature, this limitation is no consolation for anyone who is hit by it.

---

3. For a more extensive treatment see Jörg Jeremias, *Der Zorn Gottes im Alten Testament: Das biblische Israel zwischen Verwerfung und Erwählung* (2nd ed.; BThSt 104; Neukirchen-Vluyn: Neukirchener, 2011).

2.

According to the majority of scholars, Deut 9–10 rests upon Exod 32 in its original form, that is, upon the older layers of Exod 32 that exclude the special tradition of the fighting Levites (vv. 25–29), probably Aaron's self-defense in his dialogue with Moses (vv. 21–24), and the intercessory prayer of Moses (vv. 7–14). The latter case is not as evident as the first ones. Although Exod 32:7–14 is certainly an addition to Exod 32, it uses the same Deuteronomistic language as Deut 9–10 and has many phrases in common with Deut 9:12–14, 25–29. Therefore, opinions differ on how the close relatedness of these two texts is to be explained. We shall come back to this special question at the end of our considerations.

If we compare Deut 9–10 with its model Exod 32, we meet *two fundamental differences*:

(1) In Deut 9–10, the wrath of God is no longer limited to the guilt of the golden calf, but is expanded to include Israel's mistrust of God in the wilderness.
(2) While Moses' prayer in Exod 32 is successful in the beginning (vv. 10–14) it is rejected by God at the end (vv. 31–34). All of Moses' many prayers in Deut 9–10 are successful.

The first difference is decisive for the interpretation of Deut 9–10, with which I shall begin, followed by a discussion of the second, decisive for the understanding of Exod 32.

3.

In *Deut 9* the wrath of God is extended to respond not only to the fabrication of the golden calf, but also to the many situations of Israel's rebellion against God in the wilderness. Moses' reflection upon Israel's early history starts in v. 7: "Remember this and never forget, how you provoked the Lord your God to anger in the desert. From the day you left Egypt until you arrived here you have been rebellious against the Lord."[4] The Horeb episode follows immediately afterward (v. 8) and covers most of Deut 9: "At Horeb you aroused the Lord's wrath...." But verse 7, quoted

---

4. Citations of biblical texts are taken from the NIV.

above, stresses the permanence of Israel's guilt. In Hebrew the sentence for this reason is constructed very artificially with a participle and the verb היה (מַמְרִים הֱיִיתֶם: "You were permanently rebellious"). And when, after Moses' reflection upon his destruction of the golden calf, the theme of the rebellion in the wilderness is resumed, the text reads: "You also made the Lord angry at Taberah,[5] at Massah.... You have been rebellious against the Lord ever since I have known you" (vv. 22, 24). By including the wilderness narratives into the subject of the wrath of God, the author evidently intends to exclude Israel's possible claim for righteousness during the time before and after the fabrication of the golden calf (Deut 9:1–6). To be sure, for Deut 9 the golden calf is the unsurpassable peak of God's people's guilt. But the golden calf is by no means just an episode. It is accompanied by chains of guilt during the wilderness wanderings that would themselves call for God's destruction of Israel—if not for Moses.[6]

But the implicit scope of God's wrath in Deut 9–10 reaches far beyond Israel's mistrust in the wilderness. This is shown primarily by its very *sophisticated use of terminology* for God's wrath. True, there is a "Leitwort" (M. Buber) for this wrath in Deut 9, a root dominating the whole chapter, which is קצף. It occurs three times in the *hiphil* with Israel as subject ("to arouse God's wrath"; vv. 7, 8, 22) and once in the *qal* with YHWH as subject ("to be angry, full of wrath"; v. 19). The root of this "Leitwort" is rather rare compared with other phrases for wrath—for the *hiphil* there are only two other references in the whole OT, while the *qal* with YHWH as subject occurs only once in the historical books. Apparently the traditional term אף of the model Exod 32 is replaced consciously, possibly in order to use a phrase which is specific for God's wrath at the time of Moses.

---

5. Again, a construction with היה and a participle; literally: "You were permanently provoking YHWH to anger."
6. Some recent authors such as Eep Talstra ("Deuteronomy 9 and 10: Synchronic and Diachronic Observations," in *Synchronic or Diachronic? A Debate on Method in Old Testament Exegesis* [ed. Johannes C. de Moor; OTS 34; Leiden: Brill 1995], 187–210) and Norbert Lohfink ("Deuteronomium 9,1–10,11 and Exodus 32–34," in *Gottes Volk am Sinai: Untersuchungen zu Ex 32–34 und Dtn 9–10* [ed. Matthias Köckert and Erhard Blum; VGWTh 18; Gütersloh: Chr. Kaiser/Gütersloher Verlagshaus, 2001], 41–87), judge that vv. 7–8 and 22–24 are later additions to an original separate Horeb narrative. I doubt that such a narrative ever existed in Deut 9–10 and I see no compelling reasons for this literary-critical operation. But Talstra and Lohfink are right in their disagreement with the far-reaching literary separations of other scholars. To my mind, only Deut 10:6–7 and 8–9 can be demonstrated as additions with certainty.

On the other hand, there are two phrases for God's wrath in Deut 9 that occur only once or twice but that coordinate the chapter with events related much later:

(1) The root אנף in the *hitpael*, "to be enraged" (used only with God as subject) is usually directed against single persons who have become guilty (as is true in Deut 9 for Aaron [v. 20]). It is directed against God's people as a collective in the OT only twice: in Deut 9:8 and in 2 Kgs 17:18. With regard to the connections mentioned below this may not be fortuitous; in that case Deut 9:8 for a careful reader of the OT would already aim at God's wrath destroying Samaria and Jerusalem.

(2) More evident is the root כעס in the *hiphil* with Israel as subject ("to provoke God to anger") in v. 18b.[7] The root is characteristic for describing Israel's guilt (and the guilt of its kings) during the divided monarchy. It is used in a typical Deuteronomistic manner from 1 Kgs 14 to 2 Kgs 23 nearly twenty times (and otherwise predominantly in the Deuteronomistic passages of the book of Jeremiah). When this root occurs in Deut 9, every trained reader of the OT is urged to relate it to the sins of Jeroboam I, Ahab, and Manasseh.

(3) There is at least one textual hint proving that the relation between God's wrath during the time of Moses and God's wrath leading to the destruction of Samaria and Jerusalem is intended. As already quoted above, in Deut 9:7 Moses introduces his reflection upon Israel's guilt during his lifetime: "Remember this and never forget, how you provoked the Lord your God to anger in the desert. From the day you left Egypt until you arrived here, you have been rebellious against the Lord." By far the closest parallel to this judgment serving as a link is found in God's speech through a prophet in 2 Kgs 21:15: "They have done evil in my eyes and have provoked me to anger from the day their forefathers came out of Egypt until this day." 2 Kgs 21:10–16, however, is the decisive prophetic

---

7. For the peculiarities of this root, which D. J. McCarthy calls the "provocation formula," see his "The Wrath of Yahweh and the Structural Unity of the Deuteronomistic History," in *Essays in Old Testament Ethics* (ed. James L. Crenshaw and John T. Willis; New York: Ktav, 1974), 97–110.

announcement of the destruction of Jerusalem and its temple in Deuteronomistic thinking.[8]

What is the intent of this kind of *expansion of the scope of God's wrath* in Deut 9–10? One aim, of course, is to intensify the correspondence of God's wrath against the golden calf and his wrath against "the sins of Jeroboam," which was intended from the very beginning of the tradition of the golden calf. More importantly, this expansion aimed to answer the question of how Moses' successful prayer in Deut 9–10 should be interpreted in the light of the destruction of Jerusalem and God's holy temple. True, every reader understands that in its refusal of the only living God, Israel would have been lost and annihilated already at Mt. Sinai/Horeb without Moses' intercessory prayer. But how far did this prayer reach?

To answer this question we have to look at the second "Leitwort" in Deut 9–10. The outcome of God's wrath in Deut 9 is constantly Israel's "destruction"/ "annihilation" (שמד in *hiphil* with God as the subject occurs five times: 9:8, 14, 19, 20, 25; cf.10:10), which is avoided by Moses. Lohfink, to his merit, observed that this phrase plays an important role in the books of Kings in relation to God's wrath as well,[9] but that there is a significant difference: it is used either concerning guilty kings whose "houses" (that is, families and clans) are annihilated (1 Kgs 13:34; 15:29; 16:12), or the nations who formerly possessed Israel's land and who were less guilty than Manasseh was (2 Kgs 21:9), but never in relation to Israel.[10] Instead, two other phrases that are synonymous take its place. God's wrath leads to his הסיר מעל פני יהוה ("removal from the presence of YHWH"; 2 Kgs 17:18, 23; 23:27; 24:3) or to his השליך מעל פני יהוה ("thrusting from the presence of YHWH"; 2 Kgs 17:20; 24:20). Though, of course, the loss of the temple and of the land meant a terrible experience of the wrath of God, Israel was not annihilated in spite of its exceeding guilt. Thus, Moses' intercessory prayer remained effective for all future Israel, even for the generations in and after the exile. Moses' reflection in Deut 9–10 ends:

---

8. For the linkage between Exod 32:30–31 and 2 Kgs 21:17, see n. 17 below.

9. Norbert Lohfink, "Der Zorn Gottes und das Exil: Beobachtungen zum deuteronomistischen Geschichtswerk," in *Liebe und Gebot: Studien zum Deuteronomium* (ed. R. G. Kratz; FRLANT 190; Göttingen: Vandenhoeck & Ruprecht, 2000), 138–155; 143–145.

10. Compare, in contrast, the repeated threat of Israel's annihilation (*hiphil* of שמד) by God in Deut 28 (vv. 20, 24, 45, 48, 51, 61, 63).

"Now I stayed on the mountain forty days and nights, as I did the first time also. It was not his will to destroy you." The same idea is repeated in 2 Kgs 14:27: "Since the Lord had not said he would blot out the name of Israel under heaven, he saved them by the hand of Jeroboam son of Jehoash." In my opinion Lohfink is right when he stresses that in these passages a new concept of the wrath of God is created, according to which God's wrath no longer leads to the annihilation of the guilty, but, though terrible for those being hit by it, spares his chosen people and leads "only" to their loss of the land.[11]

4.

Studying *Deut 9–10* first and then returning to Exod 32, the reader is irritated initially by the fact that the very clear picture of Moses' repeated successful prayer by which he saves his people from destruction seems to be obscured in Exod 32. Why is Moses' intercessory prayer in Exod 32 successful only at his first time of praying, but refused by God at the second time? The help to answer this question provided by a diachronic reading becomes obvious. It is an undisputed result of critical scholarship that Moses' successful prayer in Exod 32:7–14 belongs to the later layers of the chapter; it bursts with Deuteronomistic phraseology very close to Deut 9–10, and apparently wants to answer the rejection of Moses' older prayer in vv. 30–34.

Why then is Moses' prayer rejected by God in *Exod 32:30–34*? Before answering this question it is important to note that the hermeneutical horizon of Moses' prayer in vv. 30–34 is not yet the wrath of God and not yet the imminent annihilation of his people as in the later passage, vv. 7–14. In vv. 30–34 the context proves that Moses goes too far in what he asks from God. His intention "to make atonement for your sins" (v. 30) is not quite clear. The *piel* of כפר has a meaning that differs from the later cultic use of the verb in the priestly writings. This is shown already by the fact that Moses is the subject of the verb and not God. In his actual prayer (v. 32), which realizes his intention of "making atonement," Moses chooses two alternative requests: either God will forgive Israel's "great sin"[12] or Moses wishes his name to be blotted out of God's book of the living.

---

11. Lohfink, "Der Zorn Gottes," 150–51.
12. The explanation of this sin at the end of v. 31 ("they have made themselves gods of gold") presupposes Exod 20:23 and is probably a later addition; cf. Christoph

Since God answers only the second alternative (v. 33), it becomes clear that the first part asks for something impossible: Israel's sin is far too "great" to be forgiven. But also the second part of Moses' prayer is refused by God. This probably implies an "exchange [of] his life for their [i.e., Israel's] forgiveness,"[13] or even "eine Lebensersatzleistung durch stellvertretende Totalhingabe."[14] Recently the offer of Moses' life has been understood as meaning that Moses simply wanted to be in solidarity with his people and to suffer the same fate as them, that is, to meet the expected death of all members of the people.[15] But this latter interpretation is hardly fitting—at least for the older text— since the divine answer to Moses ("whoever has sinned against me I will blot out of my book") by no means aims at the destruction of the whole people.[16] Still the late passage of the Levites fighting for God (vv. 25-29) presupposes that some of the people were guiltier than others. It is only the first prayer of Moses in the Deuteronomistic style that reckons with a reaction of God destroying his whole people. In any case, at the end God, in spite of Israel's "great sin," clings to his promise of the land for his people and postpones punishment (v. 34)—probably the fall of Samaria in 722 is glimpsed in this announcement.[17]

In light of his rejected request at the end of the chapter, how is Moses' successful prayer in *verses 7-14* to be interpreted? These verses appar-

---

Dohmen, *Das Bilderverbot: Seine Entstehung und seine Entwicklung im Alten Testament* (BBB 62; Frankfurt: Athenäum, 1987), 117-18.

13. Childs, *Exodus*, 571.

14. Hartmut Gese, "Die Sühne," in idem, *Zur biblischen Theologie: Alttestamentliche Vorträge* (Munich: Mohr Siebeck, 1977), 82-106 (88).

15. Bernd Janowski, *Sühne als Heilsgeschehen: Studien zur Sühnetheologie der Priesterschrift und zur Wurzel KPR im Alten Orient und im Alten Testament* (WMANT 55; Neukirchen-Vluyn: Neukirchener, 1982), 144. He is followed by Michael Widmer, *Moses, God, and the Dynamics of Intercessory Prayer: A Study of Exodus 32-34 and Numbers 13-14* (FAT 2/8; Tübingen: Mohr Siebeck 2004), 130-134. Cf. also Umberto Cassuto, *A Commentary to the Book of Exodus* (Jerusalem: Magnes, 1967), 423.

16. See most recently Michael Konkel, *Sünde und Vergebung: Eine Rekonstruktion der Redaktionsgeschichte der hinteren Sinaiperikope (Exodus 32-34) vor dem Hintergrund aktueller Pentateuchmodelle* (FAT 58; Tübingen: Mohr Siebeck, 2008), 142.

17. See Lothar Perlitt, *Bundestheologie im Alten Testament* (WMANT 36; Neukirchen-Vluyn: Neukirchener, 1969), 209. This may be true also for the dark final v. 35; cf. Erhard Blum, *Studien zur Komposition des Pentateuch* (BZAW 189; Berlin: de Gruyter, 1990), 57, 217. We should note also that the phrase "to commit a great sin" (חטא חטאה גדלה, v. 30; cf. v. 31) has its only parallel in 2 Kgs 21:17 and may thus very well hint at the destruction of Samaria (and Jerusalem).

ently do not want to change the older tradition of the refusal of Moses' request by God, but want to help the readers of the story to understand this refusal correctly.

The main difference between verses 7–14 and verses 30–34 has already been hinted at. While verses 30–34 speak of a divine punishment against a vague number of guilty people, verses 10–14, in contrast, aim at God's plan to annihilate Israel—except of course Moses, who stayed with God when Aaron and Israel built the golden calf, and whom God wants to make a new Abraham (compare v. 10b with Gen 12:2). And only when this new horizon of annihilation of Israel—no longer God's but Moses' people (v. 7)—is introduced, God's intention is directed by his wrath. God's wrath and the possible annihilation of Israel as its effect belong together. In view of verses 10–14 it makes good sense that verses 30–34 never speak of God's wrath. Instead, their subject is the punishment of the guilty (v. 33).

Thus, the first aim of verses 7–14, the passage following immediately the description of Israel's guilt, is to secure from the very beginning that the aim of God's refusal of Moses' request in verses 30–34 is not to destroy Israel. It is Moses, the only just one among the Israelites, who prevents God from carrying out his primary intention. The text of verse 10 is so bold as to say that God is unable to destroy his people without Moses' approval. God has to say, "Now leave me alone so that my anger may burn against them and that I may destroy them." Moses stands, so to speak, in God's way and has to move, if Israel is to be destroyed.[18] But Moses will not move. He has lots of arguments to offer for God's incapacity to destroy his own people. And the reader, of course, is to understand that Moses' arguments are in fact God's own. Already the older tradition in verses 30–34 knew of his promise to give Israel the land. This led him to postpone his punishment.

But we have touched so far only on the first of two major differences between verses 7–14 and verses 30–34. The second one is overlooked by traditional exegesis even more than the first. In verse 32 Moses asks God for forgiveness and his intercession is refused; in verse 12 he asks for God's repentance and he is heard. These two requests are by no means identical,

---

18. Josef Scharbert (*Heilsmittler im Alten Testament und im Alten Orient* [QD 23/24; Freiburg: Herder, 1964], 97) comments adequately: Moses must "sozusagen das Volk erst zur Bestrafung freigeben…, wenn Jahwe zur Ausführung seines Verwerfungsbeschlusses freie Hand haben soll."

as most interpreters think.[19] The difference between them is shown most clearly in the visions of Amos. In his first vision of the terrible swarms of locusts who threaten "to strip the land clean" Amos asks for God's forgiveness to save his people, yet his request is answered by God's "repentance" (Amos 7:1-3). In his second vision, of a cosmic drought, Amos no longer dares to ask for God's forgiveness, but only begs for God's ending the event. He is again answered by God's "repentance," the change of his intention (vv. 4-6). In the third and fourth vision there is no longer room for prophetic intercession; Amos must become only God's mouthpiece.

What, then, is *the difference between God's forgiveness and his repentance*? The logic of Amos 7 is apparently very similar to that in Exod 32. If God could have answered Amos's request for forgiveness in Amos 7:2 in a positive way, Israel would be free from any calamity; their guilt would be "carried away," as Exod 32:32 puts it. In Amos 7, as in Exod 32, "repentance" is an act of God in a situation in which forgiveness is no longer possible. When God "repents," he refrains from destroying his people as he intended to do because of their guilt without measure; the reason for his change of mind is his promise (Exod 32) and his compassion with helpless people (Jacob being "so small"; Amos 7:2, 5). The third and fourth visions of Amos show that there is a limit also for God's "repentance."

Thus, "repentance" is God's utmost force to save His people, when forgiveness is no longer possible for him and their destruction seems inevitable. "Repentance" corresponds to God's devastating wrath. It is his very last means to prevent his wrath (which more and more becomes a power of his own) from burning and exterminating everyone, as already Hosea in Hos 11:8-9 had shown. The OT never speaks of God's changing his mind and "repenting," when some ordinary calamity is in view.[20] From the very beginning it does so only when the existence of God's people is at stake. Deuteronomy 9-10 follows this path of Exod 32:7-14. Though it does not

---

19. Also by Childs (*Exodus*, 563: "Moses secures God's forgiveness in v. 14") and notably by R. W. L. Moberly (*At the Mountain of God* [JSOTSup 22; Sheffield: JSOT, 1983], 52-53). The only exegete I know who distinguishes these two meanings clearly is Erik Aurelius (*Der Fürbitter Israels: Eine Studie zum Mosebild im Alten Testament* [CBOT 27; Stockholm: Almqvist & Wiksell, 1988], 93-96); but see also Widmer, *Moses, God*, 139.

20. I have tried to demonstrate this limitation in my book *Die Reue Gottes: Aspekte alttestamentlicher Gottesvorstellung* (BThSt 31; 2nd ed; Neukirchen-Vluyn: Neukirchener, 1997).

use the phrase "repent" for God, it has Moses praying to God repeatedly forty days and nights with only one aim: to prevent God from destroying Israel (Deut 9:18-19, 25-29; 10:10).

Exodus 32:7-14 and Deut 9-10 agree that Israel survived the guilt of the golden calf only because of Moses. Without his intercession the wrath of God would have annihilated his people. Deuteronomy 9-10 adds that there is a long chain of guilt, starting with Israel's mistrust of God in the wilderness and ending with the sins of Jeroboam, Ahab, and Manasseh, which equally called for God's wrath and which would have lead to Israel's death without Moses.[21] All of these statements, of course, primarily point to the quality of the guilt of Israel, who experienced God like no other nation did and still viewed themselves as permanently rejecting him.

5.

Exodus 32 in its final form and *Deut 9-10* can be interpreted only in relation to each other. This is demonstrated most clearly by the fact that Exod 32:7-14 and Deut 9:12-14, 25-29 not only run parallel, but show many identical phrases and whole parts of sentences. Either both texts have a common author[22] or one must be dependent on the other. My previous thoughts have shown that priority should be sought with Exod 32:7-14.[23]

---

21. Thus, in view of Israel's "great sin," the two reflective expressions of God's will in Deuteronomistic literature, thinking that on first glance seem to be contradictory, in fact belong together: "It was not his [i.e., God's] will to destroy you" (Deut 10:10) and "the Lord was not willing to forgive" (2 Kgs 24:4b). Compare also the successful prayer of Moses: "Turn from your fierce anger, relent and do not bring disaster on your people!" in Exod 32:12 with 2 Kings 23:26: "The Lord did not turn away from the heat of his fierce anger, which burnt against Judah because of all Manasseh had done to provoke him to anger."

22. Hans Christoph Schmitt, "Die Erzählung vom Goldenen Kalb Ex 32* und das Deuteronomistische Geschichtswerk," in his *Theologie in Prophetie und Pentateuch: Gesammelte Schriften* (BZAW 310; Berlin: de Gruyter, 2001), 311-25 (317-19).

23. This is the opinion of the majority of scholars. The reasons are given most clearly by Reinhard Achenbach in *Israel zwischen Verheißung und Gebot: Literarkritische Untersuchungen zu Deut 5-11* (EHS 23/422; Frankfurt: Peter Lang, 1991), 346-68; Suzanne Boorer, *The Promise of the Land as Oath* (BZAW 205; Berlin: de Gruyter, 1992), 297-306; and N. Lohfink, "Deuteronomium 9,1-10,11 and Exodus 32-34," 54-61. I would stress (1) that God's important assertion that Israel is no longer his own but Moses' people is in harmony with the context of Exod 32 (v. 1, 23), while it occurs surprisingly in Deut 9:12, and (2) that Deut 9-10 avoids consciously the

Yet the influence apparently was no one way street. Exod 32:9 is identical with Deut 9:12[24] and is characteristic for Deut 9–10, not for Exod 32; and Exod 32:13 most probably presupposes Deut 9:27, since it stands in a position after Moses' final request for God's repentance and adds to Deut 9:27 God's oath to the fathers to give Israel the promised land.[25]

Thus, by reading Exod 32 with its Deuteronomistic addition in vv. 7–14, the careful interpreter is urged to have Deut 9–10 in mind. This means that he or she is to be conscious of two facts stressed in the verses taken from Deut 9: (1) The golden calf is not the only reason for God's wrath against Israel; God's people are a "stiff-necked people" with a permanent intention to rebel against God; and (2) Moses in his fear of the anger and the wrath of God against Israel (Deut 9:19) not only once but several times climbed up Mount Sinai/Mount Horeb in order to pray for forty days and nights, and he was heard every time, especially because of God's binding oath to the fathers.

6.

Exodus 32 offers an exegete the chance to observe how the subject of the wrath of God is introduced into a context which did not know of it before. It is only the (exilic or early postexilic) Deuteronomistic passage (vv. 7–14) that speaks of the wrath of God, but it does so in a repeated way (three times), with an apparent stress upon the new subject. True, Exod 32, read without these later verses, tells of an unparalleled and disgusting guilt of the people of God, too, which God is unable to forgive (v. 33). He has just been rejected by his people in the very hour of his basic revelation, because they prefer to venerate a visible God that they themselves fabricated.[26] True, the punishment of the guilty is very hard, especially if the

---

undeuteronomic phrase "to bring up (עלה, *hiphil*) out of Egypt" (Exod 32:7, 8, 23; 33:1, 12, 15), which in Deuteronomy occurs only once (20:1). Yet the most recent *Habilitationsschrift* on this question by Konkel (*Sünde und Vergebung*, 154–62) pleads for the priority of Deut 9–10, as had Dohmen (*Das Bilderverbot*, 128–32) and many earlier exegetes. For me the reasons given are not at all convincing.

24. The only difference is the addressee of God's speech: Moses in Exod 32; "me" in Moses' reflection in Deut 9.

25. For more detailed explanations see Peter Weimar, "Das Goldene Kalb," *BN* 38/39 (1987): 117–60; 124–25; Jan Christian Gertz, "Beobachtungen zu Komposition und Redaktion in Exodus 32–34," in *Gottes Volk am Sinai*, 88–106, 100–101.

26. Cf. Blum, *Studien zur Komposition des Pentateuch*, 191: "Der Abfall in Ex

announcement of a postponed judgement (פקד; v. 34) aims at the end of the state and the destruction of Samaria (and Jerusalem) with its huge casualties. Still, Exod 32 in its original form never hints at the possibility that Israel might cease to exist.

It is only by the addition of verses 7-14 and by the introduction of the new subject of God's wrath of God that this possibility is made visible. Even more, the introduction of this new subject intends nothing else but to invite the reader to glance at this possibility—in order to exclude it. God's wrath is stressed with only one intention: to deny once and forever that it may burn up and devour his whole people. As in Exod 32:7-14, so also in Deut 9-10, no other consequence of God's wrath is in view than the destruction and annihilation of Israel. (True, in the latter chapters of 2 Kings, as we have seen above, a new definition of God's wrath is given which does not lead to the extermination of his people, but to the destruction of Samaria and Jerusalem. But this definition is not valid for either Exod 32 or Deut 9-10.) In this context Moses grows to an unparalleled figure. It is only Moses, the only just man in Israel, who protects Israel from God's burning anger. Israel would be lost without Moses, since their texts tell them they deserve death in the light of their guilt. This exaltation of Moses serves the same purpose as the introduction of the wrath of God into the context: *the idea of the wrath of God is introduced only to deny the possibility of its appearance*, in spite of Israel's incomparable guilt. In other words, the rise of God's wrath is excluded as a possible misunderstanding of Moses' rejected prayer and of God's announcement of coming judgment in Exod 32:30-34.

On the other hand, Deut 9-10 expands God's wrath at Mount Sinai to all the situations of Israel's mistrust in God during their long wanderings in the wilderness (and also, as we have seen, to the guilt of the kings of the northern kingdom and of Manasseh). Moses has to climb the mount several times to stay there for forty days and nights without eating and drinking in order to prevent God's wrath from burning. And since Deut 9-10 is cited in the final form of Exod 32:7-14, a reader of Exod 32 has to take the expansions into account, too. In the end, they were implied in the rise of the tradition of the golden calf from the very beginning.

---

32 nach der in Ex 24 gewährten Gottesunmittelbarkeit trägt strukturell durchaus die Züge eines 'Sündenfalles.'"

Thus, the introduction of the wrath of God into Exod 32 creates a very ambiguous feeling for a reader of the chapter. On the one hand, he or she has to understand that not only the incomparable guilt of God's rejection by the fabrication of the golden calf calls for God's destroying wrath, but also Israel's daily mistrust of God during the time of Moses, and even more so in the time afterwards. On the other hand, he or she is assured that not only during Moses' lifetime but also afterwards he prevents God's wrath from burning. Israel becomes guilty and must be punished by God, in the far past as in the present, but the existence of God's people is not threatened by God, who remembers Moses' prayer and his own promise.

The Contrastive Unity of Scripture:
On the Hermeneutics of the Biblical Canon*

Bernd Janowski

"Toward Reading and Understanding the Christian Bible" is the subtitle for our symposium on the hermeneutics of canon. The problem indicated is as old as the Bible itself. Consider what Philip asks the unnamed Egyptian court official who reads from the book of Isaiah on the road from Jerusalem to Gaza. When Philip hears him reading he asks, "Do you understand what you are reading?" (Acts 8:30). The text of Isa 53:7–8[1] is so obscure to the Ethiopian that he asks in return, "About whom does the prophet say this, about himself or about someone else?":

> Then an angel of the Lord said to Philip, "Get up and go toward the south to the road that goes down from Jerusalem to Gaza." (This is a wilderness road.) So he got up and went. Now there was an Ethiopian eunuch, a court official of the Candace, queen of the Ethiopians, in charge of her entire treasury. He had come to Jerusalem to worship and was returning home; seated in his chariot, he was reading the prophet Isaiah. Then the Spirit said to Philip, "Go over to this chariot and join it." So Philip ran up to it and heard him reading the prophet Isaiah. He asked, "Do you understand what you are reading?" He replied, "How can I, unless someone guides me?" And he invited Philip to get in and sit beside him. Now

---

* Translated by Daniel R. Driver.

1. On the scriptural citation of Isa 53:7–8, see Rudolf Pesch, *Die Apostelgeschichte (Apg 1–12)* (EKKNT 5/1; Neukirchen-Vluyn: Neukirchener, 1986), 292–93; Jürgen Roloff, *Die Apostelgeschichte* (NTD 5; Göttingen: Vandenhoeck & Ruprecht, 1988), 141. On the Septuagint version of Isa 53 see Martin Hengel, "Zur Wirkungsgeschichte von Jes 53 in vorchristlicher Zeit," in *Der leidende Gottesknecht: Jesaja 53 und seine Wirkungsgeschichte* (ed. Bernd Janowski and Peter Stuhlmacher; FAT 14; Tübingen: Mohr Siebeck, 1996), 49–91 (75ff.).

the passage of the scripture that he was reading was this: "Like a sheep he was led to the slaughter, and like a lamb silent before its shearer, so he does not open his mouth. In his humiliation justice was denied him. Who can describe his generation? For his life is taken away from the earth." The eunuch asked Philip, "About whom, may I ask you, does the prophet say this, about himself or about someone else?" (Acts 8:26–34)

The answer that he gets is remarkable. Philip does not say, "This word is fulfilled in Jesus," or, "The suffering servant in Isa 53 is Jesus Christ." Instead, starting from this passage Philip begins to preach the gospel of Jesus:

> Then Philip began to speak, and starting with this scripture, he proclaimed to him the good news about Jesus. As they were going along the road, they came to some water; and the eunuch said, "Look, here is water! What is to prevent me from being baptized?"[2] He commanded the chariot to stop, and both of them, Philip and the eunuch, went down into the water, and Philip baptized him. When they came up out of the water, the Spirit of the Lord snatched Philip away; the eunuch saw him no more, and went on his way rejoicing. But Philip found himself at Azotus, and as he was passing through the region, he proclaimed the good news to all the towns until he came to Caesarea. (Acts 8:35–40)

This little scene leads us directly to the theme of "canon hermeneutics." For although the text remains indeterminate at the decisive point and virtually provokes questions about its meaning, Philip has obviously understood what was read and passed on understanding successfully.[3] The question of

---

2. Later manuscripts insert an expanded v. 37 here. See Pesch, *Die Apostelgeschichte*, 294.

3. This leaves the reader with "the task of reconstructing the section of the Servant Song from which the story of Jesus can be construed" (Pesch, *Die Apostelgeschichte*, 292–93). Cf. Karl Kertelge, "'Verstehst du auch, was du liest?' (Apg 8,30)," in *Glauben durch Lesen? Für eine christliche Lesekultur* (ed. A. T. Khoury and L. Muth; QD 128; Freiburg: Herder, 1990), 14–22 (14); Thomas Söding, *Mehr als ein Buch: Die Bibel begreifen* (Freiburg: Herder, 1995), 383ff.; and Peter Müller, *"Verstehst du auch, was du liest?" Lesen und Verstehen im Neuen Testament* (Darmstadt: Wissenschaftliche Buchgesellschaft, 1994), 12, 92. The "lacunae or places of indeterminacy" do not denote gaps of uncertainty in the text, but a "composite need" in which the reader comes into play. See Müller, *Verstehst du?*, 130; Stefan Schreiber, "'Verstehst du denn, was du liest?': Beobachtungen zur Begegnung von Philippus und dem äthiopischen Eunuchen (Apg 8,26–40)," *SNTU* 21 (1996): 42–72 (70 n. 106); and Helmut Utzschneider and Stefan Ark Nitsche, *Arbeitsbuch literaturwissenschaftliche Bibelauslegung: Eine*

why this is so, more exactly, will concern us first. We will then ask about aspects of the formation history and interpretive history that are material to the hermeneutics of the biblical canon. A brief summary will come at the end.

What Is "Canon Hermeneutics"?

Let us begin with a basic issue. Reading, as defined by literary scholarship, is "a conscious and intentional, primarily internal (i.e., mental) action of an individual in the complex processes of visual intake and perception, especially of language in the form of written of signs, working together with mental understanding to generate meaning."[4] A taxonomy of different possible reading types includes: distanced and critical, identifying and cursory, close or word-based, or sense-based reading. Less concerned with pragmatic reading, professional literary reading devotes special attention to ambiguous texts in view of the complex strategies that are often needed to disambiguate them.[5] Acts 8:26–40 falls into this category. The question that the Ethiopian court official puts to Philip—of whom the

---

Methodenlehre zur Exegese des Alten Testaments (Gütersloh: Gütersloher Verlagshaus, 2001), 156–57, 178ff.

4. Gabriele Müller-Oberhäuser, "Lesen/Lektüre," in *Metzler Lexikon Literatur- und Kulturtheorie: Ansätze—Personen—Grundbegriffe* (ed. Ansgar Nüning; Stuttgart: Metzler, 2004), 379–80.

5. In recent literary studies of the act of reading and the meaning constituted by textual sense, it is sometimes so greatly emphasized that the *intentio auctoris/operis* (the sense given by the text and its author) threatens to disappear behind the *intentio lectoris* (the sense constituted by the reader)—if it is not noted that "the score of the text itself ... [prevents] arbitrarily subjective appropriations," as Hubert Frankemölle has it in *Matthäuskommentar 1* (Düsseldorf: Patmos, 1999), 76, following Wolfgang Iser's thesis of text as "structured parameters for its reader" (*Der Akt des Lesens: Theorie ästhetischer Wirkung* [Munich: Fink, 1990], 175); cf. Hubert Frankemölle, "Hermeneutik," in *Handbuch theologischer Grundbegriffe zum Alten und Neuen Testament* (ed. Angelika Berlejung and Christian Frevel; Darmstadt: Wissenschaftliche Buchgesellschaft, 2006), 245–46. That the activity of the reader can scarcely be overestimated in the process of understanding is also common knowledge now in biblical studies. See also, *inter alia*, Jörg Frey, "Der implizite Leser und die biblischen Texte," *ThBeitr* 23 (1992): 266–90; Söding, *Mehr als ein Buch*, 383ff.; Frankemölle, *Matthäuskommentar*, 37ff., 73ff.; Helmut Utzschneider, "Text-Leser-Autor: Bestandsaufnahme und Prolegomena zu einer Theorie der Exegese," *BZ* 43 (1999): 224–38; Christoph Dohmen, "Schriftauslegung," in *Neues Bibel-Lexikon* (ed. Manfred Görg and Bernhard Lang; Zürich: Benziger, 1991–2001), 3:513–18.

prophet Isaiah speaks (Acts 8:34)—is not answered directly, but rather on the basis of Isa 53:7–8. with a general reference to the "good news about Jesus." The text is hermeneutically instructive because it raises the problem of understanding.

> He applies himself to reading the text and deciphering its literal sense. He then asks about the christological implications of a scriptural (Old Testament) text. He draws attention to the way its claim poses a challenge to the reader to respond to this claim. And he also knows that an understanding that follows the text's claim must stand in accordance with its testimony.[6]

Following this trail a little further, the story told in Acts 8:26–40 can be applied to the rudiments of understanding, since the news of Jesus that Philip proclaims on the basis of the scripture in Isa 53:7–8, and "that at the same time goes beyond Isaiah,"[7] is as it were a sequel to the book of Isaiah. This should not be taken to imply that the servant songs are prophecies of Christ, or that the *Ebed YHWH* and Jesus Christ take orders from a "higher power," as if they are so closely interrelated that "God himself set into relationship two events separated by many centuries of history."[8] The servant songs open up an appropriate understanding of the Christ event, but this arises subsequently. That is, it arises in the wake of a complex history of transmission and reception, one grounded in actual situations with experiences and patterns sufficiently embodied in the texts that they remain within the reader's or hearer's grasp. Put differently, the servant songs "let the Christ event be understood as an act of God in the historical depths of divine action, and vice versa: *seen from a later vantage*, the Christ event reveals the final meaning of the divine act prefigured in the

---

6. Söding, *Mehr als ein Buch*, 384.

7. Erich Zenger, *Das Erste Testament: Die jüdische Bibel und die Christen* (Düsseldorf: Patmos, 1991), 128.

8. Gerd Theißen, "Neutestamentliche Überlegungen zu einer jüdisch-christlichen Lektüre des Alten Testaments," *KuI* 10 (1995): 115–36 (124); see also, *inter alia*, Ernst Kutsch, "Sein Leiden und Tod—unser Heil: Eine Auslegung von Jes 52,13–53,12," in *Kleine Schriften zum Alten Testament* (ed. Ludwig Schmidt and Karl Eberlein; BZAW 168; Berlin: de Gruyter, 1986), 169–96 (195); Hans-Jurgen Hermisson, "Das vierte Gottesknechtslied im deuterojesajanischen Kontext," in *Der leidende Gottesknecht*, 1–25, esp. 24.

formulations of the servant songs."[9] Because they refer to God's eschatological dealings with Israel and the world, and so speak of the same God, the servant songs can therefore bring the Christ-event to appropriate expression.[10] "In this sense, as a figure in whom God's eschatological work comes to expression, the servant of the servant songs is a 'type' of the servant of God, Jesus Christ."[11]

If the Christ event cannot be understood without the Isaiah text, as Acts 8:26–40 implies, important consequences follow for canonical hermeneutics. The term that plays a central role, but simultaneously poses a problem, is "type." I have just used this term with reference to Hans-Jurgen Hermisson. It allows one to give the voice of the servant of God in the *Ebed YHWH* songs in relation to the servant Jesus Christ precisely as a figure of God's eschatological dealings, to the extent that Jesus Christ is the "type" of the servant of God. In common understanding "type" is understood as the "prefiguration" of an event that occurs within a God-ordered, linear saving action that spans both testaments. In such a way Gerhard von Rad speaks

> of a type, if it concerns one of those singular prefigurations (shadowings) of New Testament facts in the OT; where outlines of the Christ event emerge already in the OT, we identify a type. As for the relationship between the servant songs and the New Testament picture of Christ, we must say that we can hardly classify the correspondence of type and antitype except to put it in the category of miracle.[12]

---

9. Odil H. Steck, "Gottesvolk und Gottesknecht in Jes 40–66," *JBTh* 7 (1992): 51–75 (53), emphasis added. See also Hermisson, "Das vierte Gottesknechtslied," 23–24.

10. See Bernd Janowski, *Die rettende Gerechtigkeit* (vol. 2 of *Beiträge zur Theologie des Alten Testaments*; Neukirchen-Vluyn: Neukirchener, 1999), 249–84.

11. Hermisson, "Gottesknechtslied," 24, emphasis original; cf. Hermisson, "Jesus Christus als externe Mitte des Alten Testaments," in *Jesus Christus als die Mitte der Schrift: Studien zur Hermeneutik des Evangeliums* (ed. C. Landmesser et al.; Berlin: de Gruyter, 1997), 199–233 (230–31); Bernd Janowski, *Stellvertretung: Alttestamentliche Studien zu einem theologischen Grundbegriff* (SBS 165; Stuttgart: Katholisches Bibelwerk, 1997), 95–96; Janowski, *Die rettende Gerechtigkeit,* 263 n. 67.

12. Gerhard von Rad, review of Joachim Begrich, *Deuterojesaja-Studien*, *VF* (1940): 58–65, cf. von Rad, *Theologie des Alten Testaments* (Munich: Chr. Kaiser, 1993), 2:387ff.

This approach has not gone unchallenged,[13] including in the case of our example. As Ernst Kutsch has remarked on the interpretation of Isa 53, "we cannot say: the servant (his fate) is a prefiguration or shadowing of Jesus Christ. This is not contained in the text, but merely imported."[14] It is brought to the text only subsequently, in order to stress the continuity of God's action with the *Ebed YHWH* and with Jesus Christ. Just as "the servant songs in the Old Testament context ... [let] the Christ event be understood in the historical depths of divine action," so also "the Christ event" is revealed "later, when viewed from the final meaning of God's action, which is prefigured in the formulations of the servant songs."[15]

When viewed from the final meaning, the temporal or, more precisely, the canon and reception-historical aspect that is implicitly expressed in this phrase is constitutive.[16] If one follows the generally accepted definition of typology, then the event of God's self-revelation that finds its full realization in Jesus Christ, according to Christian understanding, would have the character of a self-contained and linearly extended salvation story with a beginning, climax, and conclusion. According to the understanding presupposed here, however, its character is eschatologically oriented and therefore, "because of its dynamic, remains essentially open salvation history until the achievement of this [final] goal."[17] It is also in consideration of this "history of God's guidance with Israel"[18] that the canonical continuity of the Old and New Testament properly comes into play. Erich Zenger

---

13. See the critique of of Manfred Oeming, *Das Alte Testament als Teil des christlichen Kanons? Studien zu gesamtbiblischen Theologien der Gegenwart* (Zürich: Pano-Verlag, 2001), 63ff. and 91ff. On typological exegesis see the summaries in Antonius H. J. Gunneweg, *Vom Verstehen des Alten Testaments: Eine Hermeneutik* (GAT 5; Göttingen: Vandenhoeck & Ruprecht, 1988), 150ff. and 175ff.; Peter Stuhlmacher, *Vom Verstehen des Neuen Testaments: Eine Hermeneutik* (GNT 6; Göttingen: Vandenhoeck & Ruprecht, 1979), 63–64; Henning Graf Reventlow, *Hauptprobleme der Biblischen Theologie im 20. Jahrhundert* (EdF 203; Darmstadt: Wissenschaftliche Buchgesellschaft, 1983), 16ff.; and Ludwig Schmidt, "Alttestamentliche Hermeneutik und Biblische Theologie," in Hans-Jochen Boecker et al., *Altes Testament* (Neukirchen-Vluyn: Neukirchener, 1996), 323–44, esp. 331ff.

14. Kutsch, "Sein Leiden," 196.

15. Steck, "Gottesvolk," 53.

16. See Frankemölle, "Hermeneutik," 245–46.

17. Ernst Haag, "Biblische Theologie IIA," in *LThK* 2:428–30 (429), cf. Janowski, *Die rettende Gerechtigkeit*, 285–96 (293–94).

18. Haag, "Biblische Theologie," 429.

has proposed the term "canonical dialogism."[19] In borrowing the expression, I limit myself to the proposal for determining the relationship of the two testaments as a "tradition- or revelation-historical continuum,"[20] lest the fact of the double output of the scriptures of Israel in the Jewish Bible on the one hand and in the Christian Old Testament on the other hand[21] not be taken into account.[22]

---

19. Erich Zenger, "Heilige Schrift der Juden und der Christen,"in *Einleitung in das Alte Testament* (ed. Erich Zenger et al., 6th ed.; KStTh 1/1; Stuttgart: Kohlhammer, 2008), 11–33 (19ff.).

20. See Hartmut Gese, *Vom Sinai zum Zion: Alttestamentliche Beiträge zur biblischen Theologie* (BEvTh 64; Tübingen: Chr. Kaiser, 1989), 11–30 (30); Peter Stuhlmacher, *Schriftauslegung auf dem Weg zur bibischen Theologie* (Göttingen: Vandenhoeck & Ruprecht, 1975), 128–66 (138); cf. also Stuhlmacher, *Wie treibt man Biblische Theologie?* (BThSt 24; Neukirchen-Vluyn: Neukirchener, 1995), 83ff.

21. This formulation suggests that the theory of the "double output of the Old Testament in Judaism and Christianity" (Koch) must be nuanced. As it happens there are not just two, but many more "outputs" of the scriptures of Israel. See Hubert Frankemölle, "Schrift/Schriftverständnis," in *Handbuch theologischer Grundbegriffe*, 42–48, esp. 46, and Matthias Morgenstern, "Halachische Schriftauslegung: Auf der Suche nach einer jüdischen 'Mitte der Schrift,'" *ZThK* 103 (2006): 26–48. Also see the older discussion in Rolf Rendtorff, *Kanon und Theologie: Vorarbeiten zu einer Theologie des Alten Testaments* (Neukirchen-Vluyn: Neukirchener, 1991), 54–63; Koch, "Der doppelte Ausgang des Alten Testaments in Judentum und Christentum," *JBTh* 6 (1991): 215–42; Zenger, "Heilige Schrift," 11ff.; Janowski, *Die rettende Gerechtigkeit*, 255ff.; Walter Groß, "Ist biblisch-theologische Auslegung ein integrierender Methodenschritt?" in *Wieviel Systematik erlaubt die Schrift? Auf der Suche nach einer gesamtbiblischen Theologie* (ed. F.-L. Hossfeld; QD 185; Freiburg: Herder, 2001), 110–49, esp. 135–36; and Groß, *Das Judentum: Eine bleibende Herausforderung christlicher Identität* (Mainz: Matthias Grünewald, 2001), 9–56.

22. At this point some (esp. Jon D. Levenson, in "Warum Juden sich nicht für Biblische Theologie interessieren," *EvT* 51 [1991]: 402–30) have recently brought charges against a total biblical perspective, which is said to contain the "seeds of anti-Judaism" and therefore to be unsuitable for Jewish-Christian dialogue. According to Rainer Albertz ("Religionsgeschichte Israels statt Theologie des Alten Testaments! Plädoyer für eine forschungsgeschichtliche Umorientierung," *JBTh* 10 [1995]: 3–24 [13]): "The more the Old Testament theology makes a cause out of interpreting the Old Testament in relation to the New, the more that theology is in danger of pocketing the OT as Christian. The effort to prove the New Testament selection and reinterpretation of Old Testament traditions to be historically proper easily leads to a distortion of Israelite religion, because it consciously or unconsciously determines the selection and evaluation of the material. The theology of the Old Testament thus carries the seeds of anti-Judaism in itself.... The insight of B. S. Childs is probably inescapable: theology of

After all, between the Old and New Testaments one finds not only the continuity of tradition, but also profound breaks with tradition.[23] Reference to the latter has led Ulrich Luz to postulate an asymmetric relation of the two testaments.[24] As Brevard S. Childs has it,

> One of the major objections to the Tübingen form of Biblical Theology (Gese, Stuhlmacher) is that the Old Testament has become a horizontal stream of tradition from the past whose witness has been limited to its effect on subsequent writers. The Old Testament has thus lost its vertical, existential dimension which as scripture of the church continues to bear its own witness within the context of the Christian Bible.[25]

The undeniable asymmetry or discontinuity between the two testaments shows the capacity of the Old Testament—as one can show with the Psalter, for example—to be semantically open, through a repeated relecture, to the New Testament (as, *mutatis mutandis*, to the Mishnah and Talmud), and this openness is no detraction. Semantic openness differs from a "tradition- or revelation-historical continuum" and is one of the prerequisites for the reception of Old Testament traditions in the New Testament, and thus for overall biblical intertextuality.

---

the Old Testament is "essentially a Christian discipline" and therefore confessionally limited. This makes it unsuitable for Christian-Jewish Dialogue." In spite of a similar perception of these problems, Rendtorff (*Kanon und Theologie*, 1–14) draws different conclusions. See also Janowski, *Die rettende Gerechtigkeit*, 285–96 (295–96).

23. For example, see Theißen, "Neutestamentliche Überlegungen," 123.

24. On the rationale see Janowski, *Die rettende Gerechtigkeit*, 261; cf. Ulrich Luz, "Ein Traum auf dem Weg zu einer Biblischen Theologie der ganzen Bibel," in *Evangelium-Schriftauslegung-Kirche* (ed. J. Ådna et al.; Göttingen: Vandenhoeck & Ruprecht, 1997), 279–87 (283).

25. Bernhard Childs, *Biblical Theology of the Old and New Testaments: Theological Reflection on the Christian Bible* (Minneapolis: Fortress, 1992), 77 (= 1:102 in *Die Theologie der einen Bibel* [2 vols.; Freiburg: Herder, 1994–1996]), cf. Childs, "The Canon in Recent Biblical Studies," *ProEccl* 14 (2005): 26–45. Elsewhere Gese also speaks of "canon historical continuity": "As the formation of New Testament tradition adjoins a still-growing Old Testament, the New Testament does not artificially tie on to a completed Old Testament, but is itself a canon historical continuity" ("Alttestamentliche Hermeneutik und christliche Theologie," *ZThK* 9 [1995]: 65–81 [69]). See also Janowski, *Die rettende Gerechtigkeit*, 260–61 and the literature discussed there.

The eventual combination of both testaments in the two-part Christian Bible[26] does not arise simply from the idea of historical continuity between Israel and the Church. Instead, it stems primarily from the intent to assert theological continuity.[27] Continuity is not the final sense! It is the result of the canonical process, which led to the merging of both Testaments.

> Behind the definition of canon out of which the duality of the testaments originates there lies a deep objective need to document the new thing that happened in the societal dimension of God's kingdom in a new canon—and yet not in substitution and dissociation, but as a carrying to completion.[28]

Before we continue on this track, let us take a step back again to consider the problem posed by traditional ways of reading and understanding the Christian Bible. Among the relevant basic models,[29] the one that holds most interest at present is the attempt to reduce the theological significance of the Old Testament to a preparation for and promise of the Christian message, or an "advance depiction and pre-figuration (type) of the reality that comes to its completion and full figure (antitype) in Jesus."[30] The devaluation of the Old Testament associated with this model (or trend) of interpretation is known and, from a contemporary perspective, obsolete. Still, the typological interpretation of history, regardless of the persistent ambiguity of the term "typology,"[31] retains a *particula veri*. For just as the promise–fulfillment scheme can be applied to matters inside the Old Testament,[32] so typology is integral to the historical narrative of Israel.

---

26. See Janowski, *Die rettende Gerechtigkeit*, 257ff.
27. Cf. Childs, *Die Theologie*, 1:97.
28. Norbert Lohfink, "Eine Bibel—Zwei Testamente," in *Eine Bibel—Zwei Testamente: Positionen Biblischer Theologie* (ed. C. Dohmen and T. Söding; UTB 1893; Paderborn: Schöningh, 1995), 71–81 (76, cf. 74).
29. See Zenger, "Heilige Schrift," 16ff., and Theißen, "Überlegungen," 121ff.
30. Zenger, "Heilige Schrift," 17.
31. The ambiguity comes from (among other things) the way the term "typology" is almost exclusively used in the sense of a prevalence of the New over the Old Testament. See Theißen, "Überlegungen," 134ff.; Frankemölle, *Matthäuskommentar*, 69–70, among others. Moreover, "typology" is, on the basis of structural analogies between Old Testament and New, in danger of becoming a tradition-historical principle, and thus again a species of a continuum of tradition (see Schmidt, "Alttestamentliche Hermeneutik," 332).
32. See Zenger, *Erste Testament*, 126–27; Georg Braulik, "Die Tora als Bahnlesung:

Examples include the exodus theology of Second Isaiah, the relationship of creation and new creation, the liturgical significance of the Passover festival, the expectation of an eschatological savior figure like Elijah or the figure of Moses.³³ In each case it is a matter of deriving "analogies of things to come"³⁴ from past experience. If we wish to apply this understanding of typology to the relationship of the two testaments and the question of the direction in which the Christian Bible is read, we must above all be clear that the Old Testament is

> no shadowy antetype of an ultimate reality that comes to light only in the NT. Often enough the NT is but a shadowy image of an OT prototype: the creation of the inner new man (in the NT) is a typological echo of the mighty creation; the exodus of the baptist in the desert is an echo of the great Exodus!³⁵

In such cases the willful testimony of the New Testament is incomprehensible without constant reading along in the Old Testament. Norbert Lohfink addresses the category of "fulfillment" as it pertains to the "stepping into the light" or, as the case may be, the "carrying to completion" of the Old Testament: "Ever is the New defined not as new, but as stepping into the light the Old."³⁶ Instead of the prevalence of the New over the Old Testament, the relationship concerns the analogy of experience in the Old

---

Zur Hermeneutik einer zukünftigen Auswahl der Sonntagsperikopen," in *Bewahren und Erneuern: Studien zur Meßliturgie* (ed. R. Meßner et al.; ITS 42; Innsbruck: Tyrolia, 1995), 50–76 (52 n. 19); Theißen, "Überlegungen," 122ff.

33. Cf. Frankemölle, *Matthäuskommentar*, 69–70.

34. Theißen, "Überlegungen," 125.

35. Ibid., 126; cf. Lohfink, "Eine Bibel," 75–76; and Johann Marböck, "Das Alte Testament und die jüdischen Wurzeln des Christentums," *ThPQ* 147 (1999): 9–19, esp. 12ff.

36. Lohfink, "Eine Bibel," 75, cf. 76, 79–80; Zenger, *Erste Testament*, 126–27; and also in view of the category "promise," Christoph Dohmen (*Von Weihnachten keine Spur? Adventliche Entdeckungen im Alten Testament* [Freiburg: Herder, 1998], 93): "Promises are thus not settled when they are fulfilled. They hold true as promises, are maintained as promises—indeed, they stand out, rise up and thus their status is recognized. We Christians do not believe, however, that the promise of the Messiah in the Bible of Israel and the wait for the Savior has been fulfilled in Jesus of Nazareth and his birth, as we remember at Christmas, such that all the Messianic hope of the Bible was settled and our salvation brought to its full end."

and in the New Testament, and thus how to conserve or reformulate past experience so as to interpret and confirm the present in its light.[37]

Compared to the still common devaluation of the Old Testament witness as oriented to the material, the social, the this-worldly, and Israel (vs. the New Testament to the spirit, the individual, the hereafter, and the nations), and thus as a mere "precursor" or "preface" to the New Testament,[38] early Christianity and the early church had no other scriptures than the Bible of Israel until the middle of the second century.[39] The first Christians testified to who Jesus was for them out of Israel's Bible. They read it "not as a forerunner of their own gospel, but as its basis."[40] They took it to be their authoritative voice and exegetical horizon. The term "authoritative" points to the problem of the canon again, insofar as the canon sets an "authority [rule]" for a sensible world that was also the world of early Christianity. By resorting to the (nascent) Bible of Israel through which—and none other!—the twoness of the Christian Bible was founded, the New Testament authors uphold an understanding of the Christ event that is a "final, decisive salvation of God set forth 'according to the scriptures,' or in other words, arising from the Bible of Israel, which was known and recognized and presumed authoritative."[41] Therefore, the early Christian hermeneutics of the Old Testament belongs to the very origins of Christian theology and has not been grafted on subsequently.

---

37. Cf. Karl Löning, "Die Memoria des Todes Jesu als Zugang zur Schrift im Urchristentum," in *Christologie der Liturgie: Der Gottesdienst der Kirche—Christusbekenntnis und Sinaibund* (ed. K. Richter and B. Kranemann, QD 159; Freiburg: Herder, 1995), 145: "Typology in itself is a form of application of biblical statements. The consequence of 'scriptural' interpretation of the death and resurrection of Jesus is not primarily that we read different content in the Old Testament, but that one reads it with a new immediacy, as touching 'us'" (cf. Frankemölle, "Schrift/Schriftverständnis," 46–47).

38. See Zenger, *Erste Testament*, 120ff. Yet in a recent publication on the topic, Carl Heinz Ratschow ("Schrift, Heilige. V. Systematisch-theologisch," *TRE* 30:423–32), expresses the view that the New Testament is the measure of the canonicity of the Old Testament (428ff., esp. 429, nn. 11–31!). When Ratschow recalls "the deep connection of both testaments," he defines it by pointing out that "the Old Testament was the certificate of 'promise' for the New Testament fulfillment" (429). No word on the existing promise–fulfillment scheme in the Old Testament, and not a word about the fact that the term "fulfillment" must be nuanced.

39. See now the overview by Dietrich-Alex Koch, "Schriftauslegung II: Neues Testament," *TRE* 30:457–71.

40. Löning, "Memoria," 145.

41. Zenger, "Heilige Schrift," 14; cf. Frankemölle, "Schrift/Schriftverständnis," 46.

One could illustrate with further examples such as the Emmaus story of Luke 24:13–35.[42] More fundamentally, however, we now turn to ask about aspects of the formation history and interpretive history that pertain to the hermeneutics of the biblical canon.

On the Hermeneutics of the Biblical Canon

The Old Testament books are, as I have pointed out elsewhere, not simply documents of the time about which they report, but of the time from which their authors (or authors' circles) hail.[43] This distinction between narrated time and time of the narrator is of fundamental importance for the formation of biblical tradition.[44] It permits history to be understood as a cultural form rather than as a set of brute facts, that is, as "history of meaning" and thus a deeply human affair, with social and religious historical sequence in the background and the discourses of meaning in the foreground.[45] One can thereby imagine the formation of Old Testament tradition as an active river with a main channel and various tributaries:

> Its bed shifts and carries sometimes more, sometimes less water. Texts fall into oblivion while others are added, and they can be extended, shortened, rewritten, anthologized, all in varying combinations. Little by little structures take shape out of the center and periphery. Certain texts acquire central rank because their of particular significance, are copied and cited more often than others, and finally become a kind of classic epitome of normative and formative values.[46]

---

42. See the references in Janowski, "'Verstehst du auch, was du liest?' Reflexionen auf die Leserichtung der christlichen Bibel," in Hossfeld, *Wieviel Systematik erlaubt die Schrift*, 358ff.

43. See Janowski, "Kanon und Sinnbildung: Perspektiven des Alten Testaments," in *Schriftprophetie* (ed. F. Hartenstein et al.; Neukirchen-Vluyn: Neukirchener, 2004), 15–36.

44. For example, see Utzschneider and Nitsche, *Arbeitsbuch*, 161ff., 181–82, 184 and elsewhere.

45. On this double discourse structure of the biblical tradition see also Christof Hardmeier, "Systematische Elemente der Theo-logie in der Hebräischen Bibel: Das Loben Gottes—Ein Kristallisationsmoment biblischer Theo-logie," *JBTh* 10 (1995/2001): 111–27, esp. 112 n. 6.

46. Jan Assmann, *Das kulturelle Gedächtnis: Schrift, Erinnerung und politische Identität in frühen Hochkulturen* (Munich: Beck, 1997), 92.

The "current" of tradition is a metaphor for its gradual but steady shaping. In its course, structures gradually take shape out of center and periphery, out of main texts and secondary texts, out of questions taken up again and again and carried along, and of others that are only hinted at and abandoned. The process of shaping is meaningful to the extent that a tight connection obtains between the form of canon's tradition and the specific perception of religious truth expressed in it. In the biblical tradition's formation there must be something that lends coherence, and beyond that also a direction, so that the meaning produced by religious and social interaction is purposeful, and can develop in line with the emergence of a central subject.[47]

To clarify my meaning, I follow Jan Assmann in the assumption that "history is formed not just as it is remembered and retold, but even as, amidst the spirit of the narration, history is *shaped* while made and experienced, and *molded* out of fictions of coherence."[48] The meaning of the history that makes it memorable and narratable—in the case of the Old Testament, YHWH's turning to Israel and Israel's response to YHWH[49]— is folded into the history itself, as experienced by its contemporaries and as reflected in the literary evidence left by the discourses of meaning.[50] In other words, even the experiences themselves are organized semantically,

---

47. By this "central subject"—the so-called "middle of the Old Testament"—I mean the presence and the work of YHWH in (and through) Israel, and the historical life of Israel in the community of faith in its God; see Janowski, *Die rettende Gerechtigkeit*, 273ff.; Janowski, *Theologie und Exegese des Alten Testaments/der Hebräischen Bibel: Zwischenbilanz und Zukunftsperspektiven* (SBS 200; Stuttgart: Katholisches Bibelwerk, 2005), 87–124 (99ff.); Ludger Schwienhorst-Schönberger, "Einheit und Vielheit: Gibt es eine sinnvolle Suche nach der Mitte des Alten Testaments?" in *Wieviel Systematik erlaubt die Schrift*, 48–87; Hubert Frankemölle, "Einheit/Vielheit," in *Handbuch theologischer Grundbegriffe*, 145–46.

48. Jan Assmann, *Ägypten: Eine Sinngeschichte* (Munich: Hanser, 1996), 20, emphasis added. On the expression "fictions of coherence" see the critical remarks of Jörn Rüsen, "Was heißt: Sinn der Geschichte?," in *Historische Sinnbildung: Problemstellungen, Zeitkonzepte, Wahrnehmungshorizonte, Darstellungsstrategien* (ed. K. E. Müller and J. Rüsen; Hamburg: Rowohlt Taschenbuch, 1997), 17–47 (45 n. 39).

49. See Janowski, *Theologie und Exegese*, 101–2, 122.

50. By this discourse is meant the actual speech that "summarizes the various speeches of and to God in the transmitted texts themselves, and as such is fixed in the eye and contemplates the speech as symbolic action in interactive relationship" (Hardmeier, "Systematische Elemente," 113). For more detail see Janowski, *Theologie und Exegese*, 110ff.

so that they are a prerequisite for consciousness of history and historical experience.[51] Important corollaries for the question of the canon's emergence arise from this observation.

ASPECTS OF THE HISTORY OF FORMATION

Critical to the materialization of the Old Testament canon is the fact that the Old Testament does not represent a closed system of theology, but is the deposit of diverse experiences of God. Initially, such experiences assumed the faintly formed mold of the communicative memory of Israel and Judah (oral tradition, early inscriptions)[52] before they solidified within the framework of more complex processes of decision-making and selection, in institutionalized forms of mnemonics (literacy, successive updating), and finally, as fixed components, became constitutive of the identity of biblical and postbiblical belief in YHWH (canonization, a fixed text).[53]

---

51. Cf. Assmann, Ägypten, 20. This thesis touches on the assumption of Hans-Peter Müller ("'Tod' des alttestamentlichen Geschichtsgottes? Notizen zu einem Paradigmenwechsel," *NZSTh* 41 [1999]: 1–21 [20]), that a latent meaningfulness inheres in reality, so that the question of meaning can be asked of it. See also Janowski, *Theologie und Exegese*, 89–90.

52. On the "model of oral-written formation" of ancient Israelite literature, which seeks to displace the traditional dichotomy between "orality" and "literacy," see the important observations of David M. Carr, *Writing on the Tablet of Heart: Origins of Scripture and Literature* (New York: Oxford University Press, 2005), and Carr, "Mündlich-Schriftliche Bildung und die Ursprünge antiker Literaturen," in *Lesarten der Bibel: Untersuchungen zu einer Theorie der Exegese des Alten Testaments* (ed. H. Utzschneider and E. Blum; Stuttgart: Kohlhammer, 2006), 183–98.

53. Cf. Christoph Dohmen and Manfred Oeming, *Biblischer Kanon warum und wozu? Eine Kanontheologie* (QD 137; Freiburg: Herder, 1992), 97ff.; Jan Assmann, *Fünf Stufen auf dem Wege zum Kanon: Tradition und Schriftkultur im frühen Judentum und seiner Umwelt* (MTV 1; Münster: LIT, 1999), 11ff.; Ludger Schwienhorst-Schönberger, *Studien zum Alten Testament und seiner Hermeneutik* (SBAB 40; Stuttgart: Katholisches Bibelwerk, 2005), 99–112 (104); Manfred Oeming, "Das Hervorwachsen des Verbindlichen aus der Geschichte des Gottesvolkes: Grundzüge einer prozessualsoziologischen Kanon-Theorie," *ZNT* 6 (2003): 52–58; Gunther Wanke, "Kanon und biblische Theologie: Hermeneutische Überlegungen zum alttestamentlichen Kanon," in *Gott und Mensch im Dialog* (ed. M. Witte; BZAW 345; Berlin: de Gruyter, 2004), 1053–61; Frankemölle, "Einheit/Vielheit," 145–46; and Bernhard M. Levinson, "'Du sollst nichts hinzufügen und nichts wegnehmen' (Dtn 13,1): Rechtsform und Hermeneutik in der Hebräischen Bibel," *ZThK* 103 (2006): 157–83 (162ff.). One question that arises in this context concerns the material conditions for the formation of the

The process of the historical formation, interpretation and reception of Israel's Bible/the Old Testament can be represented as follows:

Literary genesis in ancient Israel

- Oral or written precursors to the tradition in the family context
- Literary formation as "systematics of actual speech"

} Individual texts (e.g., wisdom sayings), narrative cycles (e.g., Abraham-Lot), textual associations (e.g., creation-flood)

→ Genesis of biblical "literature of tradition" from various social and biographical situations

"Canonical process" as productive reception (from the seventh century)

- Revision(s), extrapolation(s)
- Modification(s), adaptation(s)
- Actualization(s), annotation(s)

} Aggregation of individual books or parts of the canon

→ Process of "collective reasoning" across individual traditions (the Pentateuch, former prophets, prophetic books, Psalms, etc.)

"Canonization" as a binding, fixed text (from the exilic period)

- add nothing + take nothing away, cf. Deut. 4:2, 12:32, and elsewhere
- Techniques of inner-biblical demarcation (rearticulation, chiastic quotation, recasting of lemmas) in place of updating, etc.

} Canon (MT/LXX) as a coherent framework of meaning

→ Close of the canon ("canonization"), though not by means of institutionalized bodies or synods

---

biblical canon. In the record of work on the matter Karel van der Toorn ("From Catalogue to Canon? An Assessment of the Library Hypothesis as a Contribution to the Debate about the Biblical Canon," *BiOr* 63 [2006]: 5–15) has recently put forward the thesis that the canon "derives from the list of books available in the library, namely, the library of the temple in Jerusalem" (ibid., 7). Thereafter the catalog of the Second Temple library, to which there are references in 2 Macc 2:13–15, for instance (cf. 1 Sam 10:25 and 2 Kgs 22), would become a precursor of the later canon.

External forms of interpretation/reception

- Not updating, but duplication(s)
- Diachronic and synchronic interpretation } Interpretation by the particular believing, receiving community
- Reception in different contexts
→ Adoption of the biblical tradition(s) through forms of "participation" (perspective of participant vs. observer)

As this overview shows, the canonical text "emanates from its own history of reception and interpretation and at the same time drives it forward."[54] Particular aspects of the "canonical process" (the formation of Israel's Bible/the Old Testament as canon) need to be considered in more detail below, including (a) the discursive nature of the tradition, (b) the synthesis of the product, and (c) the coherence of the canon.

The Discursive Nature of the Tradition

The materialization of the Bible's traditional literature[55] proves to be an explication of talk about God, which is an essential function of theology. This explication of talk about God is an account of the faith that, from the time of Deuteronomy (7th c.), occurs in increasingly discursive form, namely, through the use of terms, the composition of didactic sentences, the cultivation of arguments, and the practices of scribal interpretation.[56] In

---

54. Levinson, "'Du sollst nichts hinzufügen,'" 183.
55. The term "traditional literature" has prevailed in biblical literature on law; for its definition and use see especially Hardmeier, "Systematische Elemente," 125ff. and, as an overview, Hardmeier, "Literaturwissenschaft, biblisch," *RGG* 4/5 (2002): 425-29, as well as Blum, "Notwendigkeit und Grenzen historischer Exegese: Plädoyer für eine alttestamentliche 'Exegetik,'" in *Theologie und Exegese des Alten Testaments/ der Hebräischen Bibel: Zwischenbilanz und Zukunftsperspektiven* (ed. B. Janowski; SBS 200; Stuttgart: Katholisches Bibelwerk, 2005), 11-40, esp. 28ff., and Carr, "Mündlich-Schriftliche Bildung," 184: "I take the term traditional literature to mean texts that are passed from generation to generation, which transcend their original historical context and are in use for generations."
56. This process is of course much more complex than can be described here; see the references in Janowski, *Theologie und Exegese*, 110ff.; Levinson, "'Du sollst nichts hinzufügen,'" 157ff.; and Andreas Schüle, "Kanonisierung als Systembildung: Überlegungen zum Zusammenhang von Tora, Prophetie und Weisheit aus systemtheo-

this sense I agree with Christof Hardmeier about the "discursive character of biblical tradition,"[57] which is to understand the fact of the different and sometimes contradictory statements about YHWH and Israel as aspects of a "systematics of actual speech"—a systematics in which "the various speeches of and to God are in the transmitted texts themselves, and as such they are held up to the eye, and so are contemplated as an event in symbolic-interactive relationship."[58] The relational event is borne by an assertion of validity arising solely from of the subject matter—YHWH's turning to Israel and Israel's response to YHWH—at once driving and guiding the process by which the Bible's traditional literature is created and formed.[59]

The significantly distinct content of everyday life provides the basis for the variety of talk about God found in the structure of the Old Testament experience of God. If a concept of God is understood as the culturally shaped explication of transcendent experience(s),[60] then these explications occur in the Old Testament with great polyphony and rich imagery. YHWH is, to name just a few examples, the creating, blessing, saving, commanding, judging, angry, or forgiving God, and he is the shepherd, king, judge, father, mother, warrior, "lion," or doctor.[61] Polyphony in Old Testament speech about God is a reflection of God's unity in the diversity of its expression, in utterances that are indeed always shaped by culture. To understand biblical revelation is therefore always also to understand a culturally shaped configuration.[62]

---

retischer Perspektive," in *Luhmann und die Theologie* (ed. G. Thomas and A. Schüle; Darmstadt: Wissenschaftliche Buchgesellschaft, 2006), 211–28.

57. Hardmeier, "Systematische Elemente," 113. On this Old Testament hermeneutic of discouse, see also Erich Zenger, "Exegese des Alten Testaments im Spannungsfeld von Judentum und Christentum," *ThRev* 98 (2002): 357–66, esp. 363ff.

58. Hardmeier, "Systematische Elemente," 112–13, see also Hardmeier and Regine Hunziker-Rodewald, "Texttheorie und Texterschließung: Grundlagen einer empirisch-textpragmatischen Exegese," in *Lesarten der Bibel: Untersuchungen zu einer Theorie der Exegese des Alten Testaments* (ed. H. Utzschneider and E. Blum; Stuttgart: Kohlhammer, 2006), 13–44, esp. 21.

59. Cf. Georg Steins, "Kanonisch lesen," in *Lesarten der Bibel*, 45–64, 52.

60. Cf. Schwienhorst-Schönberger, *Studien zum Alten Testament*, 103ff.

61. See ibid., 106ff.; Rolf Rendtorff, *Thematische Entfaltung* (vol. 2 of *Theologie des Alten Testaments: Ein kanonischer Entwurf*; Neukirchen-Vluyn: Neukirchener, 1999–2001), 181ff.; Zenger, "Exegese des Alten Testaments," 363, and Janowski, "Gottesbilder," in *Handbuch theologischer Grundbegriffe*, 229–31.

62. See also Michael Welker, "Biblische Theologie II: Fundamentaltheologisch," *RGG* 4/1 (1998): 1549–53 (1552).

The Synthesis of the Product

Critical to the canonical process is the further observation that the biblical texts were not simply collected. Rather, they were selected, commented upon and supplemented. Since this process of redaction holds theological significance for the emergence of the Old Testament as a collection of scripture, one must pay careful attention to the "interfaces"[63]—like Deuteronomy, the Deuteronomistic History or the Priestly writings—that became crucial to the editors of Old Testament texts and to the process of canon formation.

The key term "redaction" speaks to the "handling of a given text as part of the written tradition and its transformation into a new whole."[64] Redaction history illuminates the "process of the emergence of texts in their literary and material dimension"[65] and, in contrast to religious- and tradition-historical reconstruction of preliminary stages, it brings out the synthesis of the product by following the emergence of a text from its beginnings through all literary stages up to its existing form (final form). At each stage, redaction history asks about the historical, religious and socio-historical implications. None of these putative precursors is passed on unchanged; all of them have been edited with a later perspective, usually exilic or postexilic. Redaction, though, does not mean the eradication of older texts or concepts so much as the reformulation of their original meaning under new conditions of understanding.[66]

---

63. On the term "interfaces" see Ernst-Joachim Waschke, *Der Gesalbte: Studien zur alttestamentlichen Theologie* (BZAW 306; Berlin: de Gruyter, 2001), 253–66 (257). The period of the 7th-6th centuries B.C. may well be such an "interface" for the formation of Old Testament traditions, and thus for the formation of the Old Testament theology in the sense of a "theology in the Old Testament." On this matter see Rudolf Smend, *Die Mitte des Alten Testaments: Gesammelte Studien 1* (BEvTh 99; Munich: Chr. Kaiser, 1986), 104–17 (113).

64. Reinhard G. Kratz, "Redaktionsgeschichte/Redaktionskritik I: Altes Testament," *TRE* 28:367–78 (367).

65. Ibid.

66. Cf. ibid., 370, as well as Kratz, *Das Judentum im Zeitalter des Zweiten Tempels* (FAT 42; Tübingen: Mohr Siebeck, 2004), 126–56.

The Coherence of the Canon

If redaction history brings to light the diversity of the biblical tradition in its literary and material dimension, the question is unavoidable: how can the diversity be reconciled with the thesis of canon as a coherent framework of meaning? Does the canon create that sense of cohesion in the first place, all on its own, or does it mark out something inherent in it, and so make visible the enrichment and nuancing of sense laid open by redaction history?[67] Of the several aspects contained in this question, one that is particularly relevant here is the (fluid) crossover from canon formation to canon closure.

Canon closure is the act by which the texts receive their normative form and function and, instead of being productively "updated," are "written off" and interpreted externally.[68] As scripturalized cultural memory the canon is a complex entity. It "seals" the historically evolved sense of a pluriform collection of scriptures and at the same time unlocks it anew. Although outwardly closed through the containment of things selected and the exclusion things rejected, it remains open to new cultivations of meaning (polysemy) thanks to its internal multivocality (polyphony) and

---

67. On this alternative, see Groß, "Auslegung," 116ff., 128ff., 139ff., etc. In a critical examination of the thesis of Norbert Lohfink ("Alttestamentliche Wissenschaft als Theologie? 44 Thesen," in Hossfeld, *Wieviel Systematik erlaubt die Schrift*, 13–47), that all the books of the canon together make a canonical collective statement, Groß challenges: "Whoever intended the gathered meaning, engendered this universal referentiality, or thought this theological thought? Neither the authors of the individual books nor the last recent editors. Perhaps the person responsible for the canonization? About their identity, criteria and intentions we of course know nothing at all" ("Auslegung," 129). As justified as these questions are, in my view, the question of the hermeneutic function of the canon for the understanding of the biblical texts ("canonical sense") is far from settled. Instead, it may be pursued more fundamentally and extensively than before. See Georg Steins, "Der Bibelkanon als Denkmal und Text: Zu einigen methodologischen Aspekten kanonischer Schriftauslegung," in *The Biblical Canons* (ed. J.-M. Auwers and H. J. de Jonge; BETL 163; Leuven, 2003), 177–98; Steins, "Kanonisch lesen," esp. 48ff.; Thomas Hieke, "Vom Verstehen biblischer Texte: Methodologisch-Hermeneutische Erwägungen zum Programm einer 'biblischen Auslegung,'" *BN* 119/120 (2003): 71–89, esp. 75ff.; Hieke, "Neue Horizonte: Biblische Auslegung als Weg zu ungewöhnlichen Perspektiven," *ZNT* 6 (2003): 65–76.

68. See also Zenger, "Der Prozeß der Pentateuchredaktion," in *Einleitung in das Alte Testament*, 124–35, in connection with Assmann, *Gedächtnis*, 93ff.

the complex architecture of its parts.[69] The earlier texts and text layers do not simply act as prerequisites for understanding the "final texts" created by the editors, but are themselves of theological significance.[70] As a collection of pertinent texts for comparison, the canon constitutes the "framework within which the various voices speak out," but it "does not take their place."[71] The guiding insight here is that the canon is a complex quantity that represents something of a contrastive unity.[72] In this, it accords with the polyphony of Old Testament speech about God, which reflects God's unity in the diversity of its expression.

Aspects of the History of Interpretation

If, against this backdrop, one proceeds to ask about the interpretation of the biblical canon, one must be sure to make allowance for the diversity named above: at the level of individual texts and textual relationships through the reconstruction of their religious, social, and theological implications, at the level of the books and parts of the canon through the venture of "collective reasoning,"[73] and at the level of the closed canon through the opening up of polyphonic and contrastive talk about God, which always aims to become the new address of God to humans.[74] The biblical canon "calls for reshaping, it demands interpretation, it puts piety to the test, it tolerates no priority, it sanctions opposition, it justifies diversity of opinion and it gives the critical spirit a permanent place."[75] Pursuit of our question at the third level leads to the following aspects: (a) the intention of the text, (b) the limits of interpretation, and (c) the believing and receiving community.

---

69. On the dialectic between closing and opening sense, see Schwienhorst-Schönberger, *Studien zum Alten Testament*, 271–79.

70. See also Groß, "Auslegung," 139–40 and elsewhere.

71. Ibid., 134, cf. 129ff., 139ff.; and Waschke, "Zur Frage," 263ff.

72. Cf. Zenger, "Heilige Schrift," 19ff.; and Frankemölle, "Schrift/Schriftverständnis," 47.

73. On the practice of this "collective reasoning" see Sæbø, "Vom 'Zusammen-Denken' zum Kanon: Aspekte der traditionsgeschichtlichen Endstadien des Alten Testaments," *JBTh* 3 (1988): 115–33 (121ff.); cf. also Janowski, *Theologie und Exegese*, 120–23.

74. Cf. Waschke, "Zur Frage," 261 and Frankemölle, "Hermeneutik," 246.

75. Levinson, "'Du sollst nichts hinzufügen,'" 183.

The Intention of the Text

The phrase "interpretation of the canon" is an interpretive concept with a view to the Bible, Jewish or Christian, that is appropriate to its respective canonical profile.[76] A basic assumption in this is the fact that the Bible itself sets guidelines for its reading and understanding. Above all the guidelines include, as we have seen, the phenomenon of productive reception, that is, the fact that in the process of the Bible's formation

> new texts are not always produced in isolation and later edited and brought together. Rather, though the tradition permits an element of conservation to be seen, it is more often one of participation. Thus the foundations of "canon" are laid down in terms of a canonical process. Recognition of a binding character of scripture, which points to the constitutive function of the subject that the text as such acknowledges, is articulated in the canonical process.[77]

The term "productive reception," which characterizes the emergence of the Bible's traditional literature, and which in turn contains strategies of the so-called steering of the reader [*Leserlenkung*],[78] accords with the term for the appropriation of the resulting tradition by the latter-day exegete. Forms of participation are in play on both sides, on the one hand in view of the conditions of the emergence of the Bible, on the other in view of the modes of their interpretation. "Participation" designates the perspective of the par-

---

76. As only specific texts are only ever interpreted in specific contexts, it would be more appropriate to speak of "biblical interpretation" instead of "interpretation of the canon," i.e., to speak of the interpretation of the (Jewish or Christian) Bible. See also Hieke, "Neue Horizonte," 65ff. and the literature cited there.

77. Christoph Dohmen, "Biblische Auslegung: Wie alte Texte neue Bedeutungen haben können," in *Das Manna fällt auch heute noch: Beiträge zur Geschichte und Theologie des Alten, Ersten Testaments* (ed. F.-L. Hossfeld and L. Schwienhorst-Schönberger; HBS 44; Freiburg: Herder, 2004), 174–91. See also Dohmen, "Der Kanon des Alten Testaments: Eine westliche hermeneutische Perspektive," in *Das Alte Testament als christliche Bibel in orthodoxer und westlicher Sicht* (ed. I. Z. Dimitrov et al.; WUNT 174; Tübingen: Mohr Siebeck, 2004), 239–303; and Hieke, "Vom Verstehen," 75–76, with reference to Martin Buber.

78. Ibid., 66: "Reflection on the reading process is above all about uncovering the structures and strategies for steering readers found in the text itself, i.e., to show which criteria the text established for an appropriate and 'economic' reading."

58 THE BIBLE AS CHRISTIAN SCRIPTURE

ticipant[79] who has a lively interest in actualization and application of the biblical tradition. Precisely how one determines the network of relationships in the three types of intent—the *intentio auctoris*, the *intentio operis* and the *intentio lectoris*—need not and cannot at present be explained in detail.[80] Decisive for the interpretation of the biblical canon as a coherent framework of meaning is the determination of *intentio operis*, that is, the determination of the present text's communicated sense—namely, in the context of the canon. For the canon or, more precisely, canonization

> sets the frame of reference because it fixes concrete canon formations. In this connection it is interesting to observe that further fixation, which manifests itself above all, for the Hebrew Bible, in the textual security of the Masoretic tradition, broaches the issue of the basic understanding of the canonical texts themselves.[81]

The Masora, for example, with its reading instructions and aids for understanding, has in mind a reader who turns from the given text to other texts in the canon, and therefore "moves ever back and forth in order to understand the texts in the corpus of the scriptures."[82]

The Limits of Interpretation

Is the biblical text vulnerable to the arbitrariness of its interpreters, who can "do anything" with it? Or are there limits to interpretation? Regardless of the multidimensionality of the individual texts, their openness or surplus of meaning, there is a "clear *intentio operis* that one can take as textual meaning based on linguistic convention, without which verbal commu-

---

79. On the difference between the perspectives of participant and observer, see Dohmen, "Biblische Auslegung," 177.
80. See ibid., 179ff. and the literature given there; see further Hieke, "Vom Verstehen," 71ff.; idem, "Neue Horizonte," 65ff.
81. Dohmen, "Biblische Auslegung," 182–83; and also Hieke, "Neue Horizonte," 65–66.
82. Dohmen, "Biblische Auslegung," 183, and also Steins, "Kanonisch lesen," 48ff. The Psalter offers a particularly vivid example of this form of canonical understanding of a text: see Zenger, "Der Psalter im Horizont vor Tora und Prophetie: Kanongeschichtliche und kanonhermeneutische Perspektiven," in *The Biblical Canons*, 111–34; and see the demonstration in Janowski, "Kanon," 29ff.

nication is impossible."[83] The limits of interpretation are thus set neither by the author of the text, nor by its later exegete, but by the biblical canon, insofar as it "represents the textual world that constitutes, as a whole, the witness of the faith community, which is the very 'word of God in human word.'"[84] The canon has such importance because it is the hermeneutical framework that encompasses and preserves the individual texts, but also gives them room for an effective deployment and contrastive dialogue.[85] It marks "the first and privileged context ... in which a biblical text is understood."[86] The universal content of the biblical tradition, which comes up in the form of contrasting dialogue, is nothing other than the "historical self-movement of God in his turning to the world"[87] or, more succinctly, "God and his facing action."[88] An interpretation that strives to support this insight and verifies suitable suggestions for interpretation against the text itself[89] is more likely to meet the intention of the text (*intentio operis*) than an interpretation that does not.

The Believing and Receiving Community

An additional facet, finally, is the insight of recent research that the Bible of Israel historically has a "double output" in the Jewish Bible (along with the Mishna, Talmud and Midrash) on the one hand, and in the Christian Old Testament (along with the New Testament) on the other.[90] But this

---

83. Dohmen, "Biblische Auslegung," 186; see also the nuanced remarks of Blum, "Notwendigkeit," 30ff.

84. Dohmen, "Biblische Auslegung," 187.

85. Cf. Zenger, "Heilige Schrift," 19ff.; and Rochus Leonhardt and Martin Rösel, "Reformatorisches Schriftprinzip und gegenwärtige Bibelauslegung: Ein interdisziplinärer Gesprächsbeitrag zur zeitgemäßen Schrifthermeneutik," *ThZ* 56 (2000): 298–324, esp. 310ff., 317ff.

86. Hieke, "Neue Horizonte," 65; cf. Steins, "Bibelkanon," 177ff.

87. Steck, *Gott in der Zeit entdecken: Die Prophetenbücher des Alten Testaments als Vorbild für Theologie und Kirche* (BThSt 42; Neukirchen-Vluyn: Neukirchener, 2001), 101 n. 42.

88. Ibid., 71; cf. Janowski, *Theologie und Exegese*, 101.

89. To ask in the manner of Hieke, "Vom Verstehen," 73: "Does the text (at which places, with which signals, structures, etc.) yet cover the proposed reading? Is the interpretation consistent with the context, or is the text only perceived from "one side," in isolation (made into a pericope)? Is the limit of its use exceeded, because the interests of the readers become too dominant?"

90. See n. 21, above.

means that the Bible of Israel knows "different modes of extrapolation and 'completion,' of which the New Testament is only one possibility."[91] And with the Mishnah, Talmud and Midrash, Judaism has developed a form of receiving biblical traditions that is as independent as the Christian one, and that contains different elements of truth.[92]

If Christians take this insight seriously and credit the enduring relationship between Israel and the promises of God bestowed upon her, we must at the same time see that in each case Jews and Christians read the scriptures in a canon that presupposes another group identity—whether the church or the synagogue. A first exegetical point of reference is the textual world of the Bible, which is thematized through historical analysis of the Bible's traditional literature.[93] To this, then, a second criterion for biblical interpretation is provided by the respective community of faith and reception. Since "canon" implies that the relevant textual profile sets a coherent structure of meaning—whether as Old and New Testament, or as the Bible of Israel with Mishnah, Talmud and Midrash—or again, since canon sets the true and binding account of a community of faith's life experiences and values,[94] the task for us as Christians lies in reading the two-part Christian Bible as the one canonical text, and in learning from it instructions for the practical conduct of life.[95] This two-part Christian Bible is the historical result of the canonical process, which cannot simply be attributed to history. After all: "The canon is the appropriate external form of the inner intention to make the truth of the witness binding for the writings in question."[96]

---

91. Luz, "Ein Traum," 281.
92. Cf. Hermann Spieckermann, *Gottes Liebe zu Israel: Studien zur Theologie des Alten Testaments* (FAT 33; Tübingen: Mohr Siebeck, 2001), 173–96, esp. 193–94.
93. See n. 38 above.
94. Cf. Gunther Wanke, "Bibel I," *TRE* 6:1–8, esp. 2, and see Dohmen and Oeming, *Biblischer Kanon*, 43ff.
95. However, it is worth considering how often "unclear" it is "which canon, among canons where the differences are not slight, must set the basis in different churches, and why" (Oeming, *Biblische Hermeneutik*, 82; see also Georg Steins, "Das Lesewesen Mensch und das Buch der Bücher: Zur aktuellen bibelwissenschaftlichen Grundlagendiskussion," *StZ* 221 (2003): 689–99.
96. Spieckermann, "Verbindlichkeit," 176, cf. Thomas Söding, "Der Kanon des Alten und Neuen Testaments: Zur Frage nach seinem theologischen Anspruch," in *The Biblical Canons*, xlvii–lxxxviii; Söding, *Die Einheit der Heiligen Schrift: Zur Theolo-*

Summary

For a long time, researchers have handled the issue of the biblical canon as a purely historical question about the timing and occasion for the collection's formation, and so have constantly revisited the idea of some decree by an institutional body or synod (the so-called "Council of Jamnia")[97] contending for or against the inclusion of individual books. This construct has not proven its worth, however. Only recently has biblical scholarship discovered that the phenomenon of the biblical canon cannot be reduced to the determination of a specific limit for the collection—although differences between the Masoretic and the Alexandrian canon, for example, are by no means arbitrary![98] Questions must also be asked about the internal motivation and substantive coherence that led to the emergence of the biblical canon (its formation-historical aspects). For "the hallmark of canon is deeply rooted in the biblical texts; it is not recognized when a formalistic concept of canon from a later time governs the examination."[99]

How to read and understand this complex structure called "canon" (or "canons")—aspects of the history of interpretation—is the task of the consequential rediscovery of the biblical canon in more recent exegesis. Although there are reservations about the new approach, some quite legitimate, due to the lack of contours for a canonical reading of the Bible,[100] still the "canonical turn" confronts standard exegesis with a central question:

> In terms of theological hermeneutics and textual and literary theory, what is to be salvaged from the historical-critical method in its customary

---

gie des biblischen Kanons (QD 211; Freiburg: Herder, 2005), passim; Wanke, "Kanon," 1056ff.; and Levinson, "'Du sollst nichts hinzufügen,'" 183.

97. See Emanuel Tov, *Der Text der hebräischen Bibel: Handbuch der Textkritik* (Stuttgart: Kohlhammer, 1997), 160; Heinz-Josef Fabry, "Der Text und seine Geschichte," in *Einleitung in das Alte Testament*, 34–59 (38–39); and van der Toorn, "From Catalogue to Canon," 7.

98. In summary see Frankemölle, "Kanon," in *Handbuch theologischer Grundbegriffe*, 264–66.

99. Steins, "Kanonisch lesen," 53.

100. See now ibid., 54ff., for aspects of how to conduct a canonical reading of the Bible.

form if it suppresses the canon as a textual and reception-historical phenomenon, or at best subsumes it as an extension of redaction criticism?[101]

The answer to this question should be clear. Probably less clear, though, is what kind of approach can prudently account for the new insights and demands without falling back into fundamentalistic narrowness.[102]

A final point. Anyone who comments on the biblical canon does so with the intention of contributing to the identity of Christian faith. Christian theology and the Christian church cannot do otherwise—not, it is fair to summarize, at any moment of their existence—than to ask about the relationship between the two testaments, and the witness passed on by them to the one God. Only when we read and theologically interpret the Old Testament in this sense, as the first part of the two-part scriptures, will we be able to speak fittingly of the one God of the two testaments. Only when we attend closely to the canonical sense of the Christian Bible will an interpretation of the canon as a whole become possible, and thereby enable a Christian canonical hermeneutic. The canon-hermeneutical work of the last twenty years is a first, promising step in this direction.

---

101. Ibid., 46.
102. See also the reflections of Schwienhorst-Schönberger, "Eindeutigkeit," 271ff.

Brevard Childs as a Historical Critic: Divine Concession and the Unity of the Canon

Stephen B. Chapman

The great contribution of historical criticism of the Bible has been its identification of diverse biblical traditions and its precision in sketching their distinctive profiles. "The God of Job is appreciably different from the God of the Deuteronomist, and either from the God of Daniel," observes John Collins.[1] Such statements are routine and uncontroversial in modern biblical scholarship, even theologically oriented scholarship.[2] Rarely asked is where the limits of such thinking might lie.[3] Surely the tradents of the book of Daniel did not actually conceive of their God as *absolutely* different from the God who figures in either Job or Deuteronomy. Does it really make sense to speak of these books as having a different "God," or even having different *theo*logies? But this kind of question is indeed exceptional in contemporary biblical scholarship, and tends to receive in response either yawns or raised eyebrows—as if the very asking of such a question has moved the conversation outside the province of history into the realm of dogmatics.

The reason for that response is that the whole force of historical criticism pushes in the direction of ever greater precision and ever more differentiation. For this reason, questions of unity are often heard as challenging

---

1. John J. Collins, *Encounters with Biblical Theology* (Minneapolis: Fortress, 2005), 22.

2. See, for example, the series *Old Testament Theology*, edited by Brent A. Strawn and Patrick D. Miller, and published by Cambridge University Press. Each volume in the series explores the "theology" of a single biblical book.

3. One significant exception is represented by Walther Zimmerli's review of the second volume of Gerhard von Rad's *Theology of the Old Testament*, VT 13 (1963): 100–111.

the entire historical-critical enterprise, when in fact the unity question is as much a historical concern as it is a theological one. Did not ancient Israel have some sense of the unity of its convictions at the same time that it experienced debates and disagreements within that common understanding? Could an incoherent jumble of political factions and ideological splinter groups truly have sustained the religion of Israel and early Judaism? Even with all of the distinctive theological emphases and possibly sharp theological divisions in the early church, must there not have been as well a core of tradition and belief that sustained Christianity and provided it with the foundation and resources it needed in order to expand so vigorously and to become a major world religion?

These too are historical questions, but historical criticism as it typically has been practiced within biblical studies encounters substantial difficulty in knowing how to pursue them, and so usually they go unaddressed.[4] I want to suggest that Brevard Childs's categories of "scripture" and "canon" can be of real assistance to biblical studies precisely in opening up avenues for increased consideration of the relationships *among* discrete biblical traditions, and for the historical investigation of the *whole* biblical tradition as it has been shaped and transmitted. Such a suggestion might imply a reading of Childs in which he is treated as a kind of historical critic, a move that many scholars would no doubt initially find implausible, forced or even absurd. And yet this is indeed how I do read and understand Childs, a brilliant scholar-teacher with whom I was privileged to study for many joy-filled years.[5] I would gently maintain that the counter-intuitive nature of this characterization of Childs as a historical

---

4. For some reflection on the issues at stake, see John Barton and Michael Wolter, eds., *Die Einheit der Schrift und die Vielfalt des Kanons: The Unity of Scripture and the Diversity of the Canon* (BZNW 118; Berlin: de Gruyter, 2003); John Goldingay, *Theological Diversity and the Authority of the Old Testament* (Grand Rapids: Eerdmans, 1987); Christine Helmer and Christof Landmesser, eds., *One Scripure or Many? Canon from Biblical, Theological, and Philosophical Perspectives* (Oxford: Oxford University Press, 2004); J. Gordon McConville, "Using Scripture for Theology: Unity and Diversity in Old Testament Theology," *SBET* 5 (1987): 39–57.

5. With this statement I certainly do not mean to imply that Childs was not also a theologian. The two identities are not necessarily mutually exclusive. As is well known, Childs was concerned that his work not be received as merely one more historical-critical proposal among others, which is why he was unhappy with the terminology of "canonical criticism." See Brevard S. Childs, *Introduction to the Old Testament as Scripture* (Philadelphia: Fortress, 1979), 82. But he objected just as much to the idea

critic lies with Childs's faulty reception rather than with his actual work. Thanks to James Barr, Childs has been understood as a Barthian theologian who inappropriately interpreted the Old Testament through a dogmatic lens.[6] Thanks to John Barton, Childs has been read as a "new critic" interested only in synchronic literary interpretation of the biblical text.[7] What both of these influential critiques share is the view that historical-critical inquiry did not function as a necessary, integral aspect of Childs's approach to the Bible. I would concede that Childs's work is not easily comprehended or digested, but the Barr-Barton reading of Childs is as obviously wrong as it is influential.[8]

What Childs was after was not the abolition of historical criticism, but a new kind of historical criticism, in which the unfair (and unhistorical!) prejudices of its past employment could be corrected and its blind spots opened up to scholarly examination. At the root of the matter for Childs was the genre question: what exactly *are* we reading? His categories of "scripture" and "canon" represented an effort to construe the nature of the biblical literature and its historical development more accurately, as well as a realization that to do so carries with it a number of methodological implications going to the heart of the field.

The essential point was once nicely formulated by C. H. Dodd: "The Bible did not descend from heaven all complete (like the Koran, as they say), and it was not dug up from some long-buried archaeological deposit (like the Egyptian Book of the Dead)."[9] Typically, biblical scholars like to

---

that historical investigation was not integral to his "approach." See his "Response to Reviewers of *Introduction to the OT as Scripture*," JSOT 16 (1980): 52–60.

6. James Barr, *Holy Scripture: Canon, Authority, Criticism* (Philadelphia: Westminster, 1983); cf. *The Concept of Biblical Theology: An Old Testament Perspective* (Minneapolis: Fortress, 1999), 378–438.

7. John Barton, *Reading the Old Testament: Method in Biblical Study* (Philadelphia: Westminster, 1984).

8. To be fair, both Barr and Barton formed their impressions of Childs's work relatively early on, prior to the appearance of Childs's culminating methodological statement, his *Biblical Theology of the Old and New Testaments: Theological Reflection on the Christian Bible* (Minneapolis: Fortress, 1992). What puzzles me is why Barr and Barton did not later revise their views of Childs.

9. C. Harold Dodd, "The Relevance of the Bible," in *Biblical Authority for Today: A World Council of Churches Symposium on "The Biblical Authority for the Churches' Social and Political Message Today"* (ed. Alan Richardson and W. Schweitzer; Philadelphia: Westminster, 1951), 157.

emphasize the first part of this formulation, looking anxiously over their shoulders at the specter of religious dogmatism. What Childs did, in effect, was to take the idea expressed in the second part of Dodd's formulation just as seriously. A biblical text is different in kind from an inscription;[10] it is not a sherd recovered from the desert sands, where it lay unknown and untouched for centuries.[11] Instead it was transmitted within concrete communities of religious conviction and practice; moreover, it was combined over time with other texts so as to form a collection of related texts. As such texts were produced, assembled, and edited, they were already in conversation with each other, and they influenced one another in the course of their historical development.

Typical historical-critical formulations miss this crucial dimension of the biblical literature. The timeworn critical slogan "to read the Bible like any other book" scores an important point when it is understood as a rejection of an unhistorical, narrowly dogmatic approach to scripture. But it woefully neglects the fact that—historically!—the Bible is finally *not* entirely "like any other book."[12] What other book has been compiled, maintained, and transmitted to the contemporary world in the same way? Similarly, descriptions of the Bible as a "library" of books, or "anthology," helpfully point to the internal diversity of the biblical materials, in contrast to a naïvely viewed presumptive unity. It is better at the outset of the process of biblical interpretation to conceive of the Bible as containing "books" rather than being a single "book" (at least given the way that the term "book" is ordinarily understood). The terms "library" and "anthology" are efforts to acknowledge this internal diversity. But they also suggest that the Bible is a collection of discrete, originally independent writings only subsequently (and thus somewhat artificially) joined together by virtue of some broad interest, or compiled because they all came from a simi-

---

10. Of course, biblical manuscripts do represent historical "artifacts" as well as being "scripture" or "canon." For exploration of their artifactual character, see Craig A. Evans and H. Daniel Zacharias, eds., *Jewish and Christian Scripture as Artifact and Canon* (SSEJC 13; LSTS 70; New York: T&T Clark, 2009); Larry W. Hurtado, *The Earliest Christian Artifacts: Manuscripts and Christian Origins* (Grand Rapids: Eerdmans, 2006).

11. Childs, *Introduction*, 73: "A corpus of religious writings which has been transmitted within a community for over a thousand years cannot properly be compared to inert shreds [*sic*] which have lain in the ground for centuries."

12. R. W. L. Moberly, "'Interpret the Bible Like Any Other Book'? Requiem for an Axiom," *JTI* 4 (2010): 91–110.

lar time or place (e.g., "Ancient Writings from the Levant in the Persian Period"). Missing from such terminology is the characteristic intertextuality of the biblical writings, which in fact has been increasingly highlighted precisely in historical-critical exegetical work on individual biblical texts.[13] In other words, "library" and "anthology" do not do sufficient justice to the historical reality of the biblical writings: not their present literary-conceptual unity, not the degree of their intertextual relatedness, and not the historical process of their literary development, in which they mutually influenced and shaped one another.

In just this sense, the terms "scripture" and "canon" signify an effort by Childs to be more historically precise. Especially in light of the confusion these terms have created, perhaps he might have expressed himself differently to better effect.[14] "Canon" has been heard too narrowly as a reference to a fixed list of books. "Scripture" has been understood too broadly as simply meaning "authoritative literature." What is meant in this latter case is apparently a scriptural collection that is "not yet canon," but such usage tends to evacuate any real content from the term. Scholarship in the comparative study of religion has in fact identified a number of distinctive features belonging to "scripture"—one of which is its perceived unity.[15]

In both cases, the intertextual dimension intended by Childs has been obscured or lost altogether.[16] Ironically, however, quite a few scholars have now invoked similar language—sometimes in the very course

---

13. Norbert Lohfink, "Eine Bibel—zwei Testamente," in *Eine Bibel—zwei Testamente: Positionen biblischer Theologie* (ed. Christoph Dohmen and Thomas Söding; UTB 1893; Paderborn: Schöningh, 1995), 71–81.

14. As Childs appeared to wonder himself; see his *Biblical Theology*, 70.

15. See William A. Graham, "Scripture," in *Encyclopedia of Religion* (2nd ed.; ed. Lindsay Jones: Detroit: Macmillan Reference USA, 2005), 12:8194–205.

16. Brevard S. Childs, "On Reclaiming the Bible for Christian Theology," in *Reclaiming the Bible for the Church* (ed. Carl E. Braaten and Robert W. Jenson; Grand Rapids: Eerdmans, 1995), 10: "I would also argue that the editors shaped the biblical material throughout the various levels of its transmission by means of signs, signals, and structural features so that the reader could be guided in construing Scripture canonically, that is, kerygmatically." This dimension of Childs's work was initially perceived most clearly by Childs's student Gerald T. Sheppard; see his *The Future of the Bible: Beyond Liberalism and Literalism* (Toronto: United Church Publishing House, 1990), 29, where he highlights "how editors in the late stages of the formation of the biblical books registered their assumptions that these books belong together within a common intertext of scripture."

of mounting a critique of Childs's approach! So, for example, in an essay entitled "Before the Canon: Scriptures in Second Temple Judaism," John Collins nevertheless refers to a "core canon" of Torah and Prophets.[17] It seems that before the "canon" there was the "core canon." At issue in such a distinction is the degree of fixity assigned to the canon's boundaries. But once fixity is viewed as a matter of degree, then questions of intertextuality and unity reemerge just as strongly. Presumably there was some notion of unity at work in a "core canon" no less than in a "canon," and proposals to add more writings to that "core canon" were surely made, at least in part, by judging the extent to which they complemented the writings already accepted as part of the "core." In this way the question of unity is still not addressed, only deferred.

So how might an intertextually oriented "canonical approach" to biblical interpretation enlarge historical criticism's scope of inquiry and prompt the consideration of new historical questions? Precisely by encouraging the comparison of individual biblical traditions, and by being open to the possibility that these traditions may not necessarily have been in competition or disagreement with one another. There is a reason that reconstructed disagreement tends to meet with a positive reception in biblical studies, while reconstructed harmony is greeted as naïve or illegitimately "theological." Historical criticism pushes just as strongly toward the *Sitz im Leben* of dispute as it does to textual difference. If the diversity of the biblical witnesses and traditions is as widespread and sharply defined as many historical-critical treatments insist, then only social fragmentation and intense ideological disagreement can plausibly explain it. In just this way, oppositional "groups," "movements," and "theologies" are reconstructed on the basis of what is often little more than a seemingly distinctive literary vocabulary or style.[18]

A classic instance of this critical logic at work can be found in scholarship on 1 Samuel 8–12, the account of Saul's rise to the kingship. Certainly

---

17. John J. Collins, "Before the Canon: Scripture in Second Temple Judaism," in *Old Testament Interpretation: Past, Present, and Future* (ed. James Luther Mays, David L. Petersen, and Kent Harold Richards; Nashville: Abingdon, 1995), 232.

18. This tendency has been identified and criticized, for example, in scholarship on "deuteronomism": see Norbert Lohfink, "Was There a Deuteronomistic Movement?," in *Those Elusive Deuteronomists: The Phenomenon of Pan-Deuteronomism* (ed. Steven L. McKenzie and Linda S. Schearing; JSOTSup 286; Sheffield: Sheffield Academic Press, 1999), 36–66.

tensions do exist in the present narrative. The monarchy is presented at the outset as essentially foreign to Israel. The elders, concerned about Samuel's advanced years, request permission to adopt a royal model of governance, "like other nations" (1 Sam 8:5). Samuel, however, hears their request with displeasure, as does God, who tells Samuel:

> Listen to the voice of the people in all that they say to you; for they have not rejected you, but they have rejected me from being king over them. Just as they have done to me, from the day I brought them up out of Egypt to this day, forsaking me and serving other gods, so also they are doing to you. Now then, listen to their voice; only—you shall solemnly warn them, and show them the ways of the king who shall reign over them (1 Sam 8:7-9).

Curiously, the people continue to insist on their request even after hearing Samuel's subsequent warning (1 Sam 8:10-20), and—even more curiously—in the end God accedes (1 Sam 8:21-22).

This negative view of kingship (as being a foreign institution, which originated in Israel only as a divine concession) is largely echoed in 1 Sam 10:17-27 and 12. 1 Samuel 10:19 and 12:12, 17, 19-20 also characterize the kingship as a sinful rejection of God. Moreover, 1 Sam 10:17-27 satirizes Saul as a timid man who hides among the baggage (1 Sam 10:22). It also mocks the people as easily deceived by Saul's impressive physical proportions (1 Sam 10:23-24). Yet these "negative" sections of the narrative contrast quite sharply with 1 Sam 9:1-10:16 and 11, in which both the monarchy and Saul are instead depicted more positively. 1 Samuel 9:2 introduces Saul as an admirable physical specimen, without any hint of irony or critique: "There was not a man among the people of Israel more handsome than he; he stood head and shoulders above everyone else." Nevertheless, Saul still seems a little timid and clueless. For example, he is the one ready to give up in the search for his father's missing donkeys; he does not know about the local seer in Zuph or that it is customary to pay him for his services; he characterizes himself as "only a Benjaminite, from the least of the tribes of Israel, and my family is the humblest of all the families of the tribe of Benjamin" (1 Sam 9:21).

Yet in this counter-narrative, the idea to install Saul as king originates with God—and not as a concession but as a divinely preordained choice (1 Sam 9:16). Saul is anointed with oil by Samuel, who invokes divine agency without reservation ("The Lord has anointed you...," 1 Sam 10:1). Similarly, in 1 Sam 11 Saul heroically comes to the aid of the besieged town of Jabesh-Gilead. Like the judges of yore, Saul receives the spirit of God and rallies the tribes in defense of the town. While Saul's anointing in 1 Sam 9 is a private, even secret, affair, his anointing at the conclusion of 1 Sam 11 occurs publicly at Gilgal, where the people, Samuel, and God all appear united in their support of him and of the new institutional role he inhabits. These episodes not only present Saul positively, they also imply that the monarchy arose legitimately in Israel to fill a genuine social need, that the monarchy was in fact divinely sanctioned.

Unsurprisingly, a long line of biblical interpreters has interpreted these tensions by reconstructing two distinct prior sources: one favorably inclined toward Saul and the monarchy, and one quite critical of both.[19] Usually the "promonarchial" source is thought to be the earlier of the two, based in part on the highly questionable assumption that "secular" material is likelier to be early and overtly theological material is probably secondary and late. However, there are also narrative considerations involved in such judgments. 1 Samuel 9 appears to interrupt an otherwise direct narrative flow from 1 Sam 8:22 to 10:17. Vocabulary, too, plays a role, since the "antimonarchial" sections employ the term "king" (*melek*) but the "promonarchial" units instead refer to Saul as "king-designate" or "(crown) prince" (*nāgîd*, 1 Sam 9:16; 10:1).[20] These tensions and distinctions within the present form of the combined narrative account are real. Even if a precise historical reconstruction of its literary formation is finally elusive, its identification as a composite account is entirely plausible and persuasive.

Yet the constant methodological pressure for greater precision and further differentiation has not treated this classic critical view too kindly. Recent scholarship is predictably inclined to reconstruct *more* than two sources behind the present form of the narrative. For example, in Werner Schmidt's mainstream *Introduction*, he postulates the existence of no less

---

19. For a sense of this earlier critical discussion, see Bruce C. Birch, *The Rise of the Israelite Monarchy: The Growth and Transmission of 1 Samuel 7–15* (SBLDS 27; Missoula, Mont.: Scholars Press, 1976); François Langlamet, "Les récits de l'institution de la royauté (I Sam. VII–XII): De Wellhausen aux travaux récents," *Revue biblique* 77 (1970): 161–200; Dennis McCarthy, "The Inauguration of the Monarchy in Israel: A Form-Critical Study of 1 Samuel 8–12," *Int* 27 (1973): 401–12; Julius Wellhausen, *Der Text der Bücher Samuelis untersucht* (Göttingen: Vandehoeck & Ruprecht, 1871).

20. For these translations of *nāgîd*, see P. Kyle McCarter, Jr., *1 Samuel: A New Translation, with Introduction, Notes and Commentary* (AB 8; Garden City, N.Y.: Doubleday, 1980), 178–79.

than five distinct traditions concerning Saul's accession to the throne—and they are all found only in 1 Sam 9–11! 1 Samuel 8 and 12 represent an additional source, according to Schmidt, comprising a surrounding deuteronomistic frame, in which the widely divergent earlier traditions have been enclosed and interpreted.[21] Such reconstructions tend to diminish the coherence of the composite narrative and imply that later inner-biblical "interpretation" has been compromising, heavyhanded, or even clumsy. However, it is fully possible to reverse the flow of this kind of argument—why not?—and view the postulated earlier sources as containing different emphases without being incommensurable, and the reconstructed later sources as sincerely attempting to combine those emphases rather than imposing a false unity—even while acknowledging the very real historical questions that cannot be fully resolved (e.g., about the exact boundaries of such "earlier" and "later" sources, and about the precise history of the narrative's formation). Could it not be that the composite narrative now found in the received biblical text is an artful specimen of nuanced theological reflection?[22] Is there any *historical* reason to reject this notion out of hand?

Actually, 1 Sam 12 is not adequately characterized as an "antimonarchial" text. What 1 Sam 12 does is to combine the positives and negatives that have been previously aired into the form of a conditional statement:

> *If* you will fear the Lord and serve him and heed his voice and not rebel against the commandment of the Lord, and *if* both you and the king who reigns over you will follow the Lord your God, it will be well; but *if* you

---

21. Werner H. Schmidt, *Old Testament Introduction* (2nd ed.; trans. Matthew J. O'Connell, with David J. Reimer; Louisville: Westminster John Knox, 1999), 153–54. For this trend, see also Timo Veijola, *Das Königtum in der Beurteilung der deuteronomistischen Historiographie: eine redaktionsgeschichtliche Untersuchung* (Helsinki: Suomalainen Tiedeakatemia, 1977); Walter Dietrich, "History and Law: Deuteronomistic Historiography and Deuteronomic Law Exemplified in the Passage from the Period of the Judges to the Monarchic Period," in *Israel Constructs its History: Deuteronomistic Historiography in Recent Research* (ed. Albert de Pury, Thomas Römer, and Jean-Daniel Macchi; JSOTSup 306; Sheffield: Sheffield Academic Press, 2000), 315–42.

22. For a recent critical treatment of 1 Samuel 8–15 as "eine fein komponierte Einheit," see Johannes Klein, "Für und Wider das Königtum (1 Sam 8–15): Figurenperspektiven und Erzählsystem," in *For and Against David: Story and History in the Books of Samuel* (ed. A. Graeme Auld and Erik Eynikel; BETL 232; Leuven: Peeters, 2010), 91–112.

will not heed the voice of the Lord, but rebel against the commandment of the Lord, then the hand of the Lord will be against you and your king. (1 Sam 12:14–15, emphasis added)

This kind of formulation is hardly random or accidental; it is repeated at the very end of the chapter: "Only fear the Lord, and serve him faithfully with all your heart; for consider what great things he has done for you. But if you still do wickedly, you shall be swept away, both you and your king" (1 Sam 12:24–25).[23]

It is in part its conditional language that leads to the characterization of this chapter as "deuteronomistic." But when that identification has been made, what has actually been determined? The conclusion that 1 Sam 12 is "deuteronomistic" is not really a historical finding, but a methodological entailment. The only historical evidence for "deuteronomism" as a sociopolitical group or movement comes from the perceived distinctiveness of some of the biblical writings. "Deuteronomistic" texts have certain verbal characteristics; 1 Sam 12 shares those characteristics; therefore, 1 Sam 12 is "deuteronomistic." Here "history" has in fact become primarily a matter of methodological consistency, even circularity, and not anything susceptible to independent verification.

More to the point, when the judgment of "deuteronomistic" has been pronounced on this chapter, what has actually been determined with respect to its contents or the contents of 1 Sam 8–12 as an entire unit? Is there not a sense in which the conditional character of 1 Sam 12 has been rendered "controlling" for the present form of the Samuel narrative? Typically, historical-critical work attempts to provide information about the originating circumstances of discrete traditions, but pays considerably less attention to the circumstances implied by their combination and the historical impact of their combined effect. The idea that God would only grudgingly agree to a monarchy, and that this monarchy would serve as a test of Israel's subsequent faithfulness—how strange this is! What kind of worldview would permit and sustain such an idea, and what are *its* historical circumstances? To what extent is this understanding of God shared with other biblical witnesses and to what degree is it unique or distinctive?

It turns out that divine concession is a major Old Testament motif, prominently distributed across various traditions and text groups (at least as these are ordinarily understood). For example, priestly tradition

---

23. Compare Childs, *Introduction*, 277–78.

features an act of divine concession at its very heart: in Genesis 9:2–6 God explicitly revokes his early stipulation that human and animal food should be exclusively vegetarian (Gen 1:29–30). Meat eating becomes permissible for both humans and animals at this point in the narrative. But it is also carefully circumscribed (i.e., blood cannot be consumed and human life remains sacrosanct; Gen 9:4–6). However, it is remarkable that the priestly tradition chose to depict God's original intention in creation as vegetarian and peaceable, given the presumed centrality of sacrifice and meat eating to bearers of that tradition.

Although the priestly unit now found in Gen 9:1–19 does not provide a reason for this divine concession, its present location just after the nonpriestly unit in Gen 8:20–23 implies a rationale. In this narrative episode Noah offers sacrifices to God, an act depicted as pleasing to God and preventing further divine judgment. The root problem at issue is said to be the human inclination toward sin, which—as the nonpriestly narrative subsequently makes even more clear (Gen 9:20–27)—the flood has not corrected. In this way, God's permission to eat meat, like the act of sacrifice, is portrayed not only as a change in divine policy, but as a concession to the human propensity for sin.

From this vantage point, one of the reasons for the ongoing restrictions with regard to sacrifice and meat eating (e.g., Deut 12:20–27; Lev 7:22–27) may well be precisely to mark such killing as concessive. By being so tightly regulated, these remain activities that require attention and care. There is an ever-present danger in allowing them to become routine and uncontrolled. Similarly, the prophetic critique of sacrifice appeals in part to the notion that sacrifice was somehow not "original" to God's instructions for Israel (Jer 7:21–26). Perhaps only on the basis of such an awareness could the biblical tradition tolerate statements calling into question the fundamental legitimacy of sacrifice (e.g., 1 Sam 15:22–23; Ps 40:6 [Heb 7]; 50:7–13; Isa 1:11–15; Am 5:21–24). Certainly the great biblical visions of the end time make a point of cancelling the concession regarding animal slaughter (e.g., Isa 11:6–9). They thereby sketch a vision of paradise restored. The integrity of creation is symbolized by peace rather than war (Isa 2:2–4//Mic 4:1–4; Hos 2:18). Peace not only completes creation— it returns creation to the original intent of its Creator. Interestingly, the restored creation will even see the end of "natural" killing such as animal predation: "the lion will eat straw like the ox" (Isa 11:8–9; cf. 65:25).

Most broadly, human killing and warfare are depicted as beginning immediately after the human exit from the garden (Gen 4:1–16) as well as ceasing at the *eschaton*. In this way, all Old Testament violence lives under the shadow of doubt. Violence is not what God wanted when the world was made, and it will not be a part of creation when God brings the world to completion. To be sure, narratives like Zech 14 include robust battle imagery in their eschatological vision of the future. But even so, such apocalyptic accounts also suggest that this violence somehow ultimately defeats violence itself and brings the creation into a state of enduring peace. Even the "ban" of destruction (*ḥērem*) is finally itself destroyed (Zech 14:11). Thus, all violence in the Old Testament finally has the character of a divine concession, something that God mysteriously permits but ultimately does not want.

Other major Old Testament traditions appear to have a concessive dimension as well. Zechariah 14 concludes by implying the end of Israel's holiness rules (Zech 14:20–21), since "every cooking pot in Jerusalem and Judah shall be sacred to the Lord of hosts." Jeremiah 31:31–34 raises a similar question with regard to covenant and torah, both of which were absent in Eden and will survive into the *eschaton* only through a process of transformation. Both factors, their absence in Eden and their eschatological transformation, might suggest that the *old* covenant and *written* torah have been given to Israel as some kind of divine strategy, that they were a means to another end (cf. Ezek 20:18–26). Yet covenant and torah are also presented in the Old Testament as genuine gifts of God (2 Sam 7; Ps 19; 119). One way to combine both emphases would be to say that God gave Israel the gifts of covenant and law because they were the socio-religious traditions that Israel needed at a particular time. But it remains quite surprising that Israel's own scriptures relativize its central traditions to any extent.

Punishment and death, especially the death of the wicked, are also not things that God ultimately wants (e.g., Lam 3:32–33; Ezek 18:23; 33:11). Once more we see how certain realities demarcate the boundaries on both sides of temporal existence: neither punishment nor death occurs within the garden (the human pair's punishment is being forced to *leave* the garden), and neither one features in the *eschaton*. So how are we to understand their prominence in ordinary human life? For the book of Ezekiel, they are divinely authorized realities that allow for the possibility of repentance (Ezek 18:24–32). Crucial, however, is the emphasis on God's lack of pleasure in this arrangement and the suggestion of divine lament that comes through some Old Testament texts so strongly (e.g., Ezek 6:9; Hos 11). It is this implication of divine struggle, of God's ends and means in conflict, that argues for the category of "concession" most persuasively. For some elusive reason, God is doing things that God does not want to do, things that are "alien" to God (Isa 28:21).[24] The nature of this concession never seems to be explored fully in the Old Testament, but by sketching a difference between the temporal world containing the conceded things and the out-of-time reality on either side of it (*Urzeit* and *Endzeit*) in which they are absent, the Old Testament grounds its understanding of divine concession most broadly in the nature of creation itself. Certain realities exist because they are simply part of creation, at least in its present state (e.g., violence, sin, punishment, death).

However, not every divine "concession" is creational. The implementation of the monarchy (1 Sam 8–12), for example, does not begin immediately after humanity leaves the garden, but only relatively late in Israel's story. Moreover, the monarchy does not survive the Babylonian exile either—not as the form of government in postexilic Judah's common life. Its purpose and function as a concession appears to be more targeted and limited in scope. The monarchy provides Israel with a gauge of its own faithfulness to God, and after the exile the monarchy is no longer useful in this same way.

Another noncreational example is provided by the tension between the book of Nehemiah and Zech 2:1–5. The Zechariah passage offers the testimony that restored Jerusalem will have no need of a wall because God will be a "wall of fire all around it." On its own narrative terms, Nehemiah's effort to rebuild Jerusalem's walls can appear impressively heroic (Neh 2:11–20; 4:7–23). But when read in light of Zech 2:1–5, Nehemiah's effort seems more ambiguous, especially with its notes of violence and internal dissension. The inclusion of both of these traditions within a single scriptural collection has the effect of posing an implicit question about Nehemiah's construction efforts: is it possible that his wall is in fact a mark of unfaith rather than faith? The Old Testament canon pushes its readers

---

24. There is a good deal of overlap in Christian theology between "concession" and "accommodation." I prefer to use "accommodation" to refer to a self-imposed limitation by God for the purpose of enhanced human understanding. Thus, the classic appeal to "accommodation" aims to explain the anthropomorphic language that scripture uses at times of God. By contrast, I am employing the term "concession" to mean a self-imposed limitation by God because of divine sensitivity to human weakness or sin. With these definitions, it could be said that "accommodation" is an epistemic concession and "concession" is a soteriological accommodation.

toward the idea that Nehemiah's success amounts to a divine concession to his situation, even as it relativizes his accomplishment.

Nor does every change in divine strategy necessarily amount to a divine concession. It could be argued that the creation of woman is presented as a divine concession in Gen 2–3, since she is not apparently part of God's original idea for the human creature. Only after God has created the human creature and given him work to do in the garden does God seem to realize that this creature needs companionship (Gen 2:15–18). At first God appears to imagine that the man could find such companionship with one of the animals, and a charming scene unfolds (Gen 2:19–20), in which God brings all the animals to the man in an effort to find him a "partner" (*'ēzer*). Only then does God create the woman from one of the man's ribs (Gen 2:21–22). Especially in light of the articulated principle "it is not good that the man should be alone" (Gen 2:18), it could be argued that the creation of the woman is a divine concession to the man's loneliness. Yet in this case the category of "concession" would be misleading.[25] There is no sense that God does not want to create the woman or that God would have preferred to create only the man. Moreover, the creation of woman still occurs in the garden, and in that way she is just as much part of God's original intention for creation as the man.

Divine "concession" instead occurs when God is depicted as agreeing to a disagreeable or less-than-ideal short-term practice in the interest of promoting God's long-range justice. Interestingly, some philosophers point to a conflict between short-term and long-term "self-interest" as lying at the heart of moral agency. "Persons" are those moral agents who must negotiate choices involving different *kinds* of self-interest.[26] A person who wants to be "brave" must sometimes enter into certain activities and simultaneously avoid others in the short term in order to be proven brave in the long run. Thus, rather than viewing the motif of divine concession

---

25. However, divine concession does appear in another form in this episode: namely, God's relinquishment of power, as indicated in the man's freedom to name each animal for himself (Gen 2:19). On this point, see Phyllis Trible, *God and the Rhetoric of Sexuality* (OBT; Philadelphia: Fortress, 1978), 93.

26. Charles Taylor, "What Is Human Agency?" in *The Self* (ed. T. Mischel; Oxford: Blackwell, 1977), 103–35. Cf. his *Sources of the Self: The Making of the Modern Identity* (Cambridge: Harvard University Press, 1989). Taylor distinguishes between "preferences," which he describes as matters of direct personal satisfaction, and "strong evaluations," or second-order determinations involving desires, goals and aspirations.

as only theologically problematic (viz., how can a sovereign God concede anything?), divine concession could be seen instead as a crucial aspect of God's narrative characterization in the Bible precisely because it communicates the fundamentally *personal* character of God.[27] Not only does God change in response to others' words and deeds, God's own negotiation of short-term/long-term concerns prompts readers to consider what it might mean to imitate God in their own negotiation of such concerns.[28]

The Old Testament portrait of God is thus a view of God as dynamic, strategic and educational. This view is in turn shared with the New Testament. The parade example for divine concession in the New Testament comes in a dominical saying about divorce. In response to a question about why divorce was permitted under Mosaic law, Jesus answers, "It was because you were so hard-hearted that Moses allowed you to divorce your wives, but from the beginning it was not so." (Mt 19:8; cf. Mk 10:5–6). Against the background of similarly oriented Old Testament texts, the reference to creation stands out. Here divorce is presented as an accommodation that God has made to human sin; divorce is not an original or ideal aspect of God's will for the world. In fact, according to Paul, the "law" as a whole was not "original" but "added because of transgressions" (Gal 3:19). In Acts, the fundamental legitimacy of the Jerusalem temple is likewise questioned (Acts 7:48; 17:24). Here and there can also be found hints of the same kind of eschatological relativization of core traditions as in the Old Testament: "But as for prophecies, they will come to an end; as for tongues, they will cease; as for knowledge, it will come to an end" (1 Cor 13:8). Somewhat surprisingly, the New Testament offers a similarly militaristic vision of the end times (Revelation), but with the same sense as

---

27. Ulrich Wilckens, *Kritik der Bibelkritik: Wie die Bibel wieder zur Heiligen Schrift werden kann* (Neukirchen-Vluyn: Neukirchener, 2012), 119.

28. For discussion of the biblical motif of *imitatio dei*, see John Barton, *Understanding Old Testament Ethics: Approaches and Explorations* (Louisville: Westminster John Knox, 2003), 15–31, 45–54; idem, "The Imitation of God," in *The God of Israel* (ed. Robert P. Gordon; Cambridge: Cambridge University Press, 2007), 35–46; Eryl W. Davies, "Walking in God's Ways: The Concept of Imitatio Dei in the Old Testament," in *True Wisdom: Essays in Old Testament Interpretation in Honour of Ronald E. Clements* (ed. Edward Ball; JSOTSup 300; Sheffield: Sheffield Academic Press, 1999), 99–115; Walter J. Houston, "The Character of YHWH and the Ethics of the Old Testament: Is Imitatio Dei Appropriate?" *JTS* 58 (2007): 1–25; Cyril S. Rodd, *Glimpses of a Strange Land: Studies in Old Testament Ethics* (Edinburgh: T&T Clark, 2001), 65–70.

in the Old Testament that eschatological violence will end divine wrath forever (Rev 15:1).

Writing in the second century, Justin Martyr identified this logic of concession at work within the Christian Bible and applied it broadly to Jewish ritual practice. God, he wrote in his *Dialogue with Trypho*, by "adopting his laws to that weak people, ordered you to offer sacrifices to his name, in order to save you from idolatry."[29] Justin proceeded also to describe the role of food restrictions (20.1-4), the Sabbath (19.6; 21.1; 27.2) and the temple (22.11) as divine concessions for the purpose of constraining idolatry. If the Israelites were going to sacrifice, it was better for them to sacrifice to the true God rather than to idols. The point of the Sabbath was similarly to restrain sin rather than to supply God's blessing. This kind of argumentation could also appeal to general New Testament characterizations of the past as a time of human faithlessness and divine forbearance (Acts 14:16; 17:30-31; Rom 3:21-26; 9:22-24). Theologically, Justin argued, such conclusions were necessary; otherwise:

> We shall fall into absurd ideas, as the nonsense either that our God is not the same God who existed in the days of Enoch and all the others who were not circumcised in the flesh, and did not observe the Sabbaths and the other rites, since Moses only imposed them later; or that God does not wish each succeeding generation of humanity always to perform the same acts of righteousness.... Therefore we must conclude that God, who is immutable, ordered these and similar things to be done only because of sinful men. (23.1-2; cf. 27.4; 30.1)

The theological problem here, of course, is that this manner of approaching the Old Testament can easily become thoroughly supersessionist, with Israel's actions understood mostly as negative examples (cf. 1 Cor 10:6) and Israel's overarching history as a history of failure.

So it is even more remarkable that this logic of concession appears quite early in Jewish tradition as well. Leviticus Rabbah also treats sacrifice as a divine concession and a divinely sanctioned means to prevent idolatry: "Since Israel were eagerly attracted to idolatry and its sacrifices in Egypt ... God said: let them always bring their sacrifices before me in the tabernacle and thus they will separate themselves from idolatry and be

---

29. Justin Martyr, *Dialogue with Trypho* (ed. Michael Slusser; trans. Thomas B. Falls; Washington, D. C.: Catholic University of America Press, 2003), 19:6; cf. 22:1.

saved" (22.6).[30] This particular interpretation of sacrifice is most famously represented in Jewish tradition by Maimonides, who further developed it and gave it a lasting place in Jewish theology.

By commanding Israel to worship with sanctuary, altar, sacrifice, and priests, Maimonides maintained, God weaned Israel away from idolatry and toward true spiritual worship:

> Through this divine ruse it came about that the memory of *idolatry* was effaced and that the grandest and true foundation of our belief—namely, the existence and oneness of the deity—was firmly established, while at the same time the souls had no feeling of repugnance and were not repelled because of the abolition of modes of worship to which they were accustomed and than which no other mode of worship was known at that time.[31]

Maimonides proceeds to distinguish between the "first intentions" and "second intentions" of God. God's "first intentions" are God's ideal and ultimate purposes. But sometimes God acts according to intermediate or "second intentions" as a concession to human weakness. In response to the rhetorical question, "How is it possible that none of the commandments, prohibitions, and great actions ... should be intended for its own sake, but for the sake of something else, as if this were a ruse invented for our benefit by God in order to achieve His first intention?," Maimonides explains his reasoning further: "God does not change at all the nature of human individuals by means of miracles."[32] In other words, it takes time for God to improve human nature, given how God has chosen to work. This position thus opens the door to a salvation-historical understanding of the biblical tradition, as in the New Testament—the idea that God was working with Israel patiently over time. One of Maimonides' chief textual warrants comes from the prophetic critique of sacrifice (he cites 1 Sam 15; Isa 1 and Jer 7). How can such texts be heard alongside the centrality of sacrifice in the Pentateuch? Sacrifice, he concludes, is "not the object of a purpose sought for its own sake," but is implemented by God for the sake

---

30. As cited in Amos Funkenstein, *Perceptions of Jewish History* (Berkeley: University of California Press, 1993), 144.

31. Moses Maimonides, *The Guide of the Perplexed* (trans. Shlomo Pines; Chicago: University of Chicago Press, 1963), 527, emphasis original.

32. Ibid., 529.

of God's first intention: "apprehending Me and not worshipping someone other than Me."[33]

What I find particularly intriguing about this shared network of concession motifs is how basic it seems to be to the fundamental theological logic of the Old Testament—on its own terms and when read together with the New Testament as Christian scripture. Early Jewish and Christian interpreters understood the Bible this way. Yet it is difficult to find treatments of divine concession in contemporary biblical scholarship.[34] Part of the reason for this silence may be that the topic is too theological for some interpreters' taste. But I actually think the more significant reason is that historical-critical scholarship (as it is ordinarily practiced) tends to separate the various traditions and text families that form the conceptual web of interlocking convictions I have briefly attempted to sketch. The focus is instead on reading priestly material against the horizon of other priestly material, nonpriestly material against the horizon of other nonpriestly material, etc. But the interpretive focus shifts decisively when the contextual frame is no longer that of a single tradition or text family. Divine concession is an especially interesting motif because it does not appear to be at home within any single tradition so much as it seems to arise in the combination and interplay among the various biblical traditions.

Presumably by the Second Temple period, priestly material and nonpriestly material were merging, and other traditions like prophecy, wisdom, and apocalyptic were also increasingly part of the scriptural "intertext." Not only were these traditions being read alongside one another, each one was also having an impact on how the other traditions were edited and transmitted. Rather than continuing to reconstruct discrete origins for diverse scriptural texts, biblical scholars will need to confront very different questions if they instead attempt to explore how those diverse scriptural texts appear to have interacted with one another within the framework of the emerging canonical corpus. These questions are just as historical, but are framed and contextualized in an alternate fashion.

In such an investigation there is real possibility for convergence of interest between canon-oriented biblical interpretation and current Second

---

33. Ibid., 530.
34. For a thought-provoking exception, see Terence E. Fretheim, "The Self-Limiting God of the Old Testament and Issues of Violence," in *Raising Up a Faithful Exegete: Essays in Honor of Richard D. Nelson* (ed. K. L. Noll and Brooks Schramm; Winona Lake, Ind.: Eisenbrauns, 2010), 179–91.

Temple scholarship. Both of these approaches or subfields presently share an interest in how the biblical corpus increasingly functioned *as a corpus* during the Greco-Roman period.[35] To this extent, one aspect of the kind of canonical approach that Childs advanced can be construed in historical terms as something like the study of "Second Temple Scriptural Hermeneutics." That Childs's project is not exclusively a formal, literary one can in fact be seen precisely in the way in which it is vulnerable to historical disconfirmation right at this point. Just what *was* the history of canon formation? How exactly *did* early Jews and Christians read these texts? How significant was their awareness of the boundaries to this corpus? What logic was involved in the editing and assembling of these scriptures into a single biblical canon? What socio-politico-theological dynamics drove the process?[36]

For this very reason Childs devoted an entire chapter to the historical formation of the biblical canon in his *Biblical Theology of the Old and New Testaments*.[37] To treat Childs's proposal as simply a contemporary theological proposal without a concomitant historical claim or foundation will not work.[38] For Childs, it was ultimately the distinctive, peculiar historical reality expressed by the ciphers "scripture" and "canon" that permitted and warranted the hermeneutical aspects of his contemporary theological position—and not the other way around, despite what several of his detractors have maintained. In other words, it is crucial for Childs that the biblical corpus really did function historically as authoritative

---

35. For examples of work in this vein, see Sidnie White Crawford, *Rewriting Scripture in Second Temple Times* (SDSSRL; Grand Rapids: Eerdmans, 2008); Mattias Henze, ed., *A Companion to Biblical Interpretation in Early Judaism* (Grand Rapids: Eerdmans, 2012); Mark S. Smith, "What is a Scriptural Text in the Second Temple Period? Texts Between Their Biblical Past, Their Inner-Biblical Interpretation, Their Reception in Second Temple Literature, and Their Textual Witnesses," in *The Dead Sea Scrolls at 60: Scholarly Contributions of New York University Faculty and Alumni* (ed. Lawrence H. Schiffman and Shani Tzoref; STDJ 89; Leiden: Brill, 2010), 271–98.

36. Jon L. Berquist, "Postcolonialism and Imperial Motives for Canonization," in *The Postcolonial Biblical Reader* (ed. R. S. Sugirtharajah; Malden, Mass.: Blackwell, 2006), 78–95, usefully provides a contrary construal with his argument that the formation of the biblical canon was *not* "religiously motivated" (83).

37. See chapter 2.1, "The Problem of the Christian Bible," 55–69.

38. *Contra* John Barton, "Canonical Approaches Ancient and Modern," in *The Biblical Canons* (ed. J.-M. Auwers and H. J. de Jonge; BETL 163; Leuven: Peeters, 2003), 199–209.

scripture.[39] Whether the scope and order of the books was exactly the same in the Second Temple period as they are today is not crucial. Childs makes clear his judgment that the boundaries of the canon were likely fuzzy to a degree and that the arrangement of the biblical books varied over time.[40]

Of course, Childs does proceed to make a further theological claim on the basis of this historical foundation. To articulate this claim, and the way in which it rests upon a historical basis, C. H. Dodd is again helpful:

> [The Bible] has indeed an archaeological aspect, for it is bound up with the life of remote epochs in the past; and in another aspect it comes to the believing reader direct from God this moment. But in plain fact the Bible is the book which you hear read in church—any church in Christendom—on any day, now or for many centuries past. We receive it from the Church: there is no other source from which we can receive precisely *these* writings in *this* setting, which make up the canon of scripture.[41]

The point here is not that the church's Bible is exactly the same as the "Bible" of early Christianity or that the church's Old Testament is exactly like the "Bible" of early Judaism. Childs explicitly allows for differences. But he does not dissolve the "Bible" of early Christianity into "Early Christian Literature" or the "Bible" of early Judaism into "Ancient Writings from the Levant in the Persian Period" either. In some concrete fashion, a process of sifting must have occurred because *eventually* the "Bible" did *not* include all of those ancient writings now known to us. Indeed—and this is simply another historical claim—the only context in which the "Bible" makes any sense as a construct is in relation to a concrete religious community. Otherwise, as has become increasingly clear from contemporary biblical scholarship, there is no adequate justification for reading only these biblical writings, and only in the particular format(s) in which they have been transmitted.[42]

---

39. Put theologically, the key point is that God chose to reveal God's self in history *by scripture*, as opposed to the typical liberal Protestant move that ties revelation to historical events alone; on this point, see Gerhard Maier, "Der Abschluss des jüdischen Kanons und das Lehrhaus von Jabne," in *Der Kanon der Bibel* (ed. Gerhard Maier; Giessen: Brunnen Verlag, 1990), 14–15.
40. Childs, *Biblical Theology*, 57–60, 74–75.
41. Dodd, "Relevance," 158, emphasis original.
42. As rather enthusiastically urged by Gabriele Boccaccini, "Is Biblical Literature

In this sense, to say that the Bible belongs to the synagogue and/or the church is not necessarily to say anything polemical or controversial at all. It is simply a fact that the "Bible" as such has no other *historical* explanation or validity.[43] To be sure, this language of possession ("belongs") runs the further risk of encouraging the domestication of scripture by religious traditions and discouraging religious communities from the ongoing work of evaluating their faithfulness *in relation to* scripture. Scripture must retain a critical authority within religious tradition if religious communities are to avoid the tendency to reproduce their identities uncritically. But only when the Bible is understood to "belong" to the synagogue and the church because it historically embodies *their* religious tradition can the Bible do its proper work of inspiring and reforming the faithful.

Still a Useful Term in Scholarship?," in *What Is Bible?* (ed. Karin Finsterbusch and Armin Lange; CBET 67; Leuven: Peeters, 2012), 50–51: "If 'biblical literature' is exclusive of non-canonical literature, it is only an obstacle to be removed. If 'biblical literature' is inclusive of non-canonical literature, why should we prefer it to something more simple and direct, as 'ancient Jewish literature'? The battle has started and we have solid canonical walls to tear down. Let's leave aside any nostalgia for the beauties of Egypt. Let our trumpets loudly sound until the walls of Jericho fall." For another perspective, see Stephen B. Chapman, "Second Temple Jewish Hermeneutics: How Canon is Not an Anachronism," in *Invention, Rewriting, Usurpation: Discursive Fights over Religious Traditions in Antiquity* (ed. Jörg Ulrich, Anders-Christian Jacobsen and David Brakke; ECCA 11; Frankfurt: Peter Lang, 2012), 281–96.

43. For further theological elaboration of this point, see Robert W. Jenson, "Scripture's Authority in the Church," in *The Art of Reading Scripture* (ed. Ellen F. Davis and Richard B. Hays; Grand Rapids: Eerdmans, 2003), 27–37.

Theological Interpretation, the Historical Formation of Scripture, and God's Action in Time

Neil B. Macdonald

Introduction

Brevard Childs was unyielding on the question of the relationship between biblical studies and systematic theology. He did not take refuge in the politics or poetics of "postmodern" rhetorical (therefore foundationless) performance. Rather, he sought quietly and effectively to make the case for the reintegration of the aforementioned disciplines on the basis of good old-fashioned dialectic, or more simply put, *argument*. Yet in systematic theology at least—and among those who likewise endorsed the theological interpretation of scripture—Childs's particular tenor on this subject, when heard (infrequently!), was at best greeted with casual uncritical agreement, but rarely if at all acted upon in practice. For those who wished to repristinate precritical biblical interpretation in a postmodern idiom (for example), Childs's commitment to the final form of the biblical text was greeted with enthusiasm. Crucially, what was overlooked was that Childs's commitment took place in a context far removed from theirs: the history of modern biblical scholarship and its fundamental insight that the Bible itself had a history which had not begun with Gen 1. It has often been said that the ultimate impact of Childs's biblical theology was to privilege the final form of the text in continuity with the great classical biblical tradition of Calvin, Luther, and Augustine. But this is to omit what is really essential and indeed foundational to Childs's vision of the academic and Christian study of the Bible: the privileging of what he called the "canonical intentionality" of scripture.[1] To read the final form of the text appropriately (in the academy at least) presupposes that one posit a historical trajectory regarding the formation of scripture. This is a historical theory which in the nature of things cannot be a "reading." It is a claim about history. Reading—interpretation—can only take place in this context. The two are not unrelated. Sometimes the "best" interpretation (perhaps the one which most effectively deals with the skeptics of modernity) favors one trajectory over another. In this chapter I wish in the main to do two things. First, I will outline what I take to be a nearly "correct" account of Childs's overall project, designed as it is to foster a positive relationship between Bible and theology. Second, I want to suggest that the concept of the historical formation of biblical tradition may have a decisive bearing on questions dear to the heart of systematic theology. The one I focus on is the relationship between God and time. The example may point the way forward for future authentic theological collaboration between systematic theology and the canonical approach to scripture.

BUT NOT EVERY THEOLOGICAL INTERPRETATION

I begin with the simple signal truth that Childs did not endorse every and all forms of reintegration. He did not give his unqualified blessing to any and all species of theological interpretation of the Bible. Paradoxically, it is because he thought theological interpretation remained foundational to the biblical project in the modern age that he opposed the fashionable (and, he thought, ultimately nonserious) notion of "reading" the Bible "subjectively," as it were. How do we know that Childs did not endorse every and any theological interpretation of scripture, did not simply and straightforwardly embrace one that took its point of departure from the givenness of the final form of the text? We know because he says so plainly himself at the end of *Biblical Theology of the Old and New Testaments*. In an autobiographical vein he wrote:

> When I first wrote my *Introduction to the Old Testament as Scripture* the major antagonist to serious theological reflection on the Bible appeared to be the diachronic legacy of nineteenth-century historical criticism. Consequently I greeted as an ally the growing twentieth-century appeal

---

1. Brevard S. Childs, *Introduction to the Old Testament as Scripture* (Philadelphia: Fortress, 1979), 79. Hereafter, *IOTS*.

to narrative theology as at least a move toward recovering a holistic reading of the Bible....

More recently it has become increasingly evident that narrative theology, as often practised, can also propagate a fully secular, non-theological reading of the Bible.... When the focus of the analysis lies in the "imaginative construal" of the reader, the text is robbed of all determinative meaning within various theories of reader response.[2]

There is much in the passage worthy of careful attention. Clearly, Childs "endorses a holistic reading of the Bible," but not unconditionally. Evidently, he also affirms narrative theology, but, again, not every example of it. His appreciation of Barth's emphasis on narrative in his *Church Dogmatics* was rooted in his conviction that for Barth narrative meant historical, not mere literary and therefore ahistorical, narrative. In his attitude toward the "imaginative construal" of the reader, one hears an echo of Calvin's impatience with those who give themselves over to a creative playing with the text at the cost of not hearing what the text itself is saying.[3] Such treatment of scripture—postmodern or "Derridean" difference, play, and diversity—is not unique to our own times. The gist of the passage seems to be that while he, Childs, had earlier advocated a synchronic over a diachronic approach to the Bible, he had indeed always qualified this assertion with the insistence that any such synchronic approach must be understood in terms of, and therefore subordinated to, the "canonical intentionality" of the Bible. And because he thought this, the diachronic approach in the form of the historical (and to that extent, "diachronic") process of the canonical shaping of the Bible came the forefront in his biblical project. To put it at its simplest: canonical intentionality entailed foregrounding the historical formation of scripture. Paradoxically, without the canonical intentionality of the Bible (in that sense the "synchronic" dimension of the text), Childs could not have countenanced the diachronic dimension.[4]

---

2. Brevard S. Childs, *Biblical Theology of the Old and New Testaments: Theological Reflections on the Christian Bible: Theological Reflections on the Christian Bible* (Minneapolis: Fortress, 1992), 723. Hereafter, *BTONT*.

3. See Karl Barth, *The Theology of John Calvin* (trans. Geoffrey W. Bromiley; Grand Rapids: Eerdmans, 1995), 390.

4. Francis Watson argues, in *Text and Truth: Redefining Biblical Theology* (Grand Rapids: Eerdmans, 1997), that it was because of his disillusionment with what had emerged in the academy in the wake of his advocacy for a theological interpretation of the canonical text, the final form of the text, that he "retreated" from his canonical

88   THE BIBLE AS CHRISTIAN SCRIPTURE

But since canonical intentionality was inextricably bound up the historical formation of scripture, the concept was in fact indispensable.[5]

No Theological Interpretation without Canonical Intentionality

What did Childs mean by "canonical intentionality?" Childs conceived of canonical intentionality as a specific and determinate kind of human-authorial intentionality. Scripture had been written by a specific community of fallible human beings, namely the fallible people who collectively went by the name of "Israel." Childs did not affirm divine inspiration in its traditional sense (certainly not in the sense that Calvin did). Childs sat easily with modernity on this point. For what it is worth, I think he would have agreed with Barth that the Holy Spirit was involved in the very genesis of scripture itself—the very *thatness* of scripture (to adapt from Heidegger, the answer to the question "why is there scripture rather than nothing" is "the Holy Spirit"). But in Enlightenment mode (the same mode that led him to reject a sixth-century origin for the book of Daniel) he held that scripture was the verbal artifact of fallible humankind: scripture is a human creation. If the Holy Spirit was the divine impetus behind the "thatness" of scripture, human beings were, if you will, responsible for the *whatness* of scripture—the content of scripture or more precisely, to use Nicholas Wolterstorff's terminology, what was humanly intentionally executed in the inscribing of the biblical text. So we do not simply read texts detached from the human beings who wrote them in historical time, who had meant something with them at their respective times, even if this something was intended for all future generations. (Childs would have been more enthusiastic about Hans Frei's adoption of "New Criticism" as a model of interpretation of biblical narrative had it not led to a dehistoricization of the Bible through treating it as something akin to an autonomous aesthetic universe cut off from historical-authorial intention.) So to reiterate: canonical intentionality was a specific kind of human-authorial intentionality. The text has determinative force precisely in the sense that

---

project in his biblical theology of both testaments—that is, retreating back to a diachronic approach (213). But for reasons that will be evident in the course of this essay, I think this is not quite right.

5. Childs (*BTONT*, 104): "I object to the diachronic approach to the Bible?"—"nothing could be further from the truth."

it has canonical-authorial force. Once we see this, we can see why Childs vehemently opposed the notion of "robbing the text of all determinative force" (*BTONT*, 723), even under the auspices of a supposed "canonical reading." For one such canonical reading could be one that takes as its sole datum the givenness of the final form of the text and subsequently constructs meaning at the behest of the creativity of the reader.

However, Childs may say that canonical intentionality is a specific kind of human-authorial intentionality, but is it really? James Barr's criticism is relevant here. He charged canonical intentionality with being a "mystic phrase" (a kind of nebulous ethereal entity!) on the grounds that to speak of the canon as itself having intentionality was a kind of category mistake.[6] Human persons have intentions; and we may speak of groups or schools having (collective) intentions. But canons do not have intentions. What then was the nature of this canonical intentionality?

Let me try to answer this question by asking another one that presupposes that the concept is compellingly coherent. What was this canonical intentionality's *intention*? Crucially for Childs it was one of witness to historical reality. What it witnessed to was God's action in time and history at different points in the people's ("Israel's") history.[7] Childs quoted Meir Sternberg's devastating critique of the validity of reading the text as a literary, as in fictional, narrative rather than as a historical one: "Were the (biblical) narratives written or read as fiction, then God would turn from the lord of history into the creature of the imagination with disastrous effects.... Hence the Bible's determination to sanctify and compel literal

---

6. James Barr, "Childs' Introduction to the Old Testament as Scripture," *JSOT* 16 (1980): 12–23, esp. 13. This seems also to be Stephen Fowl's criticism of Childs's hermeneutical assumptions based on his reading of an essay of Childs, "Recovering Theological Exegesis," *ProEccl* 6 (1997): 16–26. See Fowl's, *Engaging Scripture* (Oxford: Blackwell, 1998), 11–15. But it is quite clear from the complete corpus of Childs's thought that "the discrete voice of the Old Testament" is not a disembodied voice but the voice of human tradents and redactors. There is a determinable human intentionality whose "voice" this is.

7. This is the fundamental rationale for Childs's preference for the Reformers' understanding of *sensus literalis* over the Thomistic one. See Childs, "The Sensus Literalis of Scripture: An Ancient and Modern Problem," in H. Donner et al., eds., *Beiträge zur alttestamentlichen Theologie: Festschrift für Walter Zimmerli* (Gottingen: Vandenhoeck and Ruprecht, 1977), 80–94. This is not to exclude the possibility that metaphorical usage of the literal sense of one's words can also refer to external historical reality.

belief in the past."[8] According to Childs, then, canonical intentionality is intrinsically bound up with the notion of witness, or as philosophers might put it, truth-claiming, and indeed historical truth-claiming.

But who were the human beings that witnessed here? Biblical scholarship threw up different answers at different stages in its history. The premodern tradition said Moses was the author of the witness of the Pentateuch; Isaiah of Jerusalem wrote the book of Isaiah; Jeremiah wrote the Book of Kings; the prophet Daniel wrote the Book of Daniel in the sixth century; and so on. In contrast, in the fullness of time, the Enlightenment tradition through a process of critical textual analysis rejected the premodern stance, and instead posited the thesis that the formation of the canon had come about either as a result of documentary sources stitched together in real time or as a cumulative process of historical redactors redacting tradition history. Childs with characteristic intellectual integrity could not gainsay the latter positions. And this was so whether he sided with the view that—to give an example—the Priestly dimension of the Old Testament canon originated in an independent document, or whether it was to be understood "largely as a redactional layer of a common tradition which assumed a prior knowledge of J" (*BTONT*, 107–8). Childs in fact saw arguments for the veracity of both sides.[9] Yet even if the documentary-source hypothesis had significant mileage left in it (*pace* its critics), Childs thought the complete independence of these two literary strands "well into the post-exilic period ... quite unlikely" (113). The fundamental premise of canonical shaping—prior knowledge of the previous canonical shaping—is preserved. It is largely because of this that Childs's project is significantly different from either the premodern or the modern approach to the Bible. The premodern tradition affirmed the historical truth claims of the Bible at face value (the author the Holy Spirit does not err, nor does he lie). The modern approach dissected the same text into sources and fragments, and then proceeded to evaluate the same historical truth claims on an "atomistic" one-to-one basis, just as the premodern tradition had done. Childs did not countenance this "flat" approach. Though he held, in continuity with the critical-textual tradition, that the historical sequence of "redactors" (in the widest sense of this term) did not correspond to the order in which the Bible said God had acted—creation followed by

---

8. Meir Sternberg, *The Poetics of Biblical Narrative: Ideological Literature and the Drama of Reading* (Bloomington: Indiana University Press, 1985), 32.

9. Childs, *IOTS*, 147.

personal relationship for example—he also held that canonical shaping, far from being independent of the question of historical truth claim, had a crucial determinative dynamic effect on what the historical truth claims of the Bible actually were.

Here is the ironic beauty of Childs's approach. (Childs may have been a more unconscious ironist than his mentor Barth, but ironist he was.) It is precisely *because* the formation of the Bible had come about as a process of canonical shaping in historical time in witness to, at the very least, belief in God's actions in historical time that the concept of canonical intentionality made perfect sense. (Barr's accusation was based on the misperception that the final form of the text was the first and final word for Childs.) In fact, one should speak of the historical formation of Israel's belief in God's actions in time in its historical life (a historical formation which does not necessarily stand in a one-to-one temporal correspondence with the order in which God's actions in time happen ontically).[10] Of course, there was no such entity as the intention of the canon per se. But there is such a thing as canonical intentionality understood as a historical trajectory of textual redactors in historical time, in Israel's time. These redactors received as in a transmission process what turned out to be from the vantage point of the future (relative to them) an incomplete scriptural text. In reception of this text and in witness (sometimes reacting) to the unfolding of God's action in historical time—typified by, say, Exodus's account of the deliverance at sea, the Davidic monarchy, the Babylonian exile, the (meaning of) the giving of the Law at Sinai, etc.—they added to, or augmented, the then extant but incomplete text. In doing so, they redacted the cumulative output of a historical tradition of previous redactors, who themselves had done exactly the same thing (in algorithmic terms, we have a recursive

---

10. To repeat: if canonical shaping determines what the historical truth claims of the Bible actually are—and is not independent of them—then both the traditional premodern and the traditional modern approaches to scripture are unsatisfactory. If the historical formation of Israel's belief in God's actions in time is crucial to the theological project such that this can only be discovered from a historical study of the canonical shaping of the text, then it follows we cannot, without risk of distortion, simply assume the givenness of the final form of the text, and then seek to find ways to affirm a one-to-one correlation between, on the one hand, each truth claim of the text as it occurs sequentially and "atomistically" in the text, and, on the other, historical reality. That this happened during the course of the Enlightenment was because the unmediated focus of the Enlightenment tradition was on the "unreconstructed" premodern tradition.

historical process).[11] This meant, of course (as was said above in the case of the Priestly dimension of the Old Testament), that a redactor presently engaged with biblical text was in fact working with a received but incomplete biblical text of which the redactor therefore had prior knowledge. The ultimate effect of such a process was to privilege in some sense the final redactor's activity of canonical shaping, but only in the following sense, as Childs put it: "The significance of the final form of the biblical text is that it alone bears witness to the full history of relevation.... It is only in the final form of the text that the full effect of this revelatory history can be perceived" (*IOTS*, 75–76). But the final redactor himself or herself is only privileged in that he or she is "standing on the shoulders of giants," to use Isaac Newton's famous metaphor, affirming the full history of God's action in Israel's and the world's time and history. He or she may indeed have the stature of a pygmy relative to his or her redactional predecessors in the sense that minimal redaction has taken place.

It is because of this latter truth that (quasi-) canonical intentionality can in principle be plotted at different but cumulative stages of canonical shaping. Indeed, at each stage in the historical formation of scripture, the incomplete text could only be seen to be "noncanonical" with the benefit of hindsight, from the perspective of future completion.[12] It is in this sense that canonical intentionality is determinative for the meaning of the biblical text. As Childs puts it: "The canonical shaping serves not so

---

11. This recursive process is beautifully exemplified by Childs's commentary on Isaiah. The original historical-canonical thesis was proposed by Duhm. Duhm's thesis was essentially this. The augmentation of First Isaiah with Second Isaiah, the augmentation of First Isaiah plus Second Isaiah with Third Isaiah, were both essentially linear additive processes. For Childs, Second Isaiah not only adds to First Isaiah but redacts him, perhaps selects, rearranges, or expands the received material. And similarly, Third Isaiah does the same to that which he receives from Second Isaiah. He selects, rearranges, and expands both an already-redacted First Isaiah (by Second Isaiah), and Second Isaiah himself. The specific way in which this is done—for example, what is added and what it is added to—represents the effect of the "new" canonical intentionality in action (Childs, *Isaiah: A Commentary* [Louisville: Westminster John Knox, 2001], 1–10).

12. As Childs put it, "It is certainly true that earlier stages in the development of biblical literature were often regarded as canonical prior to the establishment of the final form. In fact the final form frequently consists of simply transmitting an earlier, received form of the tradition often unchanged from its original setting" (*Introduction*, 76).

much to establish a given meaning to a particular passage as to chart the boundaries within which the exegetical task is to be carried out" (*IOTS*, 83). It would therefore be a mistake to think that at each stage in the process of canonical shaping, *all* previous determinative meaning was redefined by the theologically active redactor.[13] The task of the reader—and certainly the biblical scholar—is to read the text itself as a historical object, which means reading it in terms of the specific trajectory of canonical shaping corresponding to the history of its formation. Insofar as one's reading is to be informed by this trajectory, the key task for the interpreter is to determine the actual process of canonical shaping that took place in historical time.

The key question in this respect may be said to be "who redacted who?" That is to say the historical *order* of redaction is crucial to the determination of meaning; which is to say, the historical order of Israel's testimony to God's soteriological action in time: "The object of historical study is Israel's own testimony to God's redemptive activity." (*BTONT*, 97) But this poses us a methodological problem. As Childs says, "basic to the canonical process is that those responsible for the actual editing of the text did their best to obscure their own identity" (*IOTS*, 78). The redactors did not explicitly tell us how the text was rolled out to canonical completion. Nevertheless, there is light on the hermeneutical horizon simply because the canonical process has left its scribal footprint on the text: "Its presence is detected by the effect on the text" (*IOTS*, 78). Insofar as one accepts a Deuteronomistic and/or a Priestly redactor, or indeed a preexilic Yahwistic redactor (as opposed to a source),[14] it can make a significant difference in the nature of the "boundaries" within which determinative meaning can be plausibly

---

13. Hence, for example in the case of the redaction of the individual stories of the primeval history, Gen 2–11, by for instance that "theologian of genius," the Yahwist (von Rad's description), one can say that even though these stories had disparate origins and perhaps even disparate intentions behind them, in the context of the Yahwist's (or whoever's) redaction and therefore in the context of canonical shaping and narrative linkage in particular, they had been deployed in order to serve a common purpose, namely, to convey a narrative description of God's character, perhaps reconceiving the divine intention in the light of present events (say, Israel's experience of being in personal relationship with YHWH in the tenth century B.C.E.). The subsequent Priestly redaction of J as argued for by Westermann and Rentdorff, for example, at creation and the flood, only serves to reinforce this point. See Childs, *BTONT*, 113.

14. See, for example, Christoph Levin, "The Yahwist and the Redactional Link Between Genesis and Exodus," in *A Farewell to the Yahwist? The Composition of the*

attributed to the text. As Childs put it in the case of the creation account, the decision to affirm either independent P and J sources or the redaction of a common tradition "greatly affects the way in which these sources relate to each other and how their variations are to be judged. Any time an exegetical appeal to intentionality is made; some interpretation of the nature of the text is obviously being assumed" (*BTONT*, 108).

In this context, whether or not one accepts the historical-redactional precedence of the Deuteronomistic redaction over the Priestly one, for example, the question remains to what extent the Deuteronomistic redaction made its presence felt in the first four books of the Pentateuch. Rolf Rendtorff holds that the Deuteronomistic redactor was a key figure in giving the outline of the Pentateuch its shape (a Deuteromonistic Pentateuch)[15]—*contra* the more traditional view that the Deuteronomistic redaction begins substantially with Deuteronomy and the Deuteronomistic history (according to this thesis, the Yahwist is *the* major influence on the Pentateuch, and the Deuteronomistic impact begins more or less with the Deuteronomistic history).[16] On the matter of Deuteronomistic or Priestly canonical precedence, Childs took a view over against the position held by James A. Sanders, that the "last redactional stage of the Pentateuch" was to be attributed to the Deuteronomist rather than P.[17] How important such questions are is measured by the impact the redactor makes on the received "final form of the text." This impact may be one that endorses or reinforces the key themes of the received text, or it may be one that takes it in a different direction. Different historical trajectories of canonical shaping may give rise to different boundaries of meaning, precisely because they testify to different canonical intentionalities plotable at different stages in historical time, but equally they may not. One may say that the

---

Pentateuch in Recent European Interpretation (ed. Thomas B. Dozeman and Konrad Schmid; Atlanta: Society of Biblical Literature, 2006), 113–43.

15. Rolf Rendtorff, *The Old Testament: an Introduction* (Philadelphia: Fortress, 1986); *The Problem of the Process of Transmission in the Pentateuch* (JSOTSup 89; Sheffield: JSOT Press, 1990; orig. in German, 1977). See also R. Norman Whybray, *Introduction to the Pentateuch* (Grand Rapids: Eerdmans, 1995) for a general introduction to this position.

16. It is always worth bearing in mind that the discernible effect of the canonical shaper one perceives in the text underdetermines in "Quinean" terms every and all theories regarding the historical formation of scripture. But this truth in itself does not undermine the rational necessity of such theories.

17. Childs, *IOTS*, 130–31.

latter prophets take the canon in a different thematic direction from the former prophets. Equally, one might say that the basic theme of the Yahwist's primeval history is not disrupted by the later Priestly redaction (Gen 6–9); or that whether the Deuteronomist left the Yahwistic and Priestly material largely untouched or not, the different trajectories of canonical shaping all say one thing: God as a judging yet desisting self in time. But all this must be a matter for empirical discovery.[18]

The Work of God in Time

I have said at various points in this chapter that scripture witnesses to God's action in time. God is in time acting in time.[19] I also implied that the concept of the historical formation of the biblical text has something decisive to say about this claim in a way that canonical readings—whose focus is only on the concept of the final form of the text—do not (the latter concept is neutral in this respect). The premodern theological tradition is testimony to the latter. Notwithstanding different views regarding which books were in the canon, the final form of the text was interpreted in terms of the following venerable classical model of God and his relationship to time. For Aquinas, as for Calvin,[20] God is timeless in the sense that all time, past, present, and future, is present to him "all at once." Under the Thomistic model of God as *actus purus*—a God who eternally, in Boethius's sense

---

18. My book *Metaphysics and the God of Israel: Systematic Theology of the Old and New Testaments* (Grand Rapids: Baker, 2006) is an example of the principle that canonical shaping determines what the historical truth claims of the Bible actually are. It did in fact delineate a historical trajectory largely free of the conception of a Deuteronomistic Pentateuch (far less a "Deuteronomistic Yahwist"). But whether an alternative trajectory such as one just cited would have led to a different conclusion regarding the identity of God as a judging yet desisting forbearing self is a moot point—though it is a matter for empirical investigation.

19. In general, if we are to pursue the reintegration of biblical studies and systematic theology that stands the test of intellectual time, a project so dear to Childs's heart, it must encompass philosophically and historically nuanced and sophisticated treatments of categories such as God, divine action, time, history, and perhaps uniquely identifying descriptions (e.g., "the one who released 'Israel' from the bondage of Egypt," "the one who raised Jesus from the dead").

20. The difference between Calvin and Aquinas in this respect is that Calvin puts greater emphasis on God decreeing from eternity not only his own actions but—deterministically—every other event in the world.

of "unending life all at once," does "everything all at once" (inclusive of incarnation and creation). God acts "all at once" such that eternity and immutability remain inviolable: God "wills change," but does not "change his will" in eternity).²¹ Nevertheless, what God wills takes place "sequentially" in our time, insofar as this is what God wills. Aquinas's God acts in history by decreeing in eternity what his actions are to be in history, inclusive of his relationship with the people "Israel." His is an "eternalist" God in this sense, whose every real act is done from eternity, in eternity. We can cite Aquinas' *Summa Contra Gentiles* as indicative of Aquinas' understanding of God's action in the world:

> Nor, if the action of the first agent is eternal, does it follow that His effect is eternal? ... God acts voluntarily in the production of things ... God's act of understanding and willing, is, necessarily, His act of making. Now, an effect follows from the intellect and the will according to the determination of the intellect and the command of the will. Moreover, just as the intellect determines every other condition of the thing made, so does it prescribe the time of its making; for any art determines not only that this thing is to be such and such, but that it is to be at this particular time, even as a physician determines that a dose of medicine is to be drunk at such and such a time, so that, if his act of will were of itself sufficient to produce the effect, the effect would follow anew from his previous decision, without any new action on his part. Nothing, therefore, prevents our saying that God's eternity existed from all eternity, whereas its effect was not present from eternity, but existed at that time, when, from all eternity, he ordained it.²²

According to this model, God determines in eternity what is to happen in time without actually acting in time himself. The physician can determine when the dose of medicine is to be taken in the future without being around at this particular time in the life of his patient. God does the same as regards making events happen in the world. So God acts on and in the world from eternity—without being in the world. Nicholas Wolterstorff

---

21. Aquinas, *Summa Theologiae*, I, q.19, a.7. See also Richard Sorabji, *Time, Creation, and the Continuum: Theories in Antiquity and the Early Middle Ages* (Ithaca, N.Y.: Cornell University Press, 1983), 241–42, for an illuminating discussion of this distinction. For an application of the distinction to creation and incarnation in terms of Aquinas's employment of Aristotle's theory of real, logical, and mixed relations such that they do not involve change in God.
22. Thomas Aquinas, *Summa Contra Gentiles*, 2.35.

illustrates Aquinas' model in terms of the childhood toy in which one releases a marble at the top of the apparatus, at which point the marble subsequently emerges at the bottom after having navigated loops, springs and trapdoors at high speed. The only action executed is the one at the beginning.[23] Just so: God determines timelessly as it were that his actions will be or are as they are at the revealing of his divine name and the "deliverance at sea." But he does not actually act in time at these historical moments.

Clearly the concept of the final form of the text, so fundamental to the premodern tradition, was interpreted in terms of reference to a timeless God. Crucial to this perspective is the following: God creates the world outside of time and "continues" (timelessly) to act in it. This has the implication that the epistemic priority of the thematic of God as creator came to determine how one understood God's (soteriological) actions in the world (the premodern theologian's first encounter as reader of scripture was with God the creator, not with God the soteriological identity). However, come modernity and Gerhard von Rad (see below), the relationship came to be reversed: it was argued that God as soteriological identity was epistemically "superordinate" to God as creator. The Bible itself had a history which did not begin with Gen 1. What effect did this have on the question of God and time? What difference did epistemic priority make if God as soteriological identity is the earliest "knowledge" "Israel" has of its God? The answer is that Israel's earliest tradition regarding YHWH has God in time such that if God is subsequently affirmed (in the history of tradition) as creating the world from outside of time, this latter must be claimed in such a way to be consistent with the epistemic priority of God in time encountering Israel in time. Indeed, the epistemic priority of God in time *in medias res*, as it were, must predispose one to think that God has always been in time (even when he creates).

Though the first tradition could (counterfactually) have been the one expressed in Gen 1 (with Moses as the originator of it, for example), for Childs it was clear that the people Israel's primal encounter with YHWH in "the deliverance at the sea" was something like this centre, from which and against which later events in the history of tradition were interpreted, and to which later narrative traditions were prefixed (Genesis traditions) or suffixed (post-"deliverance" traditions). Childs wrote: "It is generally

---

23. Nicholas Wolterstorff, "Unqualified Divine Temporality" in *God and Time: Four Views* (ed. Gregory E. Ganssle; Downers Grove, Ill.: InterVarsity Press, 2001).

agreed that the exodus from Egypt forms the heart of Israel's earliest tradition" (*BTONT*, 130). Again:

> Israel's faith developed historically from its initial encounter with God as redeemer from Egypt—the one who released Israel from the bondage of Egypt, and only secondarily from this centre was a theology of creation incorporated into its faith. (*BTONT*, 120)

In this belief Childs was indebted to von Rad's seminal paper "The Theological Problem of the Old Testament Doctrine of Creation" in which von Rad argued that Israel's affirmation of YHWH as creator was epistemically subordinate, and therefore secondary, to the primary claim of YHWH as soteriological identity.[24] What this meant of course is that Israel's primal history of tradition was an expression *inter alia* of her belief that God the soteriological identity had acted in the world *then and there*; and this, by having acted in the life of the people "Israel" then and there. This action was not just any action but one motivated on God's side by a desire to be in personal relationship with "Israel." In this sense is the first historical truth about Israel's beliefs in her God one of soteriological personal relationship. The *epistemic* priority of YHWH's soteriological identity over his identity as creator (a priority that did not have to be true—suppose the Wisdom tradition had been epistemically privileged in the historical of tradition) could be explained by the reasonable assumption that God first revealed what is central or "core" to his identity (c.f. Exod 34:6, a primitive formula which does not include reference to YHWH as creator).[25] Analogously, the epistemic priority of God in time was likewise explained by the fact that time is at the core of God's identity. If the meaning of the divine

---

24. Gerhard von Rad, "The Problem of the Old Testament Doctrine of Creation," in *The Problem of the Hexateuch and Other Essays* (London: SCM, 1984), 131–42.

25. Childs says tantalizingly: "There is no 'revelation' apart from the experience of historical Israel" (*IOTS*, 71). One could interpret this to mean that there is no "revelation" outside the historical formation of Israel's belief in God's redemptive activity in time as testified by scripture. This is so even though it implies, for example, that belief in YHWH as creator is later in historical order than belief in YHWH as a specific soteriological identity, which is to say, the belief originating in the primal encounter in Exodus that is the deliverance at the sea. It is not that YHWH is not the creator, but that epistemically his soteriological identity takes historical precedence such that this is reflected in the historical formation of scripture. This epistemic priority can be taken to be indicative of the fact that at the core of YHWH's being is a saving identity.

name is most accurately translated as "I will be who I will be," it tells us something profound about God's being: God is intrinsically—and first and foremost—a historical soteriological identity.

One could also say that the claim of God in time— that God really acts then and there, as it were—is reinforced if we endorse Barth's exegesis of the seventh day of creation: Gen 2:1–3 narrates God's getting himself into the time he has created (*Deus in mundo* as a historical precursor to *Deus incarnatus*, Jesus of Nazareth). Robert Jenson has also argued persuasively that Aquinas's analysis of divine action leads to an unacceptable separation between God's being and his actions (having effect) in the world.[26] Not unrelatedly, Jenson writes forthrightly:

> That we take God's personality seriously is vital to the religious life demanded by the gospel. The Bible's language about God is drastically personal: he changes his mind and reacts to external events, he makes threats and repents of them, he makes promises and tricks us by how he fulfils them. If we understand this language as fundamentally inappropriate, as "anthropomorphic," we do not know the biblical God. Persons do all these things, precisely to be personal, and in that the true God is personal they are ontological perfections, not deficiencies.[27]

And this means that the true God is in time. All of these characterizations of God are consistent with William Alston's conception of God as basic action (to which could be added the notion of God as basic self-determining action). They are also consistent with the notion developed elsewhere of God—YHWH—as a judging yet desisting self.[28] At the very least, God has a "personality," as Barth and Luther had it (the latter in his exegesis of Rom 3:21–26 explained God's justification by faith in terms of divine mercy *ad intra*). And this means that the true God is in time.

Conclusion

A conclusion by way of postscript: If the historical formation of biblical tradition—canonical shaping—is central to Childs's project, then it cannot be gainsaid that the project has had little impact on theological studies. A

---

26. Robert W. Jenson, *Systematic Theology* (Oxford: Oxford University Press, 1997), 1:59.
27. Ibid., 1:222.
28. See MacDonald, *Metaphysics and the God of Israel*, 117–224.

short survey of some key theological texts may make the point. Even if we look at the very best of the scholarship that both is self-consciously theological in its approach to the Bible, and that refers to Childs in some way or another, we see scant attention to the (authorial) historical formation of scripture as a determinative force in the interpretation of the biblical text. The focus is primarily about reading the final form of the text—and has very little to do with the historical formation of biblical tradition. In Stephen Fowl's edition of *The Theological Interpretation of Scripture*, Childs is only mentioned very briefly (three times), and only once in his capacity as a commentator on scripture.[29] There is no attempt in the book to place its theological interpretation in the context of some kind of objective framework of canonical shaping of the kind proposed by Childs. To be sure, the book affirms theological interpretation in its traditional sense—as one that avoids reductionist approaches and takes the reference to God's presence and actions in scripture for what they are. But there is no overall theoretical emphasis on the historical process of canonical intentionality as the supervenient theological rationale within which interpretation takes place. And since all the commentators on the Bible would affirm a classical "faith seeking understanding" paradigm—even a "rule of faith" one—it is clear that even such faith commitment is not sufficient for doing justice to Childs's methodological precepts. Indeed, we cannot escape the conclusion that exegetes faithful to the "faith seeking understanding" dictum and a holistic approach to the Bible can still produce interpretation in which "the focus of the analysis lies in the 'imaginative construal of the reader'"— as Childs puts it—rather than in the canonical intentionality integral to scripture. What of Fowl's own exposition of biblical interpretation in this respect?[30] Here again the emphasis is on the reader, but a particular kind of reader, namely, the "virtuous reader." It is essentially his or her "interpretative habits and dispositions" involving *inter alia* "practical reasoning" serving the faithful life inclusive of Christian convictions and Christian worship that shape the reading of the Bible:

> Christian interpretation of Scripture needs to involve a complex interaction in which Christian convictions, practices and concerns are brought

---

29. Stephen E. Fowl, *The Theological Interpretation of Scripture: Classic and Contemporary Readings* (Cambridge, Mass.: Blackwell, 1997).
30. Stephen E. Fowl, *Engaging Scripture: A Model for Theological Interpretation* (Malden, Mass.: Blackwell, 1998).

to bear on scriptural interpretation in ways that both shape that interpretation and are shaped by it.[31]

Fowl does in fact deal with Childs's theological project at some length. But it seems clear that it is a reading of Childs based only on his essay "Toward Recovering Theological Exegesis" (see his n. 4). There is reference to concepts such as "the final form of the text" and "literal sense," but nothing to "canonical shaping." In other words, there is nothing on "canonical intentionality" construed as the epistemic order or historical formation of Israel's belief regarding divine action, as outlined above. This would explain why Fowl's critique of Childs's emphasis on the "discrete voice of the Old Testament" would appear to be misconceived for reasons stated in this chapter (see n. 6).

There may well be many reasons for this omission in the dialogue between Childs's canonical approach and theology. But I mention two. Understanding and following Childs on canonical shaping presupposes detailed knowledge of modern biblical scholarship: the biblical text as a redacted text. Due to the cleavage between theology and biblical studies in the academy, theologians in the modern era as theological interpreters of the Bible tend not to have acquired this knowledge. Second, and perhaps more importantly, there are those affirming the primacy or superiority of precritical biblical interpretation (especially in a postmodern idiom), who have deemed the whole issue of canonical shaping an irrelevance. Readers simply respond to the final form of the text.

Childs understood the first phenomenon. But he vehemently disagreed with the second. In the example I offered on God's work in time, I hope I have given some grounds for thinking that he was right about the latter.

---

31. Fowl, *Engaging Scripture*, 8. He also writes: "I am particularly concerned that Christians learn from the best interpretative habits and practices of those who both clearly understood the purposes for which Christians interpret Scripture" (ibid., 9). Childs would of course put the emphasis on "the purposes for which Scripture was written," namely, witness to Israel's belief in God's soteriological action in time. Fowl's preference for premodern interpretation is all of a piece with his theological rationale, since it unambiguously takes place in the context of the "rule of faith." But this, as was seen above, cannot be sufficient to guarantee a reading that puts the emphasis on a historical reading.

Faith Seeking Canonical Understanding: Childs's Guide to the Pauline Letters

Leander E. Keck

The focus of Brevard Childs's 2008 *The Church's Guide for Reading Paul* is stated succinctly in its subtitle: *The Canonical Shaping of the Pauline Corpus*.[1] Thus the book is about the only Paul that now is, the New Testament Paul, not the Paul who once was, whom critics keep trying to reconstruct and portray. "Canonical shape" is one of Childs's formulations, forged in his previous studies of canon.[2] Unlike Wellhausen, who focused on the Gospels when he sensed that he had made his contribution to the understanding of the OT and "late Judaism," Childs turned to the NT in order to bring his work on "canon" to completion. Since his *New Testament as Canon: An Introduction* (1984) had discussed the fourfold Gospel corpus,[3] his last book applies the "canonical approach" (also his formulation) to the Pauline corpus, bounded by Acts and Hebrews. The entire Childs corpus pertaining to canon should be read, pondered, and engaged as a whole, for it has the potential—and to some, the danger—of transforming the study of scripture. This essay's purpose, however, is more modest: to grasp, in a preliminary way, the significance of this particular book for the study of Paul. It is appropriate to begin first, however, with an effort to understand the man and the passion of his labors.

---

1. Brevard S. Childs, *The Church's Guide for Reading Paul: The Canonical Shaping of the Pauline Corpus* (Grand Rapids: Eerdmans, 2008).

2. See, e.g., Brevard S. Childs, "The Canon in Recent Biblical Studies: Reflections on an Era," *Pro Ecclesia* 14 (2005): 26–45; also included in *Canon and Biblical Interpretation* (ed. Craig Bartholomew et al.; SHS 7; Milton Keynes, UK: Paternoster, 2006), 32–56.

3. Brevard S. Childs, *The New Testament as Canon: An Introduction* (Philadelphia: Fortress, 1984).

104   THE BIBLE AS CHRISTIAN SCRIPTURE

DISCIPLINED PASSION

Like Childs's work as a whole, *Church's Guide* engages a far wider range of themes than its subtitle suggests. Theological issues, exegetical questions, hermeneutical considerations, history of interpretation, as well as concern for the vitality of current Christian faith flow into one another to feed his vision of canon. One watermark of his work was a passion to correlate the rigorous requirements of research and writing with deep religious commitments, so that both dimensions are enriched and neither compromised. Without making the health of his own soul the measure of truth or "relevance," he worked and wrote unabashedly as a believing Protestant Christian who expected the carefully scrutinized historical evidence to expose religious phenomena that required him to engage them theologically, just as he believed that perceptive theology must address historical phenomena without blinking. He neither avoided thorny historical problems nor evaded their often unsettling implications. Precisely by writing for his peers as a scholars' scholar, he expressed his abiding concern for the church's robust fidelity to the gospel.

His long-time friend, Roy A. Harrisville, was on target in observing that "what has irritated Childs all his life is the separation between the descriptive and constructive elements of biblical interpretation, that is, between 'Biblical Theology' as a primarily historical task *and* subsequent theological reflection."[4] In Harrisville's formulation, the key word "separation" alerts us to Childs's passion to hold together dialectically (i.e., in tension) historical analysis and theological insight instead of *separating* them sequentially (first history, then interpretation, and consequently separating them substantively as well) as in much liberal theology, or *fusing* them materially (and therefore also methodologically; see *The Church's Guide*, 49), as is common in defensive conservatism and fundamentalism (16). To avoid both pitfalls, Childs developed the "canonical approach" as a hermeneutical alternative. The paradoxical result was inevitable: the more he pointed to the hermeneutical potential of the canon, the more famous he became as the Pointer. So he might not have welcomed this essay's

---

4. Roy A. Harrisville, "What I Believe My Old Schoolmate Is Up To," in *Theological Exegesis: Essays in Honor of Brevard S. Childs* (ed. Christopher Seitz and Kathryn Greene-McCreight; Grand Rapids: Eerdmans, 1999), 7.

subtitle. Nonetheless, given today's setting, the "canonical approach" *is* Childs's guide.[5]

Acknowledging Harrisville's insight entails a close look at the "canonical approach," which Childs rightly insisted was *not* a method, just as he refused to label his work "canonical criticism," a mischievous misunderstanding. Were it a method or special type of "criticism," it could take its place alongside various other modes of investigation that emerged in recent decades. Then it would be one more modification, another fine-tuning, an additional elaboration, of what is already being continuously refined—the longstanding "approach" that was deliberately noncanonical, and sometimes anticanonical. "Method" (i.e., the appropriate procedure for studying a particular phenomenon) is not at issue. What *is* at issue is precisely the "approach," the assumptions that determine one's stance toward the phenomenon; an "approach" is hospitable to a range of methods. Actually, then, the nonaggressive phrase "canonical approach" signals a clash of approaches.[6] The significance of Childs's book on the Pauline letters instantiates as well as sharpens that clash.

Clashing Approaches

One would not belittle Childs's achievement by saying that he developed the latent potential in the neglected obvious—that the two-testament Bible is the canon of the whole Christian church, and therefore is more than a major "source" for historians of the Christian religion. He saw that this elemental fact has a double significance: first, that the Bible must be understood as both a history-affected and as a history-effecting phenomenon; second, that its dual character must be allowed therefore to shape the interpreter's task from beginning to end. Only so will one reckon seriously

---

5. See Christopher Seitz's important discussion of Childs's work and its critics, "The Canonical Approach and Theological Interpretation," in *Canon and Biblical Interpretation*, 58–110.

6. More than four decades ago, Childs emphasized the decisive role of one's starting point in exegesis: "By defining the Bible as a 'source' for objective research the nature of the content to be described has already been determined." In fact, "the descriptive task lies at the heart of the theological task and is never something prior to or outside the theological endeavor" — because everything depends on how one understands *what* is being described, the subject matter to which the text points. See Brevard S. Childs, "Interpretation in Faith: The Theological Responsibility of an Old Testament Commentary," *Int* 18 (1964): 437–38.

with the kind of phenomenon that the biblical writings now are, given the "canonical shaping" they underwent *from the start,* viz., from their creation. The implications of this italicized phrase clash with the noncanonical "approach," and make Childs's view of the canon important, whether deemed promising or threatening.

To begin with, Childs's view requires an expanded, or redefined, view of the noun "canon," as well as of the verb "canonize" and the adjective "canonical." For Childs, canon as *product* (the roster of normative books) is inseparable from the long *process* that eventually produced it. "Canonization" is not reducible to an event that befell the writings, something that happened to them, an ecclesial act that made them something they had not already become (15, 43).[7] It was instead a formal acknowledgment of the writings' roles in what the church experienced as the truth of the gospel, however variously construed (61). The writings in the New Testament never lacked a "canonical" dimension; none were created to express someone's creativity; all manifest the author's sense of being authorized by the gospel, and were used in the church because it acknowledged the validity of that authorization.

The criteria that the church used to determine this validity are not as important for Childs as the fact that the writings—not only Paul's—had a criteriological function *from the start.* It was absent from neither the traditions adopted and adapted in them, nor from the sometimes detectable changes made in the writings (e.g., in editing or rearranging) en route to formal canonical status,[8] nor from the phenomenon called (pejoratively) "pseudepigraphy" (Childs's positive treatment of pseudepigraphy [159-63] draws on German Catholic scholarship). In short, some form of canonicity or normativity was operative in the creation, use, and transmission of these writings, thereby allowing them to function as the continuing criteria within the church, molding its history in worship, thought, and moral life.

---

7. So also David G. Meade: "The closure of the canon is not qualitatively different from the process of canon in the growth of tradition. It is just the final act, the logical conclusion to the process" (*Pseudonymity and Canon: An Investigation into the Relationship of Authorship and Authority in Jewish and Early Christian Tradition* [Grand Rapids: Eerdmans, 1987], 217).

8. Childs dealt with such matters in his *New Testament as Canon;* see his discussion of the Corinthian letters.

Given this expanded understanding, "approach" is the right word for Childs's *Guide*, for in conjunction with "canonical" it redefines the interpreter's stance toward the text. Whereas most biblical scholars, assuming that "canon" refers primarily to the final product (the list of officially normative writings), usually see canonization as irrelevant (at best) and therefore to be ignored, or as an impediment to unprejudiced inquiry to be overcome in the quest for the author's own meaning when the text was created, Childs valued the writings' canonicity as an important dimension of their own accumulated meanings. In this broadened view, the canonical meaning is not an addendum to the "real" meaning of the text, something of interest to church historians but not to exegetes. In short, the "canonical approach" challenged the deeprooted assumptions of the noncanonical, or anticanonical, approach that increasingly for two centuries had characterized biblical scholarship, and whose goal was ascertaining the "original" (i.e., *precanonical*) meaning intended by the author, and sometimes broadened to include the first readers' perceived meaning.

Seeing the real measure of Childs's achievement requires viewing it in light of not only the whole history of modern scholarship's debates about the canon, which he knew very well, but also knowing modern Christianity's intellectual history. Here too he was no novice (56). For this essay, however, it must suffice first to recall that the inherited noncanonical hermeneutic had been developed in order to liberate scholarly investigation of scripture from the pro-canon constraints and controls of church dogma and reactionary ecclesiastical responses to modernity's mind. Emphasizing the putative "original" (authorial) meaning was therefore a useful way to disclose a specific meaning that could be contrasted with orthodox doctrine because it was supported by scientific historiography. Thus the separation between "what it meant" and "what it means," which Childs eschewed, facilitated historical criticism's liberating victory over the dogma-governed "approach." For many liberals, what the text "still means" often turned out to be a religious principle or moral "value," philosophically some form of ethical idealism. For those who found the bloom was off this interpretation, "salvation history," fortified by "God who acts" theology (seemingly confirmed by the outcome of World War II), combined "meant" and "means." But this hermeneutic lost much of its luster in light of the gap between describing what the Israelites (or early Christians) thought or believed had happened (what it "meant") and what today's historians are prepared to think may (or may not) have happened.

Childs, however, neither looked to historical criticism to rescue real religion from fundamentalism, nor found salvation history convincing, for both failed to reckon seriously with the sort of book that critical investigation was showing the Bible to be. Dealing with that called for a different stance. The "canonical approach" is Childs's response. He found the liberating freedom to discern "what it means" precisely in the canon process that, by repeatedly updating "what it meant," yielded a canon that was designed to aid the church, through the Spirit (77). Thus the church already has a guide to its scripture, a guide built into the canon itself. This guide is to be discerned, understood, and followed; it need not be invented and promoted as (another) "new theology" or "new method."

Still, it was not welcomed everywhere. The resistance that Childs's guide encountered was more than the natural, predictable reluctance of scholars to adopt a significantly different approach to the Bible, for his stance was out of step with the *Zeitgeist* in two reciprocally reinforcing ways. On the one hand, it took shape when many found offensive the very idea of *any* literary "canon"—writings that transmitted the (alleged) heart and values of Western culture—because any such corpus was elitist and exclusionary. On the other hand, others found the *biblical* canon objectionable because of its churchly character, being persuaded that its creation was an exercise in ecclesiastical power, used to suppress what should have been supported, and vice versa. Besides, it seemed self-evident to many that viable religious life should not be subjected to the external authority of a book, especially this one, increasingly held responsible for legitimating what must be abandoned for the sake of creating a more just world.

There would have been less resistance to the guide had Childs resolved the tension between the *historical-critical* approach, which ignores the distinction between canonical and noncanonical evidence in its quest of truth about the past, and the *canonical* approach, in which the church confesses that in the canon it hears the divine truth uniquely (61). This line between the canonical and the noncanonical, implied by the confession, reminds us that we are not prophets and apostles (45). Instead, by affirming both the critical and the confessional (125, 130), Childs not only deprived each of its autonomy and absoluteness but also maintained that "tension between the divine and human interaction is essential to Scripture's function in the church" (16)—not unlike the tension in two-nature Christology. The "confession" component is constitutive for Childs's view of the biblical canon: the church confesses that "Scripture is not an inert text waiting to be rendered intelligible through the imaginative capacity of its readers. Rather,

Scripture has its own voice. Its speaking is often related to the Holy Spirit and the continuing presence of the resurrected Christ" (44).[9]

Because Childs contends that it is "quite impossible to *describe* the rise of the Christian movement without recognizing the church's understanding that in wrestling with its Scripture, it was being continually instructed by a living Lord," it is not surprising that he thinks the contrasting social and *religionsgeschichtliche* approach of Wayne Meeks shows "how high are the theological issues at stake" (63). Meeks's sociological description of the early church not only disregards its self-understanding, but also includes instead "every conceivable religious grouping as playing an equal role in its development" (62). That is, it recognizes no privileged sources (the emerging canon). Moreover, it ignores both the role of the OT, "a cognitive confessional resource for the rise of Christianity," and the gospel's "witness to a divine reality being revealed in the person of Jesus." As a result, the description is limited to "human phenomenology expressed in communal patterns of behavior," and so is "theologically one-dimensional" (57). Consequently, Childs views "the debate with Wayne Meeks to be of greatest importance."

What Childs wrote in 1994, with his eye on Old Testament study, aptly summarizes the major issues he sees also in the interpretation of Paul, and thus provides the horizon of this book: (1) "whether the Bible ... can be anything more than an expression of time-conditioned human culture"; (2) "whether any ancient text has a determinate meaning" or "interpretation is simply an exercise in ever-changing modes of deconstruction"; and (3) "whether any community of faith can claim a special relation to its Scriptures as a guide to faithful living" or whether it will "recognize only sociological forces at work" in establishing its identity.[10]

Reading the Pauline Corpus

Childs will not use the canonical approach to skip over or solve exegetical problems. He assigns it other functions, based on the hermeneutical

---

9. Long before, as an exegete "sharing himself in the reality of God's redemptive activity," Childs acknowledged the role of the Spirit, but simultaneously insisted that the presence of the Spirit "is not a method of exegesis but a divine reality promised to the church and the source of true illumination."

10. Brevard S. Childs, "Old Testament in Germany 1920–1940: The Search for a New Paradigm," in *Altes Testament: Forschung und Wirking* (ed. Peter Mommer and Winfried Thiel; Frankfurt: Lang, 1994), 244–45.

import of the way the canonizing process structured the Pauline corpus. On the one hand, to state this import, he relies on exclusions: (1) the preeminence of Romans, theologically the broadest piece in the corpus, disallows making external, nontheological (viz., historical and social) considerations the key to interpretation; (2) the references to justification in the Pastorals (2 Tim 1:9; Tit 3:5-7) culminate a living tradition of interpretation and so disallow a sharp contrast with "the historical Paul"; and (c) the interpretation of Paul's own message must not be tied so tightly to the circumstances that occasioned the letters that it either excludes appropriation by later generations or produces contradictions that prevent serious engagement with his thought today. On the other hand, he emphasizes the positive significance of the corpus: when the canonical Paul—introduced by Romans and completed by the Pastorals— is read as a whole (as the corpus intends), "the canonical structure sets up a dialectical interaction *within* the context of the corpus between the general and the specific, between the universal content of the gospel and the unique needs of each congregation" (76, emphasis added). Thus the canonical Paul generates an ongoing theological reflection, for neither the particular nor the whole is allowed to eclipse the other. The corpus does not unify or harmonize the letters either, but forms a circle (or arena, or framework) of apostolic texts within which the church hears the apostolic witness to the gospel. As the critique of Meeks's work has shown, canon as privileged context of interpretation is basic for Childs, and it underlies the importance of the Pastorals.

The significance of the Pastorals in this book can hardly be overstated. They are not "about Paul," nor do they update his thoughts. Instead, they mark a shift in the portrayal of Paul. The Pastorals not only viewed his collected letters as scripture (96-97); they also saw his teachings as "sound doctrine" (72-73). Their continuity with Paul is not a matter of their repeating his theology, which indeed "has been somewhat diluted," for their role is to "provide the hermeneutic by which Paul's ministry" can guide the ongoing church (110). Historically, "the shapers of the Pastorals stood within a growing canonical process that first included the reception of the deutero-Pauline letters (Colossians and Ephesians) and culminated in a 'trito-Pauline' corpus of the Pastorals" (165). Given the common view that the Pastorals are Paul's embarrassing stepchildren, these writings' reassessment here (drawing heavily on German Roman Catholic scholarship; see 160-66) may prove to be more influential than the emphasis on the significance of Romans at the head of the corpus, for it has long functioned as the Protestant guide to Paul. Be that as it may, what matters in the long run is whether the canonical approach is sufficiently capacious to guide scholarship, and the church as well, *away* from an unhistorical stance toward the historical Paul and *toward* a more truly historical one, one that does not evade the theological challenges built into the historicality of the Christian faith through its peculiar relation to its own past, which includes the historical Paul.

Criticism's historical Paul has many facets, but common to most is the insistence that he can be recovered by first largely abandoning the Paul of Acts, then by finding his voice only in the seven genuine letters, and finally by studying each of them in its (probable) historical sequence, as did the SBL Seminar on Pauline Theology. Ostensibly, this should have shown how Paul's theology emerged. So Romans was studied last, not according to the canonical order. But the theology of the historical Paul simply cannot be reached this way. For one thing, emphasizing the discreteness of each letter probably made it inevitable that the outcome would resemble a heap of fragments, and that some participants would claim Paul did not articulate a coherent theology into the contingent circumstances, because his thought emerged only as he wrote. Nor was it surprising that one participant concluded that the effort to find Paul's theology should be suspended for a time. As a guide for the church's understanding of the Pauline corpus (the bulk of its canon!), it is hard to imagine a more useless result, despite important observations made along the way.

To illustrate a more fruitful alternative, Childs provides eight "probes" of important exegetical issues that have dogged the noncanonical approach. Some of them concern *differences* within the corpus (Paul's apostolate, Abraham in Galatians and Romans, life in the Spirit in Romans and 1 Corinthians), some discuss *similarities* in differing contexts (Spirit-gifts in 1 Corinthians, Romans, and Ephesians; the strong and the weak in Romans and 1 Corinthians); others highlight critics' *conflicts* over basic issues (the problem of early church "offices," the unparalleled emphasis on Israel in Rom 9–11, and "the apocalyptic shape of Paul's theology"). Thereby Childs demonstrates, first, that while the canonical approach does not evade historical criticism's concerns, it avoids being dominated by the need to reconstruct the particularities of the historical Paul, and second, that reckoning seriously with the intent of the corpus's structure can suggest new modes of understanding. These "probes" show Childs the teacher, deftly walking the reader through technical scholarly debates and succinctly stating his reservations and objections.

Running through these "probes" are two themes, both unavoidable in any discussion of a body of writings produced across decades: the relation between continuity and change (a basic historical concern), and the relation between the contingency of the particular and the coherence of the whole (essential for theological analysis).

If historical criticism's issues are not dismissed as irrelevant or invalid, if the tension between criticism and confession is to be affirmed as necessary rather than assimilated into a quasi-Hegelian *Aufhebung* (synthesis), and if the canonical approach does not solve basic theological problems in the reconstruction of the theology of the historical Paul, what is gained by adopting this approach as the proper *modus operandi* for the interpretation of scripture? Childs states his own criterion of successful exegesis: "raising new perspectives for breaking out of some [!] of the impasse that has increasingly paralyzed the understanding of scripture" (81). To a considerable degree, that impasse results from the way much historical criticism has portrayed the relation of the historical Paul to "early Christianity"—the theme that is central also in the canonical approach. A few observations suffice to indicate how taking Childs's guide seriously can affect wider hermeneutical horizons.

First, although Childs does not discuss extensively the problem of language usage, it is instructive to note that in the phrase "early Christianity," the abstract noun "Christianity" is more mischievous than the ambiguous adjective "early," for while it enables one to designate this religious phenomenon as a whole, its very abstractness also encourages one to view the Christian religion as primarily a matter of ideas, and its history as the history of ideas (understandable, given the role of doctrine in the history of the Christian religion). Not surprisingly, then, where Paul's ideas are not repeated, debated, explained, and elaborated, it can appear that he was forgotten, no longer understood, or had left a limited legacy—in short, had been ineffective (or perhaps even repressed). Actually, Paul would have been ineffective if, half a century later, Christians had still been debating the issues that provoked him to write letters, or if those writing in his name had essentially repeated him. The point is not that the power of Paul's theology has been overrated, but that *our* interest in his ideas may well have beclouded a clear vision of his place in the early Christian religion as it actually was becoming. If so, in the noncanonical approach the Paul of the Pastorals has been denigrated because he was measured by the wrong criterion, and Childs's guide offers a way out of this "impasse."

Another differing perspective focuses on the historical Paul himself, and involves the impact, often indirect, of Romanticism in biblical studies as a whole, and particularly on the understanding of religion in history. Romanticism's influence in both areas still needs full investigation. Its interest in the struggles of the individual (recall its German writers' fascination with *Sturm und Drang*, and the *Bildungsroman*) offered an alternative to the earlier rationalism, and in the later years of the nineteenth century was also taken up by the *religionsgeschichtliche Schule* when it emphasized the role of the creative individual in the historical development of religion. Old Testament scholarship lionized the prophets by emphasizing their powerful religious experience as the energizer of their vocations, and some interpreters of the historical Paul wrote extensively about the apostle's individuated, intensely personal conversion experience and his subsequent life in the Spirit, easily contrasted (in effect) with the religion of the Letter (the Law). Readily, Paul's religious experience became portrayed and preached as the idealized example of vital Christian religion. To such lionization of the historical Paul, based on a problematic view of real religion and its advances in history, the canonical approach offers a helpful alternative by clearing the way for a theologically more significant relation to the Paul of early Christian history.

No one doubts that Paul's religious experience was so deeply personal that it changed his identity and authorized a vocation that somewhat transformed the faith he adopted. But the more the religion of the volcanic apostle is idealized, the more readily it is contrasted with what appears assumed and advocated by the Pastorals and Acts, sometimes labeled *Fruhkatholicismus*. "Early catholicism" is anything but a neutral description of third- (and late second-)generation Christian religion, marked by the church's claims about itself and the consequent concern for structured accountability, reliably attested tradition, sacraments, and orthodox doctrine. Rather, in the minds of wary Protestants it signals an unmistakable pejorative verdict: here is the primal "fall" of the church from its high point in the historical Paul. Even if circumstances had made the trend toward "early catholicism" inevitable or necessary for survival, it nonetheless marked a decline from Paul, if not a deliberate abandonment of his thought. If so, the church and its theology should return to the historical Paul, even though it was his letters and not the man that was canonized. Marcion, though distorting Paul deeply, was but the first Paulinist to claim him as the high ground in an attempt to purify the church of the (alleged) corrupting sub-Pauline elements that had accrued.

In short, in the disdain for "early catholicism" two hermeneutical assumptions reinforce one another: the notion that real religion is not of the Letter but of the Spirit, and the conviction that in the brief Pauline moment true religion erupted into history, as it had in Jesus, albeit differently. Built into the regret over the emergence of "early catholicism" is a (largely Protestant) longing for the earlier, allegedly simpler and purer faith and theology of Paul, reminiscent of the romantics' desire to recapture the middle ages as well as the yearning of some of them for the unmediated salvific experience of the Infinite. (It is also recognizable in some persons' perpetual search for a church deserving their attendance.) The canonical approach would make a major contribution if it has the capacity to guide the church *away* from an unhistorical attitude toward the historical Paul and *toward* a more truly historical one that reckons seriously, that is, theologically, with the historicity of the Christian community and its beliefs, rites, and ethos.

The SBL seminar's problematic outcome was not the result of distinguishing too sharply the canonical apostle from the critically constructed Paul. Rather, it was rooted in a twofold overconfidence: first, that ever more astute critical investigation *could* recover "the real Paul" from the canonical Paul—what he *really* said, intended, and was shaped by—in order to affirm the former at the expense of the latter; second, that had the recovery reached conclusions that are firm and not simply confidently stated, the results *would* have advanced significantly the interpretation of the apostle's thought for the guidance of the church and the improvement of society. The seminar's work (in which I participated) may well be recalled as another monument to biblical scholarship's hermeneutical naiveté about the generative power of critical historiography (or to naiveté's obverse, hubris).

While Childs does not repudiate efforts to anchor Paul's thought as securely as possible in the situations he addressed in his letters, he does relativize the domineering claims of such undertakings, for he sees that overemphasizing the diverse contingencies of Paul's thought can readily threaten its coherence. Instructive here is his response to J. Louis Martyn's esteemed commentary on Galatians, in which Paul's polemically-stated theology is strikingly dependent on the commentator's remarkably detailed construction of the thought of the teachers, the apostle's opponents. Childs not only thinks Martyn claimed to know more than is possible, but he also relies on the canonical function of Romans (implied in its location in the corpus) to prevent the chronologically prior Galatians from becoming the lens through which the later Romans must be read. Basic for Childs's whole vision was the work of his erstwhile colleague, Nils A. Dahl, who investigated how the early church coped with the particularity of Paul's letters in order to free them to address later, and differing, situations. Childs saw the implication: the particularity of each letter was retained, but relativized when the canonical process created the Pauline arena within all of which the church could hear not simply its favorite (legitimating) letter, but also the apostle's larger witness to the *res, die Sache*, the subject matter that evoked it.

The importance of the whole arena is especially evident in Childs's discussion of the apocalyptic dimension of Paul's thought, though he is more concerned with the function of apocalyptic than with its content. Well aware of the tangled scholarly views of "apocalyptic" (another instance of the problems created by language usage), he asks "how the subject of apocalyptic in its various manifestations—historical, literary, theological—affect[s] the reading of this [Pauline] corpus" (195). He dissents from the view that apocalyptic was "the mother of Christian theology" and its correlate, that "early catholicism" subverted "Paul's radical apocalyptic understanding of history." Childs thinks this view was "derived from a highly restricted selection of apocalyptic elements," and charges it with ignoring "the issue of canon and its development within the church" (203–7). Not surprisingly, he rejects also Martyn's radical apocalyptic interpretation of Galatians (212). Instead of beginning with "the hermeneutical assumption that apocalyptic is the primary force in the development of Paul's theology," Childs reduces its role to "an important but secondary use of images that served Paul well" (212). Accordingly, it is "a serious error" to claim that "eschatology, indeed even apocalyptic themes," have been completely lost in the Pastorals. Instead, the generating power of early Christian theology was Christology, not apocalyptic. Jewish apocalyptic thinking did enter Paul's thinking along with Old Testament traditions of "wisdom, psalmody, and liturgy," but not as "the source of the Christian faith" (215–17).

Childs's real concern, it appears, was negative: on the one hand, to prevent apocalyptic from eclipsing the rich role of the Old Testament in the construction of early Christian history, and on the other, to inhibit using apocalyptic to isolate a thoroughly apocalyptic Paul of history from the whole Paul of the corpus and from the rest of the New Testament. Still, while he sees that "the New Testament emerged from the explosive force of the death and resurrection of Jesus Christ" (216), he overlooks two elemental considerations—that by definition, "resurrection" itself is inseparable from apocalyptic thought, and that it was the apocalyptic view of "resurrection" that gave "explosive force" to the assertion that precisely the crucified *Jesus*, and only he, was resurrected. Consequently, early Christology and apocalyptic are not alternative energizers of early Christian theology, for they were conceptually intertwined. Giving due attention to this point would have actually supported Childs's refusal to isolate the apocalyptic Paul within the canon.

Childs's Challenge

Childs's canonical approach, if not simply noted as "interesting" or dismissed as "too conservative," poses a twofold challenge, one to the church (will it accept this guide?), the other to the academy (will it change some of its assumptions and ask different questions?). Before "progressive" church folk can respond positively to his canonical approach, they must overcome their anxiety-fed apprehension that following this guide will restore (and in some places, confirm) the precritical dominance of the Bible. Especially during the current Darwin anniversary, one recalls how often the church-canon nexus has been used to legitimate opposition to, and suppression of, the scholarly inquiry that is not subject to ecclesiastical power. But Childs's aim is not restoration of any *status quo ante*, but a forward-looking alternative to the distorting legacy of historicism, manifest in Christian theology's naïve reliance on "history," and in the impact of that reliance on the church. This dependence is expressed in both the passion to contrast the "historical" Paul with the canonical apostle, and in the opposite pressure to demonstrate that they are virtually identical. Childs's persistent emphasis on the dialectic/tension/balance (he uses all these terms) between the rigorously critical and the openly confessional is a persistent challenge to both the church (whether "progressive" or defensive) and the academy to forge a more adequate relation to history. The "canonical approach" has the capacity to foster such a development precisely because it is eminently historical itself.

Indeed, Childs's insistence on the ongoing indispensability of this dialectic assures the continuing validity, but not the tyranny, of the "quest for the historical Paul" who, virtually by definition, is a Paul no longer congruent with the canonical Paul. Childs neither denies the differences or harmonizes them away. Instead, he incorporates them in a historical approach that looks for continuity in differences. Thus he challenges his colleagues in academia to expand their understanding of "Pauline," so that it coheres with his expanded view of canon. As a result, the "historical Paul" is not to be played off against the canonical Paul, for in addition to the fact that the former remains more uncertain than is usually admitted, it is the latter that makes it possible (and necessary!) to talk about the former in the first place. It is almost entirely due to the creation and transmission of the diverse New Testament Paul that the complex Paul of history can be ascertained as the starting point of the "Pauline" phenomenon as a whole. In short, Childs's final book encourages critics to resume, albeit in a fresh way, the nineteenth-century discussion of "Paulinism" as a discrete, ongoing phenomenon within the Christian religion during its early, turbulent decades. Such an undertaking would involve comparing it with Johannine forms of Christian faith, with Matthean/Didachean expressions of it, as well as with "the Gnostic Paul" and the forms of the Christian religion that were hostile to Paul (more precisely, to their image of the historical Paul). Such efforts would amplify, and make more concrete, this book's view of the setting in which and for which the Pastorals were produced. Were the results to substantiate its vision, the need for, and the positive significance of, a closed canon would also become apparent. This larger, descriptive, effort was not Childs's task here, but it is ours because it is part of his legacy.

Inseparable, though distinguishable, from the descriptive enterprise is the theological task bequeathed to those who appropriate this book's perspective. Childs did not create this task, but his understanding of canon, focused here on the Pauline corpus, makes taking it up unavoidable. At issue, stated most broadly, is the defining trait of the Christian faith: its continuing relation to ascertainable and partly describable past events, concentrated decisively in Jesus but including also its own past, and epitomized here by "the historical Paul." There is nothing static about Childs's guide. To the contrary, the canonical approach calls for a ceaselessly energizing reflection on the significance of the difference between the actual Paul who once was, the critically recovered figure ("the historical Paul") who probably was, and the effective, canonical Paul who is historic. With that goes also reflection on how and why the distinction between the canonical Jesus and the Jesus of history differs from the distinction between the canonical Paul and the Paul of history. Otherwise Paul easily becomes Christianity's "Second Founder" and Jesus becomes the First Christian.

CHILDS AND THE HISTORY OF INTERPRETATION

Mark W. Elliott

This paper will attempt to lay out the main lines of a contribution made by Brevard S. Childs to the role of the history of biblical interpretation in exegesis and theology. It will first consider his achievement in the Exodus commentary, where the findings of precritical interpreters become grist for the mill of Childs's own theological interpretation. Then it will treat the work from 2004 on the history of interpretation of Isaiah, in tandem with his 2001 commentary. Lastly it will consider, by way of comparison, the need that Childs demonstrates that exegesis be fully theological and nothing less than that. At the same time it will clarify that the history of interpretation is not what makes exegesis theological but what serves to encourage yet also inform that.[1]

HISTORY OF EXEGESIS IN THE EXODUS COMMENTARY

Thirty-five years ago in his commentary on Exodus, Childs wrote: "It lies in the nature of dogmatic theology to go beyond the biblical witness and to draw out the critical implications of its testimony for the modern church in the language of its culture."[2] Yet how does one accomplish this ambitious task, which goes beyond simply establishing "the theological significance of the Exodus passage in the light of its total witness within the canon"?[3] It would seem at first glance, by the positioning of the history of interpretation section after that on the New Testament context, that one could be

---

1. Here I wish to register thanks to Christopher R. Seitz for his careful reading of and engagement with this paper.
2. Brevard S. Childs, *The Book of Exodus: A Critical, Theological Commentary* (OTL; Philadelphia: Westminster, 1973), 88.
3. Ibid., 42.

helped in this work of supererogation by consideration of the history of interpretation.[4] As he himself says, "No one comes to the text *de novo*, but consciously or unconsciously shares a tradition with his predecessors. This section therefore tries to bring some historical controls to the issue of how the present generation is influenced by the exegetical traditions in which we now stand."[5] Yet on the following page, he says: "The history of exegesis is also subsidiary to the exegesis and can be studied on its own as part of intellectual history or passed over on a first reading. The sections on Old Testament context, New Testament context, and theological reflection form the heart of the commentary."[6] It may come as no surprise that the short review in the Georg Föhrer–edited "Bücherschau" in *ZAW* includes the second but not the first quotation.[7] There seem to be two voices here in the canonical Childs: according to one, the history provides controls; according to the other, it is subsidiary. The mind of Childs on the matter is best explained as believing that there should be a dialogue between doing exegesis from the text and doing it through the history of its interpretation.

To take one important example, that of the Decalogue, after five pages on the history of exegesis, his sixth section, "Theological Reflection in the Context of the Canon," is a two-page reflection, first on the value of the history of interpretation as that which prods us to do the same for our age: "The mistake lies in assuming that there is such a thing as a timeless interpretation."[8] There he admits that of course exegesis reflects thought patterns of the age "while at the same time, if it is worthy of the name of exegesis, seeking to shape these patterns through an encounter with the biblical text." That generations' interpretations differ from one another "bears witness to the 'scandal of particularity' in which the Christian lives his life in the call to obedience." In fact, in his opinion it is a good thing that the interpretations are *particular*, even if he has his reservations about Puritans interpreting the seventh commandment as concerning

---

4. The commentary treats each chapter or pericope in six sections: (1) textual and philological notes; (2) literary, form-critical, and traditio-historical problems; (3) Old Testament context; (4) New Testament context; (5) history of exegesis; and (6) theological reflection. As James A. Wharton remarks, these are "hardly the usual topics for a critical Old Testament commentary" ("Splendid Failure or Flawed Success?" *Int* 29 [1975]: 266–76).

5. Childs, *Exodus*, xv.

6. Ibid., xvi.

7. *ZAW* 88 (1976): 145ff

8. Childs, *Exodus*, 438.

dress codes and the Reformers seeing the fourth as concerning political obedience. It would consequently be part of our particularity to take seriously historical-critical questions, and not to ignore them: a brief glance at Childs's *Introduction to the Old Testament as Scripture* and *The New Testament as Canon: an Introduction* would attest that Childs was never "ignorant." He then offers us five "exegetical controls" for this passage. Thus the Ten Commandments (1) are given in the context of God's self-revelation; (2) shape the life of the covenant community; (3) operate as both gift, pointing to the way of life and joy, and as warning against the sin which leads to death and judgment; (4) intend to engender love of God and of neighbor; and (5) require the Spirit, not an ethos of legalism. He concludes fittingly that the church "must seek to regain the significance of covenant responsibility in the context of a romantic, sentimental understanding of the religious life."[9]

Curiously, the content of these principles relates only tangentially to the things discussed in the history of interpretation section. So is that the lesson? Is the lesson of the history of interpretation merely *that* we should seek to interpret scripture *sola scriptura*, in the light of the witness of the canon in dialogue with our generation's particular questions? Did any of our exegetical forebears, Jewish or Christian, ever exegete the passage without influence from their history of interpretation? My sense is that Childs did not learn those controlling principles from the history of interpretation he reviews, but that it led him to find other guides, just as only after a trawling and sifting of the historical critical scholarship in his Introductions he arrived in a new place. Sometimes reading the history of interpretation is worthwhile because we put it behind us. In the above section the dominant influence seems to be, or sounds like, the theology of covenantal grace as taught by Karl Barth and Walther Eichrodt. There is only one other place—on Exod 17:8–16—where Barth makes an obvious contribution to the commentary.[10] Yet Barth was himself such an interpretive channel for the historical tradition of reformed (and some patristic) interpretation, that the categories of revelation, covenant, and grace have come to the fore in Childs, not because he has consciously used this tradition as a lens or a grid for exegesis, but rather because it has helped him to see the form, and to discover (rather than invent) the shape and mes-

---

9. Ibid., 439. Cf. Pieter J. Verdam, *Mosaic Law in Practice and Study Throughout the Ages* (Kampen: Kok, 1959).

10. Karl Barth, *Church Dogmatics* (Edinburgh: T&T Clark, 1957), 2.2:317.

sage of scripture for himself. This is something that Barth contributed to, or inspired, in the work of Eichrodt and Childs, as well as von Balthasar.[11]

On Exod 2:11–25, the "history of exegesis" section is missing, and there is no explicit use of the tradition to form the theological reflection that concludes that the NT has one view, that Moses was a hero, but the OT has very little of "Moses the hero." Hebrews files Moses under "faith," but "Exodus has no one rubric and describes a complex of actions ... a living and deciding among the variety of relations in which we live, seeking in the complexity of mixed sinful emotions and historical accidents to live an obedient life" (43). The two Testaments provide us with a balance, "a double perspective: faith as eschatological hope and faith as response in the present ... faith as confused action toward obedience." Here is a case where theological lessons can be learned without recourse to the history of interpretation.

Here, as I said, there is no explicit use of the tradition. And sometime, as on the previous pericope (Exod 2:1–10), the reflection is curiously sermonic in the sense of promoting a single and rather simple idea, that just as in the Gospel infancy narrative, God's providence with Israel "hangs on slender thread" or the tiniest detail, the action of a normal and otherwise anonymous woman (24). However I would argue here that the tradition has helped Childs to see the form, or the wood among the trees of the text. Childs's treatment of the exodus narrative itself (Exod 13:7–14:31) provides a clearer case of where the history of interpretation had an apparent influence on the results of exegesis: in the "theological reflections" on the exodus from Egypt, Childs concludes: "The tradition is unanimous in stressing that the rescue was accomplished through the intervention of God and God alone" (237). Yet this is actually very much Luther's and Calvin's emphasis, as Childs allows: "Surely Calvin was right in hearing the dominant note of the grace of God in a language which finds its clearest echo in the sacraments" (238).

Yet, as I have argued, Childs's attitude toward the tradition was never a subservient one. His use of the Fathers is sparing and not altogether uncritical. Melito forgot that "The New Testament not only fulfills the Old, but equally important the Old Testament interprets the New" (213). This chastising is repeated in the Isaiah book, and there even Calvin is not

---

11. On his debt to Barth, see Hans Urs von Balthasar, *The Glory of the Lord: A Theological Aesthetics* (Edinburgh: T&T Clark, 1982), 1:52–56.

spared this criticism. Sometimes Childs even seems a bit dismissive, as when he writes concerning the Passover passage (Exod 12:1–13:16) that Origen and Hippolytus provide the two main traditions of interpretation, but then does not quite say what these are. Again, this might be a sign that Childs internalized the tradition more than he described it. Without Childs's alerting us so, the Catholic tradition seems to have influenced, or at very least to chime in with, Childs's view of things, as when he writes: "The externality of God's revelation at Sinai guards the church from encapsulating God within the good intentions of the religious conscience" (384). The subject matter of this interpretation concerns not visible politics, but matters of church order that are just as visible, and this sentiment gets repeated in the theological reflection on the Tabernacle (25:1–31:18). Intercession is indispensable; the presence of God is actual not spiritual; awe and otherness are crucial; today's church, modeling itself on Israel, should learn from the biblical idiom. Overall, there is not necessarily such a big hermeneutical gulf between the two as one might think. Ecclesia antiqua speaks to ecclesia moderna.

Childs was a man of his time through being fully a son who had learned from the wisdom of the past, even as he worked with the tools of the present and engaged with its philosophical *Zeitgeist*. Although most of time Childs clearly prefers the genius of Calvin, who wrote of the third use of the law, "It must reach to the substance of the precept. It must be expanded to enjoin the opposite of that which is prohibited"[12] (434), the hinge figure in the story of Exodus interpretation seems to be Jean le Clerc (Clericus, as Childs prefers to call him). Clericus decided that the Decalogue was historically conditioned and not "the clear voice of God given to the whole assembly of mankind" (436), and also seems the first to have proposed that it was tides and winds that allowed the crossing, receiving wide opprobrium for this interpretation. On the nature of manna, Clericus stood out against the tradition: it was ordinary food, but an extraordinary provision. His became the dominant position up to the time of Kalisch in 1855, after which the consensus was that the story was a symbolic fiction. It is on this hinge that Childs wants to sit, at times a little uncomfortably. In his "Theological Reflection in the Context of the Canon" section (299–304) he is aware of trying to avoid two opposite dangers: a "'supernaturalistic' viewpoint … [that] seeks to guarantee a reality testified to in the

---

12. John Calvin, *Institutes of the Christian Religion*, 2.8.

canon by means of dogmatic controls employed outside the area of faith" (300–301), and the other extreme, whereby the biblical canon becomes subject to rationalism. Childs contends that the canon is one human witness among others and hence is reliable. The reality to which the story in Exod 15 points is not the manna, but God's providence; the same goes for the bread in the feeding of the multitude in John 6. Unlike Calvin (and Aquinas), Johannes Piscator thought some juridical laws (e.g., Exod 20:22–23:33) were still binding. Moreover, "the idealistic categories which admit divine inspiration only to what is regarded as 'eternally valid' or 'perfect' for all contexts must be firmly rejected in handling the Bible" (496). Particular and incarnate historical *realia* encourage particular interpretations, and that is a good thing. This seems a particular emphasis throughout his oeuvre for which we ought to be grateful to Brevard Childs.

Childs's decision to go it alone to provide the preacher with a resource that goes into NT, Jewish-Christian, and contemporary theological readings meant an eschewing of teamwork. In his review of Childs's *Exodus*, Wharton tells us that teamwork was what James L. Mays called for but that Childs can be defended for going it alone. For "the fact is, however, that this teamwork has not emerged." Childs, he says, "has at least confronted these disciplines afresh with their mutual interdependence, however, and challenged them to serious conversation in a new way."[13] Wharton's major reservation is that Childs tended to restrict the NT context to places where Exodus is cited. "In his desire to vouchsafe the independence and integrity of each Testament over against the other, Childs may have left the impression that their relationship is largely literary rather than theological."[14]

---

13. Wharton, "Splendid Failure," 271.
14. Ibid., 275. While the review by M. Mathias Delcor (*Bib* 57 [1976]: 432–35) is appreciative of "de l'equilibre et de la mesure" in the commentary, especially for Childs's informed conservatism regarding the place of Moses and certain archaeological questions, and that by François Langlamet (*RB* 89 [1975]: 627–28) is rather descriptive and neutral, that by Edward Lipinski (*VT* 26 (1975): 378–83) is strongly critical. Lipinski faults Childs for not being sensitive enough to the linguistic treasury of the ancient Near Eastern background and for his engagement with source-critical and traditio-historical questions being carried out only through the mediation of other scholars. In Lipinski's opinion the commentary is theological to the exclusion of being properly scientific. Childs had taken the postmodern turn, but some had not noticed. Childs's comparative lack of interest in the question of textual variants and the difference these made to subsequent interpretation "is in itself a sufficient reason to express doubts about the scientific value of a survey *per summa capita* of the his-

This seems a curious criticism and one of which the later Childs certainly could not be accused.

CHILDS AND THE HISTORY OF INTERPRETATION OF ISAIAH

Thirty years on, in his book *The Struggle to Understand Isaiah as Christian Scripture*,[15] Childs looked for pre-Enlightenment voices that sang in harmony if not in unison about the christological references of Isaiah, the authority of scripture, and the OT–NT nexus. Yet none of these voices that he selected is actually used much to determine the meaning or force of the interpretation of any verses in particular nor, for that matter, the message of Isaiah as a whole. One is left with the question: if Childs believed in theological exegesis, why did he in his Isaiah commentary of 2001 separate out the "history of interpretation" section that had graced his 1975 Exodus commentary and that there formed the bridge between source and form criticism and theological reflection? The history of interpretation perhaps benefits from a separate treatment. But does the Isaiah commentary not suffer as a consequence for not having this component?

The answer could well be that Childs never intended to repeat the trick that he had performed for Exodus. His main task was to show that the history of Christian interpretation always tried to see Isaiah as Christian scripture, that its referent was the same thing as that of which the New Testament spoke. In 1974, such a belief, albeit not uncontroversial, was not perhaps quite the minority view that it would become in Anglo-Saxon circles by 2004. Childs complains that certain approaches emphasized the text's *reception*, that is, what was done with the text, at the expense of the influence or pressure of the faithful text itself: these approaches concentrated on the disastrous cultural-political results of textual readings, and not on the nourishment that Isaiah gave the life of the church and on interpretations of the text that were often edifying. "Often the concentration falls on the misuse of biblical texts. What is missing is the ability to see

---

tory of exegesis, as done by Dr. Childs" (379). Of course, *pace* Lipinski, the lion's share of commentary writing in the premodern period was hardly stuck on textual variants or on *ipsissima verba*. Their awareness of textual variation meant that their exegesis operated at the level of sentences, images and messages rather than hinging on verbal exactitude.

15. Brevard S. Childs, *The Struggle to Understand Isaiah as Christian Scripture* (Grand Rapids: Eerdmans, 2004).

the effect of the coercion of the text itself in faithfully shaping the life of the church—its doctrine, liturgy, and practice—in such a way as to leave a family resemblance of faith throughout the ages."[16] What Childs offers therefore in *Struggle* is at least some sort of antidote, at most a constructive hermeneutical foundation for learning *theology* from Isaiah.

Building on older studies such as those by Beryl Smalley and Celsus Spicq,[17] Childs views Aquinas as replacing the Platonist spirit-letter opposition of Augustine with a move to penetrate through the text to the substance which left the text as of secondary importance—"accidental" as it were—but without losing sight of the text altogether. Childs had already voiced his appreciation of Aquinas over Augustine in his famous "Sensus Literalis" article in 1977.[18] On Isaiah, Aquinas built on Jerome in a way that he did not when working on the Psalms. Yet while the *Proemium* allows for allegorical interpretation, Childs notes that Thomas's actual interpretation of Isaiah largely eschews this: "The great bulk of his interpretation falls under the rubric *ad litteram*."[19] The *ad litteram* includes the sign of Christ's incarnation only because Isa 7:14 literally refers to a woman who is pure, and not just a *betulah*. Through such a close reading, Thomas can thus be loyal to the traditional figurative, christological sense. Also, on Isa 41:2 "the victorious one" is Abraham rather than Cyrus.

> In a real sense, Thomas's interpretation of Isa 40–66, but especially of chapter 53, is not directed primarily to the text itself—that is, not just to the words, but to their substance. He does not distinguish between literal

---

16. Brevard Childs, *Isaiah: A Commentary* (Louisville: Westminster John Knox, 2001), 5.

17. Beryl Smalley, *The Study of the Bible in the Middle Ages* (3rd ed.; Notre Dame: Notre Dame University Press, 1983); Ceslas Spicq, *Esquisse d'un histoire de l'exégèse latine au moyen âge* (BibThom 26; Paris: J. Vrin, 1944.)

18. "Sensus Literalis of Scripture: An Ancient and Modern Problem," in *Beiträge Zur Alttestamentlichen Theologie: Festschrift Für Walther Zimmerli Zum 70. Geburtstag* (ed. Herbert Donner et al.; Göttingen: Vandenhoeck & Ruprecht, 1977), 80–93. In stating that "Thomas does allow for the spiritual sense, these levels are not derived from the words as Augustine thought, but from the connections between the things signified (res^1) and second thing (res^2)" (84), Childs seems unaware that this view of signification was articulated by Augustine in *De doctrina christiana* 2. Childs's contrasting of Augustine and Thomas on creation seems a little tendentious, yet his insights, based on the work of J. S. Preus on Lyra and Gerson and the *duplex sensus litteralis*, are sound.

19. Childs, *Struggle*, 155.

and figurative senses according to the Alexandrian tradition, but passes through the words of the text to their theological substance, which inevitably transcends the verbal sense of the passage.... In this sense, one can recognize the positive application of an Aristotelian influence that overcomes some of Augustine's dualism between text and substance.[20]

Childs goes on to commend "Thomas's largely non-allegorical manner of penetrating to the figurative sense by means of an ontological, intertextual move shaped by the substance of the witness itself" (162).

If anything, the move to the realities from the textual symbol is actually properly Augustinian, but Childs seems to mean that Thomas remembers that the precise symbol is the indispensable way of access to the reality above and is not to be discarded. Childs does not mention it, but he might have been happy to note that Thomas's famous introductory sermons of 1256 come close to what one might call a canonical approach. Sometimes the history of ideas is not the strongest part of Childs's armor, but the main point is that he finds in Thomas a sound balance between word and thing.

Overall, Childs carefully and successfully selected his secondary sources. It must surely be a hard task for an Old Testament scholar to learn the rules so as to assimilate who the authorities or "hosts" within the house of church history and history of theology are, such that he might be able to feel at home there. Childs does well to object to the take on Calvin offered by one of these hosts, David Puckett. Surely, Childs argues, Calvin achieved more than a mere mediation of the "Jewish-historical" and the "Greek-allegorical." And Childs notes the similarity to Aquinas in Calvin that is often missed by Reformation historical theologians.

What we have then in *Struggle* is a history of OT hermeneutics, as distinct from a history of exegesis as was the case in the *Exodus* commentary, mediated by scholarship on Aquinas, Calvin, and others. However, this sometimes means that we spend a lot of time one or two moves away from the text of any commentary. The discourse operates more at the level of method. For example:

> Calvin's notion of the literal sense is deep enough not to need another textual level to carry a spiritual meaning by means of allegory.... In contrast to Luther, Calvin does not relate the two aspects of the literal sense

---

20. Ibid., 159.

in a dialectical fashion between the spiritual sense and the carnal, nor does he hold to an unresolved tension, a *via media*.[21]

For the mind of the author and the intention of the Spirit are identical. Further, the employment of analogy or *anagoge* to today is allowed by Calvin and, one assumes, by Childs.

> Indeed, one is frequently astonished by the ease with which the transference is made. Because of his understanding of the substance of the entire biblical witness, he can extend a particular biblical event or teaching to the selfsame Christological realities from which the church lives.[22]

In other words, because Calvin could range over the length and breadth of scripture (whose events covers two millennia), there was for him no greater distance between the "then" and the "now." Childs seems to be right when he claims that for Calvin the law's chief operation was to get believers to look toward the second coming of Christ. Childs agrees with Calvin that even if the two Testaments are joined through the one purpose of God, he is unsure about the balance of Calvin's treatment of OT and NT in his biblical theology:

> My exegetical caveat is that Calvin's approach runs the danger of projecting backward into the biblical narrative a meaning that is not derived from the Old Testament. The effect is that he christianizes the Old Testament by a form of psychologizing the unexpressed motivation of its characters.[23]

It is not the case that the direction between the Testaments ran only one way in Calvin's mind. Indeed Jeremiah in Calvin's presentation looked a bit like Paul, but then again Paul also looked a lot like Jeremiah. Both these are so because Calvin identified both of them with himself, allowing for an overlapping or a fusion of the biblical figures in his own person.

When he eventually turns to treat Calvin on Isaiah itself, Childs gives us some examples of the Frenchman's linguistic or rhetorical insight. Calvin had deep respect for the Masoretic Text, though not for the Jewish interpretations themselves—although he did make much use of David Kimchi's

---

21. Ibid., 211–12.
22. Ibid., 217.
23. Ibid.

philology. The spiritual world is not entered by an appeal to allegory; one should rather speak, with Hans Frei, of typology where a prophecy of a near event also manages to describe that of a far-off one. Childs has a very useful insight when he observes: "Calvin's reflections are thus far more oriented to pastoral care than to systematic theology" (225). Calvin was able to create such a "biblical theology formed almost entirely from the Old Testament" (226)—the hope of eternal life (Isa 36:16), salvation by grace (59:16) and faithful guidance during the whole of life (26:8).

In the last chapters of his book, Childs notes that it was Grotius (1645) who was the first to suggest interpreting the OT without reference to the NT. Another Dutchman, Vitringa, in the early eighteenth century, achieved a compromise by holding that only some amount of fulfillment of prophecy should be viewed as happening *within* the OT. Childs sees this separation between Old and New as bringing to an end the position agreed to by those as otherwise disparate as Aquinas and Calvin. Childs wishes to recall the by now almost obsolete premodern consensus. For Thomas,

> The literal sense is what the human authors intended in their writings, but because God, the ultimate author of scripture, comprehends everything all at once in his understanding, a multiplicity of sense can also be derived from the one divine intention.[24]

According to Childs, "The biblical text was never understood within traditional Christian theology as a neutral, inert object waiting for human initiative to receive a coherent meaning."[25]

Childs's view of an orthodox "family resemblance," some basic features of enduring theological concerns shaping its exegesis, is that "God's unique action in history cannot be fused with empirical history, nor can it be separated" (320). It is on the third-to-last page that Childs pins his colors to the mast:

> It is one thing to attempt to understand the Old Testament as the sacred scriptures of the church. It is quite another to understand the study of the Bible in history-of-religions categories. Both tasks are legitimate, but they are different in goal and procedure.... To understand the Bible as scripture means to reflect on the *witnesses* of the text transmitted through

---

24. Ibid., 309.
25. Ibid., 315.

130   THE BIBLE AS CHRISTIAN SCRIPTURE

the testimony of prophets and apostles. It involves an understanding of biblical history as the activity of God testified to in scripture.[26]

In other words, scripture is to be understood as a witness to *divine* history. That which mattered to these historical interpreters was not an agreed, fixed doctrine of inspiration of scripture, or even a common Christology, but a common theological *interest* in such theological matters when reading Isaiah. At the end of the book Childs writes with total clarity and considerable regret about the ostensibly ecclesiastical work of Walter Brueggemann:

> The conclusion I propose is that an investigation of the history of interpretation that focuses its analysis on the assumption that various cultural forces (historical, sociological, philosophical) are the controlling factors at work misconstrues the most central components of the church's theological reflections.[27]

THE ISAIAH COMMENTARY AND THE PLACE OF CALVIN

Childs would not do biblical theology merely through the interpretations, as Barr would demand later.[28] That would be to allow a history of religions approach, which uses the text as no more than a springboard for experience and ideology of religious traditions, no matter how true to the text. It would mean interpretation getting in the way of today's readers' direct interpretations and applications of the text. It means a mediation of the witness of scripture to the living God through another layer of theologians whom we feel bold enough to select according to our own theological or ecclesial preferences. Instead, for Childs, the interpreters simply set us an example for reading the bible canonically in our own age, which will include some amount of eisegesis, if it is to be useful, if scripture is to be heard. Therefore in Childs's *Isaiah* commentary itself the classic commentators are missing, with the exception, in two cases, of Calvin.[29] And yet,

---

26. Ibid., 321.
27. Ibid., 322.
28. James Barr, *The Concept of Biblical Theology* (London: SCM, 1999), not least his treatment of "Revelation" in ch. 27 (468–96) of that work. For more see Mark W. Elliott, *The Reality of Biblical Theology* (Bern: Lang, 2007), 55–62.
29. Brevard S. Childs, *Isaiah: A Commentary* (OTL; Louisville: Westminster John Knox, 2001).

as we shall see, there is an affinity with the historical interpreters and their theological reading of the book undergirding a number of his judgments in the commentary.

First, commenting on Isa 41, Childs mentions a "dialectic relationship" between the Testaments.[30] By "dialectic" he seems to mean that the influence on meaning is two-way, just as it was for Calvin, who gave weight to the "first" fulfilment in Cyrus (Isa 42:1–4; 323). Taking his cue from this, Childs argues that not only the Old Testament text but the relationship of prophecy to fulfilment has shaped the Christology of Matthew in Matt 12:17–21, as well as being fulfilled finally in the New. "The *Wirkungsgeschichte* [between Old and New Testaments] is clearly dialectic in movement. Jesus' healing activity is characterized as fulfilling Isaiah's prophecy. The Messiah fulfils the office of the servant in caring for the weak and fragile. Yet, conversely, it is Isaiah's portrayal that interprets Jesus' healing as bringing justice to victory and giving the Gentiles a hope" (327).

A second example in Childs's commentary concerns Isaiah 6. Calvin provided a good example in that he raised an objection against a "Christomonist" style of interpretation here. The prophet is speaking of God the Lord absolutely. Yet this God does not let himself be known without his eternal Word, who is the unique Son. Thus the Lord is Trinitarian. However, and this is the point, the trihagion in Isaiah 6 does not count as proof of this fact.

> Long ago Calvin objected to this narrow interpretation that limited the vision to the person of Jesus. Rather, he argued that in Isaiah 6 the prophet speaks of God, the Lord, in an absolute manner. Yet Calvin is quick to add that God never revealed himself to the Old Testament patriarchs apart from his eternal Word, the only begotten Son. Calvin wisely resists Christian interpreters trying to prove from the song of the seraphim that there were three persons in one essence in the Godhead.... Yet at the same time he confesses that it is indeed the triune God who is being worshipped in the OT. (60)

In other words, the Trinity did not just come into being with the New Testament in order to allow God to self-differentiate and become both Father

---

30. Cf. Brevard S. Childs, *Biblical Theology in Crisis* (Philadelphia: Westminster, 1970), 157–63, where he pioneered this idea of the two Testaments "in conversation."

and Son. The OT dispensation did not know God as Trinity, but that does not mean he *was* not Trinity.[31]

The point is not that Calvin, the only premodern allowed to join in with the host of modern commentators, is hugely significant for Childs throughout the commentary. As he would observe in *Struggle*, even Calvin could be guilty of over-Christianizing the Old Testament. But it perhaps gives us a clue that Childs himself, even where he did not name his favorite premoderns, sometimes or perhaps even more often than not, felt more affinity with their exegesis. There is a small example of this regarding the interplay of Isa 43:18 ("do not remember what happened long ago") and 26 ("recall the past with me"). According to the Dead Sea Scrolls (1QH 13,11–12), the Isaianic text taught that such a new order would destroy the old one: "The author interprets the Isaianic text as pointing to an eschatological new creation that shatters the old order." Paul was even more bold in 2 Cor 5:16–17 in his putting Old and New into opposition. However, "if this New Testament passage is correctly interpreted according to its Old Testament context, the genuinely dialectical relation between the old and the new is maintained, and the continuing threat to the Christian church from modern gnostic flights of fantasy—'imaginative construal' is the current formulation—are held in check by the biblical faith" (337). Although Thomas says very little, Calvin's view is that the people of God can only "move forward" with the understanding that God has delivered them from a past deeply mired in sin—it is not that they have begun with their own merits and God will now take them somewhere higher by his grace.[32] This sober Augustinianism keeps us humble concerning the possibilities opened up by the new creation, and appreciative of what is given in the first creation.

EVALUATION, SOME COMPARISON, AND CONCLUSION

Childs's intention was never to try to deny the validity of historical-critical method as such but simply to put it in its place—one of service, where it can operate as an auxiliary form of scholarship along with the others, such as church history, dogmatics, and biblical languages. The biblical mes-

---

31. Cf. C. Kavin Rowe, "Biblical Pressure and Trinitarian Hermeneutics," *Pro Ecclesia* 11 (2002): 295–312.

32. *Commentarius in Isaiam: Opera Iohannis Calvini* (Braunschweig: Schwetschke, 1888), 100–101.

sage reveals itself only when the ecclesial reception is considered, but that means that all possible receptions must be tested by the voice of the other Testament. So the contribution of historical Christian interpretation consists of explanations, sharpenings and recollections of the whole biblical word. For that reason it is not enough to copy the clever move by Ludger Schwienhorst-Schönbergerm when he claims that there is a vaguely "spiritual" content to the Old Testament, even when it is not explicitly christological. Such a sense is to be gained from the eating of the "leaves" of the literal sense, which serve the healing or salvation of the nations (Rev 22:2) and which, according to Jerome, in some sense are "on the way towards Christ."[33] What Childs was able to do was to show how the Old Testament was in no way foreign to Christian theology, and in fact was every bit as much a theological source as the New.[34]

Lastly, and not least because Childs was always interested in the relationship between his own work and German scholarship, let me compare the position adopted by a venerable Lutheran bishop such as Ulrich Wilckens in his recently published New Testament theology.[35] Wilckens takes spiritual exegesis seriously and welcomes its reappearance in recent times, because it offers something in favor of letting the word of scripture be heard. He speaks of an objective reality of salvation corresponding to the words of scripture. With a "typically pietistic" move he proposes that this spiritual exegesis offers a spiritual reality echoing in a spiritual polyphony. The dogmatic sense of scripture is manifest to us in that it leads into a tropological (moral) gathering of experiences and deeds in our daily lives, which resonate with the gathering of biblical texts that we read throughout the week.[36] He recommends the constant reading of the Psalter with medi-

---

33. Ludger Schwienhorst-Schönberger, "Psalm 1 in der Auslegung des Hieronymus," in *Der Bibelkanon in der Bibelauslegung: Methodenreflexionen und Beispielexegesen* (ed. Egbert Ballhorn and Georg Steins; Stuttgart: Kohlhammer, 2007), 212–30 (227–28).

34. This perhaps against a prevalent tendency of some otherwise helpful biblical theologians who come from the New Testament "side," that the Old needs to be heard through the New rather than in dialogue with it, as well as in dialogue with the interpreter's theological concerns.

35. Ulrich Wilckens, *Theologie des Neuen Testaments, II: Die Theologie des Neuen Testaments als Grundlage kirchlicher Lehre*. Teilband I. *Das Fundament* (Neukirchen-Vluyn: Neukirchener, 2007).

36. "So klingt das im Gottesdienst gehörte Wort und seine sakramental erfahrene Wirklichkeit in einer Fülle von biblischen Texten, die wir unter der Woche dazu lesen,

tation, deepening the approach to the literal sense of the text. Increasingly the voice comes to address today's reader, that is, the one voice of the same Spirit who indeed spoke in the texts of the early Christian past.[37] And this happens not independently of a connection with the richness of spiritual bible interpretation. A consideration of the anagogical sense of scripture, which reminds us that this life is only a preliminary, is also a "must" in Wilckens's scheme.

I find much here to agree with. Perhaps again, however, the dogmatic sense is somewhat underplayed, as much in the Lutheran as in the Catholic exegete (Schwienhorst-Schönberger). In reaching for the truths that scripture teaches, we need more unfolding of the mystery of God in Christ, and a treatment of objections, doubts, and despair, as well as at least some suggestions for their resolution. In other words, we need something scholastically dogmatic as well as monastic or pietistic in our interpretation of scripture. Childs has helped us in the task of knowing the challenges Enlightenment criticism of the Bible brings, but he has also shown us how Thomas and Calvin and others will not let us ignore the fact that the biblical truth needs to be rooted in our understanding in the areas of apologetics and dogmatics.

We who live after the Enlightenment might well have a problem with doing dogmatics from the Bible. This is clearly the case with John Barton: taking literally and universalising Isa 64:6 to formulate the idea that no human can ever please God, and that even good deeds are filthy rags at all times and all places, is a mistake that even Luther, who wanted to know the exact meaning of the text, sadly made. Luther interpreted everything in the light of Paul. Barton sees the Isaianic text as synecdochic and hyperbolic. "The text from Isaiah 64 only apparently supports his [Luther's] position: it is a cry of despair rather than a dogmatic definition."[38] But is

---

in einer geistlichen Polyphonie in uns weiter. Der 'dogmatische' Sinn der Schrift erschließt sich uns so, dass er wie von selbst in einer Fülle von Erfahrungen und Tätigkeiten unseres täglichen Lebens in den 'tropologischen' Schriftsinn übergeht" (ibid., 75).

37. He describes "eine meditative Dimension ... in der sich der Zugang zum wörtlichen Sinn des Textes vertieft.... Vielmehr wird die Stimme ein und desselben Geistes, der in den Texten der urchristlichen Vergangenheit der eigentlich Redende war, zur Anrede an ihren heutigen Leser" (ibid., 79).

38. John Barton, "The Fall and Human Depravity," in *The Multivalence of Biblical Texts and Theological Meanings* (ed. Christine Helmer; Atlanta: Society of Biblical Literature, 2006), 105–11 (110).

that not what biblical theology does? It is not so much about reading Isaiah through Paul as adding Paul to Isaiah, to balance grounds for grief with grounds for rejoicing. It is not about abstracting,[39] as Childs has reminded us, but about particular interpretations of particular *realia* of salvation history and the transcendent God.

Childs forces us children of the Enlightenment to think the unthinkable, that the caesura that interrupted the venerable tradition of interpretation of the OT as Christian scripture did not in fact free the OT to make more of a contribution to Western thoughts about God, nor did it help establish Judaism as a religion worthy of respect. In fact it contributed to the lethal view that it was one civilization among others best left in the sands of history, its twentieth-century children worthy of contempt and annihilation. The attempt to read the OT as non-Christian scripture quickly led to the loss of the OT from consideration as scripture. The story in which the later characters such as Brueggemann, who views prophetic poetry as a repository of "generative" symbols standing as deviations, risks becoming a tragedy in which scripture gets reduced to mottos, anthropocentric self-help, and a tool for social analysis. Childs stands with von Hofmann, Delitzsch and George Adam Smith (and probably von Rad) as enlightened critics who affirmed that the history of interpretation has much to teach us. Childs's attack should not be seen as a personal one on Brueggemann, but as on an ideology which surely has no future. The place of history of exegesis in the formation of theological exegesis is one that is a bit more significant than simply an encouragement given by historical interpreters to our theological exegesis. For as a living tradition of interpretation, it is also a help to the church's exegetical foot soldiers in seeing the form of a scriptural passage.

The one question that remains: while there is no doubt but that it was astonishingly impressive, was it right for this Old Testament scholar to march into the NT, on through the history of exegesis, finally to arrive at dogmatics? In one sense yes, because Childs was always humble enough even in his OT works to depend heavily on the close-range research of

---

39. *Contra* Russell R. Reno, "Biblical Theology and Theological Exegesis," in *Out of Egypt: Biblical Theology and Biblical Interpretation* (ed. Mary Healy et al.; Grand Rapids: Zondervan, 2004), 385–408, 399: "Childs assumes that true theology must move from 'description' of what the text says to 'analysis' of its subject matter, and this subject matter is formulated with the abstracted and scripturally thin concepts that characterize so much unsuccessful theological exegesis."

other scholars, and this is what he continued to do as he made this long march. In another sense, yes, in that to stop at each border and hand the baton over to someone else encourages the dangerous assumption that each stage is a development and yet a fairly discontinuous one in which the "anchor leg" is always dogmatics—in that respect it is fitting that the person doing the dogmatic exercise is an Old Testament scholar, one who has the OT deeply lodged in his memory and perhaps the NT and the history of exegesis deeper still. In a third sense, no, because the church and the academy alike are crying out for teamwork to be given a chance. It will mean addressing not only the shape of the commentary, but the shape of the faculty, the idea of the university, and the vocation of the church. And these last two were concerns close to the thinking heart of Brevard S. Childs.

Biblical Theology and the Communicative Presence of God

Murray A. Rae

After surveying the several attempts made by Brevard Childs to establish a foundation and a method for biblical theology, I am struck by two things in particular: by Childs's concern to study the Bible as the Word of God and by his acute awareness that those who have sought to develop what has been called "biblical theology" have not been able to settle upon a method for studying the Bible as God's Word. In what follows, I propose to support and explore Childs's first concern and then to suggest that the problem with method is in fact a function of that concern. That is to say, those who read the Bible as Christians, who read it thus in prayerful expectation that the voice of God is to be heard through scripture, should not be surprised that the *viva vox Dei* is not beholden to precisely specified methods of interpretation. The ineffable sovereignty and freedom of God in the event of divine self-communication itself confounds the academic desire to bring interpretation under strict methodological control.

The Nature of Biblical Theology

Although the whole of Childs's extensive bibliography may be regarded as contributing to the development and clarification of the enterprise called "biblical theology," the foundations, problems, and methods of biblical theology receive explicit attention in two major works in particular, *Biblical Theology in Crisis* (1970), and *Biblical Theology of the Old and New Testaments* (1992).[1] In the second of these works Childs begins by noting the

---

1. Brevard S. Childs, *Biblical Theology in Crisis* (Philadelphia: Westminster, 1970); *Biblical Theology of the Old and New Testaments: Theological Reflections on the Christian Bible* (Minneapolis: Fortress, 1992). Hereafter, *BTONT.*

ambiguity of the term itself. Biblical theology, he writes, "can either denote a theology contained within the Bible, or a theology which accords with the Bible."[2] In the first instance practitioners of the discipline of biblical theology need have no theological intent themselves, but may approach the texts gathered together in the Bible with merely antiquarian interest, content to describe what a series of ancient authors, communities, and redactors thought about God. In the second case, however, practitioners of biblical theology read the Bible with the purpose of articulating a theology that accords with the biblical witness and serves to nurture, encourage, and guide the church as it participates in God's creative and redemptive purposes for the world. Biblical scholarship of this kind is undertaken in service of God's self-communication. Its fundamental question is, what is God now saying to his people through the biblical text? Childs himself was clearly committed to this second approach. He read and studied the Bible because he understood it to be the vehicle of God's self-communication. Attention to Childs's published work reveals, however, that he does not conceive of the two approaches as alternatives. The first might be undertaken without the second, but the second certainly cannot be undertaken without the first. In other words, attentiveness to what God is now saying to the church through the biblical word requires careful and repeated attention to the theology ventured by the prophets and apostles as set forth in the Bible itself. Although Karl Barth, whom Childs read appreciatively though not uncritically, once claimed that "dogmatics does not ask what the apostles and prophets said but what we must say on the basis of the apostles and prophets,"[3] he also recognized that Christian dogmatics "must constantly keep in view" the biblical teaching as it is investigated by "exegetical theology."[4] Although Childs did not use Barth's terminology, he accepted both tasks as the responsibility of Christian biblical scholarship, and he devoted himself therefore to the task of understanding "what the prophets and apostles said" precisely in order to facilitate and encourage a faithful witness in today's church to the living voice of God.

---

2. Childs, *BTONT*, 3. The distinction made here is drawn from Gerhard Ebeling's survey of the field in "The Meaning of Biblical Theology," first published in 1960 in *Wort und Glaube* (Tübingen: Mohr Siebeck, 1960), later published in English as *Word and Faith* (London: SCM, 1963), 79–97.
3. Karl Barth, *Church Dogmatics* (Edinburgh: T&T Clark, 1975), I.1:16.
4. Ibid.

The pattern of attending first to the theology contained within the Bible before then venturing an account of what we must say on the basis of the biblical witness can be clearly seen in the sixth part of *Biblical Theology of the Old And New Testaments*. Examining a range of doctrinal themes in that section, Childs first considers the Old Testament's treatment of each theme, and second that of the New Testament. He then proceeds to offer a summary of biblical teaching before, finally, attempting a dogmatic construal for today's church of the doctrinal matter in hand. His treatment of "God the Creator," for instance, proceeds as follows: (1) the Old Testament witness; (2) the New Testament witness; (3) biblical theological reflection on creation; (4) dogmatic theological reflection on creation.[5] The method here is an expression of the conviction that what we must say (in Christian dogmatics, not to mention in preaching, in evangelism, in prophetic witness, and in pastoral care) on the basis of the prophets and apostles requires fidelity to what the prophets and apostles themselves said.

The reason for this is itself theological. The steadfastness, constancy, and enduring faithfulness of God is a persistent biblical theme. Trust in this God therefore entails the expectation that what God says now to the church will be congruent with what God has said to his people in the past. This does not mean that God will say nothing new. Nor does it mean that a particular biblical text will have a single determinate meaning. It does mean, however, that God's use of a text to speak variously to his people in different circumstances will be recognizable as God's speech precisely on account of a discernible coherence between what God says now and what God has said in the past. The lack of such coherence is a principal sign of hermeneutical error, against which the church, with the help of its scholars, must always be on guard.

Before leaving this point, we should counter a potential misunderstanding that may be generated by the way in which Childs proceeds in part 6 of *Biblical Theology of the Old And New Testaments*. The architectonic adopted there might suggest that dogmatic concerns are present only in the final section on "dogmatic theological reflection on creation," and that the earlier sections comprise a straightforward "scientific" inquiry that requires no commitment of faith. Under this assumption the work of the first three sections might be undertaken by scholars of any faith or none, leaving Christians, if they are so minded, to take the results of sections

---

5. Childs, *BTONT*, 384–412.

1–3 and apply them, as in section 4, to the pursuit of their own peculiar interests. This, however, is a mistaken view. The process of discernment by which we learn what to say on the basis of the prophets and apostles is not strictly a lineal one. Despite the pattern of Childs's thematic investigations set out above, Childs's dogmatic findings do not simply emerge at the end of his inquiries. They inform the whole process. The successive attention to the Old Testament, to the New Testament, to a summary of biblical theology, and then to dogmatic theological reflection already rests on the conviction that the texts are indeed an instrument of divine communication, that there is a true word of God to he found here, that there is a unity of sorts in the biblical witness, and that the church's interpretation of scripture requires both continual dogmatic reflection and, under the guidance of the Spirit, something along the lines of what the Reformers insisted upon by the phrase *semper reformanda*. Despite appearances, Childs's method is theologically "loaded."[6] Attention to these generative theological convictions will occupy us further below.

In his 1970 survey of the Biblical Theology movement, Childs identified five "major elements" of the movement, particularly in its North American manifestations. These were, first and above all, "the rediscovery of the theological dimensions of the Bible," second, a commitment to "the unity of the whole Bible" as witness to the reality of God, third, the conviction that "revelation is mediated through history," fourth, an appreciation of "the distinctive mentality" of the Bible, often identified as Hebrew in distinction from Greek, and finally, the distinctiveness of the Bible against its environment.[7] With respect to the rediscovery of the theological dimensions of the Bible, those involved in the movement had glimpsed with Karl Barth, Childs writes, "the strange new world" within the Bible and had become frustrated with the lack of attention in the prevailing methods of biblical criticism to the central theological content of the Bible. Critical scholarship had seemed incapable of addressing the most fundamental questions of the community of faith.

---

6. This is not a criticism. All readers bring something to the text. Good readers of texts, as we shall see further below, are those who submit what they bring to the scrutiny of the texts themselves, and who allow that they might be transformed in the process.

7. See Childs, *Biblical Theology in Crisis*, ch. 2.

What did it mean to hear in the Bible the "word of God"? Could an interpreter any longer hear God speaking through these pages? In what sense was the goal of exegesis a "divine-human encounter"? Was there a divine process at work over and above the human forces which gave it its shape?[8]

Despite the efforts to address such questions by scholars involved in the Biblical Theology movement during the middle years of the twentieth century, their endeavors left a number of pressing issues unresolved. With respect to the Bible itself, Childs explains, uncertainty remained about whether the divine revelation, thought to be mediated through scripture, should be conceived as lying in or "behind" the text. Second, the movement had failed to give a consistent or unified account of how the two Testaments of the Christian Bible were related. And third, there was doubt still about how the authority of scripture should be conceived.[9] Dispute about these questions, combined with pressures brought about by a rapidly changing theological environment in the 1960s, contributed to what Childs described as a "crisis" in biblical theology. In part 2 of his 1970 book, Childs attempts to reestablish the movement in a "fresh and disciplined" way. Beyond Childs's conviction that something along the lines of biblical theology is the only way of doing justice to the biblical texts themselves, there is urgent need also, Childs wrote, to provide nourishment for the work of church minsters who seek "some understanding of theology in its relation to the Biblical Tradition."[10]

"The first step," Childs argues, "in laying a foundation for a new Biblical Theology ... is to establish the proper context for interpreting the Bible theologically."[11] That context, he argues, is the canon of the Christian Bible. While other interpretive contexts are possible, and have a measure of legitimacy—one might, for instance, study the Bible in order to learn something about the cultural conditions of the ancient Near East—such endeavours are secondary to the concerns of the texts themselves which arose and have been treasured, not so that later generations might learn

---

8. Ibid., 33.
9. Ibid., 51–53. Childs draws attention to several other problems that attended the work of the Biblical Theology movement at that time, but I have selected for consideration those issues that have special theological importance.
10. Ibid., 95; cf. 124.
11. Ibid., 97.

something of ancient Near Eastern culture, but so that succeeding generations might be sustained in the faith to which the texts bear witness. Biblical theology rests on the conviction, Childs explains, that the biblical texts function within the community of faith as "a channel of life for the continuing church, through which God instructs and admonishes his people."[12] They are "a vehicle of divine reality,"[13] and constitute "God's special communicating of himself to his church and the world."[14] They are properly read within the context of "prayer for illumination by the Holy Spirit," through which is acknowledged "the continuing need for God to make himself known through Scripture to an expectant people."[15]

The employment of the term "canon" thus serves, for Childs, not only as a means for identifying those texts in particular that are authoritative for the Christian community, but also as a confession about God's involvement in the process by which "the authoritative writings of the church were transmitted and received in response by a faithful people of God."[16] "To speak of the canon as a context," Childs writes, "implies that these Scriptures must be interpreted in relation to their function within the community of faith."[17] Their canonical context, that is to say, is hermeneutically important. The meaning of the texts is a function of that context and will be eroded, if not altogether lost, by treating them in isolation from their canonical location and status. This is an important, yet contentious, claim to which we shall return below.

The central feature of Childs's approach to the task of biblical theology, therefore, is the conviction that God is at work in and through the process of scripture's formation, and again, in and through the processes by which the diverse texts of scripture have been received, gathered into one book, preserved, interpreted, and handed on by the community of faith through the ages. Not merely incidentally, as though the scriptural texts were formed within some other context and for some other purpose, but essentially, scripture is an instrument through which

---

12. Ibid., 99.
13. Ibid., 100.
14. Ibid., 104.
15. Ibid., 100.
16. Brevard S. Childs, "On Reclaiming the Bible for Christian Theology," in *Reclaiming the Bible for the Church* (ed. Carl E. Braaten and Robert W. Jenson; Edinburgh: T&T Clark, 1995), 1–17 (9).
17. Childs, *Biblical Theology in Crisis*, 99.

God communicates with his people. This conviction is, above all, I suggest, the distinctive mark of "biblical theology" as Childs understands it. Accordingly, the validity, and indeed the necessity, of biblical theology rests firmly upon the reality to which this conviction bears witness: *Deus dixit*. God speaks and he does so through the biblical word. The task of biblical theology, put simply, is to attend to what God says.

In what follows I will offer some theological reflections upon three aspects of biblical theology so understood: first, upon the communication of God; second, upon the unity of scripture; and third, upon "the present Word." It will be seen as a result of these deliberations that the scholarly interest in apprehending the "meaning" of the biblical texts eludes strict methodological control.

The Self-Communication of God

To say that scripture is an instrument of divine communication is to say that scripture has a role in the saving economy of the Father, the Son, and the Holy Spirit. Scripture bears witness to the actions of God through which a people is called, established, nurtured, and equipped to be an instrument and embodied anticipation of the coming kingdom of God. It is not merely accidental that scripture has this role, as though it were first formed for some other purpose and only later adopted by God for his purpose. Were that the case, then a theological hermeneutic would again and again have to defer to or even be abandoned in favor of a nontheological hermeneutic with some more primitive claim upon the biblical texts. Such has sometimes been the practice of biblical scholarship in the academy. Even scholars who concur with the intention to read scripture as "God's Word" have sometimes adopted a method that treats scripture as if it were first something other than God's Word, before handing over the fruits of their scholarship to theologians and preachers who are then supposed to make something theological out of it.

Understood in a Christian sense, however, attention to the divine address takes priority, and ought to determine the form of our scholarship from the outset. Christian biblical scholarship will not be afraid, for instance, to draw upon the long history of interpretation and faithful testimony concerning where and how God has been at work in the world in order to understand the particular testimony to that divine economy that presents itself to us in the biblical text. More traditionally put, Christian scholarship will read scripture according to the "rule of faith." The risk here of obscuring the distinctive witness of the text must be guarded against, of course, but let us be clear that there is no surer way to obscure the distinctive witness of a text than by removing it from its context in the divine economy. The distinctive witness will be better heard when a text generated by the divine economy is allowed to contradict and challenge what our adherence to the rule of faith might otherwise lead us to hope for and expect. It will only do so, however, when studied within that primary context of faith.

Christian biblical scholarship will also consider it appropriate to investigate the historical and cultural circumstances of a text's production with skills learned under the discipline of historical criticism, not merely to learn something of the text's authors, redactors, and original hearers, but also to learn something of the grace of God in entrusting his self-communication to the precarious stewardship and faltering witness of sinful human beings, and in letting that communication take shape amidst a vast range of political, cultural, and personal interests and ambitions that cloud but do not finally succeed in obscuring the radiance of the divine word.

To understand scripture as God's word of address involves the conviction that God was at work in the very formation of the texts, calling them forth as responsive witness to and instrument of his ongoing work of election, salvation, and sanctification. This action of God is identified theologically as the inspiration and the holiness of scripture.[18] "Inspiration" and "holiness" do not name qualities inherent in the texts as such; they identify the reality of God's action in calling forth and sanctifying these human instruments for the sounding of his Word. "Inspiration" means that the communicative power these texts have is imparted to them by God. "Sanctification" means that they are put to divine use. That the texts so empowered and used are now gathered together and called a "canon" constitutes in turn an affirmation of the process by which the church discerns and acknowledges the inspiring and sanctifying action of God.

It is of the utmost importance here to distinguish between the agent and the instrument of divine communication. The agent of divine communication is God who, as Barth insisted, remains Lord of revelation. The Bible, in turn, is the instrument of divine communication. The instrument alone is not sufficient for the hearing of God's voice; it requires to be

---

18. For further discussion of this point, see John Webster, *Holy Scripture: A Dogmatic Sketch* (Cambridge: Cambridge University Press, 2003).

"played" as it were, to be filled again and again with the breath, the *ruaḥ* of God. Scripture is the *living* Word of God precisely as God takes the instrument to his lips and addresses his people once more.

The warrant for treating the biblical texts as instruments of God's communication with his people comes from scripture itself. The common prophetic refrain, "Thus says the Lord," the instructions given in Deut 6:1–9, "Now this is the commandment—the statutes and the ordinances—that the Lord your God charged me to teach you," the instruction of Exod 13:8, "You shall tell your children on that day," each represent the widely attested biblical expectation that the words of scripture, received in some manner from God, shall be the means by which God's people are sustained and nurtured in faith. Likewise in the New Testament, on the basis of his apostolic appointment, Paul boldly conveys the grace and peace of God himself to those to whom he writes, while claiming to have received directly from the Lord what he now passes on to his readers (1 Cor 11: 23). Biblical theology is the activity of those readers of scripture who consent to what is heard and whose consent distinguishes them as the community of God's people. Such readers consent to Paul's claim to divine authority because they know themselves to have been summoned, commissioned, chastized, and blessed by God through the scriptural Word. Accordingly, they read scripture with the prayer that as God has made himself known to them in the past, so will he do so again through these biblical words of faith.

Furthermore, such readers, including those who undertake the task of biblical theology in the academy, do not require permission to read the Bible in this way from those who choose to proceed as if the Bible were not the instrument of God's self-communication. There is a *prima facie* case in favor of the prayerful, theological reading of scripture established by the content of the biblical texts themselves. To read otherwise is to suppose that the witness of the texts is not true, or at least to suspend judgment. In each case, however, the reader chooses to detach himself/herself from the *Sitz im Leben* within which the texts were formed and have been handed on. The texts were formed as testimonies to the being and actions of the living God. Biblical theology resists detachment from this intent, and the practitioners of biblical theology are those who share with Childs the confession that

> I do not come to the Old Testament [indeed the whole Bible] to learn about someone else's God, but about the God we confess, who made himself known to Israel, to Abraham, Isaac and Jacob.... I do not come

146   THE BIBLE AS CHRISTIAN SCRIPTURE

> to the Old Testament to be informed about some strange religious phenomenon, but in faith I strive for knowledge as I seek to understand ourselves [sic] in the light of God's self-disclosure. In the context of the church's scripture I seek to be pointed to our God who made himself known, is making himself known, and will make himself known.... I stand in a community of faith which confesses to know God, or rather to be known by God. We live our lives in the midst of confessing, celebrating and hoping. Thus, I cannot act as if I were living at the beginning of Israel's history, but as one who already knows the story, and who has entered into the middle of an activity of faith long in progress.[19]

What Childs testifies to, along with Christians throughout the ages, is that he has heard in the Bible the voice of the eternal God who makes himself known through Word and Spirit and addresses us through scripture. For Christians, reading scripture is always a matter of attentiveness to that voice. The work of Christian scholarship, accordingly, takes place in service of such attentiveness.

The Unity of the Bible

Guided by the conviction, described above, that the Christian Bible is to be understood as an instrument of divine communication, Childs is deeply concerned in *Biblical Theology of the Old and New Testaments* with developing an account of the Christian Bible's unity. Pursuing the question of unity, Childs gives approving attention to Gerhard Ebeling's claim:

> In "biblical theology" the theologian who devotes himself specially to studying the connection between the Old and New Testaments has to give an account of his understanding of the Bible as a whole, i.e. above all of the theological problems that come of inquiring into the inner unity of the manifold testimony of the Bible.[20]

As is evident through his renowned canonical approach to biblical interpretation, Childs is committed to that view. Of biblical theology he writes, "It assumes that the Christian Bible consists of a theological unity formed

---

19. Brevard S. Childs, *Old Testament Theology in a Canonical Context* (Philadelphia: Fortress, 1986), 28–29.
20. Gerhard Ebeling, *Word and Faith*, 96. Cited in Childs, *BTONT*, 7.

by the canonical union of the two testaments."[21] Although it is commonly overlooked by his critics, he is also concerned that the diversity be given due recognition: "A major task of Biblical Theology is to reflect on the whole Christian Bible with its two very different voices."[22] And further: "It would seem to me to be a major enterprise of Biblical Theology to describe carefully both the continuity and discontinuity between these two different witnesses of the Christian Bible."[23] One of the criticisms commonly leveled at the Biblical Theology movement, and indeed at all attempts to treat the Bible as a unity, is that such an approach violates the integrity of the Old Testament texts in particular. The Christian canon, it is claimed, constitutes a violation of the Old Testament texts because the dogmatic requirements of the church, according to which the content and limits of the canon are determined, impose a meaning upon them that is alien to the texts themselves.[24]

In such a climate, "the theological unity of the Old and New Testaments has become extremely fragile and it seems now impossible to combine the testaments on the same level in order to produce a unified theology."[25] Childs reported on this state of affairs in 1993, but not with approval. One of the defining marks of biblical theology, in opposition to those scholarly trends that regard the diversity of the biblical texts as subversive of canonical order and indeed of Christian faith, is a confession that in the scriptures of the Old and New Testaments the one Word of God may be heard. How then is this unity to be conceived?

One might begin by recognizing that the texts of the Christian Bible do have a common subject matter, however diverse may be their attention to it. That subject matter is the God of Israel and the fortunes of that God's people, culminating in the life, death, and resurrection of one Israelite in particular. It is true, of course, that those who wrote about and reflected upon the early stages of Israel's story had little inkling of when and how that story would come to a head, or that the ultimate good would come in the end from Nazareth. But they did succeed in establishing, articulating, and providing an enduring source of nourishment to the faith that what-

---

21. Ibid., 55.
22. Ibid., 78.
23. Ibid., 93.
24. See, for example, Philip Davies, *Whose Bible Is It Anyway?* (2nd ed.; London: T&T Clark, 2004), 14.
25. Childs, *BTONT,* 7.

ever the outcome of Israel's story, it would be an outcome in which the promise once given to Abraham would be fulfilled; all the families of the earth shall be blessed. There are episodes in Israel's history when the promise is distorted, when it is bent out of shape and takes form as nationalistic self-interest, prideful self-righteousness, or the presumption of ethnic superiority. But always there is a prophetic voice, an inspired voice, calling Israel to renewed faithfulness, to the penitent acknowledgement that it exists as a people solely on account of grace. Amongst the waywardness, amongst the misunderstanding, and amongst the disputes over what the divine promise entails, the prophetic voice proclaims that Israel's existence constitutes a sign to all nations of the creative and redemptive purposes of God. Although the texts of scripture sound forth this story in a complex polyphony, the constant theme does emerge, is returned to again and again, and provides warrant for our reading and our hearing of these texts together. Childs suggests that this common subject matter, as described so far, is accessible to historical study. "The object of historical study is Israel's own testimony to God's redemptive activity. In Israel's sacred traditions we have its particular theological testimony to those events which constituted its life before God."[26]

The fact of this common subject matter is not, however, the real basis of the Bible's unity. The common subject matter is the outcome, rather, of the singular activity of God in electing a people to be a sign of and witness to his purposes for the world. The principle of the Bible's unity is contained in the words of Gen 12:1: "Now the Lord said to Abram...." Everything in scripture has its place within the context of this divine address. Indeed, as it attends to that address, Israel learns that everything in heaven and on earth has its basis in the utterance of the divine Word. That realization is the origin of Israel's worship, of its stuttering obedience, of its lamentation in the midst of suffering and exile, of its penitence when faced with divine wrath and divine love, and of its hope that the full glory of the Lord will one day be revealed. Far from being an alien imposition upon the texts, a theological framework such as this, I suggest, is the only framework within which the particularities of the texts can be adequately comprehended.

The texts of the New Testament are likewise concerned with this subject matter. They too arise, according to the church's confession, through attentiveness to the divine Word. Only now, that Word is encountered as

---

26. Ibid., 97–98.

never before, as the Logos incarnate. The divine Word becomes flesh, takes on our human nature in the man Jesus of Nazareth, but without being changed in substance. The Word made flesh is still the one through whom all things came to be, is still the one who was before Abraham, is still the one made known to Israel as, again and again, its prophets proclaimed, "This is the Word of the Lord...." Just so, the Word become flesh is also the one through whom the wrath, the love, and the glory of God are comprehensively revealed. The New Testament is precisely a *testament* to this reality. It too is polyphonic, but the diverse voices are most distinctly heard as contributing to this theme. The hermeneutical necessity of the "rule of faith" is best understood in this way. The "rule of faith" is a statement of the theme, itself heard within the texts, but distinguished in the creeds of the church precisely in order to guide our apprehension of the biblical word.

The recognition that the Word heard in the New Testament is the same Word addressed to Israel brings us to Childs's own account of the unity of the Christian Bible. The unity of the two Testaments consists, Childs argues, in their mutual witness to the "selfsame divine reality" beyond the text. That reality is further identified in christological terms:

> [Biblical theology] has as its foundational goal to understand the various voices within the whole Christian Bible, New and Old Testament alike, as a witness to the one Lord Jesus Christ, the selfsame divine reality. The Old Testament bears testimony to the Christ who has not yet come; the New to the Christ who has appeared in the fullness of time.[27]

Childs continues, however:

> It is not the case that the New Testament writers possess a full knowledge of Christ which knowledge then corrects the Old Testament. Nor is it adequate to understand interpretation as moving only in the one direction of Old Testament to New. Rather both testaments bear testimony to the one Lord, in different ways, at different times, to different peoples, and yet both are understood and rightly heard in the light of the living Lord himself, the perfect reflection of the glory of God (Heb 1:3).[28]

Qualifications notwithstanding, the assertion that the whole of the Old Testament is a witness to the one Lord Jesus Christ is a considerable claim

---

27. Ibid., 85. Cf. 721.
28. Ibid., 85.

to digest, in view of the fact that Jesus of Nazareth is unknown in the Old Testament and vast swathes of the Hebrew Scriptures pay little attention to Israel's messianic hope. The claim that the Old Testament constitutes a witness to Christ requires a great deal of further explanation with respect to the Pentateuch, for example. Even where the messianic hope becomes explicit, in the servant songs of Isaiah, for instance, the identification of the suffering servant with Jesus of Nazareth must not be allowed to obscure the fact that Jewish readers of these texts have taken them to refer to a range of other subjects and, in some cases, have explicitly denied that they can be applied to Jesus.[29]

How does one argue, then, that the whole Bible constitutes a witness to the one Lord Jesus Christ? First, I think, by acknowledging that this claim is a confession of faith. It requires a paradigm shift, a conversion indeed, to see that in Jesus of Nazareth the Bible's account of the God of Israel and of his creative and redemptive purposes for the world as testified to in the Old Testament comes to a head. Such conversion is brought about as, by Word and Spirit, God makes himself known to individual readers of scripture and declares himself to be the subject of scripture's story, reveals himself as the one who appointed Israel as his people, who called that people to be his witness in the world, and who "in these last days has spoken to us by a Son" (Heb 1:2). Recognition of the unity of scripture is given to those who have heard that *viva vox Dei*, who have been called by name, and who, on account of that calling, have learned to know the Lord's voice. There is no way to avoid the fiduciary character of this claim. Biblical theology is a venture of faith. Proponents of biblical theology ought not to avoid or disguise the fiduciary character of their endeavors. Faith consists in the life lived, the thinking done, and the scholarship undertaken, in thankful acknowledgement of God's self-communicative presence. It therefore trusts gratefully in the promise that we shall be led into all truth (John 16:13).[30] Any hermeneutic developed outside of this context of faith is a hermeneutic that functions as if the biblical testimony were not true, as if,

---

29. See, for instance, the *Sefer Hizzuk Emunah* of Rabbi Isaac ben Abraham of Troki (various editions). Even among Jewish interpreters the identity of the "suffering servant" has been attributed to a range of subjects. I have attempted to defend the legitimacy of this hermeneutical pluralism with respect to the servant songs, and to Christian readings as well, in Murray A. Rae, "Texts and Context: Scripture and the Divine Economy" in *JTI* 1 (2007): 23-45.

30. The point is adapted from Barth, *Church Dogmatics* I.1:17.

that is, God were not involved in our knowing of him. In that case the Bible is heard no longer as God's Word, as the instrument of divine address.

Biblical theology affirms, in contrast, that the one God makes himself known through scripture. The God made known in Jesus is the very same one who spoke through the prophets of old, who by Word and Spirit called, anointed, and guided Israel to be his witness in the world. To claim that the texts of scripture bear witness to the one Lord Jesus Christ is not to suggest, therefore, that Jesus Christ is the explicit subject matter of the Old Testament texts. It is to confess, rather, that the testament offered there that the Lord has spoken is confirmed once and for all by the coming of the Christ. The Word of scripture is recognized thus as the self-communication of the eternal Word. Such, at least, is the conviction of the New Testament authors who draw on the Old Testament to confirm the identity of the Word made flesh.

The identification of the scriptural texts as canonical is the formal expression of the unity of the Bible. The church's decision does not establish this unity, nor does it bestow authority upon the biblical texts. The canonicity of the texts is not a function of the church's use of scripture, as has sometimes been argued, but of the divine use of scripture. The process by which the biblical texts were canonized by the church was not a process of authorization, therefore, but rather of recognition. If it were otherwise, if the authority of the canon were bestowed by an ecclesial decision, then the authority of scripture would be subordinate to that of the church. This was a point at issue in the Reformation debates about the authority of scripture. Luther initially supposed it to be uncontroversial that the authority of scripture was superior to that of the Pope, and was taken aback by Cajetan's assertion that "the Pope's authority ... is above a Council, scripture and everything in the church.... This was new to my ears," Luther continued, "and I said that on the contrary the Pope was not above a Council and Scripture."[31] Calvin was more forthright, saying, "To

---

31. Luther might well have been a better interpreter than Cajetan of traditional Catholic teaching on this point. Aquinas, for instance, recognizes the primacy of scripture in writing, "Faith adheres to all the articles of faith because of one reason (*medium*), namely because of the First Truth proposed to us in the Scriptures understood rightly according to the teaching of the Church (*secundum doctrinum Ecclesiae*)." *Summa Theologiae* II–II, 5, ad 2. Cited by Francis Martin, "Some Directions in Catholic Biblical Theology," in *Out of Egypt: Biblical Theology and Biblical Interpretation* (ed. Craig Bartholomew et al.; Grand Rapids: Zondervan, 2004), 65–87, 72.

submit the oracles of God to the authority of men, so as to make their validity dependent on human approbation, is blasphemy unworthy of being mentioned."[32] Zwingli likewise insisted that "all who say that the Gospel is nothing without the church's guarantee, err and insult God." As Childs puts it, "The concept of canon was an attempt to *acknowledge* the divine authority of [the church's] writings and collections."[33] Here is one of the distinctive marks of biblical theology as Childs conceives it. Biblical theology undertakes to study the Bible precisely because it has recognized these texts as authoritative—not merely authoritative in an archaeological sense, as giving authoritative insight into the culture and religious beliefs of an ancient people, but authoritative in being, both then and now, an instrument by which God presents himself to his people.

THE PRESENT WORD

While biblical theology investigates the nature and content of each Testament's ancient witness to Jesus Christ, its task does not come to an end with exegesis. Biblical theology also "wrestles theologically with the relation between the reality testified to in the Bible and that living reality known and experienced as the exalted Christ through the Holy Spirit within the present community of faith."[34] Biblical theology thus resists the customary divorce between the academic study of the biblical texts and the life of faith lived in covenant relationship with the God to whom those texts bear witness. Like theology more generally, biblical theology too is a matter of faith seeking understanding. For the community of faith, "the divine imperatives [of scripture] are no longer moored in the past, but continue to confront the hearer in the present as truth."[35] Here biblical theology arrives at its goal, to serve the community of faith in its attentiveness to scripture as the self-communication of God.

There are challenges here. To read the Bible in attentiveness to God's giving of himself, and to find by means of that divine gift that our sinfulness is pardoned and that, in Christ, we are reconciled to God requires

---

32. John Calvin, *Institutes of the Christian Religion* (trans. John Allen; Philadelphia: Presbyterian Board of Christian Education, 1936), 4.9.14 (2:447). Cf. 1.7.1 (1:85–86).
33. Childs, *Biblical Theology in Crisis*, 105, emphasis original.
34. Childs, *BTONT*, 86.
35. Ibid., 86.

something of us—repentance to begin with, and new life. This is something not customarily anticipated in the modern academy, which has long insisted that we will gain knowledge only as we maintain a proper objectivity and distance from the object of our inquiries.[36] But the Word who engages us through scripture is known in a reconciling act, an act that does not leave us as we were, but makes new persons of us. The meaning of scripture rests in that reconciling and transformative event. I employ a concept of "meaning" here in which the meaning of a text is the role it plays in a given context. To say that the divine economy is the primary and determinative context of the biblical texts is to suggest that the meaning of biblical texts emerges for the reader only as he or she becomes a participant in and is drawn into the reconciling work of God.

As we have noted earlier, such a conception does not entail that there is a singular determinate meaning of biblical texts. Because the divine economy is a continuing reality, the meaning of biblical texts will cohere with but not be confined to their meaning in their original settings. The ways in which God through scripture draws people into the outworking of his purposes and equips them to participate in the coming of his kingdom may be many and diverse. God has spoken new words through ancient texts throughout the history of his dealings with the world. The application to the person of Jesus Christ of the servant songs in Isaiah, which were first given to Israel to sustain them in exile, is but one case in point.[37] It is thus the ongoing task of biblical theology to assist the church in attending to what God is saying now to his people.

But how does one do this? Childs has sometimes expressed consternation that biblical theology has never settled on a method. But we should not be surprised at this. If it is true, as Childs attests, that the Bible is God's Word, if it is true that holy scripture is sanctified by divine use and gains its communicative power and vitality precisely as the Spirit both opens up the text and transforms the reader through encounter with the living Word of God, then it will also be true that this divine activity cannot be subjected

---

36. Postmodernism has helped, of course, to disabuse us of the illusion that our inquiries in the academy are wholly objective and value-free, but old habits die hard. We are still learning what it might mean to give due recognition to faith in the pursuit of knowledge, and we are still unsure how to proceed beyond the hesitant admission that education once was and ought still to involve the (trans)formation of character as well as the acquisition of knowledge.

37. On which, again, see Rae, "Texts and Context."

to strict academic control. Attention to the self-communication of God through the words of scripture is attention, first of all, to what God seeks to reveal of himself. It may be supposed, given the constancy of God, that what he reveals to us now will cohere with what he has revealed of himself in ages past—just so, the study of the historical particularities of the texts' original production remains important—but God may also use the texts to speak a new word for our time. The church attests that, again and again, God uses these ancient texts to speak to the particular challenges, problems, and opportunities of the present day. In this communicative event God is revealed as the primary interpreter of his Word. Barth puts the matter thus:

> If scripture as testimony to Jesus Christ is the Word of God ... who then can expound scripture but God himself? And what can man's exposition of it consist in but once more in an act of service, a faithful and attentive following after the exposition which Scripture desires to give itself, which Jesus Christ as Lord of Scripture wishes to give Himself?[38]

Biblical scholarship, accordingly, ought always to be a matter of humble service rather than of mastery. Perhaps it is true to say then that "biblical theology," above all, identifies a disposition rather than a method, a disposition along the lines expressed, for example, in the prayer with which John Calvin customarily began his lectures: "Grant unto us, O Lord, to be occupied in the mysteries of thy Heavenly wisdom, with true progress in piety, to thy glory and our own edification. Amen."[39]

Biblical theology along the lines that Brevard Childs sought to practice it belongs in this tradition. It still seeks to study the Bible in prayerful attentiveness to what is given by God through his Spirit, under the expectation that such attentiveness will contribute to our progress in faithfulness, to the edification of the church, and to the sustenance of the church's witness in the world.

---

38. Karl Barth, *The Knowledge of God and the Service of God according to the Teaching of the Reformation* (London: Hodder & Stoughton, 1938), 180–89. Cited in Webster, *Holy Scripture*, 101.

39. The prayer is cited, for example, in John Calvin, *A Commentary on Daniel* (Edinburgh: Banner of Truth Trust, 1966), 76.

The Doctrine of God Is a Hermeneutic: The *Biblical Theology* of Brevard S. Childs

C. Kavin Rowe

1.

One of the advantages of writing an invited essay is the chance it affords to explore new ways of thinking without worrying too much about the "field" for which the piece should be written.[1] This is particularly welcome in the case of an essay about the thought of Brevard Childs, who did not really have a "field" in which he worked. It is true, of course, that he was an Old Testament scholar. But it is no less true that he was a scholar of the New Testament, of the history of interpretation, of dogmatic theology, of theological ethics, and so on. This is not to say that he was equally learned in every one of these modes of inquiry. It is rather simply to make the point that the fecundity of Childs's thought is due as much to his integrated way of working and refusal to remain within a single field as it is to anything else.

As a way of honoring his commitment to the integration of theological thought, the following essay will attempt to sketch the theological underlay

---

1. The typical audience for the *Journal for the Study of the New Testament* differs, for example, from that of *Modern Theology*. Reflecting on the target audiences of various publication outlets illustrates how frequently these venues determine what we write (at least with respect to genre, scholarly apparatus, and so forth). Precisely because many of these outlets result in practice from disciplinary separation, we have good reason to be thankful for the many new ventures that are seeking to overcome a separation long repugnant to Childs: the division between biblical studies and dogmatic theology. We may think, for example, of the new *Journal for Theological Interpretation* and of the various groups at SBL that provide space for constructive efforts to bring the theological disciplines together (e.g., Christian Theology and the Bible; Theological Hermeneutics).

of the whole of his *Biblical Theology of the Old and New Testaments*.[2] The hope in so doing is threefold: to help readers of this work to understand it better than they have; to correct some misapprehensions about Childs's hermeneutical proposals as a whole; and to illustrate how the doctrine of God is inextricably tied to a particular way of thinking about the interpretation of scripture.[3]

2.

To many scholars the constructive proposals in Childs's *Biblical Theology* about how to read the Christian Bible remain a mystery. The reasons for this are probably many. For example, Childs may not have conceptualized his audience clearly enough, and hence may overlooked the fact that a great many (all?) of his readers would not share his learning in all the areas in which he makes detailed argument.[4] Thus would the amount of "background" knowledge needed to track precisely the movement of his various arguments exceed what could be expected from lesser mortals. Or, to mention another bibliographical matter, Childs works considerably in both past and contemporary German research, and his arguments thus frequently reflect an academic context that is known to many North

---

2. Brevard S. Childs, *Biblical Theology of the Old and New Testaments: Theological Reflections on the Christian Bible* (Minneapolis: Fortress, 1992). Hereafter, *BTONT.*

3. On the one hand, the essay's primary aim is not to introduce Childs's thought to those who have never studied it. I will assume familiarity with Childs's publications and main lines of thought, and will therefore make direct citations of his work only where they are obviously needed or particularly illuminating for the point under discussion. On the other hand, insofar as the essay is a "sketch" that helps to explain some of the larger matters that are at stake in reading Childs's most comprehensive book, it will simultaneously facilitate a better understanding of his work for all who care to read it carefully.

4. Cf. Christopher R. Seitz, *Word without End: The Old Testament as Abiding Theological Witness* (Grand Rapids: Eerdmans, 1998), 108-9: "The question is: is there an alternative either to rationalism on the right or left or to an experientialism of the pious, but also modern consumerist, sort? Childs's *Biblical Theology* may prove to be a book in search of an audience, and for that reason it will be judged by the widest variety of readers as learned but unsatisfactory and by an even smaller audience as the most brilliant proposal for theological exegesis offered in recent memory, but one unlikely to gain the sort of foothold necessary to transform the church in its use of scripture."

Americans only via mediation (or not at all). Or perhaps it is simply his admittedly clunky writing.

Such problems notwithstanding, I think there is a deeper reason that Childs's proposals have not found proper consideration, at least among biblical scholars: we have failed to grasp the dogmatic theological moves that fund the entirety of his conceptions about how to read the Bible. If, however, we think carefully along with Childs about reading scripture, we will discover that his thinking presupposes and articulates a particular doctrine of God. Like his theological mentors John Calvin and Karl Barth, Childs knew that to think about the Bible was to think primarily about God.[5] In order to see how reflection on the doctrine of God illumines Childs's interpretive project, however, we must first say clearly what Childs's project is not, and then, briefly, what it is.

3.

Of all the things that could be said wrongly about Childs's work, the one that is probably the most common is that Childs is an advocate of a particular method called *canonical criticism*, a method that can be placed alongside form criticism, redaction criticism, literary criticism, and so on. After all the diachronic digging and textual comparison has been done, so a common reading of his work runs, we can then—as a kind of supplemental or final move—consider our exegetical results in light of the so-called "final form" or canon. Or, in another common version, we can simply leave off the initial historical and comparative work and begin straightaway with the final form. In both cases the assumption is that canonical criticism is one method among many others that we may choose to use. Let it be said emphatically: *this is not Childs's project.*[6]

---

5. Of course, in that he begins the constructive sections of *BTONT* with the "identity of God," the structure of the book illustrates Childs's commitment to the priority of God. Cf., e.g., Childs, *BTONT*, 82, on the "primary" reality of God.

6. This fact could be realized from a simple glance at the table of contents. For example, the *Tetraevangelium* is treated in an order we find only in a twelfth-century manuscript in West Saxon (Mark, Matthew, Luke, and John). The logic that makes intelligible the order of this presentation is that which lies behind a particular view of the "synoptic problem" (Mark is earliest; Matthew and Luke use Mark, etc.). If nothing else, the treatment of the four Gospels should alert the sensitive reader to a more complex agenda than that of a simple focus on the "final form." For a list of the orders

158   THE BIBLE AS CHRISTIAN SCRIPTURE

For Childs, the entire project of canonical interpretation hinges in its intellectual suppositions not so much on a literary phenomenon, the final form of a text, as it does on the divine referent of scripture. The reason we read all these different and disparate documents together as one book, that is, is not because there is something *ipso facto* literarily pristine or exegetically satisfying about final forms—his two *Introductions* might even suggest otherwise—but because together all these various texts constitute Israel's and the church's witness to the one God.[7] Indeed, it is not only that the texts are the human witness to God but also that, in a frequent Childsean phrase, God is the reality that "*evokes* the witness" (*BTONT*, 379, emphasis added).

Because it is ultimately God who holds the documents of the canon together in one book—it is not merely a decision by Jewish and Christian communities—to reject the normative claim or hermeneutically distinctive boundary of the canon is actually to fragment the divine reality, and thus ultimately to sever our connection to God. It is also implicitly—whether we intend this or not—to offer a counterproposal about the way in which divine reality is rendered, and thus to offer a counterproposal about our connection to God, or lack of it. In Childs's way of thinking, therefore, reading canonically is not a general "solve-all-problems" exegetical program,[8] or a simple application of one type of literary criticism, or a new critical methodology. Rather, it is the necessary anthropological and ecclesial correlate to the God of Israel's self-revelation in Jesus Christ. Canonical interpretation, that is, is a positive response to the normative claim to render God inherent in the notion of Christian canon. Or, to move a little closer to Childs's own language, it is a response to the pressure exerted by God upon the interpreter of this particular book.

---

in which the Gospels occur, see Bruce M. Metzger, *The Canon of the New Testament: Its Origin, Development, and Significance* (Oxford: Clarendon, 1997), 296–97.

7. See, e.g., his remarks in Brevard S. Childs, *Introduction to the Old Testament as Scripture* (Philadelphia: Fortress, 1979), 76.

8. This seems to be another frequent misunderstanding, even among sophisticated OT interpreters. See, e.g., Walter Brueggemann, "Against the Stream: Brevard Childs's Biblical Theology" *ThTo* 50 (1993): 279–84; and of course James Barr, *The Concept of Biblical Theology: An Old Testament Perspective* (Minneapolis: Fortress, 1999). See Childs, *BTONT*, 670.

4.

Childs's insistence upon the necessary link between God and the Christian canon raises numerous important questions, but for this essay we shall deal with only two: (1) the identity of God, and (2) the relation of this identity to the two Testaments of the Bible.

(1) *Identity of God*: Childs speaks about the God of the Bible in numerous ways: "the subject matter," "substance," "reality," "*res*," and so forth. Yet, in contrast to the linguistic habits of many modern biblical scholars, "God" is not spoken of in such general terms alone. Rather, Childs specifies at point after point that the God about whom the Bible speaks in its canonical shape is the God known in the Christian church as the triune God, Father, Son, and Holy Spirit. Thus, for example, Childs can speak of the Bible's "full divine reality in its Triunity" (*BTONT*, 380), and can entitle the final section of his chapter on the identity of God "From Biblical Theology to Dogmatics: Trinitarian Theology" (*BTONT*, 375).

Childs is careful not to confuse the triune reality of God with the biblical text itself or with the historical dynamics involved in the epistemic realization of the one God's triunity. He knows, for example, that "the Bible does not contain a fully developed doctrine of the Trinity," and that "historically, the doctrine of the Trinity developed from a christological center" (*BTONT*, 375–76).[9] But he is equally clear that God cannot be spoken of in general precisely because the Bible pressures its readers to answer the question of God's identity in triune terms. To speak of the God of the Christian canon is necessarily to employ trinitarian grammar.

In speaking clearly of God as triune, Childs recognizes what many theologians have long said, namely, that trinitarian doctrine is what actually makes the Christian doctrine of God Christian (*BTONT*, 375). But he also recognizes what many theologians—and biblical scholars—in the modern world have not: the trinitarian doctrine of God is also what makes the Christian doctrine of God *biblical*.

It is true, of course, that the renewed interest in trinitarian doctrine in the twentieth century helped to fund various exegetical studies of the relation between the New Testament and the Trinity. As a whole, however, such studies were textually selective—focusing primarily on Paul or John—and built methodologically around "functional christology"

---

9. See Childs, *BTONT*, esp. 364–66.

or predication (e.g., where is Jesus actually called God?). In midcentury, Arthur Wainwright, Reginald Fuller, and Oscar Cullmann, among others, asked how Jesus and God overlapped in their function (e.g., as "Judge"), and in the 1990s Murray Harris and Raymond Brown, for example, offered careful exegetical discussion of the few cases in the New Testament where *theos* is potentially predicated of Jesus. Such studies are far from unneeded; indeed, they can illuminate well particular features of the biblical portrait of God.[10] But considered as a whole, they display a rather limited range of questions and methods. Rarely did the exegetes interested in the New Testament's doctrine of God, that is, carry their studies further and pose the broader, more difficult question about how the Trinity might relate to the Bible as a whole.[11] Stated otherwise, if the achievement of the work of Wainwright, Harris, and others is to have put at least something of the exegetical shape of the New Testament's view of God back on table, their failure is in not having done this in a hermeneutically constructive manner, or in not having connected some of their findings with an overarching conception of the God about whom they were reading. In this way, the contrast with Brevard Childs could scarcely be more striking. Unlike these earlier studies, Childs's *BTONT* not only exhibits a careful attention to a trinitarian conception of God but also demonstrates considerable reflection on what difference such a conception makes for biblical interpretation.

In what is one of the most revealing passages in the book—which is therefore worth citing almost in its entirety—Childs writes:

> It is constitutive of Biblical Theology that it takes seriously the historical forms of the biblical witnesses which are registered in the two testaments. Yet it was a fatal mistake of some forms of Biblical Theology when dealing with the identity of God to feel that it could reflect on the subject only in terms of its historical sequence. This appeal to the so-called "economic Trinity" would restrict the doctrine of God to the divine workings within a historical trajectory of past, present, and future: God, Christ, Spirit.... However, the attempt to describe God's identity merely in terms of his acts, apart from his being, is not a serious theological option for either Biblical or Dogmatic theology. The subject matter itself requires

---

10. See my earlier argument in C. Kavin Rowe, "Luke and the Trinity: An Essay in Ecclesial Biblical Theology," *SJT* 56 (2003): 1–26.
11. An exception of sorts is Karl L. Schmidt, "Le problème du Christianisme primitive," *RHPR* 18 (1938): 126–73.

that proper theological understanding move from the biblical witness to the reality itself which called forth the witness. In terms of the aforementioned division of labor, those scholars trained in dogmatic theology are often better equipped to pursue in detail the nature of God's being, especially in the light of the modern challenges to the biblical witness from various forms of philosophy. Yet it is an equally important responsibility of Biblical Theology to assure that the reflection on the being of God remains integrally related to his redemptive action within human history for the sake of Israel, the church, and the world. (*BTONT*, 370)

Leaving aside questions of the proper "division of labor" (if for no other reason than that Childs himself does not really observe it), we can discern in this passage several theologically intertwined commitments that help to structure Childs's interpretive project as a whole.

First, though he objects to a modalist historical schema (God, Christ, Spirit) as a legitimate way to talk about the "economic Trinity," Childs clearly affirms the correspondence between God's economy and "the biblical witness." Second, he affirms that this correspondence entails an obligation to take seriously the integral relation between God and "human history," or "historical sequence."[12] Third, he argues that attending to the biblical display of God's economy is not theologically sufficient in and of itself, as if we could restrict our speech about the identity of God solely to his "acts." We must instead seek to speak also of God's "being," and thus move "from the biblical witness to the reality itself which called forth the witness." Fourth, the necessity of such a move toward reflection on God's being is not simply for the sake of philosophical clarity about the challenges posed to scripture in modernity, but is, more importantly, a response to the call of the "subject matter"—which is to say nothing less

---

12. One could speak here about the doctrine of providence that accompanies the theological meaning of "historical sequence"—that is, in God's providence, he chose to create human time in such a way as to ensure that it had a linear dimension: he chose Israel before sending the messiah, became incarnate before the church worked out the doctrine of the immanent Trinity, etc. That modern thinkers have characteristically reduced time to its linear dimension and forgotten its fullness, as it were, is well explored by Matthew Levering's stimulating book, *Participatory Biblical Exegesis: A Theology of Biblical Interpretation* (Notre Dame, Ind.: University of Notre Dame Press, 2008). Levering's point is not that time does not have a linear dimension but rather that this dimension is only one "horizontal" aspect of how we should think about time (creation). There is also the "vertical" dimension to time, in which we are always and constantly participating in God's life as creator and sustainer.

than that the God who reveals himself in scripture requires reflection on who he is.

Taken together, these intertwined theological commitments reveal the attempt to work carefully with the dogmatic distinction between the economic and immanent Trinity.[13] Childs's larger point is that the identity of God is known on the basis of a biblical text that displays an undeniable historical sequence, even as this identity exceeds in "being" the witness that makes it known. Or to put it formulaically: we know from the witness of the Bible to God's acts in history that God himself exceeds ontologically the human history in which he acts redemptively; yet these two aspects of God, economic revelation and immanent reality, are not ultimately two different things, but are two ways we must think in order to speak with the requisite breadth and sophistication about the identity of the one God of the Bible.[14]

Childs's condensed articulation of the necessity to think both about God's immanent reality and his economic expression raises critical questions for scriptural hermeneutics. In relation to Childs's work, such questions can be focused rather simply: how should we read scripture so that we do justice both to "God's being" and to the "historical sequence" in which his being was made known? And, more specifically, how should we speak of the triunity of God in relation to the Old and New Testaments?

(2) *The Triune God and the Two Testament Bible*: Nowhere is Childs's programmatic commitment to the historical sequence of God's self-revelation more strikingly evident than in the structure of his *BTONT* as a whole. From the table of contents alone, we can learn that one must pass through the "discrete witness" of the Old Testament to the "discrete witness" of the New Testament before arriving at the substantive matters treated in the section entitled "theological reflection on the Christian Bible."

By "discrete witness," Childs means in practice a historically contextualized reading of the various canonical texts, which is itself the theological attempt to hear the voice of Israel and of the church in their own time and space.[15] To attend to the time and space of the voice of Israel, to stay with

---

13. See the remark cited on pp. 163–64 of this article from Childs, *BTONT*, 378.

14. This is also why Childs speaks of a "division of labor" between biblical and dogmatic theology rather than of two fundamentally different tasks: they are both concerned with the same subject matter. If the former focuses more on the economic Trinity and the latter of the immanent Trinity, they are nevertheless both reflecting on the one triune God.

15. Cf. among many other statements to the same effect: "It is incumbent on the

the importance of historical sequence, is not to deny that its voice may sound the note of promise—which of course is a notion that is concretely intelligible on the basis of a fulfillment—but it is to reject a mode of reading that would "fuse promise with fulfillment" (*BTONT*, 379).

Childs's objection to such fusion, however, is not predicated on a blind endorsement of historical criticism, or a kind of "historical consciousness" that one sees in such figures as Ernst Troeltsch or William Wrede, for example, but upon a deeper theological claim that the vertical dimension of God's self-revelation is to be taken seriously. "There is no legitimate way," writes Childs, "of removing the Old Testament's witness from its historical confrontation with the people of Israel" (*BTONT*, 379). The Old Testament testifies to the real revelation of God to Israel in time and space precisely in its function as the historical and literary reception of that revelation. To lose the voice of Israel, therefore, is not so much to violate a supposed set of the "laws of history" or the "philosophical principles" that underwrite historical-critical investigation as it is to lose the historical and literary contour of the vertical dimension of God's self-revelation in the concrete life of the Jews. The particular shape of biblical history is itself the intersection between God's self-revelation and its reception. For Childs, the economic Trinity thus functions not as a dogmatic construct with little interpretive weight—as if God's economy somehow hovered above the historically deep texture of the Bible—but as a way to speak about the God who is made known through the biblical text in just the way we have it.

Yet in consonance with his insistence upon the requirement to reflect on God's being, Childs also affirms that the interpreter is to read scripture in light of "the full-blown reality of God" (*BTONT*, 380). For all its truth, the interpretive direction entailed by an emphasis on the economic Trinity "remains one-sided and prone to error without attention to the 'immanent

---

interpreter, especially of the Old Testament, not to confuse the biblical witness with the reality itself. In order to hear the voice of each biblical witness in its own right, it is absolutely necessary to interpret each passage within its historical, literary, and canonical context" (Childs, *BTONT*, 379). Whether this interpretive moment is to be identified with historical criticism depends more on the conceptual commitments one associates with the term than it does on a common commitment to historical depth. That is, if one of the intellectual principles of historical criticism is that theological concerns should be excised from the interpretive endeavor, then obviously Childs does not favor historical criticism. If, however, such antitheological prejudice is not taken as constitutive for rigorous historical work on the Bible, then obviously Childs would be more sympathetic. And so forth.

Trinity," that is, to the nature of God's being" (*BTONT*, 378). Although it is true, for example, that the servant in Isa 53 "addresses the suffering community of Israel within the context of the old covenant" and proclaims "the message of salvation through the vicarious suffering of a divinely appointed servant," it would be theologically insufficient not to relate this figure to the divine reality toward which the biblical text aims as a whole. Thus, knowing "the will of God in Jesus Christ [opens] up a profoundly new vista on this prophetic testimony to God.... For those who confess the Lordship of Jesus Christ there is an immediate morphological fit" (*BTONT*, 382).

Childs's overall attempt to deal constructively with the economic and immanent distinction in trinitarian theology thus correlates with a dual emphasis that marks the entirety of *BTONT*: first, upon the discrete voice of each Testament (thus preserving the integrity of their historical sequence), and, second, upon their fundamental theological unity (thus preserving the integrity of their unified subject matter). To see how this dual emphasis leads directly to more specific hermeneutical proposals, we turn to Childs's language of interpretive "levels."

5.

When Childs asks if, after a careful reading of the biblical text, "we now understand the triunity of God, must not the grasp of this reality affect how we now interpret both testaments?" (*BTONT*, 379), readers new to his work would likely—and reasonably—expect a direct answer: yes. But of course, as seasoned readers of his work would know, direct answers seldom follow Childs's rhetorical questions. In this case, his "answer" is a complex discussion about the various hermeneutical levels required to interpret scripture well in light of the two more basic emphases mentioned in the previous section.

Childs is "naturally aware of the serious problems which arose when the church opted for a fourfold hermeneutic." But ecclesial misuse of the fourfold method no more obviates the need for a "multiple-level reading of scripture" than the misuse of a hammer makes it the wrong tool for driving nails. Childs does not, however, simply adopt the four different modes of reading and redescribe their respective foci in modern terms, but instead develops an interpretive grammar built around three different "levels" or "avenues" (*BTONT*, esp. 379–83).

The first level is that at which the interpreter hears "the voice of each biblical witness in its own right." At this level, "to read back into the [OT] story the person of Jesus Christ, or to interpret the various theophanies as the manifestation of the second person of the Trinity, is to distort the witness and to drown out the Old Testament's own voice" (379). There is a "historical voice" to each Testament to which we must listen if we are "to hear precisely the form of the witness as it entered into its concrete historical form" (381–82).

The second level is "another avenue into the Bible," in which the "literal/historical" reading of the first level is not contradicted, but extended. At this level, the interpreter seeks to relate the two Testaments to one another not only in terms of structural similarities and differences, but also in terms of their common "content." "Comparison" is the central mode of analysis—indeed, in a way that is materially analogous to typological reading. In relation to the identity of God, for example, at this second level the interpreter asks, "What features do the two testaments hold in common respecting the mode, intention, and goal of God's self-manifestation?" (380).

Whereas the first two levels are most appropriately understood as a movement from witness to reality—that is, from text to God—the third level of scriptural interpretation involves the reverse movement from reality to witness: "Is the concern with the full divine reality in its Triunity only the subject matter of Biblical Theology? Does it have no place within the exegesis of the biblical text? Is the hermeneutical movement of biblical interpretation only from witness to reality or can one also proceed from reality to witness?" (380) Once again, a simple answer is eschewed. In its place is a description of this third level of reading in terms that can only really be adequately understood as an encounter with God. That is to say, while Childs affirms the movement from reality to text, he does not describe this third level as a particular method—allegory, for example—but more as "a response to a living God who graciously lets himself be known" (382). Indeed, "much of the success" of this third level of reading "depends on how well God's presence has been understood" (382).

Precisely because an encounter with God cannot be limited to one piece of an interpreter's overall noetic apparatus, it would be a gross mistake to think of this third level of reading as a "final step"; exegesis, says Childs in a provocative statement, does not "proceed in stages within a fixed sequence" (381).[16] "True interpretation" is more comprehensive in

---

16. The statement is provocative because of his language of "first, second, third."

scope and "[moves] within a circle which encompasses both the movement from text to reality as well as from reality to text" (381). Let us make no mistake: for all the warning against the dangers of allegory and "retrojection," in Childs's logic all true interpretation is in fact spiritual reading: "If the church confesses that the spirit of God opens up the text to a perception of its true reality, it also follows that the Spirit also works in applying the reality of God in its fullness to an understanding of the text. The two movements cannot be separated" (382). The "reality of God testified to in the Bible, and experienced through the confirmation of God's Spirit, functions on a deeper level to instruct the reader toward an understanding of God that leads from faith to faith" (382). In short, for Childs, multileveled interpretation is but a contemporary rendition of ancient hermeneutical wisdom: all Bible reading is faith seeking understanding (*BTONT*, esp. 86).

6.

Childs's language of interpretive levels has proved difficult to understand.[17] I know of no account of his hermeneutical proposals by any biblical scholars, however, that interpret them explicitly within the framework of the trinitarian doctrine of God. My contention is that it is this framework, more so or even rather than a single method, that renders Childs's constructive moves intelligible. That is to say, in contrast to those who pigeonhole him as an advocate of "canonical criticism" or believe his project is to bring the artificially distinct categories "history" and "theology" together under one roof, my reading of Childs forgoes the attempt to find his particular method in favor of construing his overall hermeneutical habits as the outworking of a view of God. To illustrate concisely the explanatory advantage this way of reading Childs's work has over the effort to formulate his method, we can focus on the apparently contradictory statements that the interpreter both is and is not to read the OT in light of the full divine reality, that is, the triune God.

---

17. In a somewhat startling comment, even Childs himself gestures toward the inevitable difficulty that will surround our attempts to engage in or describe "true" interpretation: "The very fact that the Christian church has continued to be drawn back to allegory in a way that is not the case for Judaism could well be an indication of a genuine search for a level of exegesis which has not been satisfactorily met" (Childs, *BTONT*, 381).

As we saw in the previous section, at the first hermeneutical level, that of the discrete witness or historical voice of the Testaments, christological interpretation of the OT is inappropriate: the second person of the Trinity is not to be identified with the manifestation of God in the various OT theophanies. By the third level, however, the entire Bible is to be read in light of the full reality of the triune God. If we attempt to hold these two interpretive moves together in a single or stepwise methodology, we shall—at least on the face of it—have to judge these contrary claims to be blatant contradictions. Put simply: On the one hand, if the God of the entire Bible is the triune God, then the manifestations of God in the OT are of *this* God, and the attempt to bracket out the Trinity from OT interpretation would sever the biblical text from the reality of God himself. On the other hand, if the God manifested in the OT is not the triune God in his full reality, then the triune God is not the God of the *entire* Bible, and the unity of the Testaments at the level of their subject matter would be undone. Either way, Childs would seem to endorse incompatible theological claims.

If, however, we reread his language of levels with an interpretive framework that is cognizant of the theological importance of the distinction between the economic and immanent Trinity, then his project appears in a different light. This is not to say that such a distinction solves all the difficulties we might encounter in Childs's proposals, but it is to point out that to think from the economic side of God's triunity is to think in such a way as to take seriously the historical contour of the biblical text in which the triunity of God is not fully apparent in the life of Israel during the time of the OT—and that to think from the immanent side of God's triunity is to think in such a way as to take seriously the eternality of God's triunity required to sustain the Testaments' unity at the level of their subject matter. In short, to move too quickly or simplistically to one side or the other would be to dissolve the tension necessary to speak rightly about the concrete salvific expression of God's eternal reality. The movement from text to *res* charted in levels one and two, therefore, just is the movement from the economic to the immanent Trinity. Insofar as interpreters follow this movement, they reproduce in their own reading the epistemic path of the church from scripture to doctrine. And the movement from *res* to text spoken of in level three just is the movement from the immanent to the economic Trinity. Insofar as interpreters follow this movement, they reproduce in their own reading the ontologically grounded path of the church from doctrine to scripture.

If this way of interpreting Childs is accurate, the tension in his proposals turns out to mirror the tension between epistemology and ontology that accompanies the distinction between the economic and immanent Trinity—which is to say that the economic and immanent Trinity can be distinguished in thought and speech (hence Childs's reticence to adopt a blatant christological reading of the OT), but in reality can never be separated or apportioned to different departments of theological study (hence Childs's reticence to rule out a christological reading of the OT). This tension, therefore, is not a final one, as if God were consigned to appear ever as economic or immanent and not simply as himself; indeed, the unity of the economic/immanent tension is nothing less than the reality of God himself. So, too, for Childs the tension between the different levels of interpretation is not final, as if one had always to choose between reading at the first or third levels. And so, too, it is God himself, rather than a particular methodological construct, who provides the final unity of the different interpretive levels: "The true expositor of the Christian scriptures is the one who awaits in anticipation toward becoming the interpreted rather than the interpreter. The very divine reality which the interpreter serves to grasp, is the very One who grasps the interpreter. The Christian doctrine of the role of the Holy Spirit is not a hermeneutical principle, but that divine reality itself who makes understanding of God possible" (*BTONT*, 86–87).

Thus, rather than a contradiction or an ultimate failure to unify "historical criticism" with "theological interpretation," Childs's project displays the attempt to work hermeneutically on the basis of the inescapable complexity involved in describing the unity of the triune God. His claim for the theological importance of the "historical voice" may not, at the end of the day, fully satisfy those whose interpretive tendencies lean more heavily toward the immanent Trinity, just as his insistence that the OT must be read in the direction from *res* to witness may not satisfy those whose interpretive tendencies lean more heavily toward the economic Trinity. But perhaps that is just Childs's point with the imagery of the circle: to describe fully the identity of the God to whom the Bible points, we must be on the move, speaking now about the historical voice (economic) and now about the total *res* (immanent), all the while keeping in mind that these different modes of exegetical speech are in fact about the *same* reality, the One whose patient self-revelation and redemptive acts in concrete human history (economic) are always and ever the saving disclosure of the being of the triune God (immanent).

7.

In this brief article I have suggested that in order to understand the depth of the argumentative moves in Brevard Childs's *Biblical Theology of the Old and New Testaments*, we need to read the book as the hermeneutical outworking of a trinitarian doctrine of God. Doing so allows us to see that many of the central interpretive proposals depend for their viability—and, indeed, their intellectual sense—on the constructive tension that exists when one inhabits the economic/immanent distinction as a way to work with the relation between the biblical text and the reality to which it points. Whether or not Childs has ultimately succeeded in this attempt, it is undeniable that his effort to think clearly about the intersection between the triune God and the biblical text by which we know this God creates the right space in which theological thinking about the interpretation of scripture should be done. Childs's work, that is, is not about hermeneutics in general, but about the particular kind of hermeneutics required in light of the complex texture of God's self-revelation.[18] Biblical scholars who are not accustomed to reflecting on dogmatic distinctions for help with their exegesis may be somewhat puzzled at all the talk about the Trinity and the Bible. But then again, as Childs himself knew well, to read the Bible well is to read it in light of the God to whom it points.

---

18. An interesting corollary of the interconnection between the doctrine of God and biblical hermeneutics is that where our hermeneutics differ from Childs's, we may reasonably expect to find differences in how we conceive of the doctrine of God. Conversely, if we disagree with Childs about the way to frame the trinitarian doctrine of God, we should reasonably expect to disagree with him about how to read the Bible. To say it bluntly, the idea that we could simply analyze Childs's hermeneutical proposals without simultaneously grappling with a trinitarian notion of God is an error: but it is just this error that characterizes so much of the work on Childs's thought ("canonical criticism" and the like).

A Shared Reality:
Ontology in Brevard Childs's Isaiah Commentary

Mark Gignilliat

Introduction

This essay suggests that a significant feature of Childs's Isaiah commentary is its explicit and implicit challenge to think through the theological dimensions of Isaiah in light of its shared subject matter with the New Testament. Our attention will focus on this aspect of the commentary via two points of entry. First, this essay will critically engage a few aspects of Hugh Williamson's published reviews of Childs's *Isaiah* and *The Struggle to Understand Isaiah as Christian Scripture*. Williamson's stated concerns about Childs's approach help to clarify what is at stake in theological exegesis. Then our attention will focus on a few key places in the commentary where Childs attends to the theological character of the book in light of its shared subject matter with the New Testament. A few introductory comments are in order.

Brevard Childs was aware of the overworked genre of biblical commentary. In the preface to his *Isaiah* (2001) he mentions as much when reflecting on the ever-increasing numbers since the publication of his *Exodus* in 1974.¹ Why one more commentary on a book like Isaiah in the face of the detailed historical, philological and text-critical works of Wilderberger, Elliger, Oswalt, and others? Childs provides his readers with a characteristically sharp and straightforward rationale: "In my judgment, what is needed is a fresh interpretive model that does not get lost in methodological debates, and that proves to be illuminating in rendering

---

1. Brevard S. Childs, *The Book of Exodus: A Critical, Theological Commentary* (OTL; Philadelphia: Westminster, 1974).

a rich and coherent interpretation of the text as sacred scripture of both church and synagogue."[2] Childs sought to provide a holistic reading of Isaiah, a reading where the main line of thought and force of expression were not lost in the fray of methodological debate.

Moreover, Childs did not shy away from identifying the kind of text he was engaging as "sacred scripture." Such a claim is neither an *aperitif* nor a *digestive*. Rather, it is situated at the center of the exegetical task. He clarifies the hermeneutical significance of such a claim in the conclusion of his *Biblical Theology*:

> The basic theological argument developed in this Biblical Theology is that the unity of the two testaments is primarily a theological one. Attempts to focus on merely formal elements of religious continuity or discontinuity appear to me inadequate.... Rather what binds the testaments indissolubly together is their witness to the selfsame divine reality, to the subject matter, which undergirds both collections, and cannot be contained within the domesticating categories of "religion." Scripture is also not self-referential, but points beyond itself to the reality of God. The ability to render this reality is to enter the "strange new world of the Bible."[3]

This understanding of the text as sacred scripture provides the warrant and necessity for reading Isaiah in light of its shared subject matter, or in Childs's terms, shared reality with the New Testament. Isaiah witnesses to the one God of the two Testaments. Because this is so, the exegetical task itself must be shaped by such a confession.

Childs's stated intention for writing another commentary in no way attenuates his broad and deep knowledge of Isaiah scholarship. Childs had taught Isaiah since 1954. His detailed and disciplined attention to secondary scholarship provided him a command over the major shifts in critical approaches to Isaiah during the twentieth century—literary criticism, form criticism, redaction criticism, and rhetorical analysis. He was also aware, though disparaging, of recent postmodern, reader-centered approaches to

---

2. Brevard S. Childs, *Isaiah: A Commentary* (OTL; Louisville: Westminster John Knox, 2001), xi.
3. Brevard S. Childs, *Biblical Theology of the Old and New Testaments: Theological Reflections on the Christian Bible* (Minneapolis: Fortress, 1992), 721 (see also 345, 724). Hereafter, *BTONT*.

reading Isaiah (e.g., Conrad's).[4] Childs was a master of the field and could make direct or side comments with ease to various interlocutors whom he thought in need of correction or redirection. Nevertheless, Childs did not want to let a commentary on a sixty-six chapter book become bogged down in the minutiae of scholarly debate. In this regard, von Rad's semipopular Genesis commentary was Childs's exemplar, rather than the trenchant and detailed three-volume work of Westermann. Childs was after something different in his Isaiah commentary.

A DIFFERENT KIND OF COMMENTARY

But what exactly was different? In reviews both of Childs's *Isaiah* and *The Struggle to Understand Isaiah as Christian Scripture*, Hugh Williamson queries in the same direction. The first review is a pointedly critical review of Childs's *Isaiah*.[5] Williamson affirms Childs's concern to negotiate the complex relationship between the synchronic and diachronic aspects of the text, even though Williamson finds Childs confusing on this front. Williamson understands Childs's terminology, "coercion of the biblical text," as simply redaction criticism under a *nom de plume*.[6]

---

4. Edgar Conrad, *Reading Isaiah* (OBT; Minneapolis: Fortress, 1991).
5. H. G. M. Williamson, review of Brevard S. Childs, *Isaiah*, *ThTo* 59 (2002): 121–24.
6. Without chasing this rabbit too far, Childs's trouble with redaction critics is not their identification of a depth dimension in the text. Rather, it is the confidence often attached to their diachronic reconstruction, the necessity afforded this reconstruction, and the tendency to attenuate the hermeneutical imprint made on the final form of the material as itself an associative achievement and not just the final stage in the tradition-building process whose intention is located in the final redactor/tradents. One of many examples where Childs, while affirming a complex compositional history, distances his approach from redaction criticism's governing instincts is found in his critical engagement with the *Denkschrift* hypothesis (Childs, *Isaiah*, 44): "Crucial to the redactional method is the hermeneutical assumption that the biblical text is only correctly interpreted when texts are calibrated according to a reconstructed editorial process." The end of such an approach—in this case, the particular notion that eschatological elements are only located in the postexilic redaction, e.g., Isa 5:30—is "a critically reconstructed redactional scheme that runs roughshod over the canonical shape of the biblical text itself." The result of a tenacious attention to diachronic reconstruction is a presentation of the text quite at odds with the self-presentation of the material in its canonical form. In itself, this kind of re-presentation faces the *historical* problem of the tradents' shaping of the material in such a way as to preserve its

Williamson raises critical concerns that are all worthy of fuller investigation. I would like to focus attention on the neuralgic point that I believe Williamson finds most sensitive: Childs's interpretive approach vis-à-vis modern critical scholars. Williamson's trouble is as follows: "He [Childs] is frequently able to show how modern studies of a topic have reached an impasse or remain in severe disagreement, only to suggest that his reading points the way forward."[7] For Williamson, those Childs criticizes are asking different questions of the text than he is, and in Williamson's estimation the different interpretive quests should be respected, not castigated. "Since Childs and those he criticizes are asking different questions (whose legitimacy at a certain level he does not deny; they simply are not engaging in theological interpretation), I find this approach disingenuous."[8]

A similar note is rung in Williamson's review of *The Struggle*.[9] After praising the depth and breadth of Childs's handling of the Christian interpretive tradition, Williamson again raises the contemporary question he feels inevitably follows Childs's line of argument—"whether any exegesis that is not confessionally Christian is automatically deficient."[10] Williamson suggests nonconfessional, modern criticism is valid on its own terms and may be of service to those involved in theological interpretation. This suggestion is readily on offer in the guild today, even if for postmodern critique the latent a priori objectivity of such an account seems reminiscent of a bygone day.[11]

---

enduring character as a witness, i.e., the text's canonical intentionality. Likewise, see Childs's comments on Isa 6:13b in relation to diachronic reconfiguration (*Isaiah*, 59). Especially important on this account is Stephen Chapman, *The Law and the Prophets: A Study in Old Testament Canon Formation* (FAT 27; Tübingen: Mohr Siebeck, 2000), 93–110. Childs understands this canonical shaping as an internal *regula fidei* providing interpretive guidelines for reading the text as sacred scripture. See Brevard S. Childs, "Speech-Act Theory and Biblical Interpretation," *SJT* 58 (2005): 383–84.

7. Williamson, review of Childs, *Isaiah*, 124.
8. Ibid.
9. H. G. M. Williamson, review of Brevard S. Childs, *The Struggle to Understand Isaiah as Christian Scripture*, RBL (2005). Online: http://bookreviews.org/pdf/4494_4551.pdf.
10. Williamson, review of Childs, *Struggle*, 4.
11. Frederick Norris's account of Gregory of Nazianzen's Christian exegesis frames the issue well: "But too often there is a modern fantasy that the paradigm against which ancient insights, whether grammatical, historical or allegorical, must be judged is the 'objective' historical, critical exegesis of the modern era. Such pristine objectivity has never existed except as an ethereal goal." Frederick Norris, "Gregory Nazianzen:

Williamson's suggestion is straightforward and the history of Christian interpretation itself would affirm it, for example, in the Reformers' use of rabbinic Hebrew grammar and lexicography.[12] Childs himself was a student of Walter Baumgartner, an avowedly nonconfessional Hebrew scholar. No student of the Hebrew text can afford dismissing Koehler/Baumgartner's lexicon because it is "nonconfessional." In short, it is a straw man (and I do not think Williamson is claiming such) to suggest practitioners of canonical hermeneutics or theological interpretation find no value in nonconfessional exegesis. In fact, nothing could be further from the truth.[13]

What then is the friction Williamson is trying to identify? I would suggest the friction is located in an aside Williamson makes when defending his perspective. "The alternative perspective, to which I want, at least, to adhere, is that such work is valid on its own terms, and although it does not express itself confessionally, it may nevertheless be of service to those who write in that vein (and indeed to myself when I do so *separately*)."[14] The *different* kind of commentary Childs is after is one that questions the bifurcation of the literal and the figural, of the exegetical and theological, of the *signum* and the *res*. Modern criticism's approach to exegesis tends to treat the literary, historical, philological, and text-critical aspects of exegesis as the task in toto, whereas Childs wants to demonstrate that for Christian exegesis this first step is not the task *simpliciter* but is indeed one step in a multilayered *single* reading of the text.

Constructing and Constructed by Scripture," in *The Bible in Greek Christian Antiquity* (ed. P. Blowers; Notre Dame, Ind.: University of Notre Dame Press, 1997), 149–50.

12. On the wide spectrum of opinions between Christian Hebraists of the early sixteenth century and their use of Jewish commentaries and philological scholarship, see Stephen G. Burnett, "Reassessing the 'Basel-Wittenberg Conflict': Dimensions of the Reformation-Era Discussion of Hebrew Scholarship," in *Hebraica Veritas?: Christian Hebraists and the Study of Judaism in Early Modern Europe* (ed. A. P. Coudert and J. S. Shoulson; Philadelphia: University of Pennsylvania Press, 2004), 181–201. Though Luther had strong misgivings about the use of Jewish scholarship, Johannes Mathesius described the translation committee meeting of 1540 as follows: "Dr. Martin Luther came ... with the Old Latin and new German Bible in addition to the Hebrew text. Herr Philip [Melanchthon] brought the Greek text, and Dr. Cruciger both the Hebrew Bible and the Targum. The professors all brought their rabbis." Quoted in Burnett, "Reassessing," 194.

13. Williamson's own very learned commentary on Isa 1–5 is a case in point.

14. Williamson, review of Childs, *Struggle*, 4, emphasis added.

Williamson appeals to the incarnational analogy as warrant for this "separate" attendance to the literal sense of the text: Christ's human nature justifies exegesis of the literal sense alone.[15] The appeal to the incarnational analogy is something of a trend among evangelical biblical scholars today who are seeking to preserve the historical and creaturely nature of the Bible.[16] It should be said that there are theological problems with the appeal to Chalcedon in this context, least of which is the fact that the Bible is not divine.[17] Nevertheless, and in light of its broad use, the incarnational analogy can be helpful in shedding light on the interpretive sensibilities of those who deploy it.

At first glance, the appeal seems to work regarding the human character of scripture in light of the human nature of Christ. Docetic accounts of both are problematic. When pressed, however, such renderings attenuate the core value the bishops of Chalcedon sought to maintain, namely, that Christ's human nature is not a single subject (*hypostasis*) whose properties can be predicated. Nestorius was concerned to protect the human nature of Jesus, a laudable effort in light of Nicene trinitarian thought and the dangers of Apollinarianism—the logos took the place of the soul/mind of the man Jesus Christ, thus attenuating Jesus Christ's full humanity. Nevertheless, his efforts were trumped at Chalcedon because his Christology failed to protect the single subject, who is Jesus Christ, fully God, fully man.[18]

---

15. The literal sense, that is, separated from its spiritual or theological sense. On the literal sense in antiquity and modernity, see Brevard S. Childs, "The Sensus Literalis of Scripture: An Ancient and Modern Problem," in *Beiträge zur Alttestamentlichen Theologie* (ed. H. Donner et al.; Göttingen: Vandenhoeck & Ruprecht, 1977), 80-93.

16. Notably, Peter Enns, *Inspiration and Incarnation: Evangelicals and the Problem of the Old Testament* (Grand Rapids: Baker, 2005); Kenton Sparks, *God's Word in Human Words: An Evangelical Appropriation of Critical Biblical Scholarship* (Grand Rapids: Eerdmans, 2008); and from a theological perspective, Telford Work, *Living and Active: Scripture in the Economy of Salvation* (Grand Rapids: Eerdmans, 2008).

17. John Webster has a good account of the problems in his *Holy Scripture: A Dogmatic Sketch* (Cambridge: Cambridge University Press, 2003).

18. In fairness, the highly intellectual Christology of Nestorius is not done justice in this rehearsal. See John McGuckin, *Cyril of Alexandria and the Christological Controversy* (Yonkers, N.Y.: St. Vladimir's Seminary Press, 2004), esp. ch. 2; Aloys Grillmeier, S.J., *Christ in Tradition: From the Apostolic Age to Chalcedon (451)* (trans. J. S. Bowden; London: Mowbray, 1964).

If we press the analogy, again for the sake of revealing hermeneutical instincts, Childs resists the Nestorian tendency to predicate an activity on the human nature of scripture alone—"separately" in the face of Chalcedon's "without separation"—apart from its hypostatic union with the divine in a single subject.[19] There is only one subject in whom the two natures are fully operative without separation or confusion, without division or change. I would suggest these instincts in Childs are what set his approach over against the "Nestorian" tendency of modern biblical criticism: the creaturely character of scripture is investigated in its own right (as a separate *prosopon*) without recourse to its indivisible connection to the single subject of the one Bible, human and divine. Moreover, and despite the success or failure of the incarnational analogy in this context, the character of the biblical witness demands from its readers attention to its creaturely reality and divine author in a single subject, namely, Holy Scripture. To isolate the one from the other runs roughshod over what Childs called the Old Testament's canonical intentionality. Childs's concern about the Old Testament's witness to the one God of the two Testaments reflects his theological commitment to a certain *kind* of Old Testament exegesis—an approach that at the end of the day cannot be separated from formal and material commitments to Christian theology. The subject matter of the biblical text puts pressure on the particular methods used to read and interpret it.

In the preface to *Isaiah*, Childs makes a strategic comment about the relationship between his magnum opus, *Biblical Theology of the Old and New Testament*, and the task of biblical exegesis. Ever concerned about trajectories set by scholarly voices, Childs was self-aware enough to concede that his *Biblical Theology* had made little impact on the field of biblical exegesis. In other words, Childs found it irksome that a work on the scale of his *Biblical Theology* would be placed on the theological bookshelf without making a fuller impact on the exegesis of the Bible.

With language reminiscent of Calvin's rationale for the *Institutes*, Childs clarifies the purpose of his *Biblical Theology*: "For my part, I have always considered biblical theology to be only an ancillary discipline that better serves in equipping the exegete for the real task of interpreting the text itself."[20] As important as the task of biblical theology is for providing

---

19. I.e., the humanity of Christ is anhypostatic to his divinity.
20. Childs, *Isaiah*, xii.

a wide-angled vision, it should never circumvent or supersede the task of attending to the biblical texts themselves. Rather, it should aid the reading of the texts in their canonical shape, cross-referencing associative relationships and shared subject matter.[21] In this canonical dynamic the communicative potential of scripture is unleashed by the power of the Holy Spirit. These governing theological instincts embedded at every turn in Childs's vast literary output reveal the necessity of ontological concerns in the task of Old Testament exegesis. For the remainder of this essay, I will probe a few key places in the commentary where Childs pursues this line of thought.

There are several junctures in the commentary where Childs focuses his attention on the theological dimension of the text or the shared reality between Old and New Testaments. Many of these instances are the usual suspects one would anticipate in Isaiah's corpus, the running chords of Handel's "Messiah" providing appropriate background music. For example, despite the oracular character of the original *Sitz im Leben* and the intention of that given moment, Isa 7:14 is now located canonically in the Immanuel traditions which extend into chapters 8 and 9. This canonical shaping of the material elicits a messianic and eschatological reading of this text that looks forward in anticipation for the messianic ruler who will sit on David's throne and bring eternal peace.[22]

Childs does not refer to the New Testament in his explication of the Immanuel traditions of Isa 7-9: an initially surprising fact. Here is a case in point where Childs allows the discrete character of the Old Testament's construal of the matter to have its own say. Whether Childs intended this or not, the net effect of such a reading for those who affirm the shared subject matter between Old and New Testaments is a loud christological presence by absence—an act of metalepsis where the reader is intended to extend the reading. Barth uses the metaphor of Jesus knocking on the door of the Old Testament. He is present even in his bodily absence. This presence by anticipation preserves the character of the Old Testament's role as

---

21. For Childs, the exegetical and theological encounter within the Old Testament presupposes "that a relation of some sort is assumed between the life and history of Israel and that of Jesus Christ" (*BTONT*, 98).

22. Reflective of this reading are the comments Childs makes on Isa 8:16–18: "Originally, Isaiah may have simply hoped for a better time in the future, but when this oracle was placed within the context of his larger literary corpus, there emerges with great force a relentless openness to the future, which has been propelled forward by an eschatological vision of the whole creation within the one divine purpose" (*Isaiah*, 76).

promise without collapsing it into fulfillment. Isaiah 7:14 is an example of many places where Childs's eschatological rereading of Isaiah elicits a kind of theological treasure trove for further biblical theological reflection.[23] The constraints of the OTL commentary format did not allow Childs the needed space to explore these dimensions more.[24] There are, however, a few places where Childs draws out the ontological connections between Old and New Testaments for the reader more fully. The two primary places are Isa 53 and 61.

CASES-IN-POINT: ISAIAH 53 AND 61

Childs addresses two issues in his theological reflection on Isa 53. The first is the historical-critical approach that locates the influence, or lack thereof, of Isa 53 in the New Testament by reconstructing the history of traditions leading to the composition of New Testament documents. "Conservative" biblical scholars like Peter Stuhlmacher and Martin Hengel tend to see the Old Testament leaning toward the New, and "liberal" scholars such as Rudolph Bultmann and Morna Hooker view it in the reverse, viewing the idea of a suffering servant as a late Hellenistic development with no place in the consciousness of the historical Jesus. Childs is quick to point out the shared interpretive instincts of both groups. "Both therefore seek to ground their positions on a historical-critical reconstruction of the history of tradition."[25]

The problems with a critical reconstruction of a unidirectional tradition—leaning toward the New or retrojected back to the Old—are manifold. First, theologically speaking, it is a dead end to play the "mind of Jesus" over against the scriptural witness. Hans Frei's slim but penetrating analysis of the identity of Jesus argues forcefully that gospel readers only have access to the aim and intentions of Jesus Christ through the storied character of the fourfold gospel—one understands Jesus' identity and "self-understanding" through his words and actions witnessed to in the gospels.[26] This means there is no "mind of Jesus" to be discovered, other

---

23. On eschatological rereading of the prophets, see Brevard S. Childs, "Retrospective Reading of the Old Testament Prophets," *ZAW* 108 (1996): 362–77.
24. Childs says so himself (*Isaiah*, 420).
25. Ibid., 421.
26. Hans Frei, *The Identity of Jesus Christ: The Hermeneutical Basis of Dogmatic Theology* (Philadelphia: Fortress, 1975).

than the one presented in the scriptural witness. Childs's understanding here reflects a thorough commitment to both the formal and the material sufficiency of the fourfold gospel.[27]

Second, the history of traditions whose tendency is to identify a single direction forward or an anachronistic look backward fails to take into account "the dynamic" at work. This dynamic is located in the canonical force of the Old Testament on the New Testament's compositional history, and the hermeneutical significance for rereading the Old Testament in light of the apocalyptic unveiling of Jesus Christ.[28] The Old Testament—Isa 40–55 in particular—had a "decisive force" in the compositional history of the New Testament. At the same time, the gospel provided a hermeneutical lens for rereading the Old Testament. The flattening of this dynamic creates hermeneutical problems in the face of the material character of Christian scripture as a two-Testament canon in dialectic relationship around a shared subject matter.

The second issue Childs attends to is the suffering servant and Christian theology. To my mind, the issues become more interesting at this point because theological exegesis of the text itself is at the foreground and not New Testament reception per se. The issues discussed above are the instincts of the canonical approach to biblical theology and the relationship of the Testaments that, for those familiar with the canonical approach, will come as no surprise.[29] At this point, Childs turns his attention to the ontological character of the witness apart from its New Testament reception. The focus on the discrete character of the Old Testament's Christian theological voice is important to the overall argument of this essay.

Childs, along with the modern critical readings, resists the identification of the suffering servant as a future prophecy or "a timeless metaphor

---

27. On the formal and material sufficiency of scripture, see Timothy Ward, *Word and Supplement: Speech-Acts, Biblical Texts, and the Sufficiency of Scripture* (Oxford: Oxford University Press, 2002).

28. Childs's later work on the New Testament spoke often of the importance of "apocalyptic" in approaching the subject matter of the New Testament and in his understanding of the canonical form of the Christian Bible as Old and New Testaments. The "in-breaking" of the gospel and the anterior character of the Old Testament as something that had to end before the new began are part and parcel of Childs's trouble with the history of traditions and *Heilsgeschichtliche* approaches to biblical theology.

29. See Christopher Seitz, *The Character of Christian Scripture: The Significance of a Two-Testament Bible* (Grand Rapids: Baker, 2011).

of the suffering nation of Israel."[30] For Childs the suffering servant is a real historical figure of the sixth century. Where Childs differs from historical-critical treatment is in his understanding of the continued canonical function of the material. Though the events attested in Isa 49:1–6 and 53:1–11 are the product of a real space/time encounter between God, the servant figure, and exilic Israel, the reception of the material in Isaiah's prophetic corpus loosens the material from its historical particularity in order to function as an enduring witness and prophetic challenge to the people of God. The servant is no longer a mere figure of the past, but a continuing theological force in the redeemed community of Israel.

Childs's discomfort with the traditional reading of Isa 53 as prophecy and fulfillment is located in this complex. His trouble is not with the net result of such a reading. In fact, Childs is also concerned about the christological character of this well-known text. The discomfort is the path chosen to arrive at the christological interpretation. The traditional reading as mortar shot prophecy of Jesus neuters the text of its own character and mutes its particular idiomatic construal. Isaiah 53 in its canonical form is not presented as a prophecy looking forward—an issue critical scholars have pointed out for some time. It is, in fact, presented as a rehearsal looking backward at something that occurred, and now in its canonical placement it functions as prophecy anticipating an unfolding in the divine economy. Childs's reading is sensitive to the self-presentation of the material. The result is a theologically textured reading, more impasto than flat brush strokes.

Isaiah 53 is an enduring account of a real historical event and is not a mythopoetic construal of an idealized figure. At the same time, the subject matter of this text relates ontologically to the person and work of Jesus Christ. That is, a figural association exists between the servant of Isa 53 and Jesus. But—and this is a crucial point to observe—the typological relationship is not a mere literary construct foisted upon the text. Quite to the contrary, the typological relationship is an ontological one; it flows out of the very nature of the thing itself. The relationship is not identified on a temporal or causal basis, what Auerbach identifies as the horizontal dimension. The figural relationship is "vertically linked" in divine providence; the identification of which is an article of faith.[31] There is one

---

30. Childs, *Isaiah*, 422.
31. Eric Auerbach, *Mimesis: The Representation of Reality in Western Literature* (50th anniversary edition; Princeton: Princeton University Press, 2003), 73–74.

divine economy in and through and with which our Triune God reveals himself. The suffering servant's role in the divine economy is a figural anticipation, ontologically related to the ultimate dénouement of God's self-presentation and self-determination to be this kind of God and not another. Childs concludes, "The morphological fit between Isaiah 53 and the passion of Jesus continues to bear testimony to the common subject matter within the one divine economy."[32] In God's divine economy, the suffering and death of an innocent one in the place of transgressors (*Stellvertretung*) is God's means for redeeming Israel and the nations. Isaiah 53 does anticipate the future, now understood retrospectively in the unveiling of Jesus Christ in the divine economy. It does so, however, on the ontological level of shared reality, not merely on the level of forward-looking prophecy.

In light of the shared reality between the Testaments, Childs's handling of Isa 61 proves interesting as well. With this well-known text—located in the lections of Advent—Childs does engage the question of Old Testament reception in the New. But he does so by allowing the canonical shape of Isaiah's own witness to expand our horizons about the kind of relationship that exists between Isa 61 and Luke 4. Admittedly, Childs's comments here are more laconic than those on Isa 53. Though brief, Childs's handling of Isa 61 in light of its shared subject matter with the New Testament is illuminating.

Childs expresses surprise that Luke 4 is not given more weight regarding the question posed earlier about the servant and Jesus Christ. After all, the "servant songs" are a modern construct proposed by Bernhard Duhm. Their application to the New Testament writers obfuscates more than clarifies matters. In the character of the canonical shape of Isaiah, chapter 61 is organically linked to themes and images from the servant material of Isa 40–55.[33] Childs leans on Beuken's account of Isa 61's relation to Isa 40–55. For Beuken, the agents in Isa 61 are the servants of the servant, or the righteous offspring promised to the servant in Isa 53:10. These figures are identified as righteous (צדיק), seed (זרע), or servants (עבד) throughout

---

32. Childs, *Isaiah*, 423.
33. See W. A. M. Beuken, "The Main Theme of 'Trito'-Isaiah: The Servants of YHWH," *JSOT* 47 (1990): 67–87; Beuken, "Servant and Herald of Good Things: Isaiah 61 as an Interpretation of Isaiah 40–55," in *Le Livre D'Isaïe: Les oracles et leurs relectures: unité et complexité de l'ouvrage* (ed. J. Vermeylen; Leuven: Leuven University Press, 1989), 411–42.

Isa 54–66. In brief, the characters who announce liberation in Isa 61 are not the servant per se, but the servant's offspring.

What do we do then with Jesus' reading Isa 61:1–3a in the synagogue, and his reference to the scriptures as fulfilled in their sight? How does this coalesce with the material as presented in Isa 61? A mortar-shot approach to prophecy and fulfillment would render such questions insignificant. The liberating agent is Jesus, full stop. But for Childs, the literary character of Isa 61 within the shape of Isaiah's unified canonical witness invites the reader to view the picture in color, with more hue and shading than previously offered. Childs concludes, "Rather, a case can be made that Jesus himself ushers in the acceptable year of the Lord, and thus the citation of Isaiah 61 encompasses the entire mission of the servant, including his life, death, and offspring."[34] Because of the coercive pressure of Isaiah's construal of the acting agents within its literary context, an invitation is on offer to reread both Isa 61 and Luke 4 in light of their shared subject matter. Though Childs does not use Augustine's ecclesial language of *totus Christus*, the material insight is present in this reading. Since Isa 61's speaking agents are the servants of the servant, and since Jesus in Luke 4 speaks of the text as fulfilled in him, then the theological force of *totus Christus* is present. Because of their shared subject matter, both texts, in the combustion of their dialectic relationship and without the one being collapsed into the other, present a robust account of Jesus' embodied person and work. Jesus can speak of himself and his ecclesial body as a single reality: "Saul, Saul, why are your persecuting me" (Acts 9:4)?

What is of hermeneutical significance is the way Isa 61's own literary and theological character—a character located in the nexus between servant and servants—provides a sharper and deeper understanding of the shared subject matter between these two texts. Put crudely, it will not do on the level of theological exegesis to say, "This text is about Jesus." Though this is in fact true, the particular character and shape of the witness demands the theological reader of scripture to ask, "In what way(s) does this text, both in its particularity and canonical association with other texts, reveal the identity and ways of God?" How does the particular literary and theological character of this text in its canonical location shape our understanding of God's revelation of himself in Jesus Christ? For these two texts, the relationship between servant and servants (offspring), or in christological terms the

---

34. Childs, *Isaiah*, 507–8.

184 THE BIBLE AS CHRISTIAN SCRIPTURE

indissoluble bond between the person and work of Jesus, is a theological judgment whose warrant is located in the mind of scripture itself. Childs's brief theological comments which follow a careful reading of the text(s) provide a theological exegetical rationale for such a judgment.

CONCLUSION

There is a challenge imbedded in Childs's Isaiah commentary, a clarion call to pick up the torch and follow on in an ongoing struggle with Old Testament exegesis in light of its shared subject matter with the New, namely, the self-disclosure of the one God who is Father, Son, and Holy Spirit. Childs indicates his concern to do justice to the shared reality of the Old and New Testaments, though he hedges because the scope of such a project becomes unwieldy, given the length of Isaiah and the constraints of the commentary's genre. I do find this aspect of Childs's commentary lamentable. Maybe as a reader I want to have my cake and eat it too. Nevertheless, I do wish Childs had attempted two things in the commentary. I would have enjoyed seeing him integrate his theological reflections into the actual exegetical material itself, and not relegate it for the most part to theological excurses. Second, it would have been helpful to see Childs engage texts on the level of shared reality that do not have a direct New Testament citation or reception, for instance, the literary shift at play in Isa 49:1–6 between Israel as servant and the servant as something other than empirical Israel.[35]

Despite these wishes, there are indicators for a "go and do likewise" challenge within the Isaiah commentary that needs to be worked out for those involved in theological exegesis. As I believe Childs would want it, he is pointing in a direction rather than situating his approach as a final destination. I believe these matters require special attention for biblical scholars who are bound by confession to a certain understanding of the identity and character of God and his sacred text.

---

35. This issue is of some importance in Childs's *Biblical Theology*, the Old Testament's Christian witness beyond the Old received in the New (*vetus testamentum in novo receptum*). A nuanced account is found in Seitz's *The Character of Christian Scripture*.

A Tale of Two Testaments:
Childs, Old Testament Torah,
and *Heilsgeschichte*

Don Collett

In what sense are the commandments of the Old Testament the expression of the true will of God for Israel and the church? Is there no continuity between the old covenant and the new? The resolution requires careful theological formulation and is far from simplistic in nature. Aspects of the relationship can be formulated both eschatologically in terms of *Heilsgeschichte* and ontologically in terms of substance. The subject matter of both biblical witnesses is ultimately christological, but the relationship is best formulated dialectically rather than in abstract terms of typology. In the light of God's action in Jesus Christ, the just demands of the law (Rom 8) have been fulfilled; however, the "just demands" are still God's will for his creation. Because of Christ's act in overcoming sin, the law, which is "holy, just and good" (Rom 7:12), is no longer held captive to pervert the Old Testament law by turning it into a false avenue toward rectification (7:13). For this reason the Christian still hears the true voice of God in the Old Testament, but it is a Scripture that has been transformed because of what God in Christ has done.[1]

With these words Brevard Childs sought to describe the distinction between Old Testament Torah and the law of Christ within the overarching theological context generated by the dialectical relationship of the two Testaments. In his many publications as a Christian OT scholar, Childs maintained a high view of and theological appreciation for OT Torah in both its broad and more restricted senses.[2] To cite but one example, in

---

1. Brevard S. Childs, *The Church's Guide for Reading Paul: The Canonical Shaping of the Pauline Corpus* (Grand Rapids: Eerdmans, 2008), 121–22.
2. I have here in mind "Torah" as a reference to the OT as a whole, as well as

a summary reflection on the theological implications of OT law, Childs writes: "The Law of God was a gift of God which was instituted for the joy and edification of the covenant people. It was not given as a burden, but as a highest treasure and a clear sign of divine favour.... The clearest sign of the brokenness of the covenant and of the alienation of Israel from God emerged when his Law became a burden and a means of destroying the nation."[3] Toward the end of his life, this positive appreciation for OT Torah, especially the Mosaic law, also found expression in his last book, published posthumously, titled *The Church's Guide for Reading Paul: The Canonical Shaping of the Pauline Corpus*. Characteristic in this respect is the concern Childs registers with J. Louis Martyn's reading of Paul in Gal 3: "Although Martyn correctly recognizes the different senses of Paul's handling of the law, in the end the positive voice of the law continues to be only the pre-Sinai voice, the law's original voice, the voice of God's promise to Abraham. The Sinai voice remains from the old aeon, the bearer of the curse, the source of death and tyranny."[4] Over against Martyn, Childs's own assessment of Paul's reading of Israel's salvation history leads him to conclude that the Mosaic law "has also a positive role for Paul."[5]

"Torah" in the more restricted sense of the Mosaic law delivered to Israel in the context of the Sinai covenant.

3. Brevard S. Childs, *Old Testament Theology in a Canonical Context* (Philadelphia: Fortress, 1986), 57.

4. Childs, *Church's Guide*, 106. See the further exposition of the hermeneutical assumptions and exegetical details accompanying Martyn's reading on pages 99–103, 119–20. Commenting on the antithesis Paul registers in Gal 3 between justification through obedience to the Mosaic law and justification by faith, Childs judges that Martyn's construal of this antithesis "threatens to identify the law with a demonic tyranny" by pressing the theme of discontinuity "to an unwarranted extreme" (104). As a result of this misreading, "Even Paul's subsequent 'apology' for the law to serve as an 'addition' because of transgression (3:19) does not fully remove its denigrating function that is further made by mention of the law's being mediated by angels (3:19) to become a vehicle of God's curse. Martyn continues to refer to the Sinai law as given 'in the absence of God,' which interpretation presses the theme of discontinuity to an unwarranted extreme (see Acts 7:53)."

5. Childs, *Church's Guide*, 103–7, quote from 107. Over against Martyn's reading of the Pauline letter collection, Childs argues that the NT process of canonical shaping placed Romans at the head of the Pauline letter collection in order to serve as a hermeneutical guide for reading those letters. The positive view of the law adopted by Paul in Rom 7 is thus not to be interpreted as a later correction of an allegedly negative view reflected in his earlier letter to Galatia (99–103, esp. 102).

While it would be presumptuous to attempt to do justice in this memorial essay to the scope of the hermeneutical issues probed by Childs in *The Church's Guide*, one issue that merits further exploration is Paul's use of the concept of *Heilsgeschichte* to interpret Israel's history, especially in connection with the negative construals of the Law of Moses it has sometimes authorized. Such construals tend to form a natural alliance with currents in New Testament scholarship that virtually identify biblical theology with NT theology, a tendency noted by Childs himself.[6] For his own part, in *The Church's Guide* Childs freely recognized that Paul made use of "salvation history" as a lens for reading OT Torah, especially in Romans, but also in Galatians.[7] His concern was not to dismiss categorically its validity as a hermeneutical category, but to alert his readers to the potential it has for distorting our understanding of the true nature of the discontinuities between the OT law delivered at Sinai and the Pauline notion of "the law of Christ," especially when it is either misconstrued vis-à-vis Paul's apocalyptical theology[8] or overburdened by enlisting it as a model for uniting the Testaments.[9]

---

6. For Childs, this raises an important hermeneutical issue, namely, "whether an emphasis on *Heilsgeschichte* tends to imply that theological reflection on the Bible always proceeds in one direction, namely, from the Old to the New. At times one gains the impression that for some biblical scholars biblical theology is New Testament theology which retains a certain 'openness' to the Old Testament as the origin of certain traditions and the source of New Testament imagery" (*Biblical Theology of the Old and New Testaments: Theological Reflection on the Christian Bible* [Minneapolis: Fortress, 1992], 17). Hereafter, *BTONT*.

7. Childs, *Church's Guide*, 211. Childs suggests that Martyn, in his reading of Galatians, "much like his mentor Käsemann, has included within the overarching umbrella of apocalyptic, subject matter that is, at best, only indirectly related to apocalyptic, such as the 'righteousness of God,' justification by faith, participation in Christ's crucifixion, and baptism into Christ." He then goes on to raise a question: "Could not one argue that a phrase such as 'the fullness of time' (4:4) derives equally well from the framework of *Heilsgeschichte* and is akin, say, to Hebrews 1:1?"

8. For example, Childs argues that a canonically misplaced understanding of Paul's apocalyptical theology in Galatians can skew our understanding of the "full richness" of Paul's "*heilsgeschichtliche* approach" to the Mosaic law in Romans (Childs, *Church's Guide*, 111–12). In addition to misunderstanding the hermeneutical role assigned to Romans by the canonical shaping of the NT (122), this also ignores the corrective the letter to the Hebrews offers for our understanding of "a historically oriented *Heilsgeschichte* within a Pauline apocalyptic vision" (251).

9. See Childs's criticisms of Oscar Cullmann's linear concept of *Heilsgeschichte*, as

Rather than attempting to address all the arguments typically appealed to in support of negative assessments of the law bestowed upon Israel at Sinai, in keeping with the spirit of Childs's own assessment of Paul's reading of OT Torah, my purpose will be twofold. First, I will interact with a few of the key NT texts typically appealed to in support of this negative assessment, namely, Paul's reading of the law in Gal 3–4 and 2 Cor 3. In the course of this interaction it will become clear that these appeals cannot be fully appreciated in their true character apart from their relation to particular construals of Israel's salvation history, the hermeneutical effect of which is either to misconstrue Paul's reading of the Mosaic law, or to identify the voice of OT Torah with the post-fall order of sin and death. By way of a constructive alternative, I will suggest that the OT Torah itself provides models for the *Christian* character of Paul's teaching on formation in Gal 4 and 2 Cor 3, models that ultimately find their ground in an abiding theological ontology of God's character and glory from which the OT Torah cannot be separated. This being the case, construals of Israel's salvation history that reduce the voice of OT Torah to its probationary and death-dealing function should be rejected, or at least substantially modified.

Following this, I will turn to a larger discussion of the hermeneutical assumptions for construing the Testaments often found riding "piggyback" on these readings of Paul. While for a number of Pauline scholars in our day, the category of "story" seems to have emerged as a successor to *Heilsgeschichte*,[10] it nevertheless remains true that the reign of salvation history as a historical model for uniting the Testaments is far from passé. A number of NT scholars not only continue to make use of salvation history as a paradigm for interpreting the ongoing significance of OT Torah in the life of the NT church, but also as a model for uniting the Testaments. In any case, as my later remarks will suggest, the hermeneutical category of story shares at least one significant feature in common with salvation history as a model for relating the Testaments. Failure to appreciate this can only lead to misunderstanding this essay's larger purpose, namely, to bring under critical scrutiny a hermeneutical framework for uniting the two Testaments that originated as a form of *Heilsgeschichte* during the nineteenth century and continues to reverberate in our own day.

---

well as his later remarks on the corrective to this perspective offered by the canonical function of the letter to the Hebrews (*Church's Guide*, 201–2, 239–40).

10. Childs, *Church's Guide*, 182.

It should be added before proceeding further that this last-mentioned topic is fully in keeping with one of Childs's major concerns in his later publications, a concern perhaps best illustrated by relating an anecdote passed on to me by Christopher Seitz some years ago. A student once approached Childs to ask his opinion of Bernhard Anderson's bestselling book *The Living World of the Old Testament*, a highly popular introduction in its day that passed through four editions.[11] Childs's witty response to the student's inquiry was, "It's better than the Bible." The anecdote serves to remind us that a popular approach or paradigm for interpreting the Bible can easily replace the Bible itself, and in this respect, *Heilsgeschichte* is no exception. It also sheds light upon Childs's own understanding of the task of biblical scholarship by reminding us that his goal as an exegete of scripture was not to create yet another "school" of biblical interpretation, but rather to stress the hermeneutical primacy of the canon's own construal over against modern substitutes.[12]

A Tale of Two Paradigms for Construing OT Torah

It may be helpful to begin by briefly discussing two approaches to relating the Testaments, one modern and the other ancient, in order to help contextualize the hermeneutical issues at stake. The arguments in late modernity over the OT Torah's nature and function take place in a number of hermeneutical contexts, one of which dominated biblical studies up until the late twentieth century. In this context, appeals to Paul often derive their authorizing logic from a particular salvation-historical paradigm for relating the Testaments. The point at issue does not concern the use of the term "salvation history" *per se*, since the term itself reflects a biblical concept. Rather, the point in dispute turns upon the hermeneutical function this category has been assigned in conjunction with the rise of historical

---

11. The book was published in the United States under the title *Understanding the Old Testament* and is now available in a fifth edition.

12. "To work from the final form is to resist any method which seeks critically to shift the canonical ordering. Such an exegetical move occurs whenever an overarching category such as *Heilsgeschichte* subordinates the peculiar canonical profile, or a historical critical reconstruction attempts to refocus the picture according to its own standards of aesthetics or historical accuracy" (Brevard S. Childs, *Introduction to the Old Testament as Scripture* [Philadelphia: Fortress, 1979], 77).

consciousness in the modern period.[13] In a modern salvation-historical approach to the Testaments, biblical theology is essentially NT theology, since *forward* movement from the OT into the NT constitutes its defining feature, whether through a doctrine of progressive revelation,[14] or via a forward-thrusting tradition history powered by a historicized theory of actualization (*Vergegenwärtigung*).[15] Native to this paradigm are the twin assumptions that the NT's use of the Old is constitutive for not only what it means to do biblical theology, but also for what it means to read the OT as Christian scripture.

It would be a mistake to limit the influence of this paradigm to the past, or to the rarified air of academic circles, for it often finds popular expression in introductions and handbooks on biblical hermeneutics. To cite but one example, a popular evangelical handbook on hermeneutics by Dan McCartney and Charles Clayton approaches the task of exegesis assuming that the NT's witness should be granted hermeneutical priority over the Old, since the "redemptive historical situation" it belongs to is "clear," while that of the OT depends upon correlation with the New before it can achieve such clarity.[16] Their remarks form an instructive contrast with statements made by James Barr in 1964:

---

13. The best account of the hermeneutical impact of modern historical consciousness upon biblical interpretation remains that of Hans Frei's 1974 masterpiece *The Eclipse of Biblical Narrative: A Study in Eighteenth and Nineteenth Century Hermeneutics* (New Haven: Yale University Press, 1974).

14. One thinks here of the approach to biblical theology reflected in the work of J. C. K. von Hofmann and the nineteenth-century "Erlangen school." The approach of the Erlangen school has important anticipations in the approach to Testamental unity found in the seventeenth-century Reformed theologian Cocceius. See the discussion in Frei, *Eclipse*, 46–50, 173–75, 180–82; cf. also the discussion of von Hofmann in Rudolf Bultmann, "Prophecy and Fulfillment," in *Essays on Old Testament Hermeneutics* (ed. Claus Westermann; trans. James L. Mays; Atlanta: John Knox, 1979), 55–58.

15. For an extended critique of the hermeneutical problems associated with von Rad's tradition-historical version of *Heilsgeschichte*, see the many essays on von Rad in Christopher R. Seitz, *Word Without End: The Old Testament as Abiding Theological Witness* (Grand Rapids: Eerdmans, 1998); Seitz, *Figured Out: Typology and Providence in Christian Scripture* (Louisville: Westminster John Knox, 2001); Seitz, *Prophecy and Hermeneutics: Toward a New Introduction to the Prophets* (Grand Rapids: Baker, 2007); cf. also the earlier work of Joseph Groves, *Actualization and Interpretation in the Old Testament* (SBLDS 86; Atlanta: Scholars Press, 1987).

16. Dan McCartney and Charles Clayton, *Let the Reader Understand: A Guide to Interpreting and Applying the Bible* (Wheaton, Ill.: Bridgepoint, 1994), 193–94.

> It is an illusory position to think of ourselves as in a position where the New Testament is clear, is known, and is accepted, and where therefore from this secure position we start out to explore the much more doubtful and dangerous territory of the Old Testament.... [This] is not possible, for quite theological reasons.... Insofar as a position is Christian, it is related to the Old Testament from the beginning.[17]

While it is certainly true that the NT offers a corrective to certain misreadings of the OT (though not the OT per se), it is also true that the OT offers a corrective to misreadings of the NT.[18] Salvation-historical paradigms that hermeneutically privilege the NT over the Old place pressure upon the reciprocal nature of the relation between the two Testaments,[19] and in so doing adopt a stance for relating the Testaments that naturally gives rise to a hermeneutical *non sequitur*, namely, that the NT's use of the OT provides the primary category or indispensable lens for hearing the OT's christological voice, as though the OT needed to be correlated to the NT in order to have a Christian voice at all.[20]

This way of relating the two Testaments stands in stark contrast with that of the early church. The early church fathers did not do exegetical battle with the Judaism of their day by arguing about "the end of the story." Rather, the battle lines were almost exclusively drawn around "the beginning of the story" in the OT, and not only the question whether that story pointed to Christ, but also whether its verbal form and shape was christomorphic in its own right, and on its own semantic level, apart from its relation to the NT. Just as significant for our purposes is also the fact that the battle with Arianism in the early church centered round a dispute over

---

17. James Barr, cited in Seitz, *Figured Out*, 5.
18. See especially Childs's comments on the continuing significance of Sinai's voice for the NT in *Exodus: A Commentary* (London: SCM, 1974), 382–84.
19. Cf. Childs, *BTONT*, 17. Reflecting on the fact that an emphasis upon *Heilsgeschichte* as a model for relating the Testaments "tends to imply that theological reflection on the Bible always proceeds in one direction," Childs counters with the observation that "a strong case can be made that Biblical Theology of both Testaments must issue in theological reflection which also moves in the reverse direction from the New Testament back to the Old, and that such crucial theological dialectic is threatened by any uncritical appeal to a unilinear, one-directional trajectory into the future."
20. For a critical discussion of the way in which this hermeneutical practice works itself out in contemporary NT scholarship at large, see Christopher Seitz, *The Character of Christian Scripture: The Significance of a Two-Testament Bible* (Grand Rapids: Baker, 2011), 137–56, especially his remarks on 139–43.

the meaning of the phrase in Prov 8:22 rendered by the LXX as "The Lord *created* me at the beginning of his ways."[21] The controversy over this text in the early church highlights the fact that premoderns believed one could read the OT as Christian scripture directly in light of Christ, quite apart from the interpretive filters provided by the NT.[22] Thus it becomes apparent that it was the OT's status as a christological witness in its own right that triggered the Arian controversy.[23] In other words, the early church did not understand the Bible in terms primarily defined by the NT, or its reading of the Old,[24] but rather as a two-Testament enterprise in which both Testaments, while differently instrumental in their witness to Christ, were equidistant from the one Triune God revealing himself in Christ by his Spirit.[25]

---

21. Arius appealed to this text in support of his claim that Christ was not divine, and thus used it to underwrite what might be called "the Arian rule of faith," to wit, "there was when he was not." On the reception history of Prov 8 leading up to the Arius-Athanasius debate, see Frances Young, "Proverbs 8 in Interpretation (2): Wisdom Personified," in *Reading Texts, Seeking Wisdom* (ed. D. Ford and G. Stanton; Grand Rapids: Eerdmans, 2004), 102–15.

22. Prov 8:22 is not cited in the NT, though a few scholars have suggested that the Pauline phrase "the firstborn of all creation" in Col 1:15 may be alluding to it.

23. For a helpful historical overview and account of the exegetical issues at stake, see Jaroslav Pelikan, *The Emergence of the Catholic Tradition 100–600* (vol. 1 of *The Christian Tradition: A History of the Development of Doctrine*; Chicago: University of Chicago Press, 1975), 191–210; cf. also C. F. Burney, "Christ as the APXH of Creation," *JTS* 27 (1926): 160–77.

24. One might also question whether patristic versions of "salvation history" privilege the NT over the OT after the manner of contemporary "story-shaped" approaches to reading the ante-Nicene fathers (e.g., Paul M. Blowers, "The *Regula Fidei* and the Narrative Character of Early Christian Faith," *ProEccl* 6 [1997]: 199–228). Any attempt to establish lines of continuity between the early church and modernity at this point is bound to go astray unless it reckons with the hermeneutical impact registered by modern historical consciousness upon the contemporary church's understanding of salvation history. Borrowing language from Frei, one might say that the distance between Irenaeus' version of salvation history and that of the modern church represents "a voyage from one world to another" (cf. Frei, *Eclipse*, 90).

25. On this see Brevard S. Childs, "Does the OT Witness to Jesus Christ?" in *Evangelium, Schriftauslegung, Kirche* (ed. Jostein Ådna et al.; Vandenhoeck & Ruprecht, 1997), 57–64.

OT Torah and Salvation History:
The Law and Paul's Concern for Christian Formation

Turning now to Paul's reading of the Mosaic law in Gal 3-4, it is helpful to begin by reflecting on the theological significance of Gal 4:19 for Paul's larger view of the OT witness. There Paul speaks of his anguished desire to see Christ "formed" (μορφωθῇ) within the Galatians. At first glance it would seem that what Paul has to say in the verses following 4:19 has nothing to do with his concern that Christ be formed within them. Rather, it appears that in keeping with the general tenor of his remarks on the law's function in Gal 3, in these closing verses of Gal 4 he is simply mounting yet another polemic against Judaizing attempts to pursue justification by works. To be sure, this is part of Paul's purpose in his allegorizing use of Sarah and Hagar in which they "stand for" two covenants.[26] But this is to view the matter in an entirely polemical and negative light.

In terms of the OT's own canonical rubrics, Paul refers to texts from both the Law and the Prophets to authorize his understanding of Christian formation (4:22, 27). Thus in addition to adding another plank in his argument against justification by works, in Gal 4:19-31 Paul is also grounding his understanding of Christian formation in the theological grammar

---

26. For an overview and analysis of the issues at stake in Paul's use of allegory, see Mark Gignilliat, "Paul, Allegory, and the Plain Sense of Scripture," *JTI* 2 (2008): 135-46; cf. also John David Dawson, *Christian Figural Reading and the Fashioning of Identity* (Los Angeles: University of California Press, 2002). Earlier attempts to use purely historical criteria to draw a sharp distinction between two forms of figuration in scripture (viz., typology and allegory) have now been discredited on a number of fronts. Higton's discussion of Barth's and Frei's approach to figuration helpfully demonstrates the way in which figuration *preserves* historical meaning (see Mike Higton, "The Fulfillment of History in Barth, Frei, Auerbach, and Dante," in *Conversing with Barth* [ed. J. McDowell and M. Higton; Burlington, Vt.: Ashgate, 2004], 120-41). Such arguments work well for explaining figurative forms such as typology in which historical meanings are often assigned a comparatively high profile. However, his discussion fails to reckon with the way in which the canonical process *also* critically circumscribes and adjudicates historical meaning for theological purposes. Viewed from a canonical perspective, figural moves in the canonical process not only carry forward, but also limit the contribution historical meaning and context make to scripture's final form. Childs's insistence on allowing the canon the critical freedom to limit the semantic contribution made by historical meaning to canonical meaning leaves more breathing room for allegorical limit cases, in which the profile assigned to historical meaning has been lowered and relegated to the background.

established by the Torah and the prophets.[27] From this it would appear that more is going on in the OT with respect to Israel than Bultmann's celebrated notion that OT Israel's salvation history is *Verscheitern*,[28] a miscarriage or abortion, in short, a failure history. Read in the context of Gal 4, Bultmann's construal of the OT's salvation history raises a question: if the OT offers us nothing *positive* by way of an understanding of Christian formation, how then do we make sense of what Paul is doing in Gal 4 when he appeals to Gen 21 and Isa 54 in the context of an expressed concern for Christian formation?

In Gal 4, Paul proceeds on the assumption that salvation history under Abraham (a history that the Mosaic economy does not obliterate or erase[29]) is not *merely* the story of Israel's failure. It is *also* the story of how the law functioned as a revelation of God's glory, character, and will that served to guide Israel in her transformation into God's image, of which Moses and the prophets were an OT model or paradigm.[30] *Contra* Bultmann, the Israel of God in the OT was not merely a herd of swine that sought justification by works and failed. As God once reminded Elijah and as Paul reminds us,[31] in the OT account of Israel's *Heilsgeschichte* there was also an Israel who trusted in the promise given to Abraham and whose hearts

---

27. For a discussion of the theological grammar of "The Law and the Prophets" that arises from the OT's own canonical process of structuring biblical revelation, see Christopher Seitz, *The Goodly Fellowship of the Prophets: The Achievement of Association in Canon Formation* (Grand Rapids: Baker, 2009), 26–30, 62–63, 67–71, 90–92; cf. also especially Stephen B. Chapman's book, *The Law and the Prophets: A Study in Old Testament Canon Formation* (FAT 27; Tubingen: Mohr Siebeck, 2000), 113–31, on the significance of Deut 34:10 and 18:15-22 for establishing this grammar and structure in the OT witness.

28. See Bultmann, "Prophecy and Fulfillment," 50–75; cf. also Leonhard Goppelt, *Typos: The Typological Interpretation of the Old Testament in the New* (trans. D. H. Madvig; Grand Rapids: Eerdmans, 1982), 11–14. Goppelt notes an important precedent to Bultmann's notion of *Verscheitern* in the work of confessionally Reformed scholar Patrick Fairbairn: "For Fairbairn, the prophetic character of the OT is not based on its being a preliminary stage in a process of evolution, but on the contrast between divine calling and human failure. Israel, especially the house of David, was called to realize the promise given to Abraham (Gen 12:3). Both failed. *In this way* God is pointing to the future (13–14, emphasis added).

29. Gal 3:17.

30. See for example Meredith G. Kline, *Images of the Spirit* (Grand Rapids: Baker, 1980), privately reprinted by the author in 1986.

31. See 1 Kgs 19:9-18; cf. Rom 11:1-6.

were being formed in obedience to God's Torah through the instruction and catechesis provided by the law.[32] It is helpful in this context to remember that the Hebrew word "Torah" can be translated as "instruction" as well as "law," a fact which also points to the multidimensional character of OT law.

Again, my thesis is that the theological tendency to construe the Mosaic law's function in negative terms is tied to deeper erroneous assumptions about Paul's entire project in Gal 3–4, assumptions that are in turn driven by a particular construal of Israel's salvation history. On this view, the revelation of law in the OT primarily serves to teach us as NT saints the *wrong* way to go about pursuing the question of transformation into the image of Christ. Granting for the time being a provisional status to my thesis, let us ask why many accounts of the law understand its OT function in largely negative terms, introducing sharp and even polarizing distinctions between the OT law of Moses and "the law of Christ" Paul refers to in Gal 6:2.

As most NT scholars would agree, the law Paul has in view in Gal 3 is the law given at Sinai. It also seems clear that, for the Paul who writes to Galatia, law and gospel represent two antithetically opposed approaches to justification, approaches typified by the OT covenantal economies of Moses and Abraham. Recognizing the obvious truth of these, however, does not take us to the heart of the hermeneutical issues involved in Paul's reading of OT Torah. We may gain access to these issues by asking a question: Is it Paul's intention in his exposition of the law's function in Gal 3 to provide us with a normative or exhaustive account of the function of the law in the OT? The problem is that modern day readers of Paul often operate on the basis of the (false) assumption that in Gal 3 he seeks to provide a totalizing definition of the OT law's essence that excludes other functions for the law in both the Old and the New Testaments.

One might begin to offer a critical response to this assumption from the NT side of things by focusing upon the rather one-sided Paulinism underwriting such an approach. A canonical hermeneutic hears Paul in concert with Matthew, John, and other NT readers of the OT Torah, rather than construing Paul's reading of the law's function in Gal 3–4 as definitive for the law's purpose and function in the larger NT. A canonical reading of Paul's teaching on the law thus actively resists the modern tendency to

---

32. Deut 6:4–9.

limit the NT's understanding of law to what Paul says in Gal 3–4, thereby creating a canon within a canon and falling into the one-sided Paulinism characteristic of radical Lutheranism. However, a larger study of the law's function in the NT vis-à-vis other apostolic voices clearly lies beyond the scope of this essay. Suffice it to note at this juncture that the fact that such a one-sided Paulinism goes unquestioned by modern readers of Paul's letter to the Galatians is troubling, not least because it foreshortens the NT's own presentation of the issue.

At the same time, even if one had only Gal 3–4 rather than the larger NT witness to arrive at Paul's understanding of the law, the notion that he is providing a monolithic definition of law in these two chapters would still not follow. For the purposes of his polemical argument with the Galatian Judaizers, Paul is focusing upon a particular segment of salvation history in Gal 3, namely, the segment spanning the covenantal economies of Abraham and Moses. To make this reading exhaustive of the law ignores the law's role in its prefall context.[33] Those who regard Paul's view of the law in Gal 3–4 as a definitive account of the law's function are not only ignoring the decidedly polemical and occasional character of his remarks, but also the abbreviated character of the salvation history he chooses to focus upon in order to make his case against the Judaizers. This salvation-historical period is not exhaustive of the law's administration and function in the OT, nor did Paul intend it to be viewed as such.

ABRAHAM'S OBEDIENCE AND ISRAEL'S GUIDANCE:
GENESIS 17 AND EXODUS 15–18

That Paul is not providing a definitive account of the OT concept of Torah in Gal 3 becomes evident when we take our point of standing *within* the segment of salvation history he is describing. Paul's view of Christian formation in Gal 4 is clearly rooted in the Abrahamic promise,[34] yet it is also clear from the Genesis narrative itself that this formation, while rooted in the Spirit's power, does not exclude a place for the law's role as a continuing "guide" for what it means to walk with God, as Gen 17:1 suggests in

---

33. That is, its Adamic context in the garden. Cf. the remarks of Brevard Childs in *OT Theology in a Canonical Context*, 51. Childs takes the revelation of God's law provided by Gen 2:16 as evidence for the claim that "God has expressed his will *from the beginning*" (emphasis added). See further the discussion below.

34. Sarah "stands for" or allegorizes the Abrahamic covenant (Gal 4:24–30).

reference to Abraham, a foundational figure (along with Moses) in Israel's salvation history. By what standard is Abraham to walk before God and be blameless, if not the law as the revelation of God's glory, character, and will? Here it would seem that Abraham's call to covenantal obedience in Gen 17:1 cannot be detached from the law's formative aspect as a rule or guide, that is, the law as an expression of God's character, image, and will for his people. The fact that this reference to Abraham's covenantal obedience falls within the salvation-historical period under review in Gal 3–4 carries with it the suggestion that it is not Paul's intention in Gal 3:19–24 to deny the law's continuing function as a rule or guide in Israel's *Heilsgeschichte*.

Moreover, as others have noted, this salvation-historical period also envisions God's guidance of Israel in the wilderness, a period that stands between Israel's deliverance from Egypt and his subsequent guidance of Israel in the land. That the notion of "guidance" during this period cannot be separated from the Mosaic notion of Torah as a disclosure of God's righteous character is evident from the references to the law and the anticipations of Sinai found in the wilderness stories in Exod 15–18, stories which precede the giving of the Mosaic law proper in Exod 19–24. References and allusions to the law in these stories clearly presuppose some form of its existence prior to its formal promulgation at Sinai.[35] Regardless of the historical sequence of chapters 15–18 vis-à-vis chapters 19–24, the larger narrative sequence of Exod 15–24 clearly discourages a reading of the Sinai law that would limit its significance for Israel to the disclosure given at Sinai in chapters 19–24.[36] In terms of the narrative's final form, the Sinai Torah now functions as a theological lens for reading the wilderness stories. The burden of proof therefore rests with those who wish to argue that in Gal 3:19–24, Paul not only has in view the law's death-dealing function, but also law or Torah in the broader sense, namely, the law as a disclosure of God's character and formative guide to his will. That Paul also had Torah in this broader sense in view in the salvation-historical period under review in Gal 3–4 is unlikely, not only because this broader function of Torah finds expression in the covenantal economy of Abraham, but also

---

35. Exod 15:25–26; 16:4, 23–30; 17:1; 18:14–20.

36. For a helpful discussion of the literary-critical issues at stake, see Nathan MacDonald, "Anticipations of Horeb: Exodus 17 as Inner-Biblical Commentary" in *Studies on the Text and Versions of the Hebrew Bible in Honour of Robert P. Gordon* (ed. D. Lipton and G. Khan; VTSup 149; Leiden: Brill, 2011), 7–19.

because the stories in Exod 15-18 suggest that the Sinai Torah functions as a norm for God's guidance of Israel in the wilderness.

Abraham's call to walk in covenantal obedience in Gen 17:1 and God's guidance of Israel in the wilderness raise another question: Which Israel does Paul have in view in Gal 3:19-24? The Israel who, like Abraham, trusts in the promise and seeks to walk before God in holiness, or the Israel who, like the Judaizers of Paul's day, seeks to be justified, not by faith in the promise, but by obedience to the law? The answer is surely the latter. It is just here, however, that we must keep in mind the potential salvation-historical frameworks have for promoting reductionist readings of OT Torah in the life of Israel. Some will object to my appeal to Exod 15-18 on the ground that the function of the law in these chapters is bound up not with providing guidance to Israel, but with its probation. Biblical theologians of various stripes have typically interpreted the stories of Israel's testing in Exod 15-18 by drawing parallels between Adam's testing in the garden and Israel's testing in the wilderness (and rightly so).[37] As the paradigm for a new humanity God is raising up through Abraham, Israel's testing in the wilderness is viewed as a reenactment of Adam's probation, a probation which Israel, like Adam before it, ultimately failed. This reading of Exod 15-18 has merit, and it is not my purpose here to question its legitimacy *per se*.

However, whatever else one may say about the merits this reading has our for understanding of the Pentateuch's larger coherence and shape, especially its teachings on the covenants, this reading often functions as part of larger case for identifying the Mosaic law's function in the life of Israel with its theological role in its probation. The role of OT Torah in Israel's life in the land, as well as in its guidance in the wilderness, thus becomes indistinguishable from its probationary and death-dealing function under Moses. As a result, the voice of the OT Torah itself gets conflated with the way Israel's disobedience in the wilderness serves as a dark foil for highlighting Christ's obedience during his temptation in the wilderness (Matt. 4:1-11). Coupled with an appeal to Paul's reading of the law in Gal 3-4, the conclusion is then drawn that the law's function in the OT was bound up with Israel's probation, a probation which Israel utterly failed. In this way the OT Torah itself gets folded into Bultmann's notion of Israel's failure history (*Verscheitern*).

---

37. See for example the old classic by Ulrich W. Mauser, *Christ in the Wilderness: The Wilderness Theme in the Second Gospel and Its Basis in the Biblical Tradition* (London: SCM, 1963).

OT Torah as a Proclamation of God's Name

The difficulty with this reading of OT Torah is that the problem Paul is pursuing vis-à-vis the law in his letter to the Galatians does not concern the continuing validity of Torah in the broader sense, that is, Torah as a disclosure of God's character and formative guide to his will. For this reason we must avoid reading a totalizing view of the law's nature and purpose into Paul's discussion of the law's pedagogical function in Gal 3:19–24, a function which turns out to be death-dealing, and which therefore decisively closes the door to the possibility of being justified through obedience to the law.

Torah for Paul is a broader concept than covenant, because Torah as the historical disclosure of God's name is grounded not in covenant in the first instance, but in God's eternal character and being (Exod 33:13, 18–19; cf. 34:5–7).[38] Torah is thus grounded in a particular theological *ontology*, from which it cannot be separated. The Mosaic covenant is one particular polity or instantiation of Torah. Thus, when the Mosaic covenant is fulfilled by Christ, the OT Torah does not self-destruct, nor does it drop off like a booster rocket, to be replaced by the law of Christ.[39] Rather, as an abiding revelation of God's eternal glory, character, and will, it continues to sound its notes alongside and through the NT witness.[40] "The

---

38. The narratives of Torah not only reflect *what* YHWH has done, but also disclose *who* he is. Stated differently, the ways of YHWH disclose his identity or name.

39. As Childs reminds us in Exodus commentary, for the writer of Hebrews, "The thunder of Sinai continues to address the church in terms of obedient acts to one's fellow humans, done in response to God's claim, and measured by God's criteria. The externality of God's revelation at Sinai guards the church from encapsulating God within the good intentions of the religious conscience. Thus Exod 19 provides the major content to the New Testament's witness that God is a consuming fire. The weakness of the Old Testament is not in creating a primitive concept of God, but in the failure of Israel to respond in righteousness. The new covenant is not a substitution of a friendly God for the terror of Sinai, but rather a gracious message of an open access to the same God whose presence still calls forth awe and reverence" (*Exodus*, 384).

40. The deeper theological logic authorizing this claim rests upon the ontological identification of Christ the eternal *logos* with the God of Israel. It is on the basis of this theological ontology, authorized in the first instance by reading Israel's scriptures in light of Christ, that Irenaeus speaks of Christ as follows: "This is He who, in the bush, spoke with Moses and said, 'I have surely seen the afflictions of my people who are in Egypt, and I have come down to deliver them.' This is He who ascended and descended for the salvation of the afflicted, delivering us from the dominion of the

law of Christ" Paul speaks of in Gal 6:2 does not replace the Torah in this sense, nor in the sense of a *nova lex*, but rather serves as its transformed embodiment, a transformation which reflects the fact that the God of Israel has fully identified himself with the incarnate and risen Jesus.[41] In the NT economy defined by this incarnate and risen Lord, one meets with the eternal Author of the law, and thus the One who exhausts its intentions and purposes. For this reason, obedience to the *earthly* Jesus and obedience to Torah in its broader sense can no longer be distinguished, as they were under the OT economy, when Christ the eternal *logos* disclosed himself to Israel in a manner congruent with his invisibility in the bosom of the Father. The revelation of Christ the eternal *logos* disclosed in the incarnate and resurrected Jesus in the NT, while not prejudicial to this invisibility,[42] nevertheless bears witness to a transformation of the entire covenantal polity by which the Mosaic law was administered.[43]

Egyptians, that is, from all idolatry and ungodliness, and saving us from the Red Sea, that is, from the deadly turbulence of the heathen and from the bitter current of their blasphemy.... He caused a stream of water to gush forth abundantly from a rock in the desert, and the rock is Himself ... killing the unbelievers in the desert, while leading those who believed in Him and were infants in malice into the inheritance of the patriarchs, which, not Moses, but Jesus <gave us an inheritance>; who saves us from Amalek by stretching out His hands and leading us into the Father's Kingdom" (John Behr's translation of Irenaeus' *Demonstration*, cited in Seitz, *Character of Christian Scripture*, 198 n. 9).

41. See the discussion of Isa 45:21-24 vis-à-vis Phil 2:6-11 in Seitz, *Figured Out*, 131-44. In addition to Seitz's thought-provoking analysis, it should also be noted that in the gospel narratives, especially Luke, Jesus' personal identity is disclosed and expanded through the use of the title *Kyrios*, the LXX word which translates the divine name YHWH in the OT. For a discussion of the way in which this title implies an ontological relationship between Jesus and the God of Israel, see C. Kavin Rowe, *Early Narrative Christology in Luke: The Lord in the Gospel of Luke* (Grand Rapids: Baker, 2009); cf. also his discussion in "Biblical Pressure and Trinitarian Hermeneutics," *ProEccl* 11 (1997): 295-312, esp. 301-6.

42. The *kenosis* at Christ's incarnation described by Paul in Phil 2:7 is thus not to be understood as prejudicial to this invisibility. For an interesting discussion of the patristic debate over the nature of Christ's invisibility in the OT, see Juan Ochagavia, *Visibile Patris Filius: A Study of Irenaeus' Teaching on Revelation and Tradition* (OrChrAn; Rome: Pontifical Institute, 1964).

43. See the nuanced discussion of Childs vis-à-vis J. Louis Martyn's reading of the Mosaic law in *Church's Guide*, 117-22. Childs summarizes his own reading of the character of the law of Christ as follows: "The law of Christ is a transformed understanding of the Mosaic law. Not only has the law of Moses been shown to be provi-

OT Torah and Formation in God's Image

In terms of the broader sense of Torah, a sense grounded in God's character, every revelation of God's law word or Torah is a revelation of his glory, character, and will, and this also has direct theological significance for the law's prefall function. The law "images" God in that it discloses his righteous character, and for this reason older theologians rightly argued that the act of creation by which God formed Adam and Eve in his image entails the conclusion that the law of God must have been written in some sense upon their hearts.[44] In addition to this disclosure (though not prior to it), an external expression of the law in the Garden was also given through the sanction described in Gen 2:17. It thus becomes impossible to identity the law's function with death-dealing, because both its inward and outward expression in the garden were given prior to the entrance of the reality of sin. In this context, it is helpful to remember Paul's statement in Rom 7:7 that "the law is not sin."[45]

Thus, when it comes to defining the nature and essence of the law, our final reference point cannot be Paul's exegesis of the law in Gal 3-4. Rather, our ultimate reference point for defining the nature and essence of the law must be God's character as disclosed in the Torah. Because this disclosure encompasses Adamic humanity as well as Abraham and Moses, a fully formed and comprehensive view of the law in the OT must

---

sionary (Rom 5:20; Gal 3:23-27), but also the law of Christ is qualitatively different because of the event of Christ's death and resurrection. It is not an extension of the Mosaic law; the entire grounds for which the law as established by God for his elect people have been altered by the Christ event. It is not only a fulfillment of the Abrahamic promise—indeed, God is faithful to his promise—but, according to Rom 13, it is also an ontological transformation of the Mosaic law. The law of Christ stands in an analogical relationship to the law of Moses only in one respect. The law of Christ remains a divine imperative for Christian behavior. It covers the entire spectrum of human existence over which God is sovereign. The Christian lives under this transformed law, in the sense not of a *nova lex* but of the active presence of Christ's Spirit leading the Christian, both individually and communally, in obedience. The Christian is admonished to pursue the law of Christ in loving behavior toward all persons. It is directed toward the future, and manifests the fruits of the Spirit in overcoming the old law" (121).

44. Many Reformational confessions of the sixteenth and seventh centuries acknowledge this.

45. Cf. also Rom 7:12.

also be in accordance with its original purpose and significance in the prefall world. That purpose cannot be defined in the first instance with reference to the reality of sin, because sin was not originally on the scene. More importantly, the entrance of sin into the world does not redefine the original mandate and purpose of the law, namely, that of guiding the creaturely task of imaging God's glory through the exercise of his kingship over creation. Rather, the entrance of sin makes it necessary to pursue that purpose through other channels, namely, the Abrahamic promise adumbrated in Gen 3:15. The promise of the gospel does not redefine the original nature and purpose of the law in the prefall world in this respect. It simply achieves that purpose through other means. Viewed from this perspective, redemption in the OT is nothing less than recreation and reformation in the creaturely image God originally bestowed upon Adam and Eve.[46] In that formation project the revelatory mediation of God's character through the law fully retains its place, both in the postfall world of OT Israel and in the NT world of the church.

To sum up, whatever else Paul intends to prove by focusing upon the salvation-historical period spanning the covenantal economies of Abraham and Moses, it is unlikely that his intention in foregrounding the law's death-dealing function under Moses was to provide a definitive account of OT Torah. The law is not sin, but rather a gift reflecting God's goodness toward his people Israel, in that Israel enjoyed a revelation of his moral righteousness that other nations did not.[47] Even though Israel turned this blessing into a curse through disobedience, this transformation is the result of its abuse at the hands of apostate and wicked Israel. It by no means requires the false conclusion, drawn by some, that the Mosaic administration of the law was not a gift, but a curse. For this reason, it is misguided to identify the voice of the OT law with its "ministration of death" in the history of Israel subsequent to Sinai. Rather, the law had a dual function

---

46. Formation or sanctification thus means restoration for the sake of realizing the full *creaturely* potential Adam was created to exercise and enjoy. It is not to be confused with the notion often inherent in "deification" or *theosis* as a model for understanding Christian formation, namely, the idea that sanctification is a matter of the saints becoming more godlike or divine in some quasi-ontological sense. See for example the recent attempt to repristinate this model for Christian formation in Jason Byassee's *Praise Seeking Understanding: Reading the Psalms with Augustine* (Grand Rapids: Eerdmans, 2007).

47. See Deut 4:5-9.

at Sinai, both as a guide that figures God's righteousness to a redeemed people (the law as a *figure* of God's righteousness), and as a "pedagogue" to assist in the proclamation of the Abrahamic promise to future generations, albeit often in a negative fashion (the law in the service of *promise*).

In Gal 3-4 Paul focuses on this latter function of the law, namely, the law's pedagogical role in leading us to Christ by undercutting the possibility of justification by works. Although in this context the law's pedagogical function is primarily negative in character, this by no means exhausts every aspect of the metaphor Paul is using in Gal 3:24. The *positive* pedagogical purpose and role of the law in "imaging" God's righteousness to his redeemed people remains fully in place. Addressing the broader aspect of OT Torah as disclosure of God's character and normative guide to his will is simply outside Paul's immediate purview in Gal 3-4. What Paul wishes to rule out in Gal 4:19-31 is not this broader aspect and function of the law, but rather the notion that justification by works can serve as a basis for Christian formation. Christians are not justified by faith and then sanctified by works.[48] For the Paul who writes in Galatians, formation or recreation in Christ's image means nothing less than living out of one's justification.[49] The same Spirit who enables us to embrace the promise by faith also enables us to live out of that faith.[50] Paul is thus keen to make the case from the OT that the theological grammar of the law and the prophets grounds Christian formation not in the works of the law, nor even the law per se, but in the enabling power of God's Spirit.

Interestingly, in his commentary on Galatians, Calvin's reading of Paul's allegory interprets the children of Sinai as hypocrites who are expelled from the people of God. He argues that such hypocrites are characterized by the fact that, like the Judaizers of Paul's day, they "make a wicked abuse of the law, by finding in it nothing but what tends to slavery."[51] Here Calvin is careful to distinguish the *nature* of the law, which is good,

---

48. Gal 3:1-3.

49. While Paul's remarks in Gal 3-4 take place in the context of a debate over justification rather than union with Christ per se, a canonical reading of his teaching on justification vis-à-vis Romans reminds us that his views on justification (Rom 1-5) must be understood in relation to his views on union with Christ (Rom 6-8). Thus the fact that Paul foregrounds the issue of justification in Gal 3-4 in no way negates what he teaches about justification's relation to union with Christ in Romans.

50. Col 2:6-7; cf. Phil 2:12-13.

51. John Calvin, *Commentaries on the Epistles of Paul to the Galatians and Ephesians* (trans. W. Pringle; Grand Rapids: Baker, 2005), 138.

righteous, and holy,[52] from its *effects* upon the wicked who abuse it. Calvin is careful not to blame the failure of the OT's formation project on the law itself, but grounds that failure instead in the "wicked *abuse* of the law."[53] In any case, his approach to OT Torah forms an instructive contrast with certain forms of modern Lutheranism that radically obscure this distinction by conflating the nature of the law either with the age of sin or with its effects on the wicked, thereby wrongly concluding that Paul directly identifies the law with the power of sin, that the law's essence is curse, and that its function in Israel's salvation history is wholly defined in terms of its death-dealing function.

FRANCIS WATSON'S READING OF PAUL AND OT TORAH

Failure to recognize that Torah as a disclosure of God's name is grounded not in the death-dealing *economia* of the age of sin and death, but in a theological ontology reflective of God's eternal character and being, also lies at the heart of the tendency in modern Lutheran eschatologies to conflate the law's essence with its death-dealing function. On this approach, the eschatology of the law ultimately takes its bearings not from God's eternal character and glory, but from the age of sin inaugurated by Adam's fall. This *a priori* dogmatic move effectively historicizes the law by fostering the judgment that the term "law" applies only to the official function of the law in time, and not to its eternal reality or *res*. Thus, the entire complex of ideas in the OT associated with the term "law" partakes of a decidedly noneschatological character, inasmuch as

---

52. Rom 7:12.
53. Space does not permit me to address the distance that exists between Calvin and modern approaches to relating the two Testaments. Suffice it to say for now that Calvin himself never made use of "salvation history" as a hermeneutical category for reading Gal 4 after this fashion, let alone subordinating the OT to the NT. His approach to uniting the Testaments is illustrated by the ontological rationale he invokes for unifying the Testaments in the context of a figural reading of Israel's land blessings. For Calvin, the two Testaments find their unity in one substance, namely, Christ himself. See Calvin, *Institutes of the Christian Religion* (ed. J. T. McNeill; trans. F. Battles; Philadelphia: Westminster, 1960), 2.11.1 (1:449–51); cf. the remarks of James Samuel Preus on Augustine's views of OT *promissio* in *From Shadow to Promise: Old Testament Interpretation from Augustine to the Young Luther* (Cambridge: Harvard University Press, 1969), 16–21.

their official reign or office is terminated by Christ's death and passes off the stage at his second coming.[54]

A similar theological move underlies Francis Watson's recent attempt to interpret Paul's reading of the death-dealing function of the Mosaic covenant in 2 Cor 3 as a construal of the OT Torah in its entirety.[55] According to Watson, through a reading of Num 11–25 Paul came to see that Torah is "necessarily entangled with sin and death," a conclusion Watson judges to be undergirding Paul's theological stance on Israel's salvation history in Rom 7 and 1 Cor 10. Indeed, as far as Paul is concerned, the Torah climaxes in the law's curse, a claim Watson grounds in Paul's reading of Deut 27:26 in Gal 3:10.[56] Throughout his discussion of Paul's reading of OT Torah, Watson proceeds upon the dubious assumption that the OT citations Paul chooses reflect theological judgments about the OT Torah as a whole, and not simply the Mosaic law's death-dealing function and effect.[57] He virtually identifies the theological voice of Torah with the postfall order of sin and death, and in so doing closes ranks with Ernst Käsemann and Gehard Forde by following "the traditional Lutheran emphasis in ascribing the law completely to the old aeon."[58] Paul's reading of Moses' veil in 2 Cor 3 thus becomes a symbol of the OT Torah's identification with this postfall order, a history that is passing away: "For Paul, the law has a historical origin, and is *in no sense* eternal or timeless."[59] In this way Watson wholly economizes the law and leaves it bereft of any ongoing significance for the church as a disclosure of the OT righteousness of God now manifest through the gospel of the risen Christ.

---

54. See Gerhard Forde, *The Law-Gospel Debate* (Minneapolis: Augsburg, 1969), 184; cf. also his discussion in *Christian Dogmatics* (ed. C. Braaten and R. Jenson; Philadelphia: Fortress, 1984), 2:391–470.

55. See Francis Watson, *Paul and the Hermeneutics of Faith* (London: T&T Clark, 2004), 273–313 (281–82, 295–96). Watson understands the story related in Exod 34:29–35 "as a parable of the Torah—its deadly impact, its passing glory, and its veiling" (282; cf. also his extended remarks on 295–96). This totalizing construal of the Torah more or less requires him to exclude the book of Genesis from the Torah proper, leaving Paul with a Torah essentially constituted by Exodus, Leviticus, Numbers, and Deuteronomy (see his remarks on 276–77, esp. 277 n. 13).

56. Ibid., 276.
57. Ibid., 275–76.
58. Childs, *Church's Guide*, 105.
59. Watson, *Paul*, 278, emphasis added.

Watson thus concludes that, for the Paul who writes in 2 Cor 3, the function of Moses' veil was to conceal not merely the provisional nature of the covenantal polity of Moses, but the fading glory of the entire OT dispensation, especially the Torah.[60] This pressure to conflate the Mosaic covenant with the OT Torah per se does not arise from either the *sensus literalis* of Exod 34:29-35, Paul's reading of the Mosaic covenant in 2 Cor 3, or the canonical Paul who also penned Romans. Rather, it appears to derive from a dogmatic construal that Israel's salvation history in the Torah *per se* has been identified with the postfall order of sin and death.[61]

Childs's discussion suggests that this move on Watson's part might have been precluded had he availed himself of the exegetical brakes provided by the "continuing dialectic between a historical critical and a canonical reading of the biblical text."[62] In Mesopotamian iconography, the gods of the ancient Near East were often depicted with horn-crowned heads in order to symbolize their glory, a motif that appears to have influenced the theophany described in Hab 3. The use of the Hebrew noun *qeren* (horn) in the theophanic imagery of Hab 3:4 appears to refer to shafts of light that symbolize the "divine glow" or glory of deity.[63] It seems probable that the verb *qrn* used in Exod 34:29-30 to speak of Moses' countenance also evokes this motif. The glory of God reflected in the "horning" countenance of Moses in verses 29-30 is thus closely linked with the didactic content of the Sinai Torah mediated to Israel through Moses in verses 31-32. It is therefore doubtful at best that in 2 Cor 3 Paul is identifying *this* aspect of the Sinai Torah with the fading glory of the Mosaic covenant, since it continues to bear witness to the enduring glory of the same triune ontology undergirding Paul's new covenant understanding of the transformation effected by Christ the Spirit-Lord in 2 Cor 3:17-18.

---

60. According to Watson himself, this conclusion ultimately stems from Richard Hays's "crucial insight" that in 2 Cor 3 "a metaphorical fusion occurs in which Moses *becomes* the Torah" (ibid., 282 n. 13, emphasis original).

61. Watson attributes this dogmatic conclusion to Paul's reading of the Torah (ibid., 276), but there is good reason to query whether Watson's Paul escapes the dogmatic assumptions underwriting J. Louis Martyn's Paul, or simply leaves us with a Paul whose theologically negative reading of the Torah is now further mandated by the Torah itself. Viewed from this perspective, Watson lends additional support to Martyn's reading of the law by enshrining that reading in the self-witness and authority of the Torah itself.

62. Cf. Childs's discussion of Watson in *Church's Guide*, 128-31, quote from 130.

63. See Childs, *Exodus*, 604 n. 29, 609-10, 618-19; cf. Kline, *Images*, 61-62.

More important for the purposes of this discussion is the fact that, in a manner akin to his teaching on Christian formation in Gal 4, Paul's model for transformation into Christ's image in 2 Cor 3 finds it ground in the OT Torah, in this case Exod 34. By direct reference to the unveiled and transformational character of Moses' experience before God's glory at Sinai, Paul's christological reading of Exod 34 makes the point that, by virtue of the Spirit's ministry, NT Christians now stand where Moses once stood, beholding the glory of God in the face of Christ with unveiled faces.[64] In other words, Paul interprets the unveiled face of Moses in Exod 34 as an OT paradigm for the restoration of God's image in fallen humanity through the blessings of the new covenant, a reading predicated upon a theological ontology that identifies Christ with the glory-image of the God of Israel.

HEILSGESCHICHTE AND THE CHRISTIAN CHARACTER OF OT FORMATION

If the OT Torah itself provides models for the *Christian* character of Paul's teaching on formation in Gal 4 and 2 Cor 3, how then does one account for construals of Israel's salvation history that reduce the voice of OT Torah to its probationary and death-dealing function? Such a constructive role for OT Torah would not be possible if Paul's views on Torah were indistinguishable from the law's death-dealing function at Sinai or, for that matter, from its attachment to a larger, negative pedagogical function in the salvation history spanning the covenantal economies of Abraham and Moses. To be sure, Israel's formation occurred in a manner appropriate to the OT's economy as *logos asarkos*, that is, an economy in which Christ is mediated to Israel as the "Word not yet made flesh." Israel had a different historical experience of Christ than that of the NT saints, as the Christology of John's prologue reminds us, for NT saints experience Christ as the "Word made flesh" or *logos ensarkos* (John 1:1, 14).[65] Yet while Israel's christological

---

64. But we all, with unveiled face beholding as in a mirror the glory of the Lord, are being transformed into the same image from glory to glory, just as from the Lord, the Spirit (2 Cor 3:18 NASB).

65. In a recently published collection of essays, Bruce McCormack worries that the theological limitations inherent in the patristic categories *logos asarkos* and *logos ensarkos* will leave us with two Christs instead of one (see his *Orthodox and Modern: Studies in the Theology of Karl Barth* [Grand Rapids: Baker, 2008], 185). In order to emphasize that it is the embodied, *crucified* Christ who saves, McCormack borrows a

experience was an experience appropriate to the nature of the OT economy, and therefore rendered on a different semantic level and through different idioms than those of the NT, it nevertheless partook of the same reality (*res*) enjoyed by NT saints, namely, the Triune God disclosing himself in Christ by his Spirit. Thus the historical experience of OT Israel differed in kind but not in substance (*res*) from the christological experience of the NT saints. This has always been the catholic church's confession, and modern versions of *Heilsgeschichte* or salvation history that regard the OT as christologically deficient or as a mere prelude to the NT must not be allowed to obscure this confession.

A troubling feature inherent in salvation-historical paradigms that privilege the NT over the Old is their virtual exclusion of the presence of Christ the preincarnate Word, or *logos asarkos*,[66] not only from the

---

different set of terms from Heinrich Heppe's *Reformed Dogmatics* to suggest that the Latin terms *logos incarnandus* (the word to be incarnate) and *logos incarnatum* (the word incarnate) are better suited for the task at hand, provided that we also understand that the *logos incarnandus* is not to be equated with the "hidden God" of the *decretum absolutum*, or eternal decree. McCormack's larger worry seems to be that traditional patristic terminology opens to the door to equating the *logos asarkos* with a disembodied "hidden God" behind the gospel of the incarnation. This is obviously not the place to enter fully into this debate. One wonders, however, whether this is simply McCormack the dogmatician speaking, failing to appreciate the theological and figural significance of the language employed by the OT's sacrificial laws, albeit in terms of a semantics appropriate to the nature of the OT economy as promise. After all, such laws are not simply the accident of some deeper metaphysical substance, but the OT's *own* testimony to our utter need for Christ the Passover lamb. McCormack's dogmatic critique reflects a distinct failure to appreciate the exegetical realism at work in patristic readings of the OT's sacrificial system, especially their christological reading of the book of Leviticus. The same criticism might also be leveled in response to his worry that the "in se" dimension of God's sovereignty somehow constitutes a threat to the gospel of the incarnate and crucified Christ. Given the oneness of Christ's being with the God of Israel, the OT's own testimony to God's character as faithful and true (Num 23:19; cf. 1 Sam 15:29) puts to rest any idea that the "in se" dimension of God's sovereignty (cf. Deut 29:29) might contradict or even reverse the teachings of Christ's gospel in some future state.

66. The early church's distinction between Christ the *logos asarkos* and Christ the *logos ensarkos* presupposes the *etiam extra carnem*, that is, the existence of the eternal Son outside of and prior to his life in the flesh. The union of the two natures in the incarnation does not constitute the one person (*contra* McCormack), but rather presupposes it. In other words, the human flesh of Christ derives its personality from the person of the eternal *logos*. The union of the human nature with the eternal *logos* is

OT's account of creation and election, but also from Israel and its institutions. Rather, the OT merely functions as a dark foil for highlighting the NT's decisive christological voice, while the hermeneutical significance of Christ's pre-existence for the canonical shaping and formation of the OT's literary witness is rendered null and void.[67] However, contrary to what these modern versions of salvation history would lead us to believe, the NT is *not* the reification of the OT. It does not operate as a displacing witness that fully captures and exhausts the OT's essence, such that it now represents the OT's objectified replacement. The NT is neither the reifi-

---

thus in-personal. In this way the church not only asserted the ontological primacy of the divine over the human, but also gave expression to the logic of John's prologue: "In the beginning was the word ... and the word *became* flesh." For a helpful discussion, see Edward David Willis, *Calvin's Catholic Christology: The Function of the So-Called Extra Calvinisticum in Calvin's Theology* (SMRT; Leiden: Brill, 1966).

67. The result is an aberrant understanding of OT Christology vis-à-vis the NT-styled "Christotelism" by its advocates (e.g., Peter Enns, *Inspiration and Incarnation: Evangelicals and the Problem of the Old Testament* [Grand Rapids: Baker, 2005]). Christotelism of this sort inevitably undercuts the witness to Christ rendered through God's providential ways with Israel in OT history. Recognition of this Christ-shaped providence allowed the early church to affirm the presence of a *visible* witness to the cross of Christ in the sensible nature of Israel's historical experience, as registered in its scriptures, while at the same time recognizing there were not multiple incarnations, but only one (cf. John 1:14). By grounding the OT's christological witness in the shape of God's providential performances in Israel per se, the recognition of which is made possible by the Incarnation (understood here in the more comprehensive sense as Christ's entire earthly life, ministry, death and resurrection), the early church united both Testaments in terms of the "figurating form" of Jesus Christ. In this way, a visible or "ocular" witness is given in the OT to realities that later manifest themselves in the form of Christ's earthly ministry, especially those which find concentrated expression in Christ's cross, while the uniqueness of the Incarnation as a post-OT event is not undercut, but preserved and understood as a figural paradigm for uniting both Testaments. See especially the discussion in Ephraim Radner, *The End of the Church: A Pneumatology of Christian Division in the West* (Grand Rapids: Eerdmans, 1998), 26–35, esp. 29 n. 48; cf. also his discussion of the figuralist hermeneutics of Blaise Pascal in *Spirit and Nature: The Saint-Médard Miracles in 18th-Century Jansenism* (New York: Herder & Herder, 2002), 141–54. For a slightly different approach to the visible nature of OT's figural witness to Christ, see John Behr's discussion of Origen's notion of the "body of scripture" in *The Way to Nicea* (Yonkers, N.Y.: St. Vladimir's Seminary Press, 2001), 172–78, esp. his remarks on p. 174. Origen's account places more stress upon the witness to Christ rendered by the visible form of the "body" of OT scripture, rather than the christomorphic shape of God's providential performances in Israel's history.

cation of the Old, nor on the other hand merely an appendix to the Old, still less a Second Temple text with a DNA that primarily derives from its historical environment. Its genre is perhaps best described in terms of *a transformed OT* that receives its place alongside the Old on analogy with and in accordance with the Old's antecedent authority (1 Cor 15:3-4).

HEILSGESCHICHTE AND THE RISE OF BIOLOGICAL SCIENCE

In turning now to a discussion of the rise of *Heilsgeschichte* as a model for relating the Testaments, it is instructive to note the interesting comments Walter Conser Jr. makes in another context with respect to John Williamson Nevin's approach to theology:

> Every era has its particular marks, its images, metaphors, and signs that capture its standpoint and express its message. The organic metaphor was one of the central images for the romantic movement which played such a significant role in nineteenth-century arts, letters, and science. Protestant theology was no exception to this influence, and Nevin's writings are suffused with biological allusions, organic metaphors, and developmental images. Nevin also used these linguistic conventions to express more formal theological points.[68]

In keeping with the spirit of his age, Nevin made use of the biological concept of "organicism" to develop an ecclesiology that would combat sectarianism by restoring the historical or visible unity of the church. So also, a number of biblical theologians in both the nineteenth and twentieth centuries have exploited the concept of "organicism" to develop a salvation-historical paradigm designed to provide an historical rationale for unifying the two Testaments.[69]

---

68. Walter Conser Jr., "Nevin on the Church," in *Reformed Confessionalism in Nineteenth-Century America: Essays on the Thought of John Williamson Nevin* (ed. S. Hamstra and A. Griffioen; Lanham, Md.: Scarecrow Press, 1996), 105.

69. On the confessionally Reformed side, see Geerhardus Vos, *Biblical Theology: Old and New Testaments* (Grand Rapids: Eerdmans, 1948). The works of the NT scholar Richard B. Gaffin Jr. and of the OT scholar Meredith G. Kline have self-consciously built upon Vos's approach to redemptive history, albeit with different results. By way of contrast, Gerhard von Rad broke with this emphasis upon "organicism" and developed a version of *Heilsgeschichte* that sought to exploit the forward-thrusting character of actualization (*Vergegenwärtigung*) in connection with tradition history.

One might well ask just how the unity of the Testaments came to stand in need of restoration in the first place. Apart from coming to terms with the rise of an approach to the Bible in which "history" as a temporal medium became the all-controlling category for its interpretation, it is impossible to understand the preconditions that gave birth to this restoration project. Historicism severed the ontological link uniting the two Testaments, leaving the modern church with purely economic categories for making sense of their unity. As a result, ontological rationales for the unity of the Testaments have been in retreat since the eighteenth century, and claims for the Trinity as the unifying reality (*res*) for both Testaments have followed suit.

Natura abhorret vacuum, and a number of Protestant evangelicals stepped into the vacuum generated by this retreat with the noble intention of restoring the unity historicism had dissolved. In the place of the ontological categories traditionally presupposed by the church's trinitarian rule of faith,[70] economic categories of various flavors began to present themselves as potential candidates for restoring the lost unity of the Testaments. Various rationales competed with one other in the quest to place a repair patch on the "broken Bible" bequeathed by modernity to the church, though in retrospect it now seems clear that historical rationales emerged as victor. As a result, one now routinely finds historically-oriented rationales assuming the place once occupied by the theological ontology of the church's Triune confession, for example, redemptive-*historical*, salvation-*historical*, the *historical* contexts provided by late Second Temple Judaism, not to mention a plethora of literary rationales for unifying the Testaments as well.[71]

Interestingly, Childs notes that while von Rad "was very critical of J. C. K. von Hofmann's *organic* concept of *Heilsgeschichte*," he nevertheless "succeeded in reformulating many of Hofmann's central ideas for a post-Wellhausen age" (Brevard Childs, "Gerhard von Rad in American Dress," in *The Hermeneutical Quest: Essays in Honor of James Luther Mays on his 65th Birthday* [ed. Donald G. Miller; Allison Park, Penn.: Pickwick, 1986], 82, emphasis added).

70. For example, the ontological rationale reflected in the patristic and medieval church's distinction between *signum* and *res*. In patristic exegetical practice, this distinction served to insure that the text of scripture and its theological subject matter, that is, the Triune God disclosing himself in Christ by the Spirit, were kept together. See Childs, *BTONT*, 80.

71. A brief list of some of the more prominent options now on offer should prob-

The crucial point to note at this juncture is that, in their efforts to rebuild and reconnect historicism's "broken Bible," salvation-historical approaches in the modern period offered no critical resistance to this trend, but sought instead to meet this trend *on its own terms*. This hermeneutical strategy, in turn, had a direct impact on the church's understanding of the nature and role of the theological concept of revelation.[72] As an age of biology, organism, and developmentalism, the nineteenth century was fascinated with the notion of relations, and the newly emerging "organicism" that accompanied the rise of the biological sciences led many romantics to embrace the idea that all relations were internal rather than external in character.[73] Under pressure from the external threat of historicism, conservative salvation-historical exegetes therefore refashioned the biblical concept of revelation in terms of an organically unfolding process of *historical development*, a fact which helps explain the strong emphasis upon the historically *progressive* character of revelation in late nineteenth-century versions of *Heilsgeschichte*.

In the hands of those who sought to closely correlate revelation with history, revelation and historical process came to share in a symbiotic relationship.[74] Biologically construed, historical development in scripture

---

ably include the categories of story, narrative, great themes of the Bible, intertextuality, and inner-biblical exegesis.

72. For a discussion of the hermeneutical factors associated with the emergence of "revelation" as a technical term in the modern period, see Frei, *Eclipse*, 51–53. Frei notes that the theological concept of revelation was formerly understood not as the subject matter of scripture, but as that which testified to scripture's true subject matter, namely, Christ himself. Modernism redefined revelation's function by detaching it from its instrumental role of rendering Christ through scripture and transposing it into an independent framework of its own. The effect of this was to transform the concept of revelation into a central topic in its own right. In this way the category of revelation came to occupy the place formerly occupied by the ontological Christ in biblical hermeneutics. See also John Webster, *Word and Church: Essays in Christian Dogmatics* (Edinburgh: T&T Clark, 2001), 25 n. 41.

73. Romantic hermeneutics embraced the organic logic inherent in the notion of "correlationalism," a hermeneutic Barth famously attacked in his attempts to restore a theological ontology of revelation for scripture. In any case, along with Childs, Barth rightly saw that the OT requires one external correlation above all others to do its sense making, and that correlation is not with the NT in the first instance, but with the Triune God revealing himself in Christ by his Spirit. On this view, the NT is not so much the goal of the OT as it is the OT's surprising fulfillment.

74. See Vos, *Biblical Theology*. See also Bultmann's remarks on von Hofmann's

was now understood as a process of unfolding in which later stages were understood to be potentially present in earlier stages, as the blossom is potentially present in the bud. Precisely because one could say that the later stage was present in the earlier stage, albeit in a potential rather than actual sense, one could argue for the basic continuity of biblical history. Applied to the relation between the Testaments, this salvation-historical paradigm implied that the OT and the NT mediate the same reality, not simply in terms of different textual instrumentalities, but in terms of a later textual instrumentality that is more concrete or real than its earlier counterpart. Thus the NT's literary witness was not simply *differently* instrumental, but *more* instrumental in its witness to Christ than the OT's.[75]

---

version of salvation history: "His thesis is that it is not the *words* of the Old Testament that are really prophecy, but the *history* of Israel, to which the Old Testament testifies.... Prophecy is rather history itself, insofar as this is a movement leading to a goal, and constantly bears within itself this goal as prophecy or promise. In fulfillment, history is understood as prophecy, in the significance of its movement becoming clear" (Bultmann, "Prophecy and Fulfillment," 55–56).

The hermeneutical effect of the shift from scripture's "*verba*" to a developmental or telic account of "history" as the context for prophetic revelation was to demote the status of the OT's witness from that of a christological "charter document" to a pre-Christian "prologue." Von Hofmann's developmental account of history should not be confused with a theological account of providence in which the words of scripture (*signum*) do their sense-making through things (*res*), that is, historical realities that reflect God's providential ways with Israel, and in so doing, disclose his identity to Israel.

75. The point at issue here does not concern the *epistemological* question whether, in light of the incarnation, the apostles enjoyed a fuller understanding of scripture's christological subject matter than did the prophets. By virtue of their location in the economy of the Word not yet made flesh, many prophets and righteous people longed to see and hear what the apostles saw, and did not see it (Matt 13:17). At the same time, as Christopher Seitz rightly reminds us, what we see in the OT as the consequence of our place in time is not a warrant for quantifying the extent of OT Israel's experience of Christ, especially inasmuch as we are outsiders looking in on a relationship between God and Israel that was not generally available, which Israel enjoyed as insiders (Deut 4:7–8, Ps 147:19–20; cf. John 4:22). That being said, the issue proper concerns the *ontological* status of the OT's christological sense in its own right. Instead of regarding the christological sense of both Testaments as equally real, though differently instrumental, *Heilsgeschichte* often construes the move from the OT's christological sense to the NT's christological sense in terms of a move "from shadow to reality," or what R. Kendall Soulen elsewhere refers to as a form of "horizontal Platonism." On this approach the OT's christological sense becomes an empty shadow, while the NT represents the real or true expression of Christ's eternal identity (R. Kendall Soulen,

By way of contrast, in the early church's ontological approach to Testamental unity, the unifying contribution made by revelation in both Testaments ultimately traced back to the fact that it proceeded from the same reality or subject matter, namely, the Triune God himself. Stated differently, it was not revelation *per se* which served to unify scripture, but revelation's subject matter, namely, God the Father, Son, and Holy Spirit. In the transformation of revelation's role effected by nineteenth-century versions of *Heilsgeschichte*, however, revelation now served to unify scripture, not because it proceeded from the same triune reality in both Testaments, but because it was closely associated with the concept of historical development and progress. In this way, the developmental logic driving nineteenth-century models for understanding salvation history came to dominate twentieth-century models for restoring the unity of the two Testaments.

While the hermeneutical impact of these newly minted rationales for unifying scripture is often overlooked or simply ignored, the net effect of their various "bridging strategies" was to blur the distinction between the two Testaments, effectively fusing them into a single, unbroken salvation history.[76] The biological concept of *organism* as a metaphor for negotiating the Bible's unity suggests that the OT "unfolds" into the NT in a manner analogous to an unbroken, organic development "from bud to blossom." However, conceiving of the Bible's unity in terms of an organic movement

---

"YHWH the Triune God," *Modern Theology* 15 [1999]: 32–35, 50 [32 n. 22]). Such a harmonistic construction of the relation between the Testaments not only subordinates the OT's christological sense to that of the New, but also cannot do justice to the Pauline language of juxtaposition as registered in Rom 1:17 and 2 Cor 3:18, a juxtaposition in which the movement between the Testaments is "from faith unto faith" (ἐκ πίστεως εἰς πίστιν) and "from glory to glory" (ἀπὸ δόξης εἰς δόξαν).

76. The church's traditional appeal to figural logic for uniting the Testaments avoids this problem. Figuration links up with the future in terms of an account of scripture's *verba* that finds its ground in an abiding theological ontology centered in God's triune being. Because traditional figural models retained this ontological dimension in their account of the Testaments, they were not under pressure to close the historical and semantic distance between the Testaments by means of a harmonizing fusion of the NT's christological sense with that of the Old, or what Childs elsewhere describes as "illegitimate allegory" (*BTONT*, 84–88; see also 14, 78). Unlike economically grounded models, such as salvation history, that lack an enduring ontological rationale by which to guarantee figuration's forward reach, on this account of figuration the two Testaments are united, while at the same time preserving their distinctive semantic and historical characteristics.

from bud to blossom fails to do justice to the fact that there is a real sense in which the Old Testament does not "naturally" unfold or "lean into" the New Testament.[77] Rather, the canon's own material form registers and preserves a distinction between the Testaments, a distinction reflective of the fact that first witness reached its end *before* the second witness began in a new mode of accordance and fulfillment.

Heilsgeschichte and the Rise of the Modern Novel

That the category of "story" shares a common feature with "salvation history" at this juncture is apparent from the fact that both approaches for relating the Testaments often draw upon analogies between the modern novel and the Bible. However, this analogy is also misleading, because the division between the two Testaments cannot be directly identified with a mere chapter division in a novel or book, nor can its crucial hermeneutical significance be appreciated in this way. To conceive of the literary divide between the OT and the NT in terms of a chapter division weakens the literary boundaries that serve to demarcate and enforce that divide by suggesting that these boundaries are merely internal to the NT's own literary witness, rather than external to it. Thus, instead of heightening our awareness of the distinctive way in which the OT delivers its christological sense alongside the NT, the "one novel" analogy ironically decreases that awareness by suggesting that the OT has a christological sense *just insofar as* it comprises a series of chapters that transition more or less seamlessly into the NT. Is the OT "Christian scripture" just insofar as it comprises part of a larger novel that includes the NT? Or is it Christian scripture in its own right, albeit in a manner and idiom differently instrumental than the NT?

Herein lies the problem with likening the Bible to the modern literary genre of the novel. Although a number of biblical scholars in our time have stressed the crucial function of "sequels" for understanding earlier parts of a "story" or "novel,"[78] the point at issue is not whether "sequels" help us appreciate more fully the significance of earlier events. They most

---

77. Brevard S. Childs, *Biblical Theology in Crisis* (Philadelphia: Westminster, 1970), 122.

78. See Francis Watson, "The Old Testament as Christian Scripture: A Response to Professor Seitz," *SJT* 52 (1999): 227–32 (229–30). Similar models and arguments may be found in N. T. Wright, *The New Testament and the People of God* (Minneapolis: Fortress, 1992), 115; see also Peter Enns, *Inspiration and Incarnation*, 152–56.

certainly do. The trouble is that in the modern genre of story or novel, the greater degree of insight offered by the sequel takes place *within* the overarching framework provided by the story or novel itself. Because the moment of discovery or "second reading" triggered by the sequel occurs within the confines of this single framework, the retrospective perspective it offers is easily conflated with the earlier reality of which the sequel speaks, thus making it difficult at best to speak of that earlier reality apart from the perspective offered by the sequel's rereading. In this way, the commendable desire to affirm the legitimacy and reality of "retrospective readings" of the OT shades off into the "retrospective fallacy," that is, an approach to relating the Testaments that allows the greater degree of theological insight on offer in the NT—newly emergent in the wake of Christ's resurrection—to place an undue strain upon the discrete integrity of the OT's christological sense.[79]

The problem with these analogies lies in their potential to blur the distinction between the Testaments registered by the canon's material form, a distinction that argues against the use of bridging strategies and modern analogies that inadvertently weaken that distinction. Moreover, the hermeneutical implications of this issue are far more significant than

---

79. It is interesting to observe at this juncture that, for Calvin, the figural significance of OT land blessings was not something that arose in the first instance as the retrospective result of a "second reading" of the OT conducted from a NT vantage point. Rather, these land blessings were understood as figures of the heavenly city *in their own right* (*Institutes of the Christian Religion* 2.11.1, 1:450–51). Commenting on this passage, Hans Frei raises a question and then answers it as follows: "Did they know what it was they enjoyed? Calvin does not say, and the enjoyment is not necessarily the same thing as the direct knowledge that this is what they were enjoying. The point is not really that the land of Canaan was a figure of the future inheritance at the time if, and only if, 'the Israelites' knew it to be such. More important is the fact that they enjoyed the land as a figure of the eternal city, and thus it *was* a figure at the time. It is not a figure solely in later retrospective interpretive stance" (*Eclipse*, 35–36). Frei fully recognized the hermeneutical dangers inherent in biblical figuration, noting that for "a person, an event, a body of laws, a rite, etc., to be both itself and real in its own right, and yet stand for something else later in time and equally real which is to fulfill it, imposes a strain especially on the earlier moment" (29). He nevertheless credits Calvin with recognizing that the OT derives its forward motion from its own figural sense, and *not* from "the wedding of that forward motion with a separate backward perspective upon it" (36), that is, from its correlation with a retrospective stance which then exercises a sort of Christian back draft upon the OT. See also his later comment regarding Calvin on p. 192.

some would have us believe, because the maintenance of a clear distinction between the Testaments serves to underscore the fact that the OT is not dependent upon correlation with the NT in order to have a Christian voice at all, or in the first place. Rather, the OT's literary integrity serves to remind us that it offers its witness to Christ off the back of its own literary form, on its own semantic level, in correlation with Christ the eternal *Logos*. In other words, the discrete character of the OT's literary witness and its character as Christian scripture go hand in hand. Recognizing this fact provides us with a much-needed means in our day to resist interpretive analogies and bridging strategies that undercut the discrete character of the OT's witness as Christian scripture in its own right.

In sum, although different analogies and models are used by historical and literary approaches to unify the Testaments, the fundamental problem with both lies in their failure to deal with the hermeneutical significance of the canon's material form as a two-Testament witness rather than a single novel, or for that matter, an organically unfolding "redemptive history" correlated to the historical process of revelation. The external stress these analogies place upon the discrete character of the OT's molecular structure, far from guaranteeing its Christian character, actually contribute to its breakdown and denaturization as Christian scripture. Rather than a *single* salvation-historical paradigm for relating the two Testaments in which the NT is privileged over the Old, what the canon of scripture actually presents us with are *two* discrete witnesses equidistant from the one Christ. The two witnesses to Christ must therefore be heard separately *and* in concert with one another.[80]

SALVATION HISTORY: IS IT REALLY BETTER THAN THE BIBLE?

In bringing this discussion to a close, I hope enough has been said to justify the conclusion that the fusing of the Testaments is itself an inevitable consequence of the loss of the church's ontological and figural rationale for uniting the Testaments. This rationale was not grounded in a general theory of divine being but in a highly particular theological ontology, one in which the first Testament marked the boundaries of the testimony to the *logos asarkos*, the "Word not yet made flesh" in Israel's history (though present through figure and promise), while the second Testament marked

---

80. On this see Childs, *BTONT*, 77–78.

the boundaries of the testimony to the *logos ensarkos*, the "Word made flesh" in the gospel era. Viewed from the perspective of John's logos Christology, the two-Testament shape of the church's canon derives from, and is fully grounded in, a particular ontology and Christ-shaped providence.

The hinge between the two Testaments formed by John's logos Christology also serves to remind us that a proper understanding of the canon's two-Testament shape is the direct correlate of a proper Christology. Errors in understanding the proper relation between the Testaments inevitably trace back to errors in Christology, as Childs himself reminds us.[81] The two Testaments cannot be conflated because there is a distinction to be maintained between the witness given to Christ prior to his incarnation and the witness that followed his incarnation. On the other hand, neither can the two Testaments be separated, for they bear witness to *unus et idem Christus*, that is, to one and the same Christ.

Time and space do not permit me to discuss further the nature of the differences between modern salvation-historical approaches to understanding scripture's unity and those of premodernity, especially the approach found in the early church fathers. Suffice it to say that premodern approaches to understanding the unity of scripture relied upon ontological and exegetical rationales rather than upon historical rationales per se. This is not to say that premodern approaches were historically disinterested, though it is doubtless true that their interest in history clearly reflects a different understanding of what counts as history. Rather, it is simply to recognize that premodern approaches did not fall prey to the modern temptation to place a burden upon history that it simply cannot bear, as though "history" could somehow operate as a substitute for God's Triune being when it comes to the matter of unifying the two-Testament witness of scripture.

Controversies over the law's function in Pauline scholarship offer us a late modern example of the potential hermeneutical frameworks have for muting the OT Torah's voice, as well as distorting the true nature of its relationship to the New. "Salvation history," it would seem, is *not* better than the Bible, though it may take us part of the way in our struggle to understand scripture's two-Testament witness. However, the notion that

---

81. Childs suggests that von Rad's attempt to exploit *Traditionsgeschichte* as a "bridging strategy" for uniting the Testaments failed to do justice to the canon's two-Testament shape, precisely because he failed to develop a canonical correlate to his Christology. See Childs, "Gerhard von Rad," 77–86, esp. 85.

salvation history or its successor paradigms can serve as a substitute for a particular theological ontology for relating the Testaments, namely, the Triune God himself, is an illusion. The distorted perspective on the Testaments that emerges when we adopt a salvation-historical paradigm that privileges the NT illustrates what might be called "the funhouse mirror effect," by wrongly proportionalizing the NT's role vis-à-vis the Old. Bodies sporting huge heads and tiny feet may be amusing, but they are hardly attractive. So also, the disproportional enlargement of the NT vis-à-vis the Old fostered by modern versions of salvation history leaves much to be desired.

The power of interpretive paradigms to function as modern substitutes for the canon is an ever-present danger in biblical studies, and must be guarded against. As Childs has been faithful to teach us, the point of stressing the need for a canonical hermeneutic is to stress the primacy of canon's own construal, literary structuring, and differentiated order (*taxis*) over against alternative construals offered by external hermeneutical frameworks such as *Heilsgeschichte*. Stressing the primacy of canon's own literary indices frees scripture to speak with its own voice. In so doing, it helps avoid the problems that inevitably arise when that voice is identified with a particular construal and approach that has been culturally conditioned in terms of a given time and place. When we fail to do this, biblical theology becomes little more than the cognate spirit or expression of a given age's dominant metaphors.

Reflections on the Rule of Faith

Leonard G. Finn

I belong to a community of faith which has received a sacred tradition in the form of an authoritative canon of scripture. There is a rule of faith and practice which has been formed because God is known.
— Brevard Childs

In his recent book on Brevard Childs, Daniel Driver described the rule of faith, the *regula fidei*, as "the most central plank in canonical figuration."[1] Ironically, however, one does not find an explicitly detailed and developed understanding of the rule in Childs's major work. Driver's own extended discussion of the rule and what it specifically means for Childs is instead derived more from a study of Childs's influences—the work of Hans von Campenhausen and particularly Bengt Hägglund—than from any detailed statements by Childs himself.[2] Yet in recent decades the idea of the rule of faith has become a somewhat fashionable topic of discussion in the field of what is called biblical theology. Whether this is due to the impact of Childs's thinking about canon, or to an increased interest in the early church and *ressourcement*, or whether it is simply this moment's particular manifestation of post-Enlightenment anxiety over the ability of the scriptures to continue to broker any sort of truth, is difficult and beyond the scope of this short paper to say. However, arguably, interest in the rule of faith is often not so much interest in the concept proper, but rather a product of its seemingly inherent adaptability—as we shall see, the rule eschews any strict and final articulation of its content—and therefore an interest in reinventing and deploying it to paradigms of thinking about the

---

1. Daniel R. Driver, *Brevard Childs, Biblical Theologian: For the Church's One Bible* (Tübingen: Mohr Siebeck, 2010), 249.
2. Ibid., 250–54.

scriptures which are often antithetical to the history of the rule's working in the church.

As is suggested by the quotation from Childs with which I began this paper, the rule of faith is fundamentally about a relationship between the scriptures and the church, the community through time which has developed, passed down, received, interpreted, and cherished those scriptures. How we think about the relationship—whether we conflate the two, radically separate them (a "no creed but the Bible" position), or understand them instead dialectically, as this paper will maintain—bears directly on our construal of the rule. It is also, running ahead of ourselves slightly, about an interpretative relationship *within* the scriptures. What this paper aims to achieve then is a brief overview of the rule of faith. First, we will survey a number of popular conceptualizations of the rule that have emerged in recent years. Second, using Irenaeus' understanding of the rule as a springboard,[3] we will attempt to develop a working understanding of the rule that respects the complex dialectical relationships involved.

ALTERNATIVE UNDERSTANDINGS OF THE RULE

The problem that current interest in the rule of faith seeks to overcome is a modern problem, beginning with the rise of Enlightenment thought. Hans Frei's analysis of the breakdown of the literal sense of the scriptures—or rather, the breakdown of western Christendom's ability to read them according to the literal sense—remains the classic exposition of what was lost and what has been made to serve in its place.[4] In brief, Frei argues that the precritical world understood the Bible as having literally and accurately described the world. They viewed figuration or typology as simply "a natural extension of literal interpretation," and understood the Bible's reading of the world as properly encompassing its own (and all) present

---

3. Following Childs's assessment (*The Struggle to Understand Isaiah as Christian Scripture* [Grand Rapids: Eerdmans, 2004], 48): "Many of the individual parts of his argument are common to Barnabas, Justin, and Clement, but the hermeneutical coherence and depth of theological reflection arise to a different level of understanding in Irenaeus."

4. Hans W. Frei, *The Eclipse of Biblical Narrative: A Study in Eighteenth and Nineteenth Century Hermeneutics* (New Haven: Yale University Press, 1980).

experiences of that world.⁵ What transpires in the eighteenth century is described by Frei as follows:

> The depicted biblical world and the real historical world began to be separated at once in the thought and sensibility.... This logical and reflective distance between narrative and reality increased steadily, naturally enough provoking a host of endeavors to bridge the gap. Not only did an enormous amount of inquiry into the factual truth (or falsity) of the biblical stories develop, but an intense concentration as well on their meaning and religious significance, whether factual or of some other sort.... The point is that the direction of interpretation now became the reverse of earlier days.⁶

The example Frei gives is Gen 1-3. With this epistemological shift, it now does not matter so much whether one reads the text as factual or allegorical, because its meaning—the fact that there was a Creator, a beginning to creation, and a fall in humanity's state of happiness and perfection—"is detachable from the specific story that sets it forth."⁷ Meaning—whether it is now to be found in historical facts, some manner of theological philosophy, spirituality, or feeling—now refers to something outside the scriptures, to and through which the scriptures must cohere, rather than the reverse. Such is the current dilemma. "The post-Enlightenment interpreter became," Childs notes, "either critical or anticritical, but the option of a precritical assumption [is] no longer available once Pandora's box had been opened."⁸

Whether understood in this way or not, current formulations of the rule of faith are essentially attempts by the church in modernity to understand how to read its scriptures once again in the wake of this history. As a contextual prologue to discussing what Childs's (and others') handling of the rule of faith looks like, let us consider three alternative paradigms below—rule as story, rule as tradition, and rule as community⁹—which I

---

5. Ibid., 2–3.
6. Ibid., 5.
7. Ibid., 5–6.
8. Brevard S. Childs, *The Church's Guide for Reading Paul: The Canonical Shaping of the Pauline Corpus* (Grand Rapids: Eerdmans, 2008), 126.
9. I must acknowledge here the significant overall debt my thinking on this topic owes to a seminar I had with Donald Collett in the fall of 2011, specifically on the rule of faith. The influence is particularly evident in the proposed categorization

will suggest are finally inadequate because they each, in their respective ways, recapitulate the shift Frei has described: the rule—and with it the meaning and coherence of the scriptures—is conceived in each as something external.

RULE OF FAITH AS A STORY

Story, narrative, and drama have obvious appeal in that narrative structure is an organizational principle easily grasped by anyone. Indeed, from the point of view of apologetics or evangelism in the practice of the church, there is perhaps much to commend story as a helpful means of articulating certain aspects of the Christian faith to those unfamiliar with it. As a hermeneutical framework for biblical interpretation, however, it is deeply flawed. Paul Blowers is representative of the issues at stake.[10] He writes:

> The Rule of Faith (which was always associated with scripture itself) served the primitive Christian hope of articulating and authenticating a world-encompassing story or metanarrative of creation, incarnation, redemption, and consummation. I will argue that in the crucial "proto-canonical" era in the history of Christianity, the Rule, being a narrative construction, set forth the basic "dramatic" structure of a Christian vision of the world, posing as an hermeneutical frame of reference for the interpretation of Christian Scripture and Christian experience, and educing the first principles of theological discourse and of a doctrinal substantiation of Christian faith.[11]

In other words, the rule of faith is a metanarrative, a grand plot, that can be discerned in the scriptures that then provides coherence to the Christian life: the rule "offers believers a place in the story by commending a way of

---

schema for alternative conceptualizations of the rule, which follows Collett's breakdown and argument.

10. Paul M. Blowers, "The *Regula Fidei* and the Narrative Character of Early Christian Faith," *ProEccl* 6 (1997): 199–228. We could also easily have considered N. T. Wright, who has certainly influenced Blowers's thinking and that of others on this approach; Blowers, however, is not only representative, but he specifically addresses this approach's hermeneutics within the framework of the development of the understanding of the rule within the early church.

11. Ibid., 202.

life framed by the narrative of creation, redemption in Jesus Christ, and new life in the Spirit."[12]

There are a number of serious problems with this conceptualization of the rule as grand narrative from creation of the cosmos to the living Christian believer today. First, the canonical shape of the scriptures—two Testaments, each encompassing a variety of genres and ordered in schemes other than chronological—actively resists a storyline construal; to then read the scriptures through such a hermeneutical reduction is ultimately to read against their own coherence.[13] Second, it is not even clear that the scriptures are the necessary foundation of the rule for Blowers, for whom its basis in early church history is located in oral tradition, performance, and the incorporation of the believer into the drama's final act.[14] Third, and finally, the authoritative function of canon—that is, its role as defining the limits of normative scriptures for the church—has been erased in Blowers's conflation of what the scriptures say with what the church does or (in his language) performs.

RULE OF FAITH FROM TRADITION

Craig Allert and William Abraham may serve as representatives of this particular paradigm of the rule. Like Blowers, they resist a normative role for the scriptures, but their resistance is contingent upon a particular understanding of an antecedent rule present in the church. Whereas story at least in principle derives from the scriptures, Allert's and Abraham's positing of tradition (in their respective understanding of that term) establishes a rule external to and over the scriptures.

Allert's position (and Abraham's) is rooted in a narrow understanding of canon, which conceives of it only as a final definitive list of books and only in the sense of there being a New Testament. "Technically," he writes

---

12. Ibid., 214.
13. A good deal of Blowers's argument makes the case that Irenaeus and the church fathers worked with a narratival understanding of the rule or the "hypothesis" of the scriptures; see ibid., 210–20. For a strong case against Blowers's argument on this matter, see Nathan MacDonald, "Israel and the Old Testament Story in Irenaeus's Presentation of the Rule of Faith," *JTI* 3 (2009): 281–98. MacDonald writes, "On no occasion does Irenaeus fill out the space between the first and second 'heads' with a rehearsal of OT history ... [and, citing Blower,] we do not find 'a drama gradually unfolded with a coherent plot, climaxing in the coming of Jesus'" (286).
14. Blowers, "*Regula Fidei*," 204–5.

on this point, "when we talk of the fathers and *the* Bible, we are speaking anachronistically because the fathers of the first four centuries did not have a common Bible to which they appealed."[15] Allert acknowledges the early church's authoritative reception of "the Hebrew Scriptures" and even notes that what would become New Testament texts are not accorded the same level of authority; nevertheless, he proceeds as though that antecedent authoritative witness had no bearing for the church—what mattered was "the apostolic preaching ... the pure doctrine of Christianity and the gospel of Jesus Christ ... carried out from the action of God through the Son and the Spirit and passed on by the apostles, bishops, deacons, and presbyters."[16] Unable to recognize that the church received the scriptures of Israel precisely as authoritative writ, Allert can only come to the conclusion that to speak of a Bible for the church is to speak of a closed New Testament canon, and so necessarily "the church existed before the Bible" and "its first goal was to settle the content of the faith, and it did this using means other than the Bible."[17] In other words, for Allert the rule of faith emerges in the church, quite apart from the body of authoritative writing the church already had.[18]

Abraham also proceeds from the point of view that canon is constituted by a list; however, his argument takes matters even further in that such list-making encompasses the whole realm of the church's practice, the church's "diverse and complex canonical heritage," which over time moves conceptually from "ecclesial canons to epistemic norms."[19] Abraham argues that "the multiple materials, persons, and practices which effectively constitute the canonical heritage of the Church were and are intended to function together as complementary means of initiating converts into the life of faith," and therefore that one or another "canon" does

---

15. Craig D. Allert, *A High View of Scripture?: The Authority of the Bible and the Formation of the New Testament Canon* (Grand Rapids: Baker, 2007), 74.

16. Ibid., 111. Contra Allert on this point, see Christopher R. Seitz, *The Character of Christian Scripture: The Significance of a Two-Testament Bible* (Grand Rapids: Baker, 2011), 193 n. 2.

17. Allert, *A High View of Scripture*, 76, 82.

18. Ibid., 125. Allert writes, "Irenaeus confirms that the church of the second century really had no need of a written canon because it already had a canon of truth. It was this Rule of Faith against which everything was measured in the second century—even the writings of the developing New Testament."

19. William J. Abraham, *Canon and Criterion in Christian Theology: From the Fathers to Feminism* (New York: Oxford University Press, 1998), 27.

not necessarily function as finally authoritative.[20] The church canonized the New Testament, he argues, but it has also canonized creeds and saints.[21] Moreover, when Irenaeus and Tertullian had to counter the Gnostics, they found "the development of a scriptural canon ... utterly inadequate" and developed a rule of faith (or rule of truth), which as "a summary of Christian teaching ... can be handed over in Christian initiation," functioning "not as an epistemic norm, but as a norm of Christian identity."[22] In short, the rule of faith for Abraham is an abstraction of the tradition as a whole. It is a reflection or summary of the entire life of the church—its scriptures, but also its creeds, its liturgical practices, its sacraments, its ecclesial structure, its saints, its iconography—which is authoritatively antecedent to any one of those "canons" and to which they ultimately derive their authority in practice. As with Allert, the Old Testament is virtually absent in understanding how the church understood the rule of faith.[23]

Worthy of mention, but distinct here, is Robert Jenson. He is perhaps a hybrid of the previous two categorizations. The rule for Jenson is "a sort of communal linguistic awareness of the faith delivered to the apostles, which sufficed the church for generations": it is therefore not a textual thing, but a "community self-consciousness" and "confidence in the guiding presence of the Spirit."[24] Unlike Allert or Abraham, Jenson recognizes the fact that the "Old Testament was scripture for the apostles and disciples before they were apostles and disciples," noting even von

---

20. Ibid., 28.
21. Ibid., 35.
22. Ibid, 36.
23. Abraham argues that the church's acceptance of the "Jewish scriptural tradition" as its own was merely a necessary response to Marcion; see ibid., 33–34. What Abraham (and Allert) miss is the historical anterior authority of the scriptures of Israel for the church—indeed for Christ himself. Following Hans von Campenhausen, Childs puts the matter forcefully: "The problem of the early church was not what to do with the Old Testament in light of the gospel, which was Luther's concern, but rather the reverse. In light of the Jewish scriptures which were acknowledged to be the true oracles of God, how were Christians to understand the good news of Jesus Christ?" See Brevard S. Childs, *Biblical Theology of the Old and New Testaments: Theological Reflection on the Christian Bible* (Minneapolis: Fortress, 1993), 226 (hereafter *BTONT*); cf. Hans von Campenhausen, *The Formation of the Christian Bible* (Philadelphia: Fortress, 1972), 63–64.
24. Robert W. Jenson, *Canon and Creed: Interpretation: Resources for the Use of Scripture in the Church* (Louisville: Westminster John Knox, 2010), 15.

Campenhausen's inappropriate use of "adoption" in discussing its reception.[25] Nevertheless, in line with Jenson's overall systematic theology, the Old Testament's fundamental role is to be read "as *narrative* of God's history with his people."[26] Within Jenson's overall systematic theology, such terms as "history" and "narrative" have particular significance, and thus Jenson is not necessarily thereby relegating the Old Testament to mere prolegomena of the New. Nevertheless, Jenson's rule of faith is not something that appears to emerge at all from the Old Testament,[27] and likewise canonical scripture is not normative (*norma normans non normata*) until after formation of the New Testament (that is, following the church's having "collected and certified the documentary relics of the apostolic message").[28] The rule of faith is, for Jenson, something that emerges then only as a result of the dual process of the canonization of the New Testament and the development of the creeds.[29] His understanding of the rule must also therefore be grouped under the general set of deficiencies found within the traditional paradigm of the rule of faith.

RULE OF FAITH IN COMMUNAL USE

The third and final alternative paradigm to be discussed here is a sociolinguistic one. I will briefly offer two rather different examples. First, in his later career, Hans Frei became concerned with an overemphasis on narrative and literary form in his work, which might suggest biblical meaning was located solely within the text itself.[30] As Michael Higton has summa-

---

25. Ibid., 14.
26. Ibid., 23.
27. "The rule of faith saved the Old Testament as canon for the church—or rather, the church for the Old Testament canon—but in the process it did not open itself to the shape of the Old Testament's own narrative, and so it could not support the Old Testament's specific role in the church's practice"; see ibid., 29.
28. Jenson comments that the "foundational order of the church's norms" do not begin with the scriptures—which appear canonical only insofar as they contain both Old and New Testaments—but rather with "antecedent ministry and creed ... [and before them] the continuous liturgy of the church." See Robert W. Jenson, *Systematic Theology* (New York: Oxford University Press, 1997), 1:26–27.
29. Jenson, *Canon and Creed*, 41. The canonical New Testament and the creeds are thus the primary dialogic place where faith is essentially understood. The Old Testament would seem to have been left behind in such a formulation.
30. As Childs succinctly notes, "Hans Frei ... ultimately sought to escape the

rized the hermeneutical move: "Frei's new starting point was a conviction that there was a strong line of continuity in *Christian uses* of the Gospels."[31] To cast this logic within terms we have been discussing (and with a corollary to midrash in the Jewish tradition), Frei argues that the rule of faith is finally an interpretive rule of reading amongst the community, the church. "Established or 'plain' readings," Frei writes, "are warranted by their agreement with a religious community's rules for reading its sacred text.... The plausibility structure in this case is a literary imitation of a religious community's authority structure."[32]

David Kelsey, on the other hand, pushes this notion of community interpretation to a subversive level. It is almost not appropriate to pair him with Frei in this regard. Kelsey's proposed understanding of the rule of faith, clearly influenced by Wittgenstein, amounts to a radical deconstruction of scripture, tradition, canon, and authority. His argument is that scripture is never authoritative in itself, but rather in its *use*. To call a set of texts "scripture" is logically to make a statement about *how they are used* by a community in an authoritative manner in the context of that community's life.[33] Like Allert and Abraham above, canonization for Kelsey is functionally the historical list-making event, "a process of selecting certain writings out of a larger literary pool." Yet his focus is not on canon, but rather on what that selected community was achieving for itself. That is, he writes, "in declaring just these writings 'canon' the church was giving part of a self-description of her identity."[34] By definition, therefore, the concepts of "church" and "scripture" cannot be understood separately; community identity and scriptural authority have been completely

---

problem of the Bible's ostensive referentiality by speaking of the narrative's self-referentiality akin to a realistic novel. To read the Hebrew Scriptures only in terms of typology is to denigrate its historical role by rendering it into a timeless narrative figuration." See Childs, *Church's Guide*, 35.

31. Mike Higton, *Christ, Providence, and History: Hans W. Frei's Public Theology* (New York: T&T Clark, 2004), 201.

32. Hans W. Frei, "The 'Literal Reading' of Biblical Narrative in the Christian Tradition: Does It Stretch or Will It Break?," in *Theology and Narrative: Selected Essays* (ed. George Hunsinger and William C. Placher; New York: Oxford University Press, 1993), 144.

33. David H. Kelsey, *The Uses of Scripture in Recent Theology* (Philadelphia: Fortress, 1975), 89–112.

34. Ibid., 105.

merged.[35] "Canon," on the other hand, needs to be carefully differentiated from "scripture": scripture is "whole," but in "an irreducible variety" of ways, dependent upon the theologian and the theological proposal being made.[36] In other words, to speak of scripture's "wholeness" is at the same time to make a statement about its use and the specific interrelationship of its parts in diversity in that use.[37] There is therefore in practice "no one standard concept 'scripture.'"[38] There is the "historical canon," that which is in its use properly part of that concept of "scripture," but there is also the "working canon" of the theologian, which does not properly belong to that concept. Likewise, even "authority" must be understood from the perspective of the theologian's specific use of scripture in authorizing proposals and in the specifics of the assessment and call for response: towards faith or transformation, logical argument, interpretation of history, etc.[39] At the end of the day in Kelsey's paradigm, the rule of faith cannot even be truly spoken of, except as a broad designation for the individual practices of those who self-identify with this community, the church, which accepts scripture as canonical and authoritative in a similarly individually determined fashion. Paul McGlasson's analysis gets to the crux of the problem. "Kelsey is doing liberal theology.... He has drastically reversed the logic of interpretation, in which the life of the reader is adjusted to the subject matter of scripture rather than the reverse," a reversal which is merely that result of Kelsey's having ignored what canon implies: namely, that "scripture is already *construed* ... already shaped theologically."[40] It is precisely with regard to that theological shape that any proper understanding of the rule of faith emerges.

To summarize, three similar problems emerge in each of the paradigms discussed. First, the scriptures are unable to broker their own meaning on their own authority. Something external to them—completely in keeping with Frei's analysis of biblical hermeneutical problem of an "eclipse"—needs to be mobilized whether a dramatic retelling or "gist" of

---

35. Ibid., 93–94.
36. Ibid., 100–104.
37. Ibid., 106.
38. Ibid., 103.
39. Ibid., 148–50, 152.
40. Paul McGlasson, *Invitation to Dogmatic Theology: A Canonical Approach* (Grand Rapids: Brazos, 2006), 66–67, 49.

the scriptures,⁴¹ the creeds and traditions of the church, or the interpretive role of the community that has received them.⁴² Second, the Old Testament—when not simply absent from consideration—plays a secondary, preliminary, or at least not contradictory role. As we shall see, this is a complete reversal of the early church reality and a critical failure in being able to grasp the rule of faith. Third, all three paradigms fail to recognize that the scriptures—in their material form, first as the scriptures of Israel and then later as a Bible with two Testaments, Old and New—are authoritative in the church for its faith because they speak in living terms to each generation about their subject matter—that is, they preach Christ, teach the character of the Triune God, and reveal the divine will. As McGlasson has expressed this relationship: "God speaks only in the here and now; yet he speaks through the instrument of scripture, which is treasured as the source of ethical instruction by each new generation of the church of Jesus Christ."⁴³ We will now turn to an understanding of the rule of faith within such an understanding of the scriptures and the church.

An Exegetical Paradigm, or "All Roads Lead to Irenaeus"⁴⁴

Understanding the scriptural hermeneutics of the early church is critical for grasping the nature of the relationship of the scriptures to the rule of faith, as the early church without a New Testament viewed the scriptures of Israel as fully sufficient for preaching Christ and developing a Trinitarian hermeneutic.⁴⁵ In this discussion, however, we will narrow our focus. Driver's analysis of the rule of faith in Childs's project, with which we began, points to a correlation with that of Irenaeus: their work reflects "a framework instead of a method."⁴⁶ Like Childs, Irenaeus never gives a

---

41. Seitz, *Character of Christian Scripture*, 193.
42. As Seitz has put the matter: "All too often in the recent period one encounters an assessment of the canon of Christian Scripture that emphasizes a development from OT to NT to rule to creeds and then seeks to understand the authority of Scripture as related to an underlying 'rule,' which in its way is said to provide a kind of creedal summary derived from Scripture, or operating independently and crucially from it, so as to provide the rationale or lens or delimiting evaluation of what the significance of Scripture might be said, perennially, to be" (ibid., 192).
43. McGlasson, *Invitation to Dogmatic Theology*, 226.
44. Driver, *Brevard Childs*, 252.
45. Seitz, *Character of Christian Scripture*, 191.
46. Driver, *Brevard Childs*, 252. Driver nuances this view slightly insofar as he

detailed definition for the rule. Sometimes narrative, sometimes creedal, Irenaeus' "differing formulations" of the rule, to borrow the assessment of John O'Keefe and R. R. Reno, "can frustrate a historian searching for a precise definition."[47] Childs's concise description of Irenaeus' use is perhaps closest for both: "In Irenaeus, the rule of faith was a summary of the apostolic faith that was held as central to the church's confession. It provided the grounds of the church's faith and worship over and against deviant Gnostic speculation. The rule was not identical with scripture, but was that sacred apostolic tradition, both in oral and written form, that comprised the church's story."[48] While not inaccurate, much is obviously still left unexplained in such a curt assessment. How are we to understand the rule of faith in and from its relationships with the various entities and practices Childs identifies: scripture, apostolic tradition, and the church in its confession, faith and worship? It is perhaps helpful to approach the matter not so much from the perspective of what the rule *is* for Irenaeus— that is, its specific content, which is variously expressed (and frustratingly so)—but rather what it *does*.

Let us expand this thought by first observing that Irenaeus sees in the scriptures themselves a coherent order and inherently relational character, which points to their own system or *hypothesis* for reading. A key text is found early in *Against Heresies*, where Irenaeus argues that the Valentinian heretics read the scriptures via an *external* hypothesis, "which neither the prophets announced, nor the Lord taught, nor the apostles delivered," and they thereby "disregard the order and connection of the scriptures, and so far as in them lies, dismember and destroy the truth."[49] John Behr observes that Irenaeus' terminology is precise here: the hypothesis of a

---

subsequently points to a move from framework towards method in Childs's work—a move from Irenaeus to Origen, to extend the analogy; see 253.

47. John J. O'Keefe and Russell R. Reno, *Sanctified Vision: An Introduction to Early Christian Interpretation of the Bible* (Baltimore: Johns Hopkins University Press, 2005), 119.

48. Childs, *Struggle to Understand Isaiah*, 47; cf. Childs, *BTONT*, 31–32. We should not simply ignore the fact that Childs uses terms such as "summary" and "story," which have been critiqued in this discussion. That the rule of faith can be accurately described as "the most central plank in canonical figuration" demonstrates that Childs has a more complicated understanding than is here expressed should be quite clear; nevertheless, the use of such terms is indicative of the larger difficulties of being able to *speak* about the rule and what it is, as will be discussed below.

49. Irenaeus, *Adversus Haereses* 1.8.1 (*ANF* 1:326).

literary work, in the context of Greek thinking, is "what the poet posits ... the basic outline" of the work, but what the Valentinians have done is use "the words of phrases from Scriptures, but ... creatively adapted them to a different hypothesis, and so have created their own fabrication."[50] Stated somewhat tautologically, the rule here is simply the understanding of the coherence proper to the scriptures that permits one then to read them coherently. Irenaeus' analogy of the mosaic of a king is often cited because it so perspicaciously makes this point about the coherence of the scriptures through the rule: just as the jewels that make up such a beautiful mosaic can be rearranged to create "the miserable likeness" of a dog or fox that might deceive someone unfamiliar with what a king rightly looks like, so the "connections, words, expressions, and parables" of the scriptures can be rearranged according to alien hypotheses and thus made to deceive those who do not know the true hypothesis to which the scriptures in themselves point.[51]

This conclusion, however, clearly pushes back against any simplistic understandings of *sola scriptura*. For Irenaeus this correct hypothesis of the scriptures emerges for the church dialectically—that is, the scriptures' coherence emerges in a particular relationship to the apostolic preaching. Behr captures this relationship well: "The coherence of Scripture, read as speaking of the Christ who is revealed in the Gospel, the apostolic preaching of Christ 'according to scripture.'"[52] Now, it should be evident that what Behr (and Irenaeus) mean by "scripture" or "the scriptures" is what is now called the Old Testament, and therefore what is being described is a relationship between the early church's kerygma and the scriptures of Israel, during a period when what is now called the New Testament was still in flux as canon. It is precisely from this encounter between Christian proclamation and the scriptures that the rule emerges.

To put the matter differently, from the earliest moments of the church there was the recognition that the Christian proclamation and the scriptures of Israel spoke about the same thing, or rather the same person, Jesus Christ who was one in being with the God of Israel who raised him from the dead on the third day according to those scriptures (1 Cor 15:3-4). The

---

50. John Behr, *The Way to Nicea* (Crestwood, N.Y.: St. Vladimir's Seminary Press, 2001), 31–32.

51. *Haer.* 1.8.1 (*ANF* 1:326); cf. Behr, *Way to Nicea*, 35–36; Childs, *Struggle to Understand Isaiah*, 47.

52. Behr, *Way to Nicea*, 36.

apostolic witness to the death and resurrection of Jesus Christ thus reflects an epistemological breakthrough that understands that shared subject matter and thereby enables the witness to the ontological reality of God already present in Israel's scriptures to be fully seen at last. The resurrection opens the eyes of those first Christians to what was already in fact in their scriptures (Luke 24:31a), and therefore it does not so much give the scriptures their coherence as enable their existing coherence to be grasped. It logically follows then that to speak of Christ is necessarily to speak of him "according to the scriptures," and likewise the apostolic proclamation properly understood is itself characterized by a dialectical engagement of the scriptures with the fact of the resurrection.[53] In other words, the grammar of the Christian proclamation is from the beginning the grammar of the scriptures of Israel. C. Kavin Rowe helpfully frames the issue at hand from another direction:

> The relation of God the Father, Jesus Christ, and the Spirit as well as the relation of Jesus' divinity and humanity had to be specified in terms consistent with the most fundamental theological thrust of the Old Testament, that of the unity and singularity of the one Creator God and the directives for exclusive worship that were inextricably bound with this God's identity. That YHWH (*kyrios*) is both God the Father and Jesus Christ leads of necessity to the question of "essence," or "being," most acutely at the point of the Christian worship of Jesus.... The early church had to find a way to account for its claims and practice, and such an accounting was necessary along ontological lines because of the continuing authority of the Old Testament.[54]

It is out of this necessary dialectical relationship of apostolic preaching and authoritative scriptures that the rule of faith emerges.

This historical understanding of the rule of faith—as grounded initially in the Old Testament without reference to the New—is antithetical to much contemporary North American evangelical temperament, as is reflected in the various formulation of the rule previously discussed.

---

53. This point should become apparent as the argument progresses; however, it is important to note up front that while the term, "dialectic," can suggest subsumption and progress, my use of the term throughout is otherwise intended to denote distinction in relationship and ongoing dynamic tension.

54. C. Kavin Rowe, "Biblical Pressure and Trinitarian Hermeneutics," *ProEccl* 11 (2002): 307.

While it is beyond the scope of this paper to explore the reasons behind the collapse of trust in the Christian witness of the Old Testament, the point needs to be made that the breakdown is ultimately an epistemological product of modernity.[55] Seitz's observations about the early church's understanding of the sufficiency of what we now call the Old Testament necessarily must hold true today: "The Scriptures of Israel are viewed as fully sufficient to preach Christ, prophesy Christ, adumbrate Christ, demonstrate Christ and the Holy Spirit both as active and functioning from beginning to end, through the various economies of the scriptures' long story."[56] Properly understood, then, the New Testament as canon captures the witness of the apostolic preaching and thereby serves, as Seitz argues:

> to clarify the nature of "apostolic" teaching as public (as against secret or private), as constraining what is meant by "apostolic" (as against claims of further apostolic), as "in accordance with the Scriptures" (as against the idea that "the apostolic" and "the prophetic" writings are subject to what were to be called "antitheses" and this at a number of points) and as confirming both the scope and anterior authority of the Scriptures and thereby laying claim to a similar status of their own, in effect producing an "Old" Testament where there had been a Scripture and a correlate, accorded witness, the "New" Testament.[57]

To return to Irenaeus, a second point that clearly emerges from this early discussion in *Against Heresies* and the analogy of the mosaic of the king is that the rule entails a dialectical relationship not only between the

---

55. Seitz's historical analysis, "Scripture Becomes Religion(s): The Theological Crisis of Serious Biblical Interpretation in the Twentieth Century," offers a helpful understanding of the collapse in Anglo-American thinking over the past two centuries; see Christopher R. Seitz, *Figured Out: Typology and Providence in Christian Scripture* (Louisville: Westminster John Knox, 2001), 13–33.

56. Seitz, *Character of Christian Scripture*, 193–94.; cf. Christopher R. Seitz, *The Goodly Fellowship of the Prophets: The Achievement of Association in Canon Formation* (Grand Rapids: Baker, 2009), 130.

57. Seitz, *Character of Christian Scripture*, 195. Behr notes in this regard that "the point of canon is not to stymie inquiry and reflection, but rather to make it possible." True inquiry and reflection are simply not possible in a Gnostic context involving "secret, oral traditions." The New Testament in its canonical public and limiting capacity serves precisely as a buttress against heretical practices and threats. See Behr, *Way to Nicea*, 38–39.

scriptures and apostolic preaching, but also between the scriptures and the church. An important passage a little later is worth quoting at length:

> As I have already observed, the Church, having received this preaching and this faith, although scattered throughout the whole world, yet, as if occupying but one house, carefully preserves it. She also believes these points [of doctrine] just as if she had but one soul, and one and the same heart, and she proclaims them, and teaches them, and hands them down, with perfect harmony, as if she possessed only one mouth. For, although the languages of the world are dissimilar, yet the import of the tradition is one and the same. For the Churches which have been planted in Germany do not believe or hand down anything different, nor do those in Spain, nor those in Gaul, nor those in the East, nor those in Egypt, nor those in Libya, nor those which have been established in the central regions of the world. But as the sun, that creature of God, is one and the same throughout the whole world, so also the preaching of the truth shineth everywhere, and enlightens all men that are willing to come to a knowledge of the truth. Nor will any one of the rulers in the Churches, however highly gifted he may be in point of eloquence, teach doctrines different from these (for no one is greater than the Master); nor, on the other hand, will he who is deficient in power of expression inflict injury on the tradition. For the faith being ever one and the same, neither does one who is able at great length to discourse regarding it, make any addition to it, nor does one, who can say but little diminish it.[58]

A number of observations regarding the relationship between the rule of faith and the church can be made. First, the church is that which, in addition to having received the scriptures,[59] has also "received this preaching and this faith." The church, we might therefore say, exists by and with the dialectical relationship between these two—the scriptures and the apostolic proclamation—described above and therefore the rule of faith. Luther's well-known definition of a church as that place where the gospel

---

58. *Haer.* 1.10.2 (*ANF* 1:331).
59. Indeed, the word "received" may even be too active. Properly understood, the church came into being holding the scriptures of Israel as its own as an *a priori* fact of its existence, as evidenced by the first recorded sermon from Peter (Acts 2:14–36). See also von Campenhausen, *Formation of the Christian Bible*, 21 n. 1. He writes, "It is important to realise that there was at first no attempt to provide any justification for taking over the old Jewish Bible and allowing it authority. There was not the slightest occasion to give the matter thought."

is truly proclaimed and the sacraments rightly administered is in essence a restatement of this principle. The rule of faith is grounded in the church's beginning and is the foundation of its continuing life.

Second, the church exists *for* this rule. It "preserves it," and through continued preaching and teaching, it "enlightens all men that are willing to come to a knowledge of the truth." We are back to the analogy of the mosaic here, for what enables one person to believe the "miserable likeness" of the dog to be a king and another to dismiss it without a second thought is clearly something the church does in its relationship to the rule. Irenaeus makes the point that there are barbarians "who, in the absence of written documents, have believed this faith." He continues:

> If any one were to preach to these men the inventions of heretics ... they would at once stop their ears and flee as far as possible, not enduring even to listen to the blasphemous address. Thus, by means of that ancient tradition of the apostles, they do not suffer their mind to conceive anything of the ... portentous language of these teachers, among whom neither Church not doctrine has ever been established.[60]

Even in the absence of the scriptures proper, the "ancient tradition of the apostles," together with "church" and "doctrine," stand for Irenaeus as that which provide the believer with the rule of faith that enables proper discernment in matters of truth.

Now there is an obvious danger of misunderstanding Irenaeus here. If it is the case that the rule of faith can be grasped at an individual level without the ability to read the scriptures proper, are they not therefore at some level unnecessary? Behr is helpful with this dilemma. The rule of faith is, as we have discussed above, "the embodiment or crystallization of scripture, read as speaking of Christ who is revealed in the Gospel, the apostolic preaching of Christ 'according to Scripture.'"[61] In that sense, it functions as what Behr terms a "first principle" of reading the scriptures.[62] The scriptures are not jettisoned as so much excess baggage upon arriving at such a first principle; rather the first principle—that is, the rule of faith—is that which the church preserves, preaches, teaches, and continues

---

60. *Haer.* 3.4.2 (*ANF* 1:417).
61. Behr, *Way to Nicea*, 36.
62. Ibid., 33–34.

to learn anew, so as to enable those scriptures to speak in a Christian way to each generation.

It follows then—and this is the third and final point to be made—that the rule enables such a Christian reading of the scriptures *diachronically* in the church. Irenaeus emphasizes the oneness of the church and its tradition: "one soul ... the same heart.... For, although the languages of the world are dissimilar, yet the import of the tradition is one and the same." The point here is that it is through the church's relationship to the rule of faith that its scriptures and its proclamation are *translatable* to the nations and from generation to generation. Positively, the rule of faith is precisely what enables the continuing dynamic relationship of the Word of God to the church which has cherished it across time and space. Negatively, it prevents both the "highly gifted ... in point of eloquence" and those "deficient in power of expression" from being a threat to the faith. It is, in other words, why in the church both second-century German barbarians and twenty-first-century North American academics can hear the Word spoken by the scriptures in their own particular languages and yet see the same beautiful image of a king.

However, at this juncture we must come back to the beginning—the scriptures—to put the relationship of the church and the rule in proper perspective. The danger here is an understanding of the relationships that would dislodge the scriptures from their continuing foundational role for the church. If the church has—even understood in the providence of God—the rule of faith and the role of preserving and teaching it, to what extent are the scriptures foundational for the life of the church in a continuing sense? Is it not the case that rule in the church becomes foundational for the proper interpretation of the scriptures? Although careful to root the coherency of the rule in the scriptures, O'Keefe and Reno potentially veer in such a direction: "Correct interpretation [of the scriptures] flows from the one extrinsically given rule to the discernment of the intrinsic scriptural logic of fulfillment in Christ. *One finds the rule in scripture if one accepts its authority from the church*."[63] Likewise von Campenhausen argues the following:

> According to Irenaeus Scripture and tradition, as regards to their doctrinal content, are in entire agreement, and *the purpose of Scripture is to confirm the teaching of the Church* against all doubts.... The one rule

---

63. O'Keefe and Reno, *Sanctified Vision*, 119, emphasis added.

and guideline ... is the "canon of truth," that is to say: the content of the faith itself, which the Church receives from Christ, to which she remains faithful, and by which she lives. By this is meant neither a *Summa* of dogmatic propositions nor an unchangeable confessional formula nor even the sacred Scripture as such, however certain it may be that the latter teaches and contains the truth. The truth is alive in the Church from the beginning; it is actualised in her, so to speak, by its own power, and is never lost to her. [His] confidence in the Church and in the Church's word exists unbroken; and, from this point of view, he had no need of a New Testament.[64]

The distinction being made in the present argument in contrast to these two positions just presented—if I am reading them correctly—is subtle but important. It is one thing to say that the church's relationship to the rule of faith is a unique one of receiving, treasuring, and conveying it through time and space, and that truly the gates of hell will not prevail against it in that role. It is another thing to say, however, that it does so on its own authority, superior to, coequal with, or even (following von Campenhausen above) merely confirmed by the scriptures. Rather, the church's relationship to its scriptures must be understood as that of a lived relationship with and under them: the church re-encounters the rule of faith in the scriptures. For Irenaeus, they are not merely confirmation of the Church's teachings according to a rule; rather, the rule of faith *is* Christ "according to the scriptures," the very king at the heart of the mosaic. To put it differently, borrowing again from Behr, the "Gospel proclaims the Coming One" and therefore it is found most appropriately "in an interpretative *engagement* with Scripture, *based upon its hypothesis*, not man's, and *in accordance with the canon and tradition delivered by the apostles*."[65] The key word here is "engagement."

If the preceding has failed to give firm definition to the rule of faith, we can perhaps come to a preliminary conclusion that the difficulty

---

64. Von Campenhausen, *Formation of the Christian Bible*, 182–83, emphasis added. As has been argued above, von Campenhausen is absolutely correct in his implicit point about the antecedent authority of the Old Testament: Irenaeus did not need the New Testament to defend the Gospel. Ironically, only a sentence earlier von Campenhausen had described Irenaeus as the "first catholic theologian" in that "he begins to appeal to the New Testament documents, that is, he explicitly names them, defends their authenticity, and declares them to be normative."

65. Behr, *Way to Nicea*, 46, emphasis added.

in—and perhaps undesirability of—precisely defining it stems from its always emerging character in the church's continuing *encounter* with its scriptures. As Childs writes:

> The Christian canon is not a fixed deposit of traditions from the past, but a dynamic vehicle by which the risen Lord continues through the Holy Spirit to guide, instruct, and nourish his people. The imperative "to search the Scriptures" reveals the need for its continuous interpretation. The activity of hearing, reading, and praying is required, indeed mandated by the Scripture itself. In every successive generation new light has been promised for those seeking divine illumination to provide fresh understanding, new application to changing cultures, and a call for repentance for persistent failure in living out the imperatives of the gospel.[66]

Childs's use here of "canon"—we might as easily replace the term with "rule"—is specifically referring to the final form of Christian scriptures; however, the dynamic quality he describes is logically reflected in the rule of faith. In effect, I might express the rule as being "Christ 'according to the scriptures'" or as "Jesus Christ is one in being with the God of Israel who sent him and raised him from the dead" or in the words of the Nicene-Constantinopolitan Creed, and so forth and so on, and while all are accurate and true expressions of the rule, none finally exhausts it. We may even draw an analogy with the gospels, as Irenaeus does: there are four gospels all expressing the one Gospel.[67]

In short, the rule permits a "terminological flexibility,"[68] which dynamically allows one to speak the faith in different words and formulations, while simultaneously prohibiting expressions—such as "Christ is a creature"— outside its lexicon and grammar. It is perhaps well described as "the conviction" about truth, faith and the reading of the scriptures deployed within the "continually changing context in which the same unchanging

---

66. Childs, *Church's Guide for Reading Paul*, 26.
67. *Haer.* 3.11.8–9 (*ANF* 1:428–29): "The Gospel is quadriform."
68. Christine Helmer, "Luther's Trinitarian Hermeneutic and the Old Testament," *ModTheo* 18 (2002): 54. Helmer's larger argument regarding Luther's hermeneutics is related to our discussion: "The *res* is conveyed as the semantic referent of a diversity of terms and descriptions.... Luther makes the point that, although language is inevitably historically located, it cannot be understood to introduce diversification into the subject at the semantic level."

Gospel is preached."[69] Following this line of understanding, David Yeago makes an important distinction in how the rule of faith ultimately functions in its dynamic role within the church over time and space:

> It is essential ... to distinguish between *judgements* and the *conceptual terms* in which those judgements are rendered. We cannot concretely perform an act of judgement without employing some particular, contingent verbal and conceptual resources; judgement-making *is* an operation performed with words and concepts. At the same time, however, the same judgement can be rendered in a variety of conceptual terms, all of which may be informative about a particular judgement's force and implications. The possibility of valid alternative verbal/conceptual renderings of identical judgements accounts for the fact that we ourselves often do not realize the full implications of the judgements we pass; only *some* of their implications are ever unpacked in the particular renderings we have given them.[70]

What makes the rule of faith so difficult to discuss—its lack of final conceptualized expression—is thus exactly its most enabling characteristic for the church: its freedom. Since any expression will necessarily be historically contingent, the rule as conviction, judgment and grammar renders it free to speak not only into Ireanaeus' second-century dispute with Gnostic heresy, but also the church's problems today. It is in this freedom, we might say, quoting Childs, that far from being "a static deposit of the past," the rule is for the church "the 'living voice' (*viva vox*) of the truth."[71]

CONCLUDING THOUGHTS

A final point should be made. In two of the three paradigms discussed in the first half of this paper, much hinged on an understanding of canon in its historical, material sense: that is, one could properly speak of canon only as and when a definitive list of books had been decided upon by the church and bound once and for all (however that is understood). In the other paradigm, rule as story, this is at least potentially implicit. To make such a categorical distinction between a canon of books and canon (or rule)

---

69. Behr, *Way to Nicea*, 14, 37.
70. David S. Yeago, "The New Testament and the Nicene Dogma: A Contribution to the Recovery of Theological Exegesis," *ProEccl* 3 (1994): 159.
71. Childs, *BTONT*, 32.

of faith is to miss the relationship that the common term, canon (κανων, "rule"), begs. Indeed, the scriptures are authoritative in that they are the canonical (i.e. ruled and ruling) material witness to the ontological reality of canon (i.e. rule) of faith or truth, which is the Triune God revealed in Jesus Christ. To speak about the scriptures canonically, then—that is, in the context of the rule of faith—is to speak in three different senses: (1) *the rule of faith active in its shaping*, encompassing "the various and diverse factors involved in the formation of the literature," reflecting the fact "that canon-consciousness lay deep within the formation of the literature";[72] (2) *the rule of faith active in its shape*, a two-Testament scripture, Old and New, relating complexly and dialectically, such that the "Old is understood by its relation to the New, but the New is incomprehensible apart from the Old";[73] and (3) *the rule of faith active in the struggle to understand it*, producing "discernable characteristic features that constitute and identify a family resemblance within ... Christian exegesis."[74] To understand the rule of faith so centrally and so comprehensively—well beyond any other paradigms noted—is ultimately to put faith in the one to whom the rule points: the providence of God through the inspiration of the Holy Spirit. It is to say with Childs, from the very beginning of this discussion, "I belong to a community of faith which has received a sacred tradition in the form of an authoritative canon of scripture. There is a rule of faith and practice which has been formed because God is known."[75]

---

72. Ibid., 70–71.
73. Ibid., 77.
74. Childs, *Struggle to Understand Isaiah*, 300.
75. Brevard S. Childs, *Old Testament Theology in a Canonical Context* (Philadelphia: Fortress, 1986), 29.

Childs and the Canon or Rule of Faith

Daniel R. Driver

In fact ... canonical criticism ... is simplistic. Basically it has only one idea: the controlling place of the canon. To others this may fall apart into several conflicting ideas, but to the canonical critic himself it is all one idea. There is of course complexity even in the canon, but all that complexity can be dealt with by the one simple idea.... The canonical principle leaves the believer at peace, alone with his Bible.
— James Barr

Criticism of my understanding of canon emerges as a recurrent theme in some of the responses of my colleagues. It is occasionally claimed that it is imprecise, unanalytical, and encompasses a variety of different phenomena. I feel that the complexity of the process being described within the OT has been underestimated, and that one is asking for an algebraic solution to a problem requiring calculus.
— Brevard Childs

Locating the work of Brevard Childs (1923–2007) can be difficult.[1] A great deal has been written about what his canonical approach amounts to, not all of it sympathetic, not all of it helpful (critics can of course be either one without being the other). The fact that many of the portraits on offer do not much resemble Childs's self-presentation tends to obscure the scholar's actual voice, and it exacerbates the attempt to situate his contribution. Nowhere is this truer than in the multitudinous detractions of James Barr (1924–2006), who charges that "canonical criticism [sic]

---

1. An earlier version of this essay appeared as the first chapter of Daniel R. Driver, *Brevard Childs, Biblical Theologian: For the Church's One Bible* (FAT 2/46; Tübingen: Mohr Siebeck, 2010). Revisions and English translations from that book's North American edition (Grand Rapids: Baker, 2012) have been incorporated into the body of the text. Thanks to Mohr Siebeck for permission to reproduce the work here.

... is simplistic," that the only thing its several features have in common is that they co-exist in the same mind.[2] For Barr the term "canon" does not stand for a workable approach to biblical exegesis, but instead masks profound confusion. Childs, on the other hand, maintains against criticism like this that he would not offer "an algebraic solution to a problem requiring calculus."[3] Readers of Childs's work and of the controversy it has provoked thus face rather stark alternatives. Is the canonical approach a methodological train wreck, or is it a sophisticated attempt to address complicated hermeneutical problems?

In answering this question some have split the difference. Childs offers important insights, it is affirmed, and yet due to the confusion in and unworkability of his program, his method must be thoroughly rebuilt. The canonical approach is flawed but can be salvaged.[4] Still others have welcomed Childs's proposals as highly salubrious. Christopher Seitz, for example, counts himself with those who judge Childs's Biblical Theology "as the most brilliant proposal for theological exegesis offered in recent memory" (if "one unlikely to gain the sort of foothold necessary to transform the church in its use of scripture").[5] But the relationship between student and teacher is less than straightforward in this instance, as evidenced by the way Seitz and Childs inform one another's work on Isaiah. Seitz dedicates his 1991 study *Zion's Final Destiny* to three honored teachers, one of whom is Childs, even as the book reconsiders Childs's main work on Isaiah up to that point (*Isaiah and the Assyrian*

---

2. James Barr, *Holy Scripture: Canon, Authority, Criticism* (Oxford: Oxford University Press, 1983), 168. Barr uses "canonical criticism" despite Childs's protests. On its limitations as a descriptor for Childs's approach, see Gerald Sheppard, "Canonical Criticism," *ABD* 1:861–66.

3. Childs, "Response to Reviewers of Introduction to the Old Testament as Scripture," *JSOT* 16 (1980): 52–60 (52).

4. Major attempts at rehabilitation include Mark Brett's *Biblical Criticism in Crisis? The Impact of the Canonical Approach on Old Testament Studies* (Cambridge: Cambridge University Press, 1991), Paul Noble's *The Canonical Approach: A Critical Reconstruction of the Hermeneutics of Brevard S. Childs* (Leiden: Brill, 1995) and Georg Steins's *Die "Bindung Isaaks" im Kanon (Gen 22): Grundlagen und Programm einer Kanonisch-Intertextuellen Lektüre* (Freiburg: Herder, 1999).

5. Christopher Seitz, *Word without End: The Old Testament as Abiding Theological Witness* (Grand Rapids: Eerdmans, 1998), 109. I follow James Barr's practice of capitalizing "biblical theology" when I mean a specific instance of the genre and not otherwise.

Crisis, 1967).⁶ Childs in turn dedicates his 2001 Isaiah commentary to Seitz but does not hesitate there to probe and challenge the argument of *Zion's Final Destiny*. It hardly simplifies matters that Childs's sharpest critics and his strongest advocates share in the testing and refinement of Childs's thought over decades.

Gerald Sheppard, another of Childs's students, aptly describes part of the challenge here. "Childs has shown an ability to change his mind on issues and approaches over time. Ambiguities or lacunae at later stages in his work cannot be uncritically clarified by appeal to earlier positions. Yet what persists from his earlier work may remain presupposed by later formulations."⁷ To take just one instance, the 1970s argument from "midrash" seen in the late addition of Psalm titles is essential background to the argument for "canonical shaping," a ubiquitous theme in Childs's oeuvre. At the same time, the term "midrash" itself is increasingly rejected. Through the 1980s Childs came to view it as a mode inappropriate for modern Christian exegetes.⁸ Then again, care should be taken not to exaggerate this change dynamic. Seitz also emphasizes major strands of continuity in Childs's work over the years, and he observes "that already in 1970 Childs had laid out the basic defining features of the approach. These have been modified only subtly or in extending efforts." He points to no less than five instances of "durable and sustained interest" to be found, starting with *Biblical Theology in Crisis*: (1) critique of historical criticism, (2) special prioritization of the final form, (3) "observations on the status of the Hebrew and Greek text-traditions," (4) critical but appreciative attention to pre-Enlightenment exegesis, and (5) "biblical theological handling of the two Testaments, in which the Old retains its voice as Christian Scripture, and Biblical Theology is more than a sensitive appreciation of how the New handles the Old."⁹ That Childs's thought develops over time does not make it a moving target.

---

6. Christopher Seitz, *Zion's Final Destiny: The Development of the Book of Isaiah: A Reassessment of Isaiah 36–39* (Minneapolis: Fortress, 1991), x: "Ironically, much of Childs's own later work on canon has had a decided influence on the sorts of questions and modifications I have proposed here, vis-à-vis his original work."

7. Gerald Sheppard, "Childs, Brevard (b. 1923)," in *Historical Handbook of Major Biblical Interpreters* (ed. Donald McKim; Downers Grove, Ill.: InterVarsity, 1998), 575–84 (575).

8. For details on this development see chapter 6 of Driver, *Brevard Childs*.

9. Christopher Seitz, "The Canonical Approach and Theological Interpretation,"

But perhaps the greatest initial difficulty confronting those who wish to understand Childs is neither the need to find him amidst his many readers, nor subtlety in the development of his thought, but rather the sheer magnitude of his project. This has a couple of aspects. First, his writings adopt a cumulative scope. *Biblical Theology in Crisis* exhibits several hallmarks of the canonical approach, yet Childs would spend the next twenty-two years advancing the purpose adumbrated there. As he remarks a decade on, just after the arrival of his landmark *Introduction to the Old Testament as Scripture* (1979),

> Most of the crucial issues such as the relationship of the two testaments and the other kinds of judgments beyond exegesis which are part of the hermeneutical task, I have not been able to address directly within the scope of an OT Introduction. [In *Biblical Theology in Crisis*] I tried to cover some of these larger issues. Only after the book had been published did I realize that the groundwork had not as yet been carefully enough laid to support a theology of both testaments. Therefore, I decided to reexamine the foundations before pursuing biblical theology any further.[10]

Introduction to the Old Testament as Scripture could only be part of the reexamination, and here in 1980 he forecasts his next two major volumes, *The New Testament as Canon: an Introduction* (1984) and *Biblical Theology of the Old and New Testaments: Theological Reflection on the Christian Bible* (1992): "This descriptive task is far from complete. A study of the New Testament from a canonical perspective would also have to be executed before one could adequately address the central issues of biblical theology."[11] Thus the publication of *Biblical Theology of the Old and New Testaments* signals the completion of a longstanding personal goal,

---

in *Canon and Biblical Interpretation* (ed. Craig Bartholomew et al.; SHS 7; Grand Rapids: Zondervan, 2006), 58–110 (59).

10. Brevard Childs, "A Response [to James Mays et al.]," *HBT* 2 (1980): 199–211 (199).

11. Ibid. See the preface to Childs, *The New Testament as Canon: An Introduction* (Philadelphia: Fortress, 1984): "I would like to emphasize that this volume is an Introduction to the New Testament. It is not a biblical theology, nor does it attempt to treat in detail the whole range of questions which involves the relation of the two Testaments. It is, of course, still my hope to have time and energy one day to address these issues" (xvi).

and one with major antecedent steps.¹² The issue is not just that Childs's work is voluminous, but that it comprises a coordinated effort. It virtually asks to be read as a corpus. Second, it is not possible to be an expert in all the modes and subject areas his writing covers—from biblical theology's history and quandaries of method, to commentary on particular biblical books, to the broad contours of each testament alone and both together, to the Bible's expansive history of reception—all of which appear to be ingredient in the task (his struggle) of understanding the form and function of the Christian Bible, Old Testament and New, as one witness to the church across its total life. Such a vision goes far beyond merely keeping abreast of scholarship on Exodus or Isaiah or Paul.

Is Childs himself difficult to understand? Some well-known scholars have said as much.¹³ I myself sympathize with Roy Harrisville and Walter Sundberg, who wonder that "almost all of Childs's critics have either misunderstood, half understood, or ignored, clumsily or artfully, what has persistently served as his primary concern."¹⁴ If anything, Childs's work is repetitive, especially in rehearsing this concern. On Harrisville and Sundberg's reading it is just this:

> For Childs the Bible is more than a classic and indispensable witness to God's concern and action, however embodied. Its understanding is more than a contemporizing of the church's traditions; its ontology more than a paradigm, and more than a documenting of the human experience. For Childs the Bible, in the context of the church's confession, is the instrument of encounter with the living God.¹⁵

---

12. Christoph Dohmen frames the matter well in his preface to Brevard Childs, *Die Theologie der einen Bibel* (trans. Manfred and Christiane Oeming; 2 vols.; Freiburg: Herder, 1994–1996), 11–14; trans. of *Biblical Theology of the Old and New Testaments: Theological Reflection on the Christian Bible* (Minneapolis: Fortress, 1992), which hereafter is abbreviated *BTONT*.

13. As Rolf Rendtorff puts it (review of Childs, *BTONT*, *JBTh* 9 [1994]: 359–69), "I do not understand what it means to claim that the Old Testament testifies to Christ (not a coming Messiah, but Jesus Christ). A hermeneutic that ignores basic historical facts is incomprehensible to me" (367).

14. Roy Harrisville and Walter Sundberg, *The Bible in Modern Culture: Baruch Spinoza to Brevard Childs* (2nd ed.; Grand Rapids: Eerdmans, 2002), 324–25.

15. Ibid., 325.

To put Childs's career thesis in other words, the historically shaped canon of scripture, in its two discrete witnesses, is a christological rule of faith that in the church, by the action of the Holy Spirit, accrues textual authority. This is the figure in the carpet, so to speak, and its outline is nothing like as difficult to spot as the one sought in the fictitious writings of Henry James's Hugh Vereker. But neither is it an easy thesis to unpack and defend. This again is part of why Childs speaks of the struggle to understand Christian scripture. The bafflement of many of his reviewers turns on the strangeness of his vision in the modern world. Terence Fretheim's conclusion is both frank and revealing: the "particular formulations" in *BTONT*, he writes, "so often reflect a world other than the one in which I live."[16] Though expressing this less directly, many others seem to feel a similar alienation, and from this perspective Childs appears as a brontosaur who survived cataclysm only to plod through a smouldering landscape. That is, the queries critics have posed often sound less like "What does he mean?" than "What is he still doing here?"

There are indeed tensions in the canonical approach even if they are not as severe as some have charged. Elsewhere I discuss whether or not their sum is an inconcinnity.[17] Here I simply want to unpack two ways of locating or framing the work of Brevard Childs. The first touches his vocation as a biblical theologian, and the second, the relationship of his notion of canon to history. Both topics show Childs's commitment to some tremendous and acknowledged challenges. Both also suggest that his approach is far from simple. I hope to give some impression of the approach's aims, what problems it identifies, and how on its own terms these are solved or mitigated. As a charitable point of departure, I also want to raise the possibility that Childs's promotion of canon as a governing framework need not be seen as dogmatism, obstinacy or the mutterings of a simpleton, but can be appreciated as a knowledgeable embrace of an intricate, knotty subject.

CHILDS AS BIBLICAL THEOLOGIAN

Childs ventured into many cognate fields over his academic career. After completing four years of doctoral work at the University of Basel—this period included a semester at Heidelberg in 1951 as well—he began teach-

---

16. Terence Fretheim, review of Childs, *BTONT*, *CBQ* 56 (1994): 324–26 (326).
17. See chapters 2 and 9 in Driver, *Brevard Childs*.

DRIVER: CHILDS AND THE CANON OR RULE OF FAITH   249

ing Old Testament at a small Wisconsin seminary (now defunct) in 1954. Four years later, in 1958, he accepted a post at Yale University, where he taught until his retirement in 1999.[18] For some years he studied Jewish midrash in earnest, first with a local rabbi and then with Judah Goldin at Yale. In the meanwhile he produced a series of form critical studies in the vein of his German-speaking instructors. Later, upon writing his introduction to the OT, he devoted no less than five years to researching an introduction to the NT. The aim was to "read as widely as possible in an effort to do justice to the integrity of this discipline."[19] His next step toward biblical theology was the comparatively slim *Old Testament Theology in a Canonical Context* (1985). After finally realizing a Biblical Theology of both testaments in the same year he was made Sterling Professor of Divinity (1992). He then returned to the OT proper by writing a technical commentary on Isaiah, despite a series of health issues that he feared would keep him from completing the task. Reprieves in his illness permitted him to give a focussed kind of attention to church history, moving far beyond his early work in the history of exegesis, for which the Exodus commentary (1974) is commonly remembered, with *The Struggle to Understand Isaiah as Christian Scripture* (2004). A notable theme in the latter title is the problem of allegory in Christian exposition of the OT. Finally, he once again turned his eye to the NT with the posthumously published *The Church's Guide for Reading Paul: The Canonical Shaping of the Pauline Corpus* (2008). The manuscript had been sent to the publisher just days before his death on 23 June 2007, at the age of 83.

How should one classify ranging work of this sort? Looking for precedents, something like Rudolf Smend's study of the work of W. M. L. de Wette presents a possibility. That study falls into two parts: there is de Wette the *Alttestamentler* (part 1), and then de Wette the *Neutestamentler* (part 2).[20] The neat division does not suit Childs very well, however, and

---

18. The best previous account of Childs's biography is found in Harrisville and Sundberg, *Bible in Modern Culture*, 309–10. Though brief, it incorporates a personal correspondence with Childs about his life. Sheppard's earlier, longer account in *Historical Handbook of Major Biblical Interpreters* is still useful but contains a few errors. See also Daniel Driver and Nathan MacDonald, "Childs, Brevard S.," *Encyclopedia of the Bible and Its Reception* 5:126–27.

19. Childs, *New Testament as Canon*, xvi.

20. Rudolf Smend, *Wilhelm Martin Leberecht de Wettes Arbeit am Alten und am Neuen Testament* (Basel: Helbing & Lichtenhahn, 1958).

actually is not broad enough. In my judgment, a more general and slightly ambiguous title is most appropriate in his case—Childs as biblical theologian.[21] All parts of his work come under the biblical theological umbrella in some way. Because the designation is contested, though, it calls for a little explanation.

To begin with, Childs freely acknowledges that difficulties attend the genres he undertook. Note what he says about the task of writing an OT Theology, for instance. The context is a symposium on Jewish-Christian dialogue held in early January 1985, the year *Old Testament Theology in a Canonical Context* appeared:

> From its inception, it was characteristic of Old Testament theology that it always had to contend with serious methodological uncertainties. Although it was often called the crowning achievement of the whole discipline, it appeared as though its leading practitioners were always glancing warily about at other subdisciplines, full of concern that some new literary, historical, or philological discovery might threaten the enterprise.... Not only was the discipline loosely defined and constantly shifting, but certain fundamental tensions continue to pose questions as to what form an Old Testament theology should take. Is this academic discipline only descriptive, or does it necessarily include an element of constructive theology? What is the relation between an Old Testament theology and a history of Israel? Are its structuring principles historical, systematic, or an eclectic combination of both? And finally: what is the relation between Jewish and Christian theological interpretations of the Hebrew Scriptures?[22]

These are all among the questions he takes up at various points in his work, although it is worth underscoring that his driving concern at this juncture is theology of just the First Testament. He admits that it would be "supremely arrogant" to propose a quick solution to a nest of problems so complex they seem to inhere in the discipline. Nonetheless, he commends an approach to scripture marked by constitutive features of Christian

---

21. Childs refers to himself as a biblical theologian at least once (*The Book of Exodus: A Critical, Theological Commentary* [Louisville: Westminster, 1974], 88).

22. Brevard Childs, "Die Bedeutung des jüdischen Kanons in der alttestamentlichen Theologie," in *Mitte der Schrift: Ein jüdisch-christliches Gespräch—Texte des Berner Symposions vom 6–12 Januar 1985* (ed. Martin Klopfenstein et al.; trans. Ulrich Luz and Eva Ringler; Judaica et Christiana 11; Frankfurt: Lang, 1987), 269–81 (271–72).

exposition, features which to his satisfaction have not been adequately pursued in the critical or postcritical era. "I would like to address some of these agonizing methodological questions in some other way."[23] A key element of the prescription is a reminder that OT theology has almost always been—is perhaps irreducibly—a Christian preoccupation. If so, the ecumenical dilemma for OT exegetes becomes how to appropriately handle a Jewish canon now functioning as OT within the operations of church theology.

Biblical theology itself—more than just Old plus New, "as if one could spend the first semester with Eichrodt and von Rad and the second with Bultmann and Jeremias!"[24]—is for Childs fundamentally a bridge-building exercise, an arena for theological reflection on the entire Christian Bible in which biblical scholarship and dogmatic theology meet to illuminate the object they share. Its "major function ... is to provide a bridge for two-way traffic between biblical exegesis and systematic theology's reflection on the subject matter."[25] Childs obviously entered this space as an OT specialist, and by his own admission he was not as successful coming up to speed in systematics as in the NT. "In spite of the challenge of trying to gain competence in both testaments, this task paled into insignificance before the difficulty of gaining entrance into the field of dogmatic/systematic theology. Anyone who has ever studied under Karl Barth is left with the lasting sense of inadequacy just from remembering the standards of thoroughness which he required of his students."[26] That is, Childs never attempted a Church Dogmatics. I doubt that his ambition ever reached that far. He made efforts at proficiency in the formal discipline of theology, although these struck him as inadequate.[27] Yet biblical theology's connecting purpose is to rejoin scripture and theology. It serves something other than dialogue for its own sake, or whatever other goals might be desirable in a strictly academic context. It arises first from a church situation, and

---

23. Ibid., 272.
24. Childs, *BTONT*, xv.
25. Ibid., 481, cf. 551. See also Christine Helmer, "Biblical Theology: Bridge over Many Waters," *CurBS* 3 (2005): 169–96.
26. Childs, *BTONT*, xvi.
27. "From my library shelves the great volumes of the Fathers, Schoolmen, and Reformers look down invitingly. I have also acquired over the years many of the great classics of the Reformed and Lutheran post-Reformation tradition. However, life is too short for a biblical specialist to do more than read selectively and dabble here and there" (ibid.).

as such it principally serves the unity of the Christian confession of one God. This ecclesial context drives Childs's concern for "the oneness of the biblical witness," or the "oneness of scripture's scope" that he insists "is not a rival to the multiple voices within the canon."[28] Exactly how to articulate scripture's unity, at both the exegetical level and the hermeneutical or theological level, admits a range of answers, but for Childs the basic confessional imperative inherent in the question is experienced and voiced at every turn.

So when Gerhard Ebeling writes of an "inner unity" to the discipline in a classic essay on the meaning of biblical theology (1955), Childs picks up the language: "The Christian church responded to [the canonical scriptures] as the authoritative word of God, and it remains existentially committed to an inquiry into its inner unity because of its confession of the one gospel of Jesus Christ which it proclaims to the world."[29] At least three points of clarification need to be made about this claim. First, it is fair to say that the Ebeling-Childs line, which foregrounds unity, reverses the priorities of J. P. Gabler, who for convenience's sake is often credited with calling biblical theology into existence. Childs admits this by calling Ebeling's definition a redefinition, and "a return to a pre-Gabler position in so far as he once again joins the historical and theological elements."[30] Gabler had advocated a sharp distinction in his inaugural lecture at Altdorf in 1787, a distinction between religion and theology, between things of "historical origin" and "didactic origin," between "the simplicity of what they call biblical theology" and "the subtlety of dogmatic theology."[31] Procedurally this entails further distinctions, not only between OT and NT, but also Paul and the gospel writers, right down to the level of each individual author.[32] Yet Gabler does not envision the final divorce of biblical from dogmatic theology, and one can only guess how he might have addressed the evaporation of his hope to eliminate "doubtful readings" of scripture in pursuit

---

28. Ibid., 719, 725.
29. Ibid., 8.
30. Ibid., 7.
31. John Sandys-Wunscha and Laurence Eldredge, "J. P. Gabler and the Distinction Between Biblical and Dogmatic Theology: Translation, Commentary, and Discussion of His Originality," *SJT* 33 (1980): 133–58 (137).
32. In order to establish proper comparisons of biblical ideas to "universal notions," he prescribes first "diligently isolating the opinions of each author" (ibid., 142).

of "the Christian religion of all times."[33] Ebeling and Childs reflect very different historical moments when compared to Gabler. Furthermore, it would be a serious mistake to assume that Childs (the only one of the three actually to attempt a Biblical Theology) nullifies all distinctions in the name of unity. We have already seen evidence of the way he accords Jewish studies, OT and NT scholarship, and systematic theology their own integrity as disciplines. His language of "discrete witnesses" is also relevant here. Perhaps it is not too trivial a generalization to say that, in the centuries between Gabler and Childs, the burden of keeping Christian theology intact came to overwhelm the need to keep its domains apart. As Ebeling's essay concludes, the concept "biblical theology," the false understanding of which caused theology—contrary to the original intention—to split up into different disciplines, when rightly understood points back again to the unity of theology—not of course a unity achieved by abolishing the different disciplines, but a unity consisting in the right theological use of the different disciplines, each of which has its own peculiar task and yet each is "theology" in the sense of participating in the scientific expression of the Word of God.[34]

The task is to hear "the inner unity of the manifold testimony of the Bible," and the call is for "the intensive co-operation of Old and New Testament scholars" and indeed of all theological specialists, including dogmaticians and church historians. Should collaboration be achieved, Ebeling submits that "'biblical theology' would not then be a rival substitute for dogmatics and would hardly correspond either to the pietistic ideal of a 'simple' theology, but would be an uncommonly complex exercise in historical theology."[35] This ideal counters the trend toward hyper-specialization and realigns a standard view of biblical theology; simultaneously, it denies the simplicity of pure notions that Gabler desired. In each of these respects Childs stands with Ebeling.

Second, Childs is quite frank about what constitutes the "inner unity," and it is far from the old enthusiasm for universal religion: a biblical theologian has to do with "inner unity because of ... the one gospel of Jesus Christ." At the center of Childs's approach, then, is a startlingly specific

---

33. Ibid., 143.
34. Gerhard Ebeling, "The Meaning of 'Biblical Theology,'" in *Word and Faith* (trans. J. W. Leitch; London: SCM, 1963), 79–97 (96).
35. Ibid. He continues, "then it would be able also for its part to assist dogmatics towards a clearer grasp of the question of what constitutes scriptural dogmatics."

confession of the lordship of Jesus Christ. To be sure, he is not the first biblical theologian to make this move. In the end there is an expressly christological side to Old Testament inquiry for one of his teachers, Gerhard von Rad, however reluctantly acknowledged by von Rad himself, however often overlooked by von Rad's other students and successors. Yet for Childs the *Christuszeugnis* of scripture's witness is fully embraced by 1992 and forms the heart of his *gesamtbiblische* theology. Sometimes the utter difficulty of the assertion sounds out loudest. "To be sure, it remains hard to specify what it means to find a reference to Christ in the Old Testament, and struggling with this problem cuts to the heart of biblical theology."[36] Just how should one move from the verbal or literal sense of the the OT to its true theological substance, identified by Childs as knowledge of God in the face of Christ? Most traditional Christian exegetes do so readily. Von Rad's hesitancy in the twentieth century, and Childs's in its own way, is symptomatic of a dilemma facing biblical scholars who feel compelled to take similar steps in a critical age. All the same, BTONT undertakes the search for, and upholds the proclamation of, one thing from two testaments, namely, the gospel of Jesus Christ.

Third, specificity about Christ puts extra strain on the biblical theologian's ecumenical obligations. If OT theology was once presumed the crown of OT scholarship, this has not been the case since about the time Childs first waved the tattered banner of biblical theology in 1970. Jon Levenson, in an essay exploring shortcomings in the OT Theologies of Eichrodt and von Rad, effectively describes the less certain climate that has gained predominance over the field of historical critical scholarship.

In North America, the emergence of religion departments and Jewish studies programs and departments has further contributed to the dethronement of Christian theology, indeed any theology, as the organizing paradigm for the study of the Hebrew Bible. As a consequence, in the elite academic world, those for whom the term "Old Testament" is more than vestigial have been put into the unenviable position of an ex-emperor who now must learn how to be a good neighbor.[37]

---

36. Brevard Childs, "Biblische Theologie und christlicher Kanon," *JBTh* 3 (1988): 13–27 (24). Compare idem, "Gerhard von Rad in American Dress," in *The Hermeneutical Quest: Essays in Honor of James Luther Mays on his 65th Birthday* (ed. Donald Miller; Allison Park, Pa.: Pickwick, 1986), 77–86.

37. Jon Levenson, *The Hebrew Bible, the Old Testament, and Historical Criticism: Jews and Christians in Biblical Studies* (Louisville: Westminster John Knox, 1993), 32.

Given these circumstances, one can appreciate why a theologically minded Lutheran Old Testament scholar like Fretheim judges *BTONT* as "a theological retrenchment"—a failure precisely in its ability to cope with the new climate—and "more as a somewhat belated end of an era than as ... an imaginative venture that charts new directions."[38] Fretheim probably underestimates the extent to which Childs broke with those he gladly claimed as his teachers (interestingly, Levenson quotes Childs in support of his critique of von Rad). But by voicing deeper misgivings about the ability of *BTONT* to address "the complex realities of the contemporary world," Fretheim makes the potentially damaging point that Childs's tendency to dismiss newer theological efforts by liberation, process, feminist or postmodern theologians puts him out of touch.[39] The canonical approach is just too traditional to have relevance or impact. Are most historic forms of Christianity automatically out of touch, though? The attempt simply to clear and restore old paths—much older than von Rad, or even Gabler—does not exclude the possibility of dialogue with those cutting other trails. Commenting from a Jewish perspective, Levenson sees potential, if only partly actualized: "Founded upon a historical particularity—the Protestant canon—Childs's method harbors a potential for respect for other historically particular traditions."[40] This despite (or seemingly because of) the fact that a frank confessionalism comes built in, with high liability for offense. "The role of canon often calls for a parting of the ways," writes Childs near the front of his last book.[41] How much capacity does Childs's work have to advance in-house or interreligious dialogue? Readers will be of different minds, though fairly quickly one confronts real limits on the possibility for consensus. There is still the option Levenson advances, that creedal particularity sets the foundation for a more substantive exchange than Gabler could have imagined, although if so, the most productive front is likely to be the one shared by people who wish to heal the breach between scripture and tradition rather than to celebrate or exploit it. Protestant though he be, it is hardly by accident that Childs has been relatively well received by certain Jewish and Catholic biblical specialists.

---

38. Fretheim, review of Childs, *BTONT*, 324.
39. Ibid., 326.
40. Levenson, *Hebrew Bible*, 122.
41. Brevard Childs, *The Church's Guide for Reading Paul: The Canonical Shaping of the Pauline Corpus* (Grand Rapids: Eerdmans, 2008), 44.

To this point I have sketched ways of locating Childs vocationally, chiefly as a biblical theologian, and of locating his work, ecclesially and ecumenically, as a body centered on the oneness of the Bible's scope and grounded in a christological confession. Naturally, more could be said on each score. First, though, another thing shown by this preliminary tour bears repeating. Childs took his project very seriously, never underestimating the difficulty of mastering so many different subject areas. Though he was uncommonly studious, he owns up to limitations in the broad personal competence he sought. We have seen the acknowledgement, too, of "agonizing methodological questions" in the operations of OT theology, as well as genuine hesitation about what it means "to find a reference to Christ in the Old Testament," particularly with respect to what has been called the double reception of the Hebrew Bible. If we can credit statements like these, if he truly feels the weight of "agonizing methodological questions" including those in the list cited above, and if with him we share an impression of the number and width of historical, religious and disciplinary chasms to be spanned, then there may be some sense in talking about calculus after all.

CANON AND HISTORY

Generosity toward constructive theological work with canon runs against the prevailing mood. The canonical approach is a nonstarter, according to a common worry, because biblical scholarship oriented by or to church teaching blocks the free investigation of historical periods and sources that is central to the biblical scholar's mandate. Robert Kraft, for example, speaks of the "tyranny of canonical assumptions." For him, and for not a few members of the Society of Biblical Literature he addresses, to speak of canon at all is to introduce a seriously distorting anachronism. "Historically responsible philological work, of course, does not pay attention to these boundaries, either as limits ... or as touchstones."[42] Kraft's view is as straightforward as it is widespread: history trumps canon.

This attitude has not helped Childs's reception, reinforcing a habit of incredulity toward the logic and self-presentation of the canonical approach visible especially in the literature on Childs's so-called method. Criticism

---

42. Robert Kraft, "Para-mania: Beside, Before and Beyond Bible Studies," *JBL* 126 (2007): 5–27 (17–18).

has been so severe at times that one senses why in his later work he wants to "resist the practice of some immediately to characterize [his] approach as 'canonical,' since the label has only engendered confusion."[43] Yet in the end he neither abandons the term nor amends his use of it along the lines suggested by his critics. Therefore, to clear the ground for a better hearing, it will be helpful to outline the trajectory of his thought on the relationship of canon and history—categories that stay in tension to the very last: in that sense canon never trumps history for him—and then to suggest the advantage of canon as an umbrella term. In other words, my purpose in this section is to clarify Childs's thought at a crucial point where it has often been misunderstood. The hope is to forestall premature dismissal of a proposal that has proved so counterintuitive that it is commonly rejected out of hand. Is not the recourse to canon a retreat from history into dogma (a "dogmatic flight from the difficulties of historical work," in the words of Manfred Oeming[44])? If not, why not? How can Childs's dogmatic (in the word's more positive sense), theological deployment of canon accommodate all that we know about the extremely complicated history of canon?

Those who instinctively associate "canonical criticism" with antihistorical dogmatism would do well to consider when and where Childs went to school. True enough, in the background was the sort of conservatism that resists the incursions of "higher" criticism. As the mature Childs puts it in a correspondence with Harrisville and Sundberg, "it took me some years to get beyond Hodge and Warfield."[45] It is hard to say exactly when he overcame the legacy of old Princeton, which he probably knew first in the Presbyterian church his family attended in Queens, New York,[46] but there is solid evidence that it happened before he had his doctorate. Like many of his peers, Childs's formal education was interrupted by World

---

43. Brevard Childs, *Isaiah: A Commentary* (Louisville: Westminster John Knox, 2001), xii. He continues, "I hope that this commentary will be judged on its own merits apart from any prior concept of what a 'canonical' reading ought to entail." The same request could well preface all of his work now.

44. Manfred Oeming, *Das Alte Testament als Teil des christlichen Kanons? Studien zu gesamtbiblischen Theologien der Gegenwart* (3rd ed.; Zürich: Pano, 2001), 204–5 (195–96 in Oeming, *Gesamtbiblische Theologien der Gegenwart: Das Verhältnis von AT und NT in der hermeneutischen Diskussion seit Gerhard von Rad* [2nd ed.; Stuttgart: W. Kohlhammer, 1987]); cf. ibid., 216 (209 in 2nd ed.).

45. Cited in Harrisville and Sundberg, *Bible in Modern Culture*, 310.

46. Childs was born in Columbia, South Carolina, on 2 September 1923, and baptized Episcopalian, but the family moved north because of the father's poor health.

War II. Anticipating the draft, he elected to start at Queens College, near home, rather than to go away to university. He was there little more than a year. In October 1942 Childs enlisted in the US Army.[47] Barely nineteen, he prepared to sail for Europe. On his sister's account, he had by then already taken a serious interest in theology, aided by the leader of a student group at Queens who helped guide his extracurricular reading.[48] Recollecting the weekly letters she exchanged with her brother during the war, the sister tells how Childs worked to teach himself Greek while aboard the RMS Queen Mary.[49] He returned to the United States in 1945 for redeployment to Japan, but Truman's atom bomb kept this from happening (he was on leave, visiting his sister, when it fell). As he waited to be demobilized, Childs completed several correspondence courses through the Army Education Program, earning enough credit through the University of Michigan to graduate with an AB and an MA in 1947. From there he went to Princeton Theological Seminary (Bachelor of Divinity, 1950), and then back to Europe, to Switzerland and Germany.

Against this backdrop, it is interesting to think about what motivated Childs's selection of material when, in the summer of 1995, he submitted a small box to the Princeton Seminary archives. In addition to later papers, letters and manuscripts, there is a syllabus from an introduction to the New Testament taught by Bruce Metzger in 1948. And there are Childs's own scrupulous notes from a course on the parables of Jesus, with Otto Piper

---

47. According to U.S. Army enlistment records (The National Archives, http://aad.archives.gov/, accessed 23 October 2009), Childs enlisted in New York on 17 October 1942.

48. Did it include Hodge or Warfield?

49. "I always have that picture, of this nineteen year old heading into war, and he was teaching himself Greek. And he said, everybody was gambling—they had crap tables going and the money was this high—and here's Bard, working away. There was something so typical about Bard's determination" (recording of a personal communication with Anne Childs Hummel, 22 November 2008). During the war, while moving from France into Germany—he was in transportation, not the infantry, though according to Hummel he advanced with the front into Germany—his sister was in school at Wellesley College. She remembers writing for advice on a required year-long course on the Bible. The course introduced her to biblical criticism, and it shook her confidence in scripture. She wrote to her older brother about the issues it raised several times, sometimes twice a week. Childs responded regularly, reassuring his sister. "It was the content of what he said, but more than that it was the assurance that this wasn't the only way to look at it, that gave me great confidence," Hummel recalls. Unfortunately, their wartime correspondence has not survived.

in 1949. Apart from a copy of his Basel dissertation (1955), the only other testament to his student days is a paper written for Walter Baumgartner in 1952, with Baumgartner's feedback in the margins. A hardworking source-critical analysis of Exod 13:17–15:21 that searches out the hand of L, J, E, or P verse by verse (at the end Baumgartner praised it as a "sorgfältige und wohlüberlegte Arbeit mit verständigem Urteil [careful and well considered work with insightful judgment]"), the paper indicates something important about the early direction of Childs's work in the Old Testament. If initially Childs inclined toward Greek and the New Testament, he left Princeton with something else in view. (By Harrisville and Sundberg's report, his influences at Princeton were "few" and "largely negative."[50]) The paper also shows clearly that Childs went to Basel for what it had to offer in the Old Testament, not for Karl Barth.[51] Finally, whatever parallels one might be tempted to draw between Childs's years of study on the European continent and those of Charles Hodge a century and a quarter before, the most obvious are disanalogous. In terms of their attitude to German criticism, the outcomes for these two learned men were fundamentally different.[52] Was there symbolism for Childs, with respect either to the famous old Princeton school or the seminary he would have remembered, in leaving this particular paper in its archives?

EARLY AND LATE ATTITUDES TO HISTORY: FROM 1952 TO 2008

Entitled "The Deliverance of Israel at the Crossing of the Sea," the Baumgartner paper bears a curious relation to Childs's subsequent work. Let me give some indication of its flavor. The piece begins by making detailed observations about the chosen text, noting alternate readings from the old Greek, the Syriac, the Samaritan Pentateuch, and so on. Exodus 13:20, for instance, is judged to be "very corrupt." In a subsequent note on literary analysis the same verse is ascribed to P, because P has the most developed geographical tradition (he is following Baentsch, Holzinger, and Noth, against Beer

---

50. Harrisville and Sundberg, *Bible in Modern Culture*, 310.
51. The relationship of Childs to Barth has been widely misunderstood. As I demonstrate in chapter 3 of *Brevard Childs*, Childs cautiously warms to Barth only later, at Yale, although he heard Barth lecture in his student days.
52. See the published form of a dissertation Childs directed: Marion Taylor, *The Old Testament in the Old Princeton School (1812–1929)* (San Francisco: Mellen Research University Press, 1992), esp. 50–55 and 74–79 on Hodge.

and Eissfeldt). Other verses are separated into two or more strands, though P is said to be hard to distinguish from E. Next, Childs reconstructs two main sources under the headings "The Account of the Yahwist" and "The Account of EP." The former lacks any account of Israelites crossing the sea. Much of the subsequent discussion concerns "geographical-historical problems," such as the meaning and location of the יַם־סוּף in different traditions. With von Rad and especially Noth, Childs decides that the "localization" of the sea is secondary, that in fact accounts of the Exodus contain two distinct localizations. All of this is standard historical-critical stuff, of course, conversant with the best research of the day. Given the approach for which Childs is now known, what is most remarkable here is his rejection of ostensibly more conservative options. Noth's account of incongruous traditions is preferred to Pedersen's case that the whole of Exod 1–14 is a historicized "passah festival." A twenty-eight-year-old Childs writes,

> It has been convincingly demonstrated that the slaughter of sheep, the smearing of its blood on the tent posts, and the eating of bitter herbs, belonged to the ancient nomadic sacrifice customs. However, while this connection is clear, the weak point in Pedersen's argument is the actual connection between the passah legend and the exodus tradition. *To be sure, in its present form, the passah legend is a preparation for the exodus*, and the passah festival is a "Gedächtnisfeier [memorial celebration]." *But an organic, primary connection fails between the traditions.* Noth sees this correctly, in my opinion, when he criticizes Pedersen at this point.... The Passah festival was originally a sacrifice customary among the "weidewechselnde Wanderhirten" before the departure for the summer pasturage. The yearly "exodus" was historified and took on the meaning of the once-and-for-all departure out of Egypt. Once the relation was created between the festival and the exodus tradition, the historifying was carried out all along the line.[53]

Apart from seven short notes on undiscussed problems, this is where the essay ends. Remarkably, its basic analysis was rehearsed twice in Childs's later work, finally being reworked for the appropriate chapter in his Exodus commentary. Two years before that, in 1972, Childs (then aged

---

53. Brevard Childs, "The Deliverance of Israel at the Crossing of the Sea (Exodus 13:17–15:21)" (graduate paper written for Walter Baumgartner, University of Basel, 1952; in the Brevard S. Childs Manuscript Collection, Princeton Seminary archives), 12–13, emphasis added.

forty-eight) also used the paper as the backbone for the fourth lecture (of five) in the James Sprunt Lectures at Union Theological Seminary in Virginia. Something had shifted, though. The title for the lecture series that year was "Canon and Criticism: The Old Testament as Scripture of the Church," and session four was called "The Crossing of the Sea in its Canonical Context."[54]

What changed? In *Brevard Childs, Biblical Theologian* I give an account of major threads of continuity and change across Childs's work. To summarize, the first of two big turns happens on the road to *Biblical Theology in Crisis*—1970 is a convenient marker. The second relates to a clarified understanding of the relationship of church and synagogue, involving concerns he sometimes calls the "mystery of Israel" and the "mystery of Christ." It happens in the early 1980s. At present, though, it is important to say that the change is more subtle than has often been supposed. The double reworking of the Basel paper is a case in point.

First, the paper was reworked for the 1972 Sprunt Lectures. Lecture 4 uses Exod 14 to explore an instance of "one of the most difficult problems of faith and history."[55] The existence of sources is presupposed. There are "two basically complete, and yet different, accounts of the event at the sea," though Childs pleads for "more flexibility in describing them than is often allowed."[56] Then, in language straight from the old postgraduate paper, the J account is given under one heading, and the P(E) account under the next. After this, however, his analysis pushes in a new direction:

> Following the source analysis, the historical critical interpreter usually makes some comparisons of the two accounts and tries then to draw historical and theological conclusions. In my judgment, before any such move it is basic to seek to understand the whole account in its final form.

---

54. Copies of all but the first lecture are housed at Princeton Theological Seminary. The first is "The Canon as a Historical and Theological Problem," and I cannot say whether its exclusion is deliberate. Papers 2, 3, and 5 are, respectively, "'II Isaiah' in the Context of the Canon," "The Canonical Shape of the Psalter," and "Daniel in the Context of the Canon." Revisions of all this material made its way into subsequent publications.

55. Childs, "Canon and Criticism: The Old Testament as Scripture of the Church" (James Sprunt Lectures, Union Theological Seminary, Richmond, Va., January 1972; in the Brevard S. Childs Manuscript Collection, Princeton Seminary archives), 26.

56. Ibid., 27. "This reservation is simply to share the feeling of many Old Testament scholars that the minute divisions have often gone beyond the evidence."

There is another witness which must be heard, namely the final redaction. How does the chapter function as a whole?[57]

This question was not asked in 1952. Quite the contrary. Now, though, he attends to "the present form of the biblical text," arguing that "the final form of the story has an integrity of its own."[58] Is the earlier account undone? Has he inadvertently joined leagues with the likes of Pedersen, or even surpassed him in the move toward harmonization?

Not necessarily. Importantly, Childs suggests "that there is a canonical integrity which cannot be identified with simply literary unity."[59] The run-up to his Exodus commentary includes other, closely related work that does not directly reprise the Basel paper. The most sophisticated is "A Traditio-Historical Study of the Reed Sea Tradition" (1970), which makes some adjustments to the slightly earlier "Deuteronomic Formulae of the Exodus Traditions" (1967, in a Festschrift for Baumgartner, actually). In the later essay Childs articulates his view that the Song of the Sea in Exod 15 is dependent on the conquest tradition: "It seems highly probable that the influence stems from the Jordan tradition which has been projected back to the earlier event rather than in the reverse direction."[60] For J, the event at the sea was part of the wilderness tradition, but through a variety of influences, including the Deuteronomic concern for centralization, it became linked (in P) to Israel's primary saving event, the Exodus, with consequences for how Passover was understood. The analysis in 1970 is more up to date. It includes Frank Cross and George Coats, for instance. Noth, though, is still preferred to Pedersen. What has been introduced to the discussion for the 1972 lecture, in full awareness of complex underlying sources, is a historical and theological account of the contribution of the redactor. "The biblical writer is aware, both of the variety within the tradition, and the two levels of divine activity, which combined ordinary [J] and wonderful [P] elements." To leave the account arrayed according to "a pattern of historical development runs counter to the intention of the final narrative."[61] At one level this is simply an historical observation. At

---

57. Ibid., 28.
58. Ibid., 31.
59. Ibid., 27.
60. Childs, "A Traditio-Historical Study of the Reed Sea Tradition," *VT* 20 (1970): 406–18 (414; cf. 410).
61. Childs, "Canon and Criticism" (Sprunt Lectures), 31.

another, the text's full history stands as a warning against the hegemony of historical development as the sole critical framework. "The canonical redaction operates as a critical judgment against such moves and bears witness how the various parts are to be understood."[62] At yet another (higher?) level—from a theological vantagepoint—the "critical judgment" of the canon aligns with scripture's witness to the church, a major theme of his Sprunt Lectures.

> The work of God is not buried in past events that are dependent on the scholar's reconstruction, but is attested plainly by the law and the prophets. That which the historian characterizes as a late literary fiction, the church confesses to be the full witness of God's redemption made possible through the continued activity of the Holy Spirit within the community of faith.... To the question, how then did God redeem Israel at the sea, the Christian can only reply: Read the scriptures. Here is found the beginning of the story of God's redemption, which brought the Church into being and continues to provide it with life.[63]

History raises some troubling theological questions for a person of faith, such as, "What if the Exodus did not 'actually' happen?" Childs acknowledges the issue without attempting to address it. What he does instead is to complexify what counts for history in the first place. After the final form, there is the long history of effects in "the community of faith"—synagogue as well as church, as he often says elsewhere, though his own native context is patent—a variegated history with its own sets of context and reality.

By 1974 all this research and reflection had been drawn into a much larger project. Chapter 9 of *Exodus*, "The Deliverance at the Sea (13:17–14:31)," repeats the basic juxtaposition of contexts.[64] It introduces a third recension of the J and P(E) accounts (the only one published), and then incorporates and builds on exegetical observations from 1972. Oddly enough, we arrive at a position from which to see the development of Childs's template for *Exodus*. Chapters start with a bibliography and a translation of the text under consideration. Most then have six sections, some omitting one or more of the last three:

---

62. Ibid., 32.
63. Ibid.
64. "There is some value in rehearsing the story according to each of the two main sources. However, the case will be made in the exegesis for the integrity of the composite accounts" (Childs, *Exodus*, 220).

264   THE BIBLE AS CANON OF THE CHURCH

1. Textual and Philological Notes
2. Literary and Traditio-Historical Problems
3. Old Testament Context
4. New Testament Context
5. History of Exegesis
6. Theological Reflection[65]

A way of investigating items 1 and 2 had been established at Basel in the early 1950s. Subsequently, for reasons that will have to be explored later, an array of biblical theological preoccupations fills out the scope of investigation. To the extent that reorientation of item 3 to the received text was novel, it must also be said that Childs's emphasis on "final form" surfaces with a broad complement of orienting theological concerns. This took time, and in the preface to *Exodus* we catch a glimpse of the route taken:

> My academic interest in the book of Exodus goes back some twenty years to an unforgettable seminar on Moses which was conducted by Professor Walter Baumgartner of Basel in the summer semester of 1952. Well-worn copies of Dillmann, Gressmann, Driver, and Noth indicate their constant use over two decades. Active work on this commentary extends over ten years. During that period I have gone through many different stages in my own thinking. Somewhere en route I discovered that Calvin and Drusius, Rashi and Ibn Ezra, belong among the giants. I have tried to show why these great expositors—the term "pre-critical" is both naïve and arrogant—need to be heard in concert with Wellhausen and Gunkel.[66]

"Somewhere en route" is vague language—maybe deliberately so. However Childs may have discovered the importance of the tradition, the essential point is twofold: Calvin and Drusius, Rashi and Ibn Ezra quite concretely fill out language of "the community of faith"; and, again, they add further historical dimension to a text that has so very many historical dimensions.

It has been said that *Exodus* represents the source-critical Childs, allegedly distinct from a new-critical or "final form" Childs known elsewhere. In truth, after Basel the acknowledgment of reconstructed biblical history never goes away.[67] Some will be surprised to learn how permanently

---

65. The scheme's rationale given in ibid., xiv–xvi.
66. Ibid., x.
67. Reconstructed history mostly means tradition history, in Continental style,

Childs commits himself to an investigation of the diachronic, even though he refuses to let it have the last word. A 2008 comment about Acts, for instance, sounds almost intensely historicist: "The canonical function of Acts in relation to the whole New Testament, but especially in relation to the Pauline corpus, can be correctly described *only* when one reconstructs the historical process leading to its canonization."[68] Yet the statement lines up with a major purpose of his final study, which is to explore the relationship of two sometimes contradictory histories of canon. Although earlier works refer to Martin Kähler's understanding of *Geschichte* and *Historie*, Childs's *Church's Guide* develops the relation of this pair of words to an extent that surpasses all of his previous discussions. The terms signal overlap and divergence "between critical, historical exegesis and confessional, canonical understanding of biblical interpretation."[69] He defines them this way: "*Geschichte* is the historical reflections on events and conditions carried on within a confessing community of faith. *Historie* is the attempt to understand events from an objective, scientific analysis, applying ordinary human experience, apart from any confessional content, as the measure of its credibility."[70] Maintaining the tension between these perspectives is essential. Those who dissolve the tension tend to give maximalist or minimalist accounts of *Historie* on the assumption that *Geschichte* stands or falls with it, evoking either way Childs's characteristic dissatisfaction with options on the "right" and "left" of the theological spectrum. Kähler's terms are therefore also linked to conservatism, which fuses *Historie* and *Geschichte*, and liberalism, which separates them permanently.[71] For Childs, in contrast to both, canon and history are neither antinomies nor twins.

Put differently, tension between *Historie* and *Geschichte* parallels a tension between secular history and sacred history, mirrored in a life spent working in the modern university for the sake of the church. In a sense the theological problematic is not new, except insofar as a different

---

although sometimes one finds judgments about "what actually happened." On the historicity of the crossing of the sea in particular, see *BTONT*, 100, cited below.
68. Childs, *Church's Guide*, 223, emphasis added.
69. Ibid., 16.
70. Ibid., 165.
71. It is interesting to see the reasons Childs distances himself from Scott Hafemann's maximalist account of Paul and history, for instance (ibid., 125–26). For a fuller account of Childs between "left" and "right" see my "Later Childs," *PTR* 38 (2008): 117–29.

and sharper dialectic emerges after the rise of critical biblical scholarship. Church fathers and reformers sometimes wondered about how to handle scripture if it came into real conflict with good science (consider Augustine's last commentary on Genesis), though none anticipate the hermeneutical reversal described in Hans Frei's *Eclipse of Biblical Narrative* (1974). Thus when Childs speaks of "canon" and "community of faith" in the singular, as opposed to the plurals commonly seen in literature oriented more exclusively to secular history, it is fair to spot a rough analog to Augustine's "city of God."[72] As a theological category, canon bespeaks the unity that governs Childs's description of the Bible's function as a testimony to one God in church and world. One might as well speak of "canon" and "canons" as *Geschichte* and *Historie*.

Then again, standing on the other side of a hermeneutical watershed, Childs's work is deeply marked by the gap that opens between what Frei calls the "history-likeness (literal meaning) and history (ostensive reference)" of biblical narrative.[73] Much as his thought overlaps with Frei's at this point, though, Childs prefers to speak of reading the Bible as "witness" instead of as "source." The most obvious departure from categories of realistic narrative: "witness" implies a confession. As Childs explains while introducing Old Testament aspects of his *BTONT*, "The contrast lies in viewing history from Israel's confessional stance, from within a community of faith, rather than from a neutral, phenomenological reconstruction. However, in spite of insisting on a basic distinction in the way of viewing history, the problem remains that a subtle relationship continues to obtain between these two perspectives." Another difference from Frei, then, as from nearly all exegetes working before the Enlightenment, is Childs's readiness to make critical judgements about the relationship of history on its canonical presentation to history as reconstructed by modern scholars. It can range from high correspondence to almost total noncorrespondence.

At times Israel's confessional witness overlaps fully with a common public testimony, and a confirmation of an event such as the destruction

---

72. Writing of *The City of God* in this connection, Childs explains: "The effect of this Augustinian typology was to develop a powerful theological thesis respecting the unity of God's purpose within history. However, history as such remained fully subordinated to theology. It is, therefore, not by chance that no serious attention to the history of Israel for its own sake emerged until the Renaissance" (*BTONT*, 196).

73. Hans Frei, *The Eclipse of Biblical Narrative: A Study in Eighteenth and Nineteenth Century Hermeneutics* (New Haven: Yale University Press, 1974), 12.

of Jerusalem in the sixth century can be elicited even from foreign and hostile nations (Ezek 26:15ff.; 36:16ff.). At other times there is virtually no relation between Israel's witness (e.g. the crossing of the sea, Exod 14) and extrabiblical sources. Usually there emerges some sort of connection, even when remote or contradictory (cf. the manna stories of Exodus and Numbers). The theological challenge is to pursue an exegesis of these passages in such a way as to avoid the rationalistic assumption of a common reality behind all religious expression or the threat of supernaturalism which would deny in principle any relation between an outer and inner side of historical events.[74]

There are good reasons why Childs calls all of this an "approach," even when he sits loose to the epithet "canonical." Hearing the confession (more than making one himself) is the bedrock:

The goal of a new approach is to seek to do justice to the theological integrity of Israel's witness while at the same time freely acknowledging the complexities of all human knowledge and the serious challenge of modernity to any claims of revelation. Whether one calls a new approach "canonical," "kerygmatic," or "postcritical" is largely irrelevant. I would only reject the categories of mediating theology (*Vermittlungstheologie*), which seeks simply to fuse elements of orthodoxy and liberalism without doing justice to either. The fact that one falls back on the problematic term "dialectic" is merely a sign that there is no comprehensive philosophical or hermeneutical system available that can adequately resolve with one proposal the whole range of problems arising from the historical-critical method.[75]

The contrast, then, is not properly between liberalism and conservatism. Instead, the need is for biblical theologians "to work in a theologically responsible exegetical fashion,"[76] a duty with at least two major dimensions. On the one hand, "the biblical material" must be handled "in a way which is critically responsible."[77] This mode gives attention to the discrete witnesses of both testaments and to their constituent parts. It also resists "biblicist, external appropriation of the various parts of the Christian Bible without the required exegetical rigour of the theological discipline."[78] On

---

74. Childs, *BTONT*, 100.
75. Ibid., 99.
76. Ibid.
77. Ibid., 94.
78. Ibid., 336.

the other hand, the material calls for a response. It makes a "coercion ... on the reader. There is a 'reader response' required by any responsible theological reflection."[79] Christians feel this coercion differently than Jews, and those who adopt an inside perspective feel it differently than those outside do. From his Christian position Childs rises to a "struggle of faith by the church and the individual Christian of today [that] continues to focus on God's promises in his word," though this too must come to expression within "disciplined theological reflection."[80]

At issue is how to let Christian discourse on the Bible be at once public and faithful. Orthodoxy can be broad, though it comes under strain once biblical history and ostensive history drift apart. It becomes an acute "struggle" when the half-measures propped up by a residual Christendom finally collapse—when emperors are deposed and face the prospect of learning to be good neighbors, or when the institutional space left for faithful pursuit of Christian theological disciplines at elite schools diminishes to such an extent that it may be wondered just how much public real estate remains. If historicists successfully overthrow the "tyranny of canonical assumptions," then Childs may indeed be known as one of the last giants of a bygone era. That remains to be seen. Whatever the outcome, the fraught ground between sacred and secular is the conceptual space Childs attempts to occupy. If the ecclesial context of his work is fundamental, as I suggest, the university context is no less important. His commitment to both institutions explains why he simply must grapple with history, including history in reconstructed rather than merely final form.

CANONS BROAD AND NARROW

Given what has already been said, it is appropriate to inquire after canon as an historical concept before offering an account of canon as a live dogmatic concept. What is canon from the vantage of *Historie*? Canons inhabit history, after all, if they are real. Can Childs's metacanon cope with the many canonical facts on the ground? Scholars of biblical canon formation regularly say that there are as many canons as there are religious communities, and there is truth in this. For many it is also axiomatic that canon must be sharply distinguished from scripture, in part because most communities

---

79. Ibid., 335. Admittedly, this is a peculiar way of using the phrase "reader response."
80. Ibid., 336.

that cherish a canon stand at some remove from the communities that produced the scriptures in it. If canon is late, relative to scripture, then there is at least a possibility that a given community's theology of its canon is arbitrary, or at least nonessential, to scholars who are trying to account for the theology in or arising from the scripture preserved in canons. It seems like a classic case where free historical investigation stands to overturn the established orthodoxy.

There are arguments for and against the strict separation of scripture from canon. In the English-speaking world the argument for such a distinction stems from Albert Sundberg's influential *The Old Testament of the Early Church* (1964), and it has been advanced in various ways by James Sanders, John Barton, Eugene Ulrich, Lee McDonald, and a host of others. Elsewhere and in an earlier day Theodor Zahn had looked for the church to have its core canon in place by the end of the first century, but Adolf von Harnack argued persuasively for a second-century date. Today there is a near consensus that the fourth century is the proper *terminus*. It is in line with this that McDonald and Sanders ask, introducing their hefty compendium *The Canon Debate* (2002), "With such a long delay in the church's use of the term 'canon' to describe a closed body of Christian scriptures, one may well ask why there was an emergence of 'canon consciousness' in the church of the fourth century C.E. and little evidence of it before?"[81] Examples of this position could easily be multiplied, and another will be given shortly.

Then again, another historical assessment sees a consciousness of canon emerging far earlier, coincident in meaningful ways with the distinct concept "scripture." In 1953 Isac Seeligmann spoke of a *Kanonbewußtsein* within the Jewish Bible itself, tacitly expressed in what might now be called innerbiblical exegesis or proto-midrash. By 1967 Childs had noted Seeligmann's argument and soon began to adapt the notion of "canon consciousness" within scripture in his own proposals.[82] A dissenting minority has followed this alternate (and prior) usage of "canon consciousness," including some of Childs's former students.[83] One also

---

81. Lee McDonald and James Sanders, eds., *The Canon Debate* (Peabody, Mass: Hendrickson, 2002), 13.
82. See chapter 6 in Driver, *Brevard Childs*, for an account of I. L. Seeligmann's "Voraussetzungen der Midraschexegese" (VTSup 1 [1953]: 150–81), and of this important essay's place in the early development of Childs's approach.
83. See the 2005 taxonomy of literature on canon in Brevard Childs, "The Canon

thinks of continental scholars such as Christoph Dohmen. Although he knows that the first clear references to the canon as a list of books do not appear until the fourth century—the Muratorian fragment aside, Athanasius lists twenty-seven canonical books of the New Testament in 367—Dohmen defends an alternate definition of canon: "rather, the term highlights the norming function of books and collections of books that are already available and designated by a variety of terms, such as scripture, holy scripture (or books), Miqra, Law, Torah, and Prophets."[84] By these lights "canon" emerges much earlier than the fourth century CE. It is something the early church inherits, in incipient form at least, from the pre-Christian synagogue.

How does one make sense of the difference between these two trajectories, each of which seeks to account for the same body of historical evidence? Possibly the single greatest difference hinges on narrow and broad definitions of canon. An anxiety shared by many who incline toward narrower usage is that broader use imports anachronistic dogma by applying the term too early.[85] In the extreme one might even say that the the ascription of canonicity always belies the historical situation. Canon is not a real concept at all but sheer ideology. And one can find representatives of this extreme view. Writing of John Van Seters's critique of the term *redactor*, Thomas Römer asserts: "I agree with Van Seters, that one should not use the term redactor for the editors of the 'final form' of a text, *since such a final form never existed.*"[86] As the remark is neither qualified nor

---

in Recent Biblical Studies: Reflections on an Era," *ProEccl* 14 (2005): 26–45; repr. in Bartholomew et al., *Canon and Biblical Interpretation*, 33–57. Of note are Stephen Chapman, *The Law and the Prophets: A Study in Old Testament Canon Formation* (FAT 27; Tübingen: Mohr Siebeck, 2000), especially 106–10, and Christopher Seitz, *The Goodly Fellowship of the Prophets: The Achievement of Association in Canon Formation* (Grand Rapids: Baker, 2009), especially 43–45, 53.

84. Christoph Dohmen, *Die Bibel und ihre Auslegung* (3rd ed.; Munich: Beck, 2006), 20.

85. As Steins rightly insists (in Egbert Ballhorn and Georg Steins, eds., *Der Bibelkanon in der Bibelauslegung: Methodenreflexionen und Beispielexegesen* [Stuttgart: Kohlhammer, 2007], 115), contra Hubert Frankemölle (*Frühjudentum und Urchristentum: Vorgeschichte—Verlauf—Auswirkungen* [Stuttgart: Kohlhammer, 2006]), an early application of the term canon is not anachronistic if the word's meaning fits the situation it describes.

86. Thomas Römer, *The So-Called Deuteronomistic History: A Sociological, Historical and Literary Introduction* (London: T&T Clark, 2007), 49 n. 10, emphasis added.

explained, it is difficult to know what he means. Manifestly final forms do exist. For the Hebrew Bible the Aleppo Codex is an obvious and splendid example. Taking this for granted, Römer appears more to mean that "final form" is an empty concept, wholly alien to the biblical situation. Canon, then, intrudes on history; or to be precise, it intrudes on the sort of history that would see editions of Deuteronomistic History (so-called) as a more basic textual and historical reality than Former Prophets. Römer's hyperbole permits a stark division between canon and history, but this actually seems rather rare among those who study canon formation. Most operate with at least a tacit awareness of their stake in the appropriateness of a community's theology of its Holy Writ. If canon is rejected, in other words, it is typically because canon is a false dogmatic concept, not because it is not history. Canon is not replaced by sheer history, typically, but by the evidently more suitable category scripture. Scripture then stands in the breach, inviting a historically chastened theology of, say, the Protestant church's Bible. An irregular exercise of negative theology takes place (not canon!) by which something deemed too rigid is supplanted by something broader and more flexible. The bifurcated use of "canon consciousness" that stems either from Seeligmann or from Sundberg is not explained by the bald rejection of dogma, in many cases, but by divergent formulations of right dogma.[87]

Adoption of a broad semantic range for canon has made Childs and those who follow him outliers in recent discussions. As a striking example, consider the impasse that halts traffic between Childs's work on the Pauline corpus (2008) and Craig Allert's *A High View of Scripture? The Author-*

Toward the end of the book comes an acknowledgment that something changes. There is a "transformation of the book of Deuteronomy [which] was the end of the Deuteronomistic History" and the beginning of the "Former Prophets" (182). Absent any explanation of this transformation, however, the reader is left with the impression that the change lacks deep logic and is therefore mostly arbitrary.

87. In addition to John Webster's skill as a dogmatician, one advantage of his "frankly dogmatic" account in "The Dogmatic Location of the Canon" is precisely that it is frank (in John Webster, *Word and Church: Essays in Christian Dogmatics* [Edinburgh: T&T Clark, 2001], 9–46). He "assumes the truth of the church's confession of the gospel, regarding that confession as a point from which we move rather than a point towards which we proceed" (11). Studies of canon formation have different goals, but relative to Webster they have a methodological weakness if an ostensibly historical category, scripture, is made a surrogate for a more obviously dogmatic category, canon, and then quietly becomes the vehicle for dogmatic judgments.

ity of the Bible and the Formation of the New Testament Canon (2007), titles that would appear to coincide as much in theme as time. Allert, a Canadian and self-described evangelical,[88] follows his more technical first monograph with a pastorally minded book about "how an understanding of the formation of the New Testament canon may inform an evangelical doctrine of Scripture."[89] Childs, as we have seen, navigates from the historical Paul to the canonical Paul with the aim of elevating regard for theological aspects of a historically shaped corpus. Both authors define "canon" early in their books, where some pretty fundamental disagreement begins. As from 1970 and counter to a "narrow, history-of-religions definition," Childs defends "a far broader definition that does justice to the theological dimension of the term. The early Christian church was never without a canon since it assumed Israel's Scriptures as normative."[90] Allert, on the other hand, takes for granted that "canon" should be restricted to mean "a closed collection of texts to which nothing can be added and from which nothing can be taken."[91] He also states flatly at one point: "The church existed before the Bible."[92] In each case, the goal is obviously sound dogma rather than no dogma. What is at stake in this in-house debate about the character of Christian scripture? And from a wider perspective—with regard to those who insist on bracketing religious commitments, insofar as that is possible—what does it matter if one broadens canon or abandons it for scripture? Is history distorted in either case? A brief comparison of Childs and Allert can shed light on both questions. Childs's approach is far from the only way to handle the difficult intersection of history and theology at the point of what the church's canon is and does, but I do hope to illustrate how the broad use of canon that has bemused so many of Childs's readers can be both theologically advantageous and historically defensible.

Falling in line behind Sanders and McDonald, then, Allert defines "canon consciousness" as the express knowledge of a closed list of canoni-

---

88. Evangelical in Allert's sense should of course be distinguished from evangelisch in the German sense (and as adopted by Webster).
89. Craig Allert, *A High View of Scripture? The Authority of the Bible and the Formation of the New Testament Canon* (Grand Rapids: Baker, 2007), 173, cf. 10. His first title is *Revelation, Truth, Canon and Interpretation: Studies in Justin Martyr's Dialogue with Trypho* (Leiden: Brill, 2002).
90. Childs, *Church's Guide*, 4 n. 4, cf. 253.
91. Allert, *High View?*, 9 n. 1, cf. 37.
92. Ibid., 76.

cal scriptures and so as something that does not properly emerge in the church until the fourth century.[93] More uniquely, he makes additional efforts to reform a semi-popular evangelical understanding of the Bible as having quite definite boundaries: sixty-six books in total, inerrant in the original autographs. Against this, Allert brings evidence of how much apocryphal literature is cited by the very Fathers who set parameters on the church's New Testament, and of how broad the Fathers' sense of inspiration tends to be. North American evangelicals need a thicker ecclesiology, he insists, by which they stand to gain an appreciation of the historically porous boundaries between canonical and noncanonical scripture, and ultimately between scripture and tradition. This is the setting for a "realization that the Bible grew up in the cradle of the church," which leads to his clam that "[t]he church existed before the Bible."[94] At this point, however, he ventures into awkward historical-theological territory. If the target is just a "Bible, Holy Spirit, and me" view of *sola scriptura*, then one can see his point. If, on the other hand, he is making a theological claim of the first order, then the claim is open to question. Even on strict historical grounds, what weight does one give to the fact that the early church took as its theological inheritance and point of reference the Jewish scriptures? Allert makes much of the notion that the church did not receive a canon, but rather scriptures on the way to canon—does this mean the church had no Bible? Or what does 1 Cor 15 mean in saying that Christ died according to the scriptures? On a few occasions, Allert refers to the "content of Christianity," but the crucial question goes unasked: before and as the NT came into being, how did the church apprehend this content? Saint Augustine can hardly settle the matter, yet it is challenging to remember that even at the brink of the fifth century he sees in the Old Testament "such a strong prediction and pre-announcement of the New Testament that nothing is found in the teaching of the Evangelists and the apostles, however exalted and divine the precepts and promises, that is lacking in those ancient books."[95] In short, in Allert's work the role of the Old Testament in the crucial first centuries of the church's life is not adequately explained.

---

93. Ibid., 52, 68, 131. Allert actually equates the consciousness of canon with datable lists. "If, as some argue, the early church consciously created and closed a New Testament canon at the end of the second century, why does the proliferation of canon lists begin to appear only in the fourth century?" (131).

94. Ibid., 76.

95. Augustine, *Contra Adimantum* 3.4 (PL 42:134). Still, as David F. Wright points

Like Allert, John Webster worries about the mislocation of canon by some Protestants as "a relatively isolated piece of epistemological teaching."[96] But from a dogmatic standpoint Webster better arbitrates the oft-emphasized correlation of canon and community. Is ecclesiology the base on which doctrines of canon and scripture build? What then of revelation, of the triune God's saving action and self-communication? "The question ... is whether it is more appropriate to speak of the people of the book or the book of the people."[97] Evidence that Allert lacks a satisfactory answer to this question, in theological and historical terms, can be seen in the trouble he has connecting second- and fourth-century definitions of canon. Tellingly, his argument pivots midway through when he backs away from the narrow "canon as list" definition posited at the outset. Allert explains:

> Even though we have here predominantly been using the word with reference to a list of texts, its initial use has nothing to do with texts.... In the latter half of the second century, "canon" for Irenaeus meant the Rule of Faith, the content of essential Christian belief. This was also true of other church fathers.... Soon the word "canon" moved from this more fluid usage to refer to concrete things, such as conciliar decisions, monastic rules, clergy, and finally to a list, index, or table—something with which a person can orient oneself.[98]

From here the discussion vacillates between apparently contradictory senses of the key term, from the plural canons of the early church to the one canon that arrives late. Allert's conclusion merely reiterates the tension, and thus falters where it might have approached a more coherent doctrine of scripture than the thin one he deconstructs.

---

out ("Augustine: His Exegesis and Hermeneutics," in *Hebrew Bible/Old Testament: The History of Its Interpretation* [ed. Magne Sæbø; Göttingen: Vandenhoeck & Ruprecht, 1996–2013], 1.1:701–30 [714]), Augustine revised this passage to read "almost nothing" in his *Retractationes*.

96. Webster, "Dogmatic Location," 9.

97. Ibid., 24. In places Allert seems to favor the latter and certainly emphasizes it strongly. For instance, "The Bible must be viewed as a product of the community because traditions of the community provide the context in which Scripture was produced" (Allert, *High View?*, 145, cf. 84–86).

98. Ibid., 78–79. Is the second century's more abstract canon of truth not something with which a person could orient oneself?

The second century has rightly been identified as very important in the canonical process.... The four Gospels rose to preeminence and a Pauline collection was circulating and received as authoritative in most congregations throughout the empire. Indeed, there was a core collection of Christian documents. But we must measure this statement and not read a later concept of written canon into the second century. It is quite likely that the formation of a closed collection of Christian writings was not paramount in the mind of the second-century church. This is indicated especially by its reaction to ... heresies: they were countered not with a written canon, but rather with the canon of truth. If the written canon was paramount, we should expect to see a preponderance of lists following these great heresies, but this is precisely what we do not see—until the fourth century.[99]

There is no reason to doubt that the meaning of "canon" (or rule) shifts in the passage of time from Irenaeus and Tertullian in the second and third centuries to Eusebius and Athanasius in the fourth. What is open to question is whether "a preponderance of lists" is the *terminus* with which the final significance of canon is to be identified. Canon is a fourth-century phenomenon by definition, in that case, and has only incidental links with earlier phenomena by the same name. Allert therefore laments "the unfortunate claim that the Bible itself is the Rule of Faith, or that when the Bible came into existence (second century), it became the Rule of Faith."[100] If there have been naive attempts to collapse the difference here—Allert finds examples among evangelical scholars—it does not follow that more informed attempts to span the gap are also unproductive. To the contrary, it is altogether unlikely that the church's two-testament canon should have no relation whatsoever to its *canon et regula fidei* in the period before questions of the New Testament's scope were settled. Allert's hiatus between two ancient canons, paralleling the modern hiatus between scripture and canon, is almost the *reductio ad absurdum* of a widespread definition.

In contrast to Allert, Childs actively exploits the polyvalence of the word "canon," which for him is an expansive cipher. For instance, in a response to reviewers of his 1979 *Introduction* he speaks of "a rule of faith called canon."[101] And already in *Biblical Theology in Crisis* he notes, "In its original sense, canon does not simply perform the formal function of

---

99. Ibid., 129–30.
100. Ibid., 83.
101. Childs, "Response to Reviewers," 52.

separating the books that are authoritative from others that are not, but is the *rule* that delineates the area in which the church hears the word of God. The fundamental theological issue at stake is not the extent of the canon, which has remained in some flux within Christianity, but the claim for a normative body of tradition contained in a set of books."[102] Childs draws this insight from a few theologians and church historians. Karl Barth is one. Another is Hans von Campenhausen, whose *Die Entstehung der christlichen Bibel* (1968) is praised by Childs in 1970 and is known to Allert in English translation (1972):

> The one rule and guideline, the only "canon" which Irenaeus explicitly acknowledges, is the "canon of truth," that is to say: the content of the faith itself, which the Church received from Christ, to which she remains faithful, and by which she lives. By this is meant neither a Summa of dogmatic propositions nor an unchangeable confessional formula nor even the sacred Scripture as such, however certain it may be that the latter teaches and contains this truth.[103]

Yet another is Bengt Hägglund, who draws the following conclusion in a 1958 study of *regula fidei* in the patristic period: "It is no accident that the Greek word for *regula*, κανών, increasingly became a firm designation for holy scripture. The original witness is therefore not only 'canonical' because it represents the authority of the prophets and apostles, but also because it is the bearer of revelation, mediating the reality of salvation."[104] Or to quote Webster again on a point that I think Childs would appreciate, "a canon which is only a useful accident, only tradition, cannot rule."[105] In terms of Allert's discussion, the second-century sense of canon as a rule of

---

102. Childs, *Biblical Theology in Crisis* (Philadelphia: Westminster, 1970), 99, emphasis added.

103. Hans Freiherr von Campenhausen, *The Formation of the Christian Bible* (trans. John Austin Baker; London: A&C Black, 1972), 182; trans. of *Die Entstehung der christlichen Bibel* (Tübingen: Mohr Siebeck, 1968).

104. Bengt Hägglund, "Die Bedeutung der 'regula fidei' als Grundlage theologischer Aussagen," *ST* 12 (1958): 1–44 (39).

105. Webster, "Dogmatic Location," 18. Further on he argues: "Unless it is set in the larger structure of divine action and its creation of human response which we call revelation, "canon" can become simply "rule"; its normative status becomes its own property, rather than a consequence of its place in the divine economy. Above all, reference to divine action falls away…. But as a function of revelation, the canon is not merely a list or code; it is a specification of those instruments where the church may

truth or faith dominates in Childs's thought, but this contains rather than rivals fourth-century and other subsequent senses of canon.

In conclusion, let me file three observations about the importance of seeing canon as *regula fidei* in Childs's last book on Paul. First, *contra* Allert: "The Christian church was never without a canon."[106] Because canon is broad rather than narrow, Childs can make tenable historical claims that avoid underestimating the role of what came to be known as the Old Testament. Second, the semantic exchange between canon and *regula* operates in the background in *Church's Guide*—it is taken for granted on the basis of earlier work—and yet without it the task of outlining the contours of the Pauline corpus falls to pieces. Sketching Paul's canonical profile is a way of getting more specific about how the parts of the corpus interrelate, and how, together with the whole company of prophets and apostles, the corpus functions in and constrains the church's christologically ordered life. Third, however, canon's dogma is no less basic than canon's history. Childs's increased specificity about the role of both parts of the Christian Bible as one *Christuszeugnis* has troubled some readers of his *BTONT*, though the category that grows to prominence in his final book is not Christology but pneumatology. A lengthy treatment of the life of the Spirit in Paul sets the stage for this claim about how Christianity's authoritative tradition is actualized in each generation of the saints: "It is the church's confession of the role of the Holy Spirit as the divine presence at work that continues to enliven and transform the written Word of Scripture into the living Word for today."[107] Plainly this is dogmatic language. It arises out of a particular Christian confession. Yet if there is just one point to underscore in view of many scholars' unease about canon as a dogmatic concept, it should be Childs's acknowledgment that canon is unavoidably a dogmatic concept. What would it mean to treat it "merely" as history? Historians have a right to banish erroneous dogma from the biblical period. If canon attaches to scripture, on the other hand, it should with the proper qualifications be allowed to stay. Is there, as some have seen, a *Kanonbewußtsein* deep in the formation of the literature itself? That depends on what a person means by canon. But in all probability church teaching and academic research on canon alike will be

---

reliably expect to encounter God's communicative presence, God's self-attestation" (28–29).

106. Childs, *Church's Guide*, 61; cf. 4 n. 4 and 253–54.

107. Ibid., 128, cf. 62–63, 77, 97, 112–38, 167, 255.

better served by those who start with plausibly robust dogmatic conceptions than by those who shy away from scant ones and so risk letting bad dogma distort their history.

Psalm 34: Redaction, Inner-Biblical Exegesis and the Longer Psalm Superscriptions—"Mistake" Making and Theological Significance

Christopher R. Seitz

Some forty years ago the *Journal of Semitic Studies* published an essay by Brevard Childs entitled "Psalm Titles and Midrashic Exegesis."[1] Childs recognized the difficulty of using the postbiblical term "midrash" for inner-biblical exegesis, but he wanted to argue that later the expansions of Davidic ascription—at Qumran, and in the LXX, Syriac Apocrypha, Targums, and Peshitta—were consistent with and had their roots within the biblical period itself.[2] Psalm titles were not supplied on the basis of independent historical information; neither was that the claim they sought to make for the psalms. Rather, the process pointed to "a learned tradition of the study of the Scripture" undertaken by a scribal school (149). Psalms as pre-existent compositions were closely studied in pietistic circles, and the details of them were matched, through prayerful reflection, with episodes known from the narratives of Samuel–Kings. In this way, the inner life of David was opened up, as the literal sense of some psalms was seen as capable of expansion through association with episodes in the life of David. It is not my intention to rehearse the details of this careful argument from Childs, but to explore one aspect of his 1971 study, that is, the character of inner-biblical exegesis and redaction through the lens of Ps 34. Here a mistake appears to be made in referring to "Abimelech" instead of "Achish."

---

1. Brevard S. Childs, "Psalm Titles and Midrashic Exegesis," *JSS* 16 (1971): 137–50.
2. The Greek tradition has supplemented the number of titles, added Davidic ascription to eight Psalms, and Jeremiah to one, and provided new historical settings. Qumran has a supernumerary Psalm. Childs notes: "The further expansion of the titles in the Syriac Apocryphal Psalms, in the Targum and in the Peshitta, testifies that the same process continued" (ibid., 143).

If redaction is responsible for the superscription of the psalm, what was intended by the reference to Abimelech, or was a "mistake" made?

First, however, we must ask what is meant by the term "redaction." To speak of redaction and a redactor is to point to a moving target in present scholarship. John Barton has spoken of what he calls "the disappearing redactor," and one might wonder if such disappearance was Barton's hope, so manifold and even contradictory are the characterizations of literary supplementation in the Bible that cluster under the title of redaction.[3] The redactor supplies "happy endings" (so Terrence Collins regarding redaction in the Book of the Twelve).[4] The redactor takes two sources that disagree and with eraser and glue wrests from them a new final text that has enough of the mark-up showing to give evidence of all this (so Propp's redactor of E and P in Exodus).[5] The redactor merges the "very good" of Gen 1 and the "fall" of Gen 2–3, and in so doing achieves a theological masterpiece (so von Rad).[6] The redactor achieves a synthesis in the preaching of Hosea and Amos, by application of key textual additions in both books, so as to preserve the particularities of each, and to insist on their common divine origin, compatibility, and inspiration (so Jeremias).[7] The redactor places texts next to one another with little in the way of literary supplementation, and so doing achieves an important effect, as seen in the movement of Pss 1, 2, and 3.[8] The redactor is a fiction, and we ought instead to think of late, wholesale works by single authors on the scale of

---

3. John Barton, *Reading the Old Testament: Method in Biblical Study* (2nd ed.; London: Darton, Longman & Todd, 1996), 56–58. See also his own reflections in "The Day of Yahweh in the Minor Prophets," in *The Old Testament: Canon, Literature, and Theology; Collected Essays of John Barton* (Aldershot, England: Ashgate, 2007).

4. Terence Collins, *The Mantle of Elijah: The Redaction Criticism of the Prophetical Books* (BibSem 20; Sheffield: JSOT Press, 1993).

5. William H. Propp, *Exodus 1–18: A New Translation with Introduction and Commentary* (AB 2; New York: Doubleday, 1999); *Exodus 19–40: A New Translation with Introduction and Commentary* (AB 2A; New York: Doubleday, 2006).

6. Gerhard von Rad, *Genesis: A Commentary* (trans. John H. Mark; rev. ed.; OTL; London: SCM, 1972). See discussion of von Rad in Christopher Seitz, *Prophecy and Hermeneutics: Toward a New Introduction to the Prophets* (STI; Grand Rapids: Baker, 2007), 155–87.

7. Jorg Jeremias, "The Interrelationship between Amos and Hosea," in *Forming Prophetic Literature: Essays on Isaiah and The Twelve in Honor of John D. W. Watts* (ed. James W. Watts and Paul R. House; JSOTSup 235; Sheffield: Sheffield Academic Press, 1996), 171–86.

8. This kind of significance is being restored in canonical readings of the Psalter.

Herodotus (so Van Seters).⁹ Even Blenkinsopp's recent publication on Gen 1–11 speaks of the redactor as a final synthetic author: "Genesis 1–11 is not just a combination of two sources pasted together like two computer files but the production of an author who worked up P and J, together with other source material, into a compelling narrative."¹⁰

And we might consider a related matter: Are the differing characterizations of redaction *due to the location of such alleged work in the canon*? That is, are narrative, wisdom, and prophetic texts offering up different examples of redaction because the literary deposit being extended is different, and is therefore handled differently? Here Childs's essay on psalm titles may speak of redaction as inner-biblical study, based on the comparison of texts; while in the narrative texts of Exodus in his 1974 commentary,¹¹ or the prophetic texts of the sixty-six chapters of Isaiah,¹² it will naturally take a different form. Lawson Stone once wrote: "The continuous reception, reinterpretation, and reformulation of the biblical tradition disclosed by form and redaction criticism undergirds Childs's notion of 'canonical shape.'"¹³ The continuous reception, reinterpretation, and reformulation of which he speaks will inevitably look different depending on the source material itself. This point probably needs underscoring.

At this point I want to turn to one specific example of inner-biblical exegesis in Childs's 1971 essay, the title supplied for Ps 34: "David Psalm. When he feigned madness before Abimelech so that he drove him out." The problem is obvious enough. The episode referred to would appear to be David's flight from Saul in 1 Sam 21, but the explicit mention of

---

One can see it throughout the earlier history of interpretation (Basil called Ps 1 the keel on a boat; Jerome spoke of the entrance to a mansion).

9. John Van Seters, "The Report of the Yahwist's Demise Has Been Greatly Exaggerated!" in *A Farewell to the Yahwist? The Composition of the Pentateuch in Recent European Interpretation* (ed. Thomas B. Dozeman and Konrad Schmid; SBLSymS 34; Atlanta: SBL Press, 2006), 143–57.

10. Joseph Blenkinsopp, *Creation, Un-creation, Re-creation: A Discursive Commentary on Genesis 1–11* (London: T&T Clark, 2011), 7.

11. Brevard S. Childs, *The Book of Exodus: A Critical, Theological Commentary* (OTL; Philadelphia: Westminster, 1974).

12. Brevard S. Childs, *Isaiah* (OTL; Louisville: Westminster John Knox, 2001).

13. Lawson G. Stone, "Ethical and Apologetic Tendencies in the Redaction of the Book of Joshua," *CBQ* 53 (1991): 28 n. 17. The quote continues, "much more decisively than structuralist or 'new critical' commitments to the final form of the text" (*pace* John Barton, *Reading the Old Testament*, 140–79).

madness—the only one in Samuel-Kings—occurred not with Abimelech but Achish. Because the problem is so obvious, the older tradition and modern criticism have seen it and offered many solutions. According to some, Abimelech is a mistake, a scribal error.[14] According to others, Abimelech is actually Achimelech, the priest of Nob from the same chapter (21:1–9), from whom David "withheld his true design"—a reading picked up in the textual tradition known to Theodoret and also certain Vulgate readings.[15] Yet there is no confusion about Achimelech/Abimelech elsewhere in the psalm titles. Psalm 52 correctly relates Achimelech, father of Abiathar, to the execution by Doeg the Edomite in 1 Sam 22. Further alternatives are that Abimelech was the Hebrew name of the Philistine Achish (Rashi's intimation, later recycled by Dahood),[16] or that Abimelech is a title, like Pharaoh or Caesar, and was used with any king of Philistia. This view is widely held in the tradition (Calvin, Aquinas). We will return to this issue shortly.[17]

---

14. Referring to the superscription, Hans-Joachim Kraus writes, "The rest of the heading makes an effort to provide a historical setting for this 'Psalm of David' and in so doing commits the error of confusing Achish of Gath with Abimelech (1 Sam 21:12–15). No internal reference to the old story of David is given anywhere in Psalm 34" (*Psalms 1–59: A Commentary* [trans. Hilton L. Oswald; Minneapolis: Augsburg, 1988], 383). The modern critical instinct may speak of a redactional/editorial error, as against one in the scribal transmission. Note how categorically Kraus denies any connection between the content of the psalm and the narratives of Samuel-Kings.

15. Clement VIII has "Ahimelech" as a correction of Sixtus V's "Abimelech."

16. Rashi also sees an association with Abimelech in Gen 20 and 26. This goes back to an aggadic midrash which states that Achish was virtuous like Abimelech. Like the patriarch, he did not wish to harm David. See the discussion in Mayer I. Gruber, ed., *Rashi's Commentary on Psalms 1–89 (Books I–III) with English Translation, Introduction, and Notes* (Atlanta: Scholars Press, 1998) 168–69. Mitchell Dahood writes, "It is quite possible that Abimelech was the Semitic name of the king of Gath" (*Psalms I: 1–50* [AB; Garden City: Doubleday, 1966], 205).

17. "Il n'y a pas de desaccord, car ou bien il eut deux noms, ou bien son nom fut Achis mais il fut de la descendance d'Abimélech" (Jean-Eric Stroobant de Saint-Eloy, ed., *Thomas D'Aquin Commentaire sur les Psaumes* [Paris: Cerf, 1996], 399). Calvin wrote: "Abimelech is here employed; and it is probable that the latter name had been the common designation of the monarchs of the Philistines, as Pharaoh was the common name of the monarchs of Egypt, and Caesar that of the Roman Emperors, which was borrowed from the name of Julius Caesar, who had first seized the imperial power among the Romans. We know that many ages before David was born, the kings who reigned in Gerar in the time of Abraham were called Abimelech. It is not, therefore, to be wondered at, that this name should be handed down from age to age

Childs speaks of a close study of the scriptures which results in redactional associations being made by means of superscriptions. By "close study," he does not mean a sort of mechanical device without any exegetical significance, such as seeing the Hebrew word for "taste" in 34:8 (טַעֲמוּ) and linking it with the word for behavior (טַעְמוֹ) in 1 Sam 21:14, or similarly linking the words "boasting" (תִּתְהַלָּל) and "feigning" (וַיִּתְהֹלֵל). Rather, two texts are associated by means of a superscription so that some specific theme of the psalm and a specific detail in the narrative presentation of David are, in consequence, mutually illumined. Now how does one imagine this taking place? Several things must be noted as we take up this question.

First, the thirteen superscriptions of this kind are rare enough that one must ask, why these particular psalms and not others? And, why only these and not more (at least in the Hebrew text)?[18] Second, the thirteen references do not follow the order of their unfolding in 1–2 Sam. The flight of David from Absalom as remembered in Ps 3 occurs after the feigning of madness mentioned in Ps 34. The next psalm superscription, in Ps 51, concerns David's encounter with Bathsheba, and then we return to the earlier story of Doeg's execution of the priests at Nob, his fate being clarified by Ps 52's judgment—something never clarified in the narratives of the Deuteronomistic History.[19] Now this might suggest that the psalms already stood in their present order, with themes like "day and night" prayer linking Pss 3–7, and the lumping together of specifically Davidic psalms in Books 1 and 2, before the process of inner-biblical reflection being noted was initiated.

How might we answer this question, then: Was the "close study" of scripture one that began with the David narratives, or one that moved initially from the base of the Psalter roughly in its present form? (Most will agree with Childs that the superscription process was a late postexilic

---

among their posterity, and become the common name of all the kings of Palestine" (John Calvin, *Commentary on the Books of the Psalms* [trans. J. Anderson; Edinburgh: Calvin Translation Society, 1845], 1:555–56).

18. See n. 2 above.

19. Childs comments, "There is an additional reason why the connection of the Psalm with Doeg was a natural one. The Book of Samuel nowhere reports on the fate of Doeg. But surely such treachery demands punishment! Once the superscription has been added, the reader knows of his certain destruction because of his deceit (v. 7 ff.)" ("Psalm Titles," 145).

development.) So, for example, does the density of reference to fear in Ps 34, encountered nowhere so clearly before in the opening psalm sequence—if that is the right way to characterize it—encourage an association with the two main episodes of fear in the David stories, having to do with the time spent in the Philistine camp of Achish (1 Sam 21:12 and 23:15)? Did a reception-history process within the development of scripture search for specific themes in the psalms and then relate them to the David of Samuel by means of superscription? Or was the movement in the other direction? Did a sense of irresolution in the story of Doeg's evil execution of the priests at Nob initiate a search for a psalm of David, already in fixed sequence, that would associate itself with that story, and also offer a word of justice and resolution, such as Ps 52 manifestly does, saying, "God will uproot you permanently. He will take you away and snatch you out of your tent, and root you out of the land of the living.... Here is the man who did not make God his stronghold, but trusted on the multitude of his riches and became strong, destroying others" (Ps 52:5, 7)?

If so, this would give partial explanation for both the selectivity and the lack of chronological concern evidenced by the present sequence of superscripted psalms. But could it not also be the case that such close study of psalms and Davidic stories was always reciprocal in character? Perhaps a psalm was thought to explore helpfully some aspect of the narrative (the fear of David in the camp of Achish), while the story of David being rescued from danger in 1 Samuel needed something more in the way of prayerful reflection, which the psalm supplies. How did David escape when in such dire straits, in the hostile camp of Achish, greatly afraid? The Psalm supplies the answer: David prayed this prayer. Why did God forgive David in the Bathsheba affair? Psalm 51 explained it as having to do with a deep confession of far greater urgency and pain than what we read in 2 Samuel. How did David avoid capture following the Ziphite revelation to Saul of his whereabouts? He begged God to save him for his own name's sake, trusted in God's defense, and promised freewill offering and sacrifice, as the seven verses of Ps 54 economically put it: "I will sacrifice a freewill offering to you.... For he has delivered me from all my troubles."

That this process might have continued indefinitely, and did partially, is a sign that the selectivity turned only on the limits of the narrative tradition itself, and the suitableness of matching the details of a specific psalm with the narrative presentation, neither overloading it artificially nor making merely superficial or word-association links, but seeking instead deeper theological penetration. The general tradition of David as author and singer of psalms was the warrant for this exploration. This even allowed psalms that did not actually fit the narrative presentation of David—the dedication of the temple—nevertheless to be free for such an association given the appropriateness of the content, in this case, of Ps 30. David could then raise his voice at that event after all, as the one constantly rescued in life by prayer and confession, giving first-person thanks to God quite literally forever (see Ps 30:12).

So why Abimelech? Why would such close study and attention to detail as we have otherwise noted in the superscripting process result in a mistake at this point? As Childs has suggested, "By substituting the name of Abimelech the author of the title is calling attention to the Abraham/Isaac stories (Gen xx and xxvi) which provide a certain parallel to the David story."[20] He then concludes in his usual cautious way, "Unfortunately the evidence is insufficient to press this theory."[21]

If, however, as we have noted, those carrying out close inner-biblical interpretation studied two textual bodies with equal and reciprocal attention, nothing would prevent them from scanning more widely. The general argument that a king of the Philistines might be called "Abimelech" as the *nomen dignitatis* of all Philistine kings is fine so far as it goes, but sounds like a form of special pleading. What is to be noted is that in the separate stories of Abraham and Isaac in Philistine territory, a king with the "title" Abimelech is encountered. Or, one and the same king, named Abimelech, across two generations.[22]

Insufficiently noted is that in both stories a key feature is fear. Like David, the patriarchs are in the enemy camp, in their case due to famine. Both think their lives are in danger. Isaac "feared to say, My wife, thinking lest the men of the place should kill me" (26:7, RSV). And Isaac prospers so much that Abimelech drives him out (לֵךְ מֵעִמָּנוּ, v. 16), an action only assumed in the literal sense account of David and Achish in 1 Sam 21–22, where David simply departs and, we are told, escaped to the cave of Adullam (over against "he drove him out" [וַיְגָרְשֵׁהוּ]) in the superscrip-

---

20. Childs, "Psalm Titles," 145. Compare Artur Weiser and hints in the tradition noted above, "In place of the Philistine king Achish of Gath, mentioned in I Sam. ch. 2, Abimelech is here referred to, probably on account of Gen. chs. 20 f.; 26" (*The Psalms: A Commentary* [OTL; Philadelphia: Westminster, 1962], 296).

21. Ibid.

22. Is the narrative implying that the same "Abimelech" fell twice for the wife-sister cunning, but all the same acted appropriately on both occasions?

tion of Ps 34). Later, of course, like his patriarchal forebear, David will prosper greatly in the entourage of Achish, in service of the Philistine army. Achish must send him forth as Abimelech did Isaac, both worried at the prospect of too long a sojourn of the favored Israel in their midst (see 1 Sam 29:6–10).

In a carefully phrased paragraph, Michael Fishbane says of typology or figural reading:

> It also reveals unexpected unity in historical experience and providential continuity in its new patterns and shapes. Accordingly, the perception of typologies is not solely an exegetical activity, it is, at the same time, a religious activity of the first magnitude. For if legal and other aggadic exegeses emphasize the verbal aspects of ongoing divine revelation, typological exegesis reveals its historical concreteness. Typological exegesis is thus not a disclosure of the sensus plenior of the text, in the manner of other forms of inner-biblical exegesis. It is rather a disclosure of the plenitude and mysterious workings of divine activity in history.[23]

The impulses teased out by Childs in a careful study of psalm superscriptions show exegetical activity, but they also, to use Fishbane's language, show religious activity, described by Stone as "the continuous reception, reinterpretation, and reformulation of the biblical tradition disclosed by form and redaction criticism" which "undergirds Childs's notion of canonical shape."[24] In the case of Abimelech in Ps 34, we may also see the figural linkage of David with the patriarchs in the context of prayer, where the themes of fear and danger emphasize "providential continuity" and "a disclosure of the plenitude and mysterious working of divine action in history." Erich Auerbach uses the language of vertical figuration, whereby a connection between separate events "impossible to establish by reason in the historical dimension" is posited as a vertical link to "Divine Providence, which alone is able to devise such a plan of history and supply the key to its understanding."[25] I have sought to speak of this dimension in my own writing as history in its own special register.[26]

---

23. Michael Fishbane, *Biblical Interpretation in Ancient Israel* (Oxford: Clarendon, 1989), 352.
24. Stone, "Ethical and Apologetic Tendencies," 28 n. 17.
25. Eric Auerbach, *Mimesis: The Representation of Reality in Western Literature* (trans. Willard R. Trask; Princeton: Princeton University Press, 1953), 73–74.
26. See especially *Prophecy and Hermeneutics*, 55–113.

In the final paragraph of the 1971 essay, Childs draws a distinction between von Rad's earlier effort to resuscitate the term "typology" along the lines of prophecy and fulfillment and what Childs identifies in the superscriptions in the Davidic psalms. In a pregnant sentence Childs writes, "A theological analogy is directed not primarily to the typological unfolding of a future-oriented tradition, but rather to the exploring of an area that has been staked out by means of a sacred text. History has retained its importance, but in the transformed state of being canonical history."[27] In the case of Ps 34, the movement is not only within the area staked out by means of the sacred texts of Psalms and 1 Samuel but also, arguably, in Gen 20 and 26. The ancestor in danger is seen to be the figural type providentially linked in canonical history to the later David of Samuel and Psalms. The movement is not only not future-oriented in the manner of von Rad's manifest misdrawing tradition process as the credenda strains toward Christ[28] but is instead a movement backward in time to see God's providential hand at work in the days of the ancestors who, like David, found themselves in places of danger and in need of prayer and of God's deliverances. If the "mistake" of Abimelech has wrongly sent the reader on a path that underscores a typological association between David and his ancestors Isaac and Abraham, what a fortunate error it has been all the same. In our view, a generic title ("Abimelech") was utilized in the superscripting process not to disturb the Achish association, but as an addition to it, to point the reader to wider canonical signification.

II

At this point I want to introduce a rival understanding of the significance of the "mistake" whereby Abimelech has replaced Achish in the title of Ps 34. In back-to-back homilies by Augustine on Ps 34 (Ps 33 in the translation tradition familiar to him), the preacher seizes on this apparent error and seeks to understand its significance on very different terms. Augustine notes that one should expect the superscription to supply Achish, as that is the name the story of Samuel–Kings gives the king of Gath before whom David feigned madness (1 Sam 21:10–15). So there is no doubt on his

---

27. Childs, "Psalm Titles," 150.
28. See the extended discussion of von Rad's proposal for a tradition-historical linkage of Old and New Testaments, and a different proposal, in Seitz, *Prophecy and Hermeneutics*, 155–87.

part: "Clearly it has been changed." But, he immediately adds, "not without reason." In the sentence previous to this he intentionally emphasizes that he will be dwelling on "the mysterious reason for the change of name," using the term *sacramentum*.[29] "The episode was recalled, yet the name was altered, and there must be some reason for this."[30]

I want to follow Augustine's reading closely, because he has recently been held up as a kind of exemplar for Christian interpretation of the Psalms (and of the Old Testament more generally), associated with what Byassee often refers to as "the return to allegory."[31] "Allegory" is never defined in any precise sense in this work, but it appears to be held up chiefly in contrast to what has gone by the label of "authorial intention" in the historical-critical mode of the last two centuries—not, in other words, in the classical conception of the older history of interpretation, where "literal sense" and/or an author's intention also covered extended senses.[32] Augustine serves as the model for a "return to allegory" and a brief treatment by him of Ps 33 (i.e., Ps 34) is held up as a positive and exciting roadsign for us to follow.[33] As Childs has himself provided a chapter in

---

29. In his commentary Aquinas also refers to a "mystical sense." What he gives under that label is a very short précis, including only incidental details from Augustine, prior to his own detailed exposition of the psalm as such. See John E. Rotelle, ed., *Expositions of the Psalms 33–50* (trans. M. Boulding; Hyde Park, N.Y.: New City Press, 2000).

30. Ibid., 15.

31. Jason Byassee, *Praise Seeking Understanding: Reading the Psalms with Augustine* (Grand Rapids: Eerdmans, 2007). Note the phrase ("return to allegory") appears as well in Childs's essay in this volume, where Childs locates the theme in the recent history of ideas, in association with typology, figural reading, and so forth. There is a vast literature to be cited here, but it is readily available elsewhere in print.

32. Brevard Childs, "Sensus Literalis: An Ancient and Modern Problem," in *Beitrage zur alttestamentliche Theologie: Festschift fur Walther Zimmerli zum 70 Geburtstag* (ed. Herbert Donner et al.; Gottingen: Vandenhoeck & Ruprecht, 1977), 80–93.

33. Byassee, *Praise Seeking Understanding*, 93–96. Relevant to our theme, he writes: "How do we make a contemporary assessment of Augustine's exegesis here? It is conceivable that the superscription describing David's feigned madness before Abimelech was a mere mistake, that its presence above Psalm 33 ought to add nothing to our reading of that psalm. It is conceivable, but to a scripturally shaped imagination, unlikely. Such a misattribution is better thought of as a gift than a mistake. A wink to the fellow initiate: read closer." Obviously our argument here is that the superscription is crucial to the appreciation of the Psalm, in relation to the canonical witness, and indeed it "adds much." In this our position is that we are following a genuine intention

this volume on allegory, it would be helpful to see if a canonical approach associated with him, and used in a modest way in his 1971 treatment of the psalm titles, joins up with this recent appeal to allegory and to the exegesis of Augustine.

Augustine proceeds with a long disquisition on "the deep and vast mystery we have here"[34] in the superscription, before he moves to commentary on the psalm itself, which in length is on the order of less than half of his treatment of the psalm title and its related text in 1 Sam 21 as such. For the purpose of our evaluation we need to reproduce the key verse of the latter as it comes to us in a form different from contemporary English translations—his Latin text, a translation of a Greek translation:[35]

> David was afraid of him [Achish, King of Gath] as well, and altered his behavior in front of them all, affecting madness. He drummed on the

---

of the canonical process. As such, we would not characterize the psalm title using the language of "mere mistake" but equally neither would we speak of "misattribution." I hope to show that Augustine's evaluation of the alteration of the name is not a wink at all. Neither is it chiefly an appeal to "read closer" in some general sense. Both ideas ("wink" and "read closer") are congenial with many of the authors—though not all—Byassee wishes to commend under the rubric of "return to allegory." But for Augustine we are not in the realm of general hermeneutics or postmodern resistance to authorial intention. The name change is for Augustine a matter of high seriousness, theologically and ecclesiologically. It has a very specific meaning: Christ departed from the Jews. Though he does not offer a detailed account of intentionality as we might wish that in the modern sense, Augustine's judgment is clearly that the alteration is "authorially intended" in the classical sense that it has a single, intended meaning from which other signification is to be drawn. See also F. Young, "Augustine's Hermeneutics and Postmodern Criticism," *Int* 58 (2004): 42–55.

34. Rotelle, *Expositions*, 13.

35. We need not pursue the text-critical issue here, viz., whether the departure in the translations goes back to a different *Vorlage*, or whether it simply results from a difficult reading shared with the MT tradition. The NIV U.K. of 1 Sam 21:13, for example, reads: "So he feigned insanity in their presence, and while he was in their hands he acted like a madman, making marks on the doors of the gate and letting saliva run down his beard." The translation is not particularly difficult, but the images are hardly everyday ones. Note that Augustine's text has the language of "drumming" and especially, "he carried himself in his hands"—a phase that makes no sense in the context being reported, one could argue—that is, unless the literal sense's only purpose is to convey a "spiritual meaning." It is the division of "literal" and "spiritual" sense-making that seems most in need of evaluation.

doors of the city and was carried in his own hands, and fell down outside the threshold, as saliva dribbled down his beard.[36]

Augustine's superscription text is straightforward: "A psalm of David, when he altered his behavior in the presence of Abimelech, and forsook him, and went away."[37]

Now what does Augustine make of the obvious discrepancy between the name Achish in the story of 1 Samuel and Abimelech in Ps 34 (33)?[38] Having begun with the idea that meaning must be sought through prayer, especially when there are difficulties, using the catch-phrase "knock and it shall be open," he turns to the general principle that OT events have a double reference—so 1 Cor 10:11, with specific reference to manna as spiritual wilderness food (1 Cor 10:3), to crossing the sea as a type of baptism (10:1-2), and to the rock that gushed forth water as Christ (10:4). Note that these citations from Paul bespeak the idea that Christ and the church are ontologically present in the events of the exodus. Literal sense and extending sense-making are complementary, because of the wider NT confession that the one God of the exodus is the Father and the Word and the Spirit. Augustine takes this general NT appeal to "allegorical sense

---

36. Rotelle, *Expositions*, 14.
37. Ibid., 15.
38. Byassee makes much of the fact that Augustine does not depart from the historical setting, and that is true so far as it goes. He describes Augustine's reasoning in this way: "This is something that really happened, and what happened has been written down, so that although the title of that psalm was assigned very mysteriously, it was, all the same, derived from an event that really occurred" (*Praise Seeking Understanding*, 94). So he soberly remarks, "Any figurative, christological sense to this psalm rests squarely on the historical reliability of the events narrated" (Ibid., 94). In actual fact, the quote from Augustine has to do not with Ps 33 but Ps 3, "when David was in flight from the face of Abessalon, his son" (Rotelle, *Expositions*, 13). As for Ps 33, Augustine states clearly, "We do not find this story precisely, but we do find an event from which the story seems to be derived" (Ibid., 14). The relation between literal and extended senses is the critical question here, not whether christological readings or figural readings are proper. They are, if they are extensions of the literal sense. Aquinas will offer that the *sens mystique* is several things at once, in respect of "altering the visage"—a sacramental referent; a changing of the old covenant before Abimelech to the "*royaume de mon Pere*" (his positive interpretation of the name Abimelech); using Isa 53, a reference to "no form that we would regard him," and so forth (Stroobant de Saint-Eloy, *Commentaire sur les Psaumes*, 399). With him we see that the spiritual sense is more than likely several things at once.

making" and, in the case of Ps 34 (33), narrows it considerably. This point is crucial, and we shall return to it below.

The basic concern, reflected in the extended treatment given to the psalm title, is the nature of the change from Achish to Abimelech in the superscription. "The letter kills, but the spirit gives life," Augustine states. So he concludes his general account of David and Goliath (the backdrop to David's flight to the camp of King Achish) as types of Christ and Satan, and then moves to the superscription proper. Why does the superscription give us Abimelech? Augustine answers that it is to underscore the etymological potential of "Abimelech" as "his father's kingdom."[39] Christ altered his presence when the Word became Flesh (John 1:14). He did this in the presence of Abimelech. According to the "spiritual meaning," he did it "in the presence of Jews."[40] We know this because the psalm title concludes, "and he forsook him and went away." This is where the "spiritual meaning" sharpens its hold on Augustine. The Jews held to the old order of Aaron, even though Christ "altered his behavior" as the Word became flesh and the order of Melchizedek was instituted. So although in times past God sent "plenty of preachers to the Israelites," he stopped: "He forsook them and went away." Romans 9 tells Augustine "at any rate few in comparison with those who were lost, for they were many. We read of thousands. Scripture says, A Remnant shall be saved (Rom 9:27); but if you look for Christians today among the circumcised, you find none."[41] Augustine reads the psalm title and interprets the literal sense as Christ bringing a new order, which was refused, so he "forsook the Jewish people and went away."[42] According to Augustine, this is the meaning of the psalm title.[43]

But what of the actual events as recorded in 1 Sam 21? Here Byassee is partly right, that Augustine assumes the historicality of the episodes of David's flight. Moreover, the ostensive reference of the scriptures is directly and uncomplicatedly rendered in the form of two different liter-

---

39. Rotelle, *Expositions*, 18.
40. Ibid.
41. Ibid.
42. Ibid.
43. Note that this is a specific meaning, not a postmodern encouragement to explore gaps and "winks" (see Young, "Augustine's Hermeneutics," 44). "While there are superficial similarities, Augustine's position is fundamentally invested in issues of truth and reference that postmodernism brackets out" (ibid., 42).

ary contexts (Ps 34 and 1 Sam 21), not necessitating recourse to a theory of editors or form-critical origins in the history of religion. That much is surely true when it comes to Augustine and history. But for him the actual sustained interest in the "historicality" (properly anachronistic in his case) is precisely in proportion to sustaining his point about Christ departing from the Jews. Indeed, some have sought to evaluate the difference between *allegoria facti* and *allegoria verbi* and their precise relationship.[44] Thus far, the emphasis (so the significance of etymology in Augustine's discussion) and word phrases falls decisively on the latter. "History" (*facti*) is simply the venue generating sentences (referring to events ostensively), which are then primary for spiritual elaborations of various kinds (via the *verbi*). So, as Christ departed "Abimelech" (the Jews) so he also "really" departed "Achish," as the historical narratives of Samuel show us. But in this frame of reference, it is hard to distinguish what "really" means in any different, more historical sense. The emphasis is on *verbi*: word associations and etymology.

The name "Achish" also provides an etymological clue for Augustine in the manner of "Abimelech," though here one must have recourse to "experts" (probably Jerome is intended). According to Jerome, the name "Achish" means "what is it?" Who asked, "What is it?"—well, a lot of people throughout the ages! But for Augustine, consistent with his reading of the superscription, the referent is "the scandal of the eucharist"[45]—that is, the incredulity recorded in John 6:53. Again Augustine narrows this to a specifically Jewish referent:

> Yet here is Christ saying, Unless you eat my flesh and drink my blood, you will have no life in you. He seems to be mad. But it is to King Achis that he seems to be mad, that is, to be stupid and ignorant. Accordingly he forsakes them and goes away; understanding has fled from their hearts, so that they cannot comprehend him.[46]

In his summary in the second homily, Augustine makes this even clearer: "Christ later instituted that sacrifice according to the order of Melchizedek in which his own body and blood are offered. He thus altered his appear-

---

44. See the compact discussion in the Childs chapter in this volume.
45. Rotelle, *Exposition*, 19.
46. Ibid., 20.

ance and behavior in respect of the priesthood, and abandoned the Jewish people, and came to the Gentiles."[47]

The remaining phrases of the verse are now available for christological significance as well. "He affected" means Christ had affection. "He drummed on the door" means that as a drum consists of stretched skin, so Christ was crucified. "The doors of the city" are the doors of our heart. The peculiarly phrased "and was carried in his own hands" (given that the MT speaks of David's being "in their hands," that is, in the camp of the Philistines) refers to Christ handing over his body in the Last Supper, "for he was holding that very body in his hands as he spoke." "He fell down" means he threw himself down in humility. And finally, what can one make of "the saliva dribbled down his beard" if it does not retain its literal sense in any typological way, but instead calls forth a direct spiritual application? Saliva is the dribbling of infants, and "eat my flesh" is baby-talk, "yet these infantile words masked virile strength, for virile strength is symbolized by the beard."[48]

Byassee comments in passing that the use of etymology is a favorite Hebrew narrative technique. But he fails to note that, when this is so, the narrative itself calls attention to it.[49] Otherwise it would just be the kind of etymologizing that anyone can undertake from outside the sense-making of the literal presentation. Moreover, the etymologizing in the case of Achish and Abimelech (strained though that is in its own right) is of a different order than that derived from translated words and lateral associations of various kinds. Moreover, in Hebrew narrative the instinct to offer an etymological signification is done in the service of drawing out some aspect of the story itself. "So Abraham called that place 'The LORD will provide'" explores an aspect of the narrative as given previously (Gen 22:1–13). In Augustine's case, the etymologizing specifically seeks to direct our attention away from the narrative as given, toward its true context.

In summarizing the work of Andrew Louth in the essay included in this volume, Childs writes that *facti* and *verbi* are two aspect of allegory in which "the *facti* is fundamental for establishing the analogy, whereas the *verbi* functions much like an embroidery of the analogy. The two extensions are complementary and not antagonistic."[50] In the case of his

---

47. Ibid., 24.
48. Ibid., 22.
49. Byassee, *Praise Seeking Understanding*, 96.
50. Brevard Childs, "Allegory and Typology within Biblical Narrative," in this

homilies on Ps 34, Augustine does not actually foreground use of the term "allegory," as if he were accessing a method that we were in turn supposed to emulate. He speaks instead of mystery, and of hidden truth, and of spiritual meaning. He does not view this level of meaning as arbitrary or as a mere invitation to follow him and do likewise, but rather he argues that the meaning is quite fixed: it pertains to Christ's movement away from the Jews, as David left Abimelech and as he went away from Achish. These episodes in the life of David (*facti*) would have no meaning of a Christian kind, according to Augustine, unless they could be attached to the single field of reference he undertakes: "Otherwise we might have thought that what the psalm recalled and related was nothing more than the event in the Book of Kings."[51] At issue here is not whether there is Christian significance in what the "psalm recalled and related" (arguably there is, according to the wider history of interpretation) so much as what the "more" is for Christian reading if it is not what Augustine has set forth and what Byassee apparently believes is the "more" we need to be concerned to emulate.

A canonical reading seeks to comprehend the intentionality of the OT witness by attending to its final form. The authorial intention of Ps 34 is not to be sought by asking what David intended according to the canons of historical verification, nor is it to be found in some pristine original situation. The superscription shows evidence of an effort to relate the life of David to correlate episodes of fear and prayer in the camp of the enemy, but also to present him as the providentially guarded elect of God. The use of "Abimelech" is not a mistake, a misattribution, or a signal of primarily hidden meaning, in the specified form that Augustine argues we must see. Rather, it points to an intentionality that asks us to follow the "canonical editor," as associations are made across the OT witness. David as God's man remains a critical component in the text's ability to make sense. A Christian reading does not hold up the discrete witness of the OT so as to deprive it of an extensional significance, nor to keep its sense-making locked in the past. By carefully noting the attention to providential linkage in time, we are sent to school so better to appreciate this dimension where it occurs elsewhere in Christian Scripture. The ultimate "filling full" of the OT in the NT is a species of typological and figural extensions already making its character known in the scriptures of Israel.

---

volume, 299–311.
51. Rotelle, *Exposition*, 19.

On modern ears. the harshness and specificity of Augustine's reading, focused as it is on Christ's forsaking the Jews, may seem striking and gratuitous. In response to Jesus, Must even dribble in the beard (of the Israelite David nonetheless) become incomprehensible baby-talk by unbelieving, immature Jews in response to Jesus? Does the NT itself require us to view incomprehension—especially in John's Gospel—as a trait peculiar to "Jews" to whom God in time ceased to go out, according to Augustine, as over against the Twelve and other followers (themselves of course Jewish)? Byassee acknowledges the problem and devotes a chapter to it, seeking various reading strategies and community reflection to mitigate it.

But one can ask whether the problem is actually of a different order. What Augustine does in Ps 34 is effectively to evacuate David and Israel from the psalm. He can only assume that without his steady Christian glossing of words and phrases—drumming on the door means crucifixion—the psalm will have no Christian application, and will be just a story in the past. But the wider history of interpretation shows that not to be so. For Calvin, David and Israel remain God's elect, and they really see Christ from within their own economy. David speaks of genuine promises made to him by God, and he is also given to see more. David is the righteous sufferer who by prayer is delivered by God, really. In this, providentially, David joins Abraham and Isaac before him. In this, providentially, he is a type of the Christ, great David's greater son.

There is one further issue that requires more attention than this chapter can unfold. Luther's psalm lectures carry on much of the Augustinian tradition, though he is clearly experimenting with hermeneutical schemes that adjust the "fourfold sense" and seek a fresh christological sense, using an older spirit-letter model in a new way. Yet over time the evacuation of David created a distinct spiritual and pastoral problem. If Christ is the voice of the psalms, and the sins and sorrows and burdens and fear and spiritual depletion we read of there are not genuinely his own, but those matters he speaks of "on behalf of the church," a potential loss looms large. In Ps 22, the Latin and Greek translations introduce the idea of sin in the opening verses: "Why are you so far from the words of my sins?" Yet clearly Ps 22 must be Christ's voice for great swaths of the tradition. So emerges the idea that "he made him to be sin who knew no sin" is at hand to explain this. Augustine and others use this concept here and elsewhere.

Luther followed much of this line of thinking, but in time, and with great spiritual relief, he discovered "the faithful synagogue." He discovered this not because he worried about harsh antisemitism, real or potential, and wanted to alleviate it, or to address it in sympathetic ways in the manner of Byassee. Anyone reading Luther will see he was swimming against a strong tide of his own on this matter. The christological evacuation of the psalms gave Luther no access to the sinful and fearful life that he knew was his own. One does not have to follow all the details of James Preus's account of this transition in Luther's exegesis to accept that Luther's own reading of the psalms clearly changed.[52] Luther gave up the "elitist view" of Israel, whereby only a tiny few ever heard the gospel in its OT idiom—an elite that, in the end, serves the purpose chiefly of illustrating a contrast between the believing church and Israel. Luther sees something in the "exceeding hope" (*superspervi*) of the faithful Israel. The faithful Israel shores up not the idea of an elite whose tiny numbers are overshadowed by the true ecclesia; rather, the faithful Israel is an exemplar for the church, a high standard of exceeding hope the Christian longs to embrace through the vicissitudes of life, life in Christ. Regarding Ps 118, he writes:

> This people also who cry out here, were not without salvation and light and grace. But the promised future they did not yet have, to which they were being held as something still to be had, to be sought, to be desired. For they were being held closed up in the faith to be revealed. So all of us (*Ita omnes sumus*) are in the midst of grace which is had and yet to be had.[53]

Preus offers this reflection:

> Luther now begins to argue that both the Church and the existence of the believer are to take the faithful synagogue as a model and norm for their faith. The promise under which the synagogue lives involves pain and anxiety because it is delayed. Luther meditates on the pathos of existence which waits entirely on God's promise. In doing so, Luther assumes the burden of giving theological expression to the perpetual crisis of faith, in every age, when God does not seem to be doing anything in the world.[54]

---

52. James Samuel Preus, *From Shadow to Promise: Old Testament Interpretation from Augustine to the Young Luther* (Cambridge: The Belknap Press of Harvard University Press, 1969).
53. Weimar Ausgabe 4.375.4–8. Citation from Preus, *From Shadow to Promise*, 221.
54. Ibid., 217.

The reading of Ps 34 offered by Augustine has so diminished the actual pathos of the Psalm—a pathos that joins David and the Church—that it is not simply a matter of tidying up harsh statements against the Jews after the fact by various communal and reading strategies. A canonical reading seeks to identify the providential work of the Triune God within the bosom of Israel, in this case, associating the genuine fear and risk of God's elect in the generations of the ancestors and the great man of prayer, King David. This is not a "Jewish" reading of the Old Testament, but a genuinely Christian one, which in turn finds the providential work of God in pure transparency as the psalms penetrate every aspect of the passion narratives. At the same time, Christ has not "forsaken and gone away from Abimelech"—the Jews—but through the scriptures of Israel continues to bear witness to himself. The knocking we must do is not in search of hidden meanings which could never have made their voice heard within God's own dispensations in Israel, but a knocking that seeks to hear the literal sense in its canonical intentionality, and in just this way, sees extended senses that are complementary and providentially overseen. This is the fulltime job of the Holy Spirit "who spake by the prophets," the inspirer of God's Word and Divine Agent in our comprehending it.

Augustine's reading of the psalms in the context of his homilies is what it is: a rhetorically charged, inventive, associative christological reading. It is not a sermon that encourages us to use our scripturally shaped imagination to interrogate gaps and "mistakes" and to go and do likewise, given the plentitude of meaning that any text may be said to generate. Augustine has a very clear and specific idea of what Ps 34 means. I am not convinced that calling it allegory, and then seeking to return us to such readings, has been sufficiently thought through. His interpretation of Ps 34 is in many ways a virtuoso performance based upon the idea that a text was changed so as to call attention to itself in ways that Augustine alone can decipher and proclaim. That other explanations are more persuasive at the level of the literal sense or canonical sense would probably not deter Augustine at all. That is because he was looking for Christ in a certain modality—the index of Jewish incomprehension—and so that is what he found in beard dribble and altered visage. Is this allegorical reading *simpliciter*? No. It is a species of a certain kind of christological excessiveness that evacuates the literal sense and the main themes of David, Israel, and fear, and disconnects the psalm from its own providential location in the revelation of the Triune God. Because Augustine has really gone as far as one can go in stretching the literal sense, I doubt that others can imitate this kind of reading. It is done not to maximize significance, but to specify and hyperfocus it on the theme of Christ's relation to the Jews. If this produces a worrisome outcome vis-à-vis modern Jewish-Christian relations, it is because the Old Testament's Christian voice has actually not be heard as clearly as it might be, precisely to the degree that it has over-stipulated the voice as Christ's on terms Augustine finds congenial. One does not correct that by offering an adjustment here and there, but by enriching what might be meant by allegorical and figural reading in accordance with the canonical intention.

Allegory and Typology
within Biblical Interpretation

Brevard S. Childs

Perhaps an initial word is in order as to how and why I arrived at this topic. During the last decade or so I have been working on an Isaiah commentary. As I drew near to completing it, it began to dawn on me with some sense of anxiety just how much I had left undone. Above all, I had not expended much time or space in considering the history of interpretation, that is, how the book of Isaiah had been received by both Jews and Christians over the centuries.

Then I saw announced a new publication by John Sawyer of Newcastle, who was an old friend going back almost forty years when we were together in Israel. He had just written a book entitled *The Fifth Gospel*, which sought to trace how the book of Isaiah had been heard and used. Immediately I purchased it and read the book with much eagerness. Indeed his book is full of interesting and learned observations starting with the NT's use of Isaiah. It also includes chapters on Isaiah's role in art and music, its use in the Middle Ages in developing the doctrine of Mariology, and sadly how its messianism was turned into a political weapon to use against the Jews. In the end, I finished his book with very mixed feelings. I realized just how different our understanding of the history of interpretation was. For Sawyer, the main forces at work in describing the church's use of Isaiah were cultural forces which had often resulted in a bizarre mishearing of the biblical text. Although I do not deny that such cultural forces were at work in different degrees throughout history, I question whether this was all that one could find. I thought that the theological side of the issues had not been adequately explored.

The questions that continued to haunt me seemed to me quite basic. Had the Christian church simply been led astray during all these years and stumbled in darkness without any serious theological guidance from this book? Is there no coercion from the text of sacred scripture providing true instruction? I had long since rejected the modern historical-critical consensus that nothing of any real exegetical significance had occurred prior to the nineteenth century, but then what kind of light was earlier present? How did and does scripture actually function for a community of faith and practice?

It was with these questions I set about seeing if one could justify speaking of a coercion, of a living theological content, present in spite of all the cultural differences at work through the centuries. Because I had been working on Isaiah, I thought that it would be wise to limit my scope by focusing largely on this one book. Isaiah was a good choice because many of the most significant Church Fathers, from both East and West, had written on Isaiah (Justin, Irenaus, Origen, Eusebius, Jerome, Cyril, Chrysostom). I was hoping in time also to sample Thomas and Nicolas of Lyra for the Medieval period, and Luther and Calvin for the Reformation. Finally, in the modern period, starting with Virtringa, Gesenius, de Wette, Delitzsch, and Duhm, I wanted to see whether there is any memory of what could be termed the Church's exegetical tradition.

After working for several months I experienced one overwhelming impression. The one component common to all the Church Fathers was the application of figurative meanings, call it allegory. I became convinced that unless one could gain a new understanding of allegory, the enterprise of recovering a useable exegetical Christian tradition seemed doomed from the start. To put it bluntly: for better or worse allegory is constitutive of patristic exegesis. But then how is one to proceed standing at the beginning of the twenty-first century?

It is generally agreed that the widespread aversion to allegory by modern biblical scholars derives from several clearly defined sources. First, the Reformers' strong attack on the abuses of allegory, especially Luther's, set most Protestants against the allegorical approach to interpretation as part of its rejection of the Roman Catholic tradition. Luther argued for the simple, natural meaning of the text, deriving its meaning from the grammatical, historical sense without the need for an additional allegorical extension that blurred the clarity of the divine Word. Secondly, the impact of the Enlightenment was also crucial to the critical rejection of tradition, but its adherents pushed with even greater force the attack on the applications of various figurative senses. They appealed to the literal sense of the text as the only legitimate goal of serious exegesis. Of course, both among Reformers and the followers of the Enlightenment, considerable confusion reigned and vestiges of the older traditions continued well into the nineteenth century.

In Roman Catholic circles stress fell on the literal sense, an approach that found its warrant in St. Thomas's hermeneutics. But at the same time various appeals to figurative senses were continued. (Raymond Brown's dissertation *The Sensus Plenior of Sacred Scripture* in the early 1950s was the last serious attempt at a defense of the figurative in North America from the Catholic side). In modern Protestantism the term allegory continued to arouse negative emotions, but appeals to "typology," such as that of Patrick Fairbairn's two-volume work, continued as a form of homiletics. However, with the growing hegemony of the historical-critical method, typology, allegorical, and other figurative senses became increasingly suspect. By the beginning of the twentieth century, even in Anglican circles, the famous volume of Bishop Trench on the parables became a "whipping boy" used to illustrate how not to interpret Scripture.

In the light of this history of a rejection of figurative senses of scripture, it becomes even more remarkable that in the post-World War 2 period there was suddenly an aggressive attempt to recover a figurative sense under the rubric of "typology." This movement was only indirectly related to the rebirth of confessional theology associated with Karl Barth in the 1920s and 1930s. Barth himself had little interest in typology, but his close friend Wilhelm Vischer did somewhat muddy the waters with the book *The Witness of the Old Testament to Jesus Christ*, which appeared in 1936.

Rather I think it is fair to say it was largely outside the arena of German confessional theology that there emerged a sudden new interest in typological exegesis. Moreover, this interest quickly gained a rather consistent profile:

(1) Typology was to be sharply distinguished from allegory. The former was embraced as legitimate; the latter as a distortion to be rejected.
(2) Appeal to typology was not viewed as a return to the precritical interpretation, but as an extension of the historical-critical method, and was not regarded as threatening to the historical nature of the biblical witness.
(3) Typology was a way of actualizing the text and making the events of scripture accessible to later readers according to patterns of promise and fulfillment, of antitype (ἀντίτυπος) and type (τύπος).

It is remarkable to recall how widespread this interest in typology became, particularly in the first decades of the post-World War 2 period.

(1) In Germany, Goppelt's book *Typos: The Typological Interpretation of the Old Testament in the New*, written in 1939, had certain antecedents in the nineteenth-century *Heilsgeschichte* of J. C. K. von Hofmann, but it did nevertheless mark a fresh beginning. Goppelt was at pains to show that typology was not to be confused with illegitimate allegory. Shortly one noticed Goppelt's influence on von Rad, H. W. Wolff, and O. Cullman, among others. Still, in retrospect one can see that in Germany typology did not develop deep roots. Before long even von Rad appeared to repudiate his essay on OT typology, and the use of terms like *Vergegenwärtigung* (actualization) and "kerygmatic" replaced typology.

(2) In France, the new typological interest received massive support from J. Daniélou. In his many books he argued with great force and learning that typology was an essential feature of all patristic interpretation. At the same time, he strongly supported the thesis that typology was an ancient Christian technique of interpretation, whereas the roots of allegory lay outside Christian tradition, entering only later from Jewish, Philonic, and Gnostic forms of exegesis. There were of course other important patristic scholars who wrote extensively on the subject of figurative interpretation and did not always agree with Daniélou (de Lubac, Guillet, Crouzel).

(3) In Britain, the newer interest in typology received a classic expression in Lampe and Woollcombe's volume *Essays on Typology* (1957). Particularly Woollcombe expended great energy in mounting an apology against the attacks on typology as being anti-historical. Far more critical of typology was the influential monograph of R. P. C. Hanson, *Allegory and Event: A Study of the Sources and Significance of Origen's Interpretation of Scripture* (1959). Hanson had many positive things to say about typology, but he contested Daniélou's sharp distinction between typology and allegory. In practice he thought that early Christian typology became swallowed up by allegory. He defined true Christian tradition as historical and Palestinian, and saw the inroads of Alexandrian allegory corrupting typology and destroying the essential connection of Bible and history. Another significant British scholar in the ongoing debate was M. Wiles, who in the end was even more critical than Hanson respecting a typological approach.

(4) In North America, typology was revived in many popular works on biblical theology under the rubric of salvation history. The dominant issue in the ensuing hermeneutical debate focused on the relation of figu-

rative interpretation to biblical history, and the reigning historical-critical method continued to provide the criteria for setting the legitimate parameters for figurative readings. Brown (*Sensus Plenior*) sought to find some place for figuration. He argued for an additional deeper meaning "intended by God," but not directly tied to the human author. But even this concession was shortly dropped by most Catholic scholars as they entered fully into the historical-critical approach as a way of freeing themselves from dogma. The most serious technical discussion of allegory in early Christianity was provided by Robert M. Grant (*The Letter and the Spirit*). Grant's contribution was in offering a highly competent historical discussion of patristic exegesis in which he traced its Greek roots. He did not attempt to enter into the theological debate, but assumed the time-conditionality of this early tradition of interpretation without either attacking or defending this method.

I think it is fair to say that by the mid-1960s the hermeneutical interest in typology had begun to fade and the initial enthusiasm of the 1950s had greatly ebbed. When figurative senses were exploited within the prevailing form-critical school, they consisted only to gage references to recurring patterns within the ongoing growth of tradition, or as elements of an assumed *Heilsgeschichte*. The strongest direct attack on typology in the 1960s was launched by James Barr (*Old and New in Interpretation*). His concern was to demonstrate that the appeal to typology arose as a hidden apologetic attempting to define biblical meaning within a theological concept of history. He thus disputed the distinction between allegory and typology and sought to give the death blow to typology as a form of misconstrued biblical theology. Barr described both allegory and typology as bringing a foreign ideology to bear on the text—he named it a "resultant system"—which was alien to the author's original intention. In retrospect one can see that Barr's contribution was largely negative, but served to bring to an end an appeal to typology which had been ill-defined and vulnerable. Barr pronounced an obituary on this exegetical approach, but he was unaware of an unexpected revival of figurative interpretation which was very soon to erupt into a new and exciting form.

The fresh approach to allegory came from the side of patristic scholars. It encompassed a group of leading Catholic scholars such as de Lubac, Crouzel, von Balthasar, among others, and patristic scholars from the English-speaking world like Frances Young, Karen Jo Torjesen, and Janet Soskice. It also included the brilliant book of Jon Whitman (*Allegory: The Dynamics of an Ancient and Medieval Technique*), who explored the historical roots in Ancient Greek and Hellenistic allegorical tradition. From the Jewish side, Michael Fishbane offered a highly illuminating study of the function of figurative, midrashic exegesis in Tannaitic Judaism. However, above all, initial credit for a highly provocative study of allegory goes to Andrew Louth's brilliant chapter "Return to Allegory" in *Discerning the Mystery* (1983), which challenged Christian theology to reflect seriously once again on allegory as an exegetical tool constitutive to Christian tradition.

During the last two decades of research, several lines of consensus have emerged in this new focus on allegory as an interpretive technique:

(1) First, it is widely agreed that the sharp post–World War II distinction between allegory and typology cannot be sustained. Already within the NT the two approaches are blurred together. Actually the term "typology" is of recent origin and does not have deep hermeneutical roots in either the Eastern or the Western patristic traditions (cf. Whitman, Young). This observation, however, is not to suggest that the concept of allegory is simple, since it embraces various aspects of figurative speech, some of which were emphasized by those who were interested in focus alone on typology. Louth (*Discerning the Mystery*, 119) accepts de Lubac's distinction between *allegoria facti* and *allegoria verbi*, according to which the *facti* is fundamental for establishing the analogy, whereas the *verbi* functions much like an embroidery of the analogy. The two extensions are complimentary and not antagonistic. Louth correctly insists that the function of allegory is related to the struggle to discern the mystery of Christ. It is a way of relating the whole of Scripture to that mystery, a way of finding a synthetic vision into the images and events of the biblical narrative (*Discerning the Mystery*, 121).

(2) The distinction between the so-called literal sense and the figurative/allegorical cannot be correctly defined in terms of historicity. In fact, the description of typology as historical and allegory as non-historical, the position defended by Daniélou and Hanson, greatly misconstrued the issues by introducing anachronistically nineteenth- and twentieth-century concerns foreign to the patristic era. Rather, the heart of the problem of allegory turns on the nature of the referentiality of the biblical text. Allegory is a figure of speech implying that its reference is something other than what is being said, and the crucial issue lies in determining the theological substance to which it points metaphorically. Young emphasizes that in Origen, for example, the multiple senses are really multiple referents (*Biblical Exegesis and the Formation of Christian Culture*, 150). Thus

he engages in his exegetical practice not by contrasting literal and figurative senses, but in his application of cross-referencing within Scripture to uncover the underlying continuity of the subject matter in all the levels.

(3) The context within which allegory functions is basic to its proper understanding. The appeal to allegory is not a device by which to avoid difficulties in the text, as is often suggested, or to allow unbridled use of human imagination. Rather, its use functions within a rule of faith (its *theoria* in Greek terminology) as the language of faith seeks to penetrate into the mystery of Christ's presence. It is a means of appropriation of a text by its faithful readers in making the ancient text their own. For all the Church Fathers, the use of figuration was assumed as a means by which the living Lord of scripture through the work of the Holy Spirit continued to address each new generation though vigorous pursuit of the deeper significance of the words of scripture.

(4) Recent patristic scholarship has also made clear that the frequent contrast between the allegory of the Alexandrians and the frequent contrast of the Antiochenes has largely been misconstrued (Theodore, Theodoret, Chrysostom). The latter were certainly not precursors of the modern historical-critical approach. Rather the controversy turned on how one properly understood scripture's context. The Antiochenes did not appeal to literalism as such, nor was it an interest in historicity against which the Antiochenes fought in Alexandrian allegory. Rather the Antiochenes resisted a type of allegory that destroyed textual coherence, that is to say, which distorted the overarching framework (its *theoria*) and thus failed to grasp its true subject matter, its *hypothesis*.

It is at this juncture in reflecting on the proper role of allegory in biblical interpretation that attention invariably and by necessity focuses on Origen, since he was the first Christian theologian who addressed specifically the hermeneutical problem of the different senses of scripture. Usually interest concentrates on Origen's treatise *On First Principles* (*Peri Archon*) 4.1–3. Here he describes his approach by analogy to human psychology. Just as there is within a person a body, a soul, and spirit, so also in scripture there is a threefold meaning: the literal, the moral, and the spiritual. The problem is that this classification appears to be only one among others used by him, and its appearance in Origen's actual exegesis is quite rare. Usually his approach lies in pursuing a twofold meaning of scripture, namely its literal and its spiritual sense. Moreover, other schemata are used, and the distinctions between the anagogic, tropological, and mystical are fluid. De Lubac (*Histoire et esprit: L'intelligence de l'écriture d'après*

Origène, 17ff.) goes so far as to suggest that the later medieval classification of a fourfold distinction ultimately derives from Origen.

For gaining clarity on the significance of allegory for biblical interpretation one needs a closer scrutiny regarding Origen's distinction between the literal and the spiritual senses. The issue is far more complex than often thought. In the past, scholars have been initially led astray by seizing on Origen's remark in *First Principles* that there are certain passages in which there is no "bodily" (literal) sense at all and that the interpreter must here seek only the spiritual. The inference has been drawn that Origen denigrated the plain or the historical sense, seeing it as unnecessary and peripheral to his real task. However, both de Lubac (*Histoire*, 92ff.) and Crouzel (*Origen* ET 61ff.) have gone to great lengths in refuting this interpretation and in pursuing the subtlety of Origen's understanding of the literal sense. The initial difficulty arises from the fact that the term "literal sense" is not defined in the same way by Origen and his modern critics. Origen means by it the raw material of the text before any interpretation is made. The result is that the literal sense for moderns is often described as the spiritual sense by Origen.

Moreover, de Lubac goes into great detail in pointing out that the denial of the literal sense by Origen is in no way a rejection of a passage's historicity. Nor can the literal sense be identified with the so-called original sense of the human author. One of the confusions that has arisen in Hanson, for instance, was the problem of explaining the enormous energy expended by Origen over the narrative details of a biblical passage—textual, geographical, historical—if his literal sense was denigrated as unimportant. Rather, de Lubac has gone a long way toward showing the organic harmony between the literal and the spiritual in Origen's exegesis, and how the spiritual sense would have been considered disembodied without its abiding relationship to the literal sense. Often when Origen speaks negatively of the literal sense, it is in the context of a debate with Jewish interpreters who would limit a passage's meaning to its plain sense and thus explicitly reject its spiritual rendering.

According to Hanson, Origen's pursuit of allegory was wrongheaded because he had imposed an alien, quasi-Gnostic system on the biblical text in utter disregard of its historical meaning. Yet Origen would have vehemently rejected this allegation. Rather he justified his procedure by appealing to the Apostle Paul's frequently referring to eight particular texts (Rom 7:14; 1 Cor 12:2, 10, 12, 16; 9:9–10; 10:11; 2 Cor 3:6, 15–16, and Gal 4:24). Origen thus found in Paul a warrant for pressing beyond the letter to the spiritual realities to which it pointed. In fact, the difficulties within the biblical text served precisely to alert the reader to the necessity of probing deeper.

Origen was committed to an understanding of scripture shared by the New Testament and the Fathers who preceded him that the sacred biblical text was the vehicle for God's continued revelation, the text in all its multidimensional shape, both literal and spiritual reality. The role of the Holy Spirit remained in the forefront of his exegesis and the continuous activity of the inspired text addressing its receivers was paramount as the text was interpreted intertextually in the light of its comprehensive witness.

One of the most illuminating recent studies of Origen's exegesis has been provided by Karen Torjesen, in *Hermeneutical Procedure and Theological Method in Origen's Exegesis*. At the outset Torjesen is dissatisfied with the usual description of Origen's exegesis that begins with his literal/historical interpretation and then shifts to his allegorical reading as if a separate step. The result is that the theological dynamic informing his exegesis is lost. Rather, by focusing on his most important extant texts (Psalms, Jeremiah, Song of Songs, Luke) she is able to demonstrate a basic consistency of his approach which even spans the different genres of scholia, homily, and commentary.

Origen's understanding of context is crucial and differs markedly from all assumptions of modern historical methodology in seeking a neutral objective historical setting of the original author. A clear example is Origen's exegesis of Ps 38 (Ps 37 LXX): "O Lord, rebuke me not in thy anger, nor chasten us in thy wrath...." Origen begins by allowing the situation of the hearer to determine the context of the psalm, but then the movement is reversed when the actual exegesis of the biblical text in turn illuminates the setting of the hearer. That is to say, the context of his literal sense of the text is interpreted at the outset theologically as concerned with the "care of souls." This theological rendering thus stands in immediate continuity with the fuller dimension of the selfsame subject matter by means of its figurative extension. Origen assumes that all of Scripture is about the presence of the Incarnated Christ, the Logos, which defines the content of the witness. The manifest forms of the Logos determine the pedagogical function of the divine presence, which is the goal of all exegesis.

Origen follows a consistent order in tracing the pedagogical movement of the Logos. Because the literal sense already is understood as an essential historical part of this pedagogical goal, the very concrete quality of the biblical narrative demands its spiritual interpretation. The two levels reflect different forms, but share a selfsame spiritual reality within a harmony on the substantive level. Obviously what Origen means by "historical" is not the same as its modern sense, since history is for him the concrete manifestation of the Logos. It is the symbolic form of truth presented universally in the Incarnation. It is the theological reality within the text, and not the naked texts that reflect the Logos engaged in a unified pedagogical reality. Origen's final exegetical step after moving the literal sense forward into its full spiritual dimension is to apply the spiritual truth to the hearer according to its "usefulness"—a technical term for Origen. Exegesis thus involves a movement directed by the inspiration of the Spirit to a divine pedagogy in a continuous movement of salvation for the reader/hearer who is continually instructed through a progress of the soul into divine truth.

In my original research project I had planned to pursue the interpretations of the various Church Fathers in Isaiah to see how they handled this one prophetic book. However, I was initially frustrated to discover that virtually all of Origen's huge multi-volume commentary on Isaiah had been lost. Fortunately, Jerome did translate into Latin nine of Origen's homilies on Isaiah, largely from chapters 6–10. Although far from adequate in representing the enormous richness of Origen's full commentary, at least it offers some impression of both the strength and the weakness of his approach.

First, Origen invariably begins his homilies by establishing a context for pursuing his understanding of the literal sense of the text. The pattern in his homilies on Isaiah closely follows that described by Torjesen. This is to say, the context either conforms to that of the reader or is closely related to it. Thus Homily 1, on Isa 6, does not focus on establishing an absolute date for Uzziah's death, but rather the death of sinful Uzziah. Immediately the inference is drawn that only the righteous can see God's glory. Origen's homily turns its full attention to admonishing his Christian audience to pursue a life of holiness in order to be capable of perceiving God's majesty. Similarly in Homily 8, chapter 10 begins by speaking of the divine judgment on those who constructed idols in Jerusalem and Samaria. Very quickly Origen moves to redirect the focus on idols to idols of the heart and thus to apply the arrogant claims of the proud rulers of Jerusalem to the pride of the present hearers who also claim to be doing great things in their day.

Secondly, Origen shows great skill in establishing the significance of the theological context by means of careful intertextual references concerning both the Old and New Testaments. In Homily 2 Origen notes that in Isa 7 the text reads *vocabis* ("you will call his name"), whereas in Matt 2, the NT text citing the book of Isaiah reads *vocabitur* ("it will be called"). Although Origen does not rule out a fortuitous textual corruption, in this case he finds a clear intentionality at work. He notes that Ahaz is not the subject of the verb, but rather the house of David, which from the NT's context means the church. Therefore he argues that the NT is prophesying that in the future there will be a faithful community of believers who will confess the name of Immanuel, that is, "God with us."

Finally, in Homily 6 Origen moves explicitly to the role of the spiritual sense when interpreting the enigmatic word of God to Isaiah: "they shall hear but not understand...." According to Origen, Israel fails to understand the divine Word because they are caught in the literal sense, and by restricting interpretation only to the latter they fail to see its deeper meaning. Just as Ahaz refuses to ask for a sign, so are those who are blinded to Jesus Christ, God's true sign of salvation.

In all his homilies on Isaiah Origen does not denigrate the literal, but from the start his interpretation is shaped toward its theological subject matter, and thus provides a basic continuity to his exposition of the true content of the biblical message.

Our time this morning is too brief to pursue Origen's exegesis in further detail. Obviously we have entered a world of biblical exegesis that is, at the very least, strange and even bizarre. Yet I would argue that there is much to be learned from it, in spite of its many problems for us moderns. Let me summarize some areas from which we can learn:

First, Origen raised the basic issue of addressing the function of Scripture for the church, which is to be a living and continuous vehicle of divine revelation. In contrast to the interpreters of the Enlightenment, he assumed that the biblical text to transcend its single historical context, and in some mysterious way through the work of the Holy Spirit to speak to its recipients a contemporary word of the presence of God.

Second, Origen struggled to do justice both to the particularity of the literal sense of the text and also to its fuller, spiritual role as a divine pedagogy in hearing testimony to the salvific work of Jesus Christ to the church and the world. Frances Young reflects Origen's concerns when she writes: "Without a form of allegory that at least allows for analogy, the biblical text can only be an object of archaeological interest" (*Biblical Exegesis*, 3).

Third, Origen raised the question as to the faithful role of the interpreter in the exercise of creative response in receiving and transmitting the truth of the Sacred Scriptures to a community of faith and practice. In his use of allegory, Origen strove to show that the extension of the figurative sense was not simply a horizontal typology, but vertical as well. Scripture, as it were, provides a keyboard for each hearer to play and to receive new variations on the one unified story of God in Christ to be rendered in liturgy, private devotions, music, and art. As just one example, is not the negro spiritual an allegory on the Christian life expressing the needs, hopes, faith of a particular part of God's people who have struggled for four hundred years to be faithful amid deep sorrow and despair?

To conclude: I am fully aware of the host of unresolved problems that remain on the subject of allegory and biblical interpretation. Our initial question continues to haunt: Has the Christian church been led astray all these years, stumbling in the darkness and ignorance, without any serious spiritual guidance from its scriptures? Had I more time I would have liked to have pursued the response to the challenges which each successive generation of the church faced: the medieval schoolmen, the Protestant Reformers, the Enlightenment, and postmodern interpretation. I strongly feel that there is a family resemblance in the responses of the Church, in spite of the enormous diversity within the Christian exegetical tradition. Obviously, much hard work still needs to be done, not least in recovering the richness in the use of the Bible often forgotten.

Perhaps a wonderful poem of John Donne best summarizes what I have been trying to say:

> My *God*, my *God*, Thou art a *direct God*, may I not say a *literal* God, a God that wouldst be understood *literally*, and according to the *plain sense* of all thou sayest? But thou art also (*Lord* I intend it to thy *glory*...) thou art a *figurative*, a *metaphorical God too*: A *God* in whose words there is such a height of *figures*, such *voyages*, such *peregrinations* to fetch remote and precious *metaphors*, such *extensions* ... such *curtains* of *Allegories*.... O, what words but thine, can express the inexpressible *texture*, and composition of the *Word* (*Devotions upon Emergent Occasions*, XIX Expostulation).

BIBLIOGRAPHY

Barr, James. *Old and New in Interpretation*. London: SCM, 1966.
Brown, Raymond. *The Sensus Plenior of Sacred Scripture*. Baltimore: Saint Mary's University, 1955.

Crouzel, Henri. "La *distinction de la 'typologie'* et de l' *'allégorie.'*" *BLE* 65 (1964): 161–74.

———. *Origen*. Translated by A. S. Worrall. San Francisco: Harper & Row, 1989.

Daniélou, Jean. *Origen*. Translated by Walter Mitchell. New York: Sheed & Ward, 1955.

Fairbairn, Patrick. *Typology*. 2 vols. Edinburgh: T&T Clark, 1847.

Fishbane, Michael, *Biblical Interpretation in Ancient Israel*. Oxford: Claredon, 1985.

Goppelt, Leonhard. *Typos: The Typological Interpretation of the Old Testament in the New*. Translated by Donald H. Madvig. Grand Rapids: Eerdmans, 1982.

Grant, Robert M. *The Letter and the Spirit*. New York: MacMillian, 1957.

Kugel, James, and Roland A. Greer. *Early Biblical Interpretation*. Philadelphia: Westminster, 1986.

Hanson, R. P. C. *Allegory and Event: A Study of the Sources and Significance of Origen's Interpretation of Scripture*. Richmond: John Knox, 1959.

Kerrigan, Alexander. *St. Cyril of Alexandria: Interpreter of the Old Testament*. Rome: Pontificio Istituto Biblico, 1987.

Lampe, G., and K. J. Woollcombe, *Essays on Typology*. London: SCM, 1957.

Louth, Andrew. *Discerning the Mystery: An Essay on the Nature of Theology*. Oxford: Claredon, 1983.

Lubac, Henri de. *Histoire et esprit: L'intelligence de l'écriture d'après Origène*. Paris: Aubier, 1950.

———. "'Typologie' et 'Allégorisme.'" *RSR* 34 (1947): 180–226.

———. "Spiritual Understanding." Pages 3–25 in *The Theological Interpretation of Scripture*. Edited by Stephen Fowl. Translated by Luke O'Neill. Cambridge, Mass.: Blackwell, 1990.

Rad, Gerhard von. "Typologische Auslegung des Alten Testaments," *EvT* 12 (1952–1953): 17–33.

Torjesen, Karen J. *Hermeneutical Procedure and Theological Method in Origen's Exegesis*. Berlin: de Gruyter, 1986.

Whitman, Jon. *Allegory: The Dynamics of an Ancient and Medieval Technique*. Cambridge, Mass.: Harvard University Press, 1987.

Young, Frances. *Biblical Exegesis and the Formation of Christian Culture*. Cambridge: Cambridge University Press, 1997.

Contributors

Stephen B. Chapman is Associate Professor of Old Testament at Duke University. His publications include *The Law and the Prophets: A Study in Old Testament Canon Formation* (FAT 27; Mohr Siebeck, 2000); "What Are We Reading? Canonicity and the Old Testament," *Word & World* 29 (2009): 334–47; "The Canon Debate: What It Is and Why It Matters," *Journal of Theological Interpretation* 4 (2010): 273–94; "Modernity's Canonical Crisis: Historiography and Theology in Collision," in *Hebrew Bible/Old Testament 3.1: The Nineteenth Century* (ed. Magne Sæbø; Vandenhoeck & Ruprecht, 2013), 651–87. He serves on the editorial board for *Siphrut: Literature and Theology of the Hebrew Scriptures* (Eisenbrauns).

Don Collett is Assistant Professor of Old Testament at Trinity Episcopal School for Ministry in Ambridge, Pennsylvania. A native of Montana, he holds degrees from Montana State University in Bozeman (B.A.), Westminster Seminary in California (M.Div.), and University of St Andrews, Scotland (PhD).

Daniel R. Driver is Assistant Professor of Old Testament at Tyndale University College, in Toronto, Ontario. His monograph on Brevard Childs (Mohr Siebeck 2010, repr. Baker Academic 2012) was the first to incorporate all of the author's published works, as well as a number of unpublished letters and papers.

Mark Elliott is Reader in Church History at the University of St Andrews, Scotland. He wrote his PhD on patristic biblical interpretation at Cambridge University (published by Mohr Siebeck in 2000 as *The Song of Songs and Christology in the Early Church, 381–451*) and has since taught at Nottingham, Liverpool Hope, and St Andrews. He has published on the history of biblical interpretation, notably *Isaiah 40–66* for the Ancient Christian Commentary Series (2007) and *Engaging Leviticus* for Wipf & Stock

(2012). He has also published in the area of biblical theology, notably *The Reality of Biblical Theology* (Peter Lang, 2007) and a book forthcoming with Ashgate. He is chair of the Biblical Theology section for the SBL's International Meeting.

Leonard G. Finn is currently pursuing a doctorate in Old Testament studies at Wycliffe College at the University of Toronto. He has an MDiv from Trinity School for Ministry in Ambridge, Pennsylvania, and an MPhil in English literature from the State University of New York at Stony Brook. He is ordained in the Anglican Church of North America, serving at Christ the King Anglican Church in Toronto, Ontario.

Mark Gignilliat has taught at Beeson Divinity School, Samford University, since 2005. Before coming to Beeson, he taught at Wycliffe Hall, University of Oxford. He took his PhD from the University of St Andrews, Scotland (2005). Gignilliat is involved in the ministry of his local church (Presbyterian) and enjoys teaching and preaching in a variety of ecclesial contexts in Birmingham, Alabama.

Bernd Janowski, born in 1943 in Stettin, Germany, studied Protestant Theology, Egyptology, and Ancient Near Eastern Studies at Tübingen from 1967 to 1972 and received his doctorate in theology in 1980. He was promoted to Professor in Hamburg (1986–1991) and Heidelberg (1991–1995). Since 1995 he has been Professor of Old Testament at the University of Tübingen, Faculty of Protestant Theology. Since 1996, he has been a full member of the Heidelberg Academy of Sciences, emeritus since 2011.

Jörg Jeremias, born 1939 in Göttingen, Germany, studied Protestant Theology and Near Eastern Languages and Cultures in Göttingen, Zürich (Switzerland), Heidelberg, Bonn, and Yale University, New Haven (USA). He earned a master's degree (STM) in Ugaritic under Prof. Marvin Pope at Yale (1961), a doctorate under Prof. Martin Noth at Bonn (1964), Assistant under Prof. Hans Walter Wolff and second doctorate (Habilitation) in Heidelberg (1969). He was professor at the Ludwig-Maximilians-Universität at Munich (1972–1994) and at the Philipps-Universität at Marburg (1994–2005), as well as Guest Professor in Jerusalem and in Hermannstadt/Sibiu (Romania) and recipient of an honorary doctorate (Klausenburg/Cluj, Romania).

CONTRIBUTORS

Leander E. Keck is Winkley Professor of Biblical Theology emeritus at Yale Divinity School, where he also served as Dean from 1979 to 1989. Before retiring in 1997, he chaired the editorial board for the *New Interpreter's Bible*. Among his publications are *Paul and His Letters*, a commentary on the apostle Paul's letter to the Romans, and *Who Is Jesus? History in Perfect Tense*. He is currently completing a study of New Testament Christology.

Neil B MacDonald (PhD, University of Edinburgh) is Reader in Theological Studies at the University of Roehampton, London. He is the author of several books, including *Metaphysics and the God of Israel: Systematic Theology of the Old and New Testaments*, and *Karl Barth and the Strange New World within the Bible: Barth, Wittgenstein, and the Metadilemmas of the Enlightenment*.

David L. Petersen is Franklin N. Parker Professor of Old Testament Emeritus at Emory University's Candler School of Theology. Prior to his appointment at Emory, he held faculty positions at the University of Illinois and the Iliff School of Theology. He has authored or edited twenty books and over sixty articles and chapters. Petersen has served on the editorial boards of the *Journal of Biblical Literature*, *Catholic Biblical Quarterly*, and the Old Testament Library. In 2004, Petersen was elected president of the Society of Biblical Literature. Petersen was the convener of the editorial board for the Common English Bible.

Murray Rae is Professor of Theology at the University of Otago and Head of the Department of Theology and Religion, where he teaches courses in Systematic Theology and Ethics. His research interests include the work of Søren Kierkegaard, theological hermeneutics, Maori engagements with Christianity, and theology and the built environment. He is editor of the Journal of Theological Interpretation monograph series, and his publications include *Mana Maori and Christianity*, *Kierkegaard and Theology, History and Hermeneutics*, and *Kierkegaard's Vision of the Incarnation*.

C. Kavin Rowe is an Associate Professor of New Testament at the Divinity School of Duke University. In addition to multiple scholarly articles, he is the author of *World Upside Down* and *Early Narrative Christology*. He was the recipient of the John Templeton Prize for Theological Promise, the Paul Achtemeier Award from the Society of Biblical Literature, a Fulbright Fellowship, and grants from both the Lilly Foundation and the Louisville

Institute. He is currently the President of the Society of Biblical Literature's Southeastern Region.

Christopher R. Seitz is Senior Research Professor of Biblical Interpretation at Wycliffe College in the University of Toronto. He was previously Professor of Old Testament at Yale University (1987–1997) and the University of St Andrews (1998–2006). He is the author and editor of sixteen books. He has completed a commentary on Colossians for the Brazos Theological Commentary series and is presently researching a commentary on Joel for the International Theological Commentary series (T&T Clark). Brevard Childs was a teacher, colleague, and close friend for over twenty-five years.

Index of Ancient Sources

Hebrew Bible/Old Testament

Genesis

1	280
1:29–30	73
1–3	223
1–11	281
2–3	76, 280
2–11	93
2:1–3	99
2:15–18	76
2:16	194 n 33
2:18	76
2:19	76 n. 25
2:19–20	76
2:21–22	76
4:1–16	73
6–9	95
8:20–23	73
9:1–19	73
9:2–6	73
9:4–6	73
9:20–27	73
12:1	148
12:2	30
12:3	194 n. 28
17:1	196, 197
19:37	12
20	282, 287
21	194
22:1–13	293
26	282, 287
26:7	285
26:16	285
26:33	12

Exodus

2:1–10	122
2:11–25	122
3	16
3:1–4:17	13, 14
3:12	14, 15
12:1–13:16	123
13:7–14:31	122
13:8	145
13:17–14:31	263
13:17–15:21	259
13:20	259
14	261, 267
15	124
15–18	197
15:25–26	197 n. 35
16:4	197 n. 35
16:23–30	197 n. 35
17:1	197 n. 35
17:8–16	121
18:14–20	197 n. 35
19–24	197
20:22–23:33	124
20:23	28 n. 12
25:1–31:18	123
32	22, 23, 28
32:1	32 n. 23
32:7	30, 33 n. 23
32:7–14	24, 28, 30, 31, 32, 34
32:8	33 n. 23
32:9	33
32:10	30
32:10–14	22, 24, 28, 30
32:12	30, 32 n. 21
32:21–24	24

-317-

Exodus (cont.)

32:23	32 n. 23	10:6–7	25 n. 6
32:25–29	24, 29	10:10	23, 27, 32, 32 n. 21
32:30	28	12:20–27	73
32:30–31	27 n. 8	12:32	51
32:30–34	28, 30, 34	18:15–22	194 n. 27
32:31–34	24	28:20	27 n. 10
32:32	28, 30	28:24	27 n. 10
32:33	28, 33	28:45	27 n. 10
32:34	29, 34	28:48	27 n. 10
33:1	33 n. 23	28:51	27 n. 10
33:12	33 n. 23	28:61	27 n. 10
33:13	199	28:63	27 n. 10
33:15	33 n. 23	34:10	194 n. 27
33:18–19	199		
34:5–7	199		
34:6	98		

Joshua

7:26	12

Judges

6	16
18:12	12

Leviticus

7:22–27	73

Deuteronomy

3:14	12		
4:2	51		
6:1–9	145		
6:4–9	195 n. 32		
9	24, 26		
9–10	24, 25 n. 6, 27, 28, 33 n. 23, 34		
9:1–6	25		
9:7	23, 24, 25, 26		
9:7–8	25 n. 6		
9:7–10:11	23		
9:8	23, 24, 25, 26, 27		
9:12	32 n. 23, 33		
9:12–14	24, 32		
9:14	27		
9:18	23, 26		
9:18–19	32		
9:19	23, 25, 27, 33		
9:20	23, 26, 27		
9:22	23, 25		
9:22–24	25 n. 6, 32		
9:24	25		
9:25	27		
9:25–29	24, 32		

1 Samuel

8	71
8–12	72, 75
8:5	69
8:7–9	69
8:10–20	69
8:21–22	69
8:22	70
9	70
9–11	71
9:1–10:16	69
9:2	69
9:16	69, 70
9:21	69
10:1	69, 70
10:17	70
10:17–27	69
10:19	69
10:22	69
10:23–24	69
10:25	51 n. 53
11	69, 70
12	69, 71, 72
12:12	69

12:14–15	72	2 Chronicles	
12:17	69	20:26	12
12:19–20	69		
12:24–25	72	Nehemiah	
15	79	2:11–20	75
15:22–23	73	4:7–23	75
20	282		
21	281, 282, 289, 291	Psalms	
21–22	285	1	280, 281 n. 8
21:1–9	282	2	280
21:10–15	287	3	280, 290 n. 38
21:12	284	3–7	283
21:13	289	19	74
22	282	22	295
23:15	284	30	285
29:6–10	286	30:12	285
		33	288, 290, 290 n. 38
2 Samuel		34	279, 281, 283, 284, 286, 287, 288, 290, 291, 293, 294, 295, 296
6:8	12		
7	74	37 LXX	307
		38	307
1 Kings		40:6	73
3:34	27	50:7–13	73
14	26	51	283, 284
15:29	27	52	282, 283, 284
16:12	27	52:5	284
19:9–18	194 n. 31	52:7	284
22	16	54	284
		118	296
2 Kings		119	74
14:27	28		
17:18	26, 27	Proverbs	
17:20	27	8:22	192
17:23	27		
21:9	27	Isaiah	
21:10–16	26	1	79
21:15	26	1:11–15	73
21:17	27 n. 8, 29 n. 17	2:2–4	73
22	51 n. 53	6	16, 131, 308
23	26	6–10	308
23:26	32 n. 21	6:13	174 n. 6
23:27	27	7	309
24:3	27	7–9	178
24:4	32 n. 21	7:14	126, 178, 179
24:20	27	11:6–9	73

Isaiah (cont.)

11:8–9	73
26:8	129
28:21	75
36:16	129
40–55	180, 182
40–66	126
41	131
41:2	126
42:1–4	131
43:18	132
43:26	132
45:21–24	200 n. 41
49:1–6	181, 184
53	42, 164, 179, 181, 182, 290 n. 38
53:1–11	181
53:7–8	37, 40
54	194
54–66	183
59:16	129
61	179, 182, 183
61:1–3	183
65:25	73

Jeremiah

7	79
7:21–26	73
31:31–34	74

Lamentations

3:32–33	74

Ezekiel

6:9	74
18:23	74
18:24–32	74
20:18–26	74
26:15	267
36:16	267

Hosea

11	74

Amos

5:21–24	73

7:1–3	31
7:2	31
7:4–6	31
7:5	31

Zechariah

2:1–5	75
14	74
14:11	74
14:20–21	74

Apocrypha/Deuterocanon

2 Macc

2:13–15	51 n. 53

New Testament

Matthew

2	309
12:17–21	131
19:8	77

Mark

10:5–6	77

Luke

4	182, 183
24:13–35	48
24:31	234

John

1:14	291
6	124
6:53	292
16:13	150

Acts

2:14–36	236 n. 59
7:48	77
8:26–40	39, 41
8:30	37
8:34	40
9:4	183
14:16	78

INDEX OF ANCIENT SOURCES

17:24	77	3:15–16	306
17:30–31	78	5:16–17	132

Romans

		Philippians	
3:21–26	78, 99	2:6–11	200 n. 41
7:2	185	2:7	200 n. 42
7:13	185		
7:14	306	Colossians	
9	291	1:15	192 n. 22
9–11	111		
9:22–24	78	2 Timothy	
9:27	291	1:9	110
11:1–6	194 n. 31		
		Titus	
Galatians		3:5–7	110
3	186, 193, 195		
3–4	188, 193, 195	Hebrews	
3:17	194 n. 29	1:1	187 n. 7
3:19	77, 186	1:2	150
3:19–24	199	1:3	149
4	188, 193, 194	6:11–7:2	11
4:19	193	11:8–9	31
4:19–31	193		
4:22	193	Revelation	
4:24–39	196 n. 34	15:1	78
4:27	193	22:2	133
6:2	195, 199		

DEAD SEA SCROLLS

1 Corinthians			
9:9–10	306	1 QH 13, 11–12	132
10:1–2	290		
10:3	290	RABBINIC AND MEDIEVAL JEWISH	
10:4	290		
10:6	78	Leviticus Rabbah	
10:11	290, 306	22.6	78–79
11:23	145		
12:2	306	Moses Maimonides	
12:10	306	*The Guide of the Perplexed*	79
12:16	306		
13:8	77	CHRISTIAN	
15	273		
		Augustine	
2 Corinthians		*City of God*	266
3	188	*Contra Adimantum*	
3:6	306	3.4	273 n. 95

Augustine (cont.)
De doctrina christiana
2   126 n. 18

John Calvin
*Commentaries ... Galatians
and Ephesians*   203 n. 51
Commentary on Daniel   154 n. 39
Commentary ... Psalms   283
Institutes of the Christian Religion
1.7.1   152 n. 32
2.8   123 n. 12
2.11.1   204 n. 53, 216 n. 79
4.9.14   152 n. 32

Irenaeus
Against Heresies   232
1.8.1   232 n. 49, 233 n. 51
3.4.2   237 n. 60
Demonstration   199 n. 40, 200

Justin Martyr
Dialogue with Trypho
19.6   78
20.1–4   78
21.1   78
22.11   78
23.1–2   78
27.2   78
27.4   78
30.1   78

Martin Luther
Weimar Ausgabe
4.375.4–8   296 n. 53

Origen
Homilies on Isaiah
1   308
2   309
6   309
8   308
On First Principles
4.1–3   305

Thomas Aquinas
Summa Theologiae
I, q.19, a.7   96 n. 21
II–II, 5, ad 2   151 n. 31
Summa Contra Gentiles
2.35   96 n. 22

Index of Modern Authors

Abraham, William 225–27
Achenbach, Hans 32
Albert, Craig 225, 226
Albertz, Rainer 43
Allert, Craig 271–274, 277
Anderson, Bernhard 189
Assmann, Jan 48–50
Auerbach, Eric 181, 286
Aurelius, Erik 31
Balthasar, Hans Urs von 122
Barr, James 65, 89, 91, 130, 158, 190, 191, 243–44, 303
Barth, Karl 87, 99, 121, 138, 140, 150, 153, 157, 178, 193, 301
Barton, John 64, 65, 77, 81, 133, 134, 269, 280, 281
Behr, John 200, 209, 233, 235–36, 239, 241
Ben Zvi, Ehud 17
Berquist, Jon L. 81
Beuken, W. A. M. 182
Birch, Bruce C. 70
Blenkinsopp, Joseph 281
Blowers, Paul M. 192, 224, 225
Blum, Erhard 29, 33, 52
Boccaccini, Gabriele 82
Boorer, Suzanne 32
Brett, Mark 244
Brown, Raymond 160, 301, 303
Brueggemann, Walter 130, 158
Bultmann, Rudolph 179, 190, 194, 198, 213
Burnett, Stephen G. 175
Burney, C. F. 192

Byassee, Jason 202, 288, 290, 291, 293–95
Campenhausen, Hans von 227, 228, 236, 239, 276
Carr, David M. 50, 52
Chapman, Stephen B. 83, 174, 194, 270
Childs, Brevard 9–16, 21–22, 29, 44, 45, 64, 66–68, 72, 82, 85, 86, 88, 90–92, 94, 98–101, 103–9, 111, 112, 115–17, 119–23, 125–31, 135–42, 146, 147, 149, 152–69, 171–93, 196, 205, 206, 211, 214, 215, 217–19, 221–23, 227–29, 231–33, 240–48, 250, 251, 253–63, 265–69, 271, 272, 275–77, 279, 281, 283, 285, 287, 288, 292, 293
Clayton, Charles 190
Coats, George 18
Collins, John J. 63, 68
Collins, Terence 280
Conrad, Edgar 173
Cooser, Walter, Jr. 210
Crawford, Sidnie White 81
Crouzel, Henri 302, 303, 306
Cullmann, Oscar 160, 187
Dahl, Nils A. 115
Dahood, Mitchell 282
Daniélou, Jean 302, 304
Davies, Eryl W. 77
Davies, Philip 147
Dawson, John David 193
De Lubac, Cardinal Henri 302, 305, 306
Delcor, M. Mathias 124
Dietrich, Walter 71
Dodd, C. Harold 65, 82

Dohmen, Christoph   29, 33, 39, 46, 50,
   57–60, 247, 270
Donner, H.   89
Driver, Daniel R.   221, 231, 243, 245,
   248, 249, 269
Ebeling, Gerhard   146, 252, 253
Eichrodt, Walther   121
Eldredge, Laurence   252
Enns, Peter   176, 209, 215
Evans, Craig A.   66
Fabry, Heinz-Josef   61
Fairbairn, Patrick   301
Fishbane, Michael   286, 304
Forde, Gerhard   205
Fowl, Stephen   89, 100, 101
Frankemölle, Hubert   39, 42, 45, 47, 49,
   50, 61, 270
Fretheim, Terence E.   80, 255
Frei, Hans   179, 190, 192, 193, 212, 216,
   222–24, 228–29, 266
Fretheim, Terence   248
Frey, Jörg   39
Fuller, Reginald   160
Funkenstein, Amos   79
Gabler, J. P.   252, 253, 255
Gaffin, Richard B., Jr.   210
Gertz, Jan C.   33
Gese, Harmut   29, 43
Gignilliat, Mark   193
Goldingay, John   64
Goppelt, Leonhard   194, 302
Graham, William A.   67
Grant, Robert M.   303
Grillmeier, Aloys   176
Groß, Walter   43, 55, 56
Groves, Joseph   190
Gruber, Mayer J.   282
Gunneweg, Antonius H. J.   42
Haag, Ernst   42
Hafemann, Scott   265
Hägglund, Bengt   221, 276
Hanson, R. P. C.   302, 304, 306
Hardmeier, Christof   48, 49, 52, 53
Harrisville, Roy A.   104, 105, 247, 249,
   257, 259

Helmer, Christine   64, 240, 251
Hengel, Martin   37, 179
Henze, Mattias   81
Hermisson, Hans-Jurgen   40, 41
Hieke, Thomas   55, 57–59
Higton, Mike   193, 229
Hofmann, J. C. K. von   190, 211, 213,
   302
Hooker, Morna   179
Houston, Walter J.   77
Hunziker-Rodewald, Regine   53
Hurtado, Larry W.   66
Iser, Wolfgang   39
Janowski, Bernd   29, 41, 44, 45, 48–50,
   56
Jenson, Robert W.   83, 99, 227, 228
Jeremias, Jörg   23, 31, 280
Kelsey, David H.   229, 230
Kertelge, Karl   38
Klein, Johannes   71
Kline, Meredith G.   194, 210
Koch, Dietrich-Alex   3, 43, 47
Konkel, Michael   29, 33
Kraft, Robert   256
Kratz, Reinhard G.   54
Kraus, Hans-Joachim   282
Kutsch, Ernst   40, 42
Lampe, G.   302
Langlamet, François   70, 124
Landmesser, Christof   64
Levenson, Jon D.   43, 254, 255
Levering, Matthew   161
Levinson, Bernhard M.   50, 52, 56
Levin, Christoph   93
Lipinski, Edward   124, 125
Lohfink, Norbert   25, 27, 28, 32, 45, 46,
   55, 66, 68
Long, Burke   19
Löning, Karl   47
Louth, Andrew   304
Luz, Ulrich   44, 60
Macdonald, Lee   269
MacDonald, Nathan   197, 225, 249
MacDonald, Neil B.   95, 99
Maier, Gerhard   82

INDEX OF MODERN AUTHORS

Martin, Francis	151	Rowe, C. Kavin	132, 160, 200, 234, 291
Martyn, J. Louis	114, 115, 186, 187, 200	Rüsen, Jörn	49
Mauser, Ulrich W.	198	Sæbø, Magne	56
McCarter, P. Kyle, Jr.	70	Sanders, James	269, 272
McCarthy, Dennis J.	26, 70	Sandys-Wunscha, John	252
McCartney, Dan	190	Sawyer, John	299
McConville, J. Gordon	64	Scharbert, Josef	30
McCormack, Bruce	207, 208	Schmidt, Karl L.	160
McDonald, Lee	269, 272	Schmidt, Ludwig	42
McGlasson, Paul	230–31	Schmitt, Hans	32
McGuckin, John	176	Schreiber, Stefan	38
Meade, David G.	106	Schüle, Andreas	52
Meeks, Wayne	109, 110	Schwienhorst-Schonberger, Ludger	49, 50, 53, 56, 133
Melugin, Roy	19		
Metzger, Bruce M.	158	Seitz, Christopher	105, 119, 157, 180, 189–91, 194, 200, 226, 231, 235, 244–45, 270, 286, 287
Moberly, R.W.L.	31, 66		
Morgenstern, Matthias	43		
Müller, Peter	38, 50	Sheppard, Gerald	13, 67, 245, 249
Müller-Oberhäuser, Gabriele	39	Smalley, Beryl	126
Harris, Murray	160	Smend, Rudolf	54, 249
Nevin, John Williamson	210	Smith, Mark S.	81
Nitsche, Stefan Ark	38, 48	Söding, Thomas	38, 39, 40
Noble, Paul	244	Sorabji, Richard	96
Norris, Frederick	174	Soulen, R. Kendall	213
Ochagavia, Juan	200	Sparks, Kenton	176
Oeming, Manfred	42, 50, 60, 257	Spicq, Ceslas	126
O'Keefe, John J.	232, 238	Spieckermann, Hermann	60
Pelikan, Jaroslav	192	Steck, Odil H.	41, 42, 59
Perlitt, Lothar	29	Steins, Georg	53, 55, 61, 244, 270
Pesch, Rudolf	37	Sternberg, Meir	90
Pines, Shlomo	79 n. 31	Stone, Lawson S.	281, 286
Preus, James Samuel	204, 296	Stroobant de Saint-Eloy, Jean-Eric	282, 290
Propp, William H.	280		
Rad, Gerhard von	41, 93, 98, 190, 218, 255, 280, 287, 302	Stuhlmacher, Peter	42, 43, 179
		Sundberg, Albert	269
Radner, Ephraim	209	Sundberg, Walter	247, 249, 257, 259
Rae, Murray A.	150, 153	Talstra, Eep	25
Ratschow, Carl Heinz	47	Taylor, Charles	76
Rendtorff, Rolf	44, 53, 93, 94, 247	Theißen, Gerd	40, 44–46
Reno, Russell R.	135, 232, 238	Torjesen, Karen	307
Reventlow, Henning Graf	42	Tov, Emanuel	61
Rodd, Cyril S.	77	Trible, Phyllis	76
Roloff, Jürgen	37	Troeltsch, Ernst	163
Römer, Thomas	270, 271	Tucker, Gene	19
Rotelle, John E.	288–90, 292, 294	Ulrich, Eugene	269

Utzschneider, Helmut 38, 39, 48
Van der Toorn, Karel 50
Van Seters, John 281
Veijola, Timo 71
Verdam, Pieter J. 121
Vischer, Wilhelm 301
Vos, Geerhardus 210, 212
Wainwright, Arthur 160
Wanke, Gunther 50, 60
Ward, Timothy 180
Warton, James, A. 120
Waschke, Ernst-Joachim 54, 56
Watson, Francis 87, 205, 206, 215
Webster, John 144, 154, 176, 212, 271, 274, 276
Weimar, Peter 33
Weiser, Artur 285
Welker, Michael 53
Wharton, James A. 120, 124
Whitman, Jon 303
Whybray, R. Norman 94
Widmer, Michael 29, 31
Wilckens, Ulrich 77, 133
Williamson, Hugh 171, 173–176
Willis, Edward David 209
Wolff, Walter 14
Wolter, Michael 64
Wolterstorff, Nicholas 97
Work, Telford 176
Woollcombe, K. J. 302
Wrede, William 163
Wright, David F. 273
Wright, N. T. 215
Yeago, David S. 241
Young, Frances 192, 289, 291, 304, 309
Zacharias, H. Daniel 66
Zahn, Theodor 269
Zenger, Erich 40, 43, 45, 47, 53, 55, 56, 58, 59
Zimmerli, Walther 63